FORGIVENESS WORK

Forgiveness Work

MERCY, LAW, AND VICTIMS' RIGHTS IN IRAN

ARZOO OSANLOO

PRINCETON UNIVERSITY PRESS
PRINCETON & OXFORD

Published by Princeton University Press
41 William Street, Princeton, New Jersey 08540
6 Oxford Street, Woodstock, Oxfordshire OX20 1TR

press.princeton.edu

All Rights Reserved
ISBN 978-0-691-17203-3
ISBN (pbk.) 978-0-691-17204-0
ISBN (e-book) 978-0-691-20153-5

British Library Cataloging-in-Publication Data is available

Editorial: Fred Appel & Jenny Tan
Production Editorial: Ali Parrington
Jacket/Cover Design: Layla Mac Rory
Production: Erin Suydam
Publicity: Nathalie Levine & Kathryn Stevens

Cover image: Sheikh Safi al-Din Khānegāh and Shrine Complex, Ardabil, Iran.
Courtesy of author

This book has been composed in Arno

Printed on acid-free paper. ∞

Printed in the United States of America

10 9 8 7 6 5 4 3 2 1

It may be that forgiveness is the major theme in history
and the will to it the largest proof of man.

KENNETH CRAGG

THE MIND OF THE QURAN (1978:128)

CONTENTS

NOTE ON TRANSLITERATION, DATES, AND NAMES

FOR TRANSLITERATING both spoken and written Persian, I follow a modified version of the transliteration scheme outlined by the journal for *Iranian Studies*. I have omitted diacritical marks for ease of reading. For Arabic terms or phrases employed by my Persian interlocutors, I similarly follow the Persian transliteration style. For proper names, I employ common English spelling. All translations are my own, except where I have indicated otherwise.

For key dates, I provide the Common Era (CE), unless for context I found it necessary to use the Anno Persico or Iranian *shamsi* (solar) calendar. In the latter case, I have provided dates in both *shamsi* and CE.

The names of my interlocutors are pseudonyms except where they are public officials or otherwise prominent individuals whose stories eclipse anonymization, such as a judge, lawyer, playwright, or social worker. Regardless of their position, I obtained the prior consent of all individuals quoted. While anonymization often can provide confidentiality and privacy to interlocutors, in this, I am likewise persuaded by Nancy Scheper-Hughes's reflections in the second edition of *Saints, Scholars, and Schizophrenics* that "we owe our anthropological subjects the same degree of courtesy, empathy, and friendship in writing that we generally extend to them face to face in the field. . . . Sacrificing anonymity means we may have to write less poignant, more circumspect ethnographies, a high price for any writer to pay. But our version of the Hippocratic oath—to do no harm, insofar as possible, to our informants—would seem to demand this" (2001:12–13). I aim to balance confidentiality and privacy with poignancy, and while this is a work of analysis and perhaps even critique, it is also a work of engagement and understanding.

ACKNOWLEDGMENTS

THIS PROJECT has been long in the making. The incubation of the ideas, their organization, and the narrative arc of the story took time to develop. Along the way, many changes, in the context of my fieldwork and the laws, kept me in a state of seeming perpetual revision. I initially thought that a lack of access to courts, cases, and interlocutors would limit my approach to a more text-based and speculative one. However, the circumstances and people I met along the way made it possible for me to sit-in on court cases and tell stories of the applications of the laws and their effects through ethnographic narratives.

Early on, in 2010, I was fortunate to have research support from the University of Washington's Royalty Research Fund that gave me time in the form of course buy-outs and research funds to go to Iran for extended research trips. Similarly, in 2011, the Fetzer Institute launched a terrific program to fund research related to love, mercy, and forgiveness. I am grateful to Lawrence Sullivan, Xiaoan Li, Jackie Stack, the Social Science Faculty Advisory Council, and the Fetzer staff, which funded my in-country research for this project over the course of several years. In 2014, the Fetzer Institute along with the University of Washington's Simpson Center for the Humanities supported an intimate workshop on Islam and Forgiveness.

My interlocutors in Iran include family members, but also friends, some whom I met at the initial stages of this project and who are now close confidants. They include Mahboubeh Ramezani, a survivor of tragedy and later social worker, whose eloquence and charisma are impossible to capture through words alone. Others, such as Leila Arshad, helped me understand the role of social workers and directed me meet to individuals who engage in forgiveness work. Farkhondeh Ehtessami shared with me her approach and the challenges in forgiveness work. The student volunteers at the Imam 'Ali Society, as well as their founder, Sharmin Meymandi Nejad, allowed me to attend their gatherings and answered many questions. I am especially grateful to all the family members who patiently discussed the difficult decision of whether or not to forgo retributive sanctioning.

Many individuals, including Goli Ebrahimi, Ali Ganji, Tohid Khakpour, and Mehrnoosh Mohtashami, helped me gather stories of forbearance and facilitated meetings with individuals, which then permitted me greater access to candid conversations with experts, government officials, family members, and others affected by murder. They are also friends with whom I had the pleasure of spending time and sharing in life's passages. Many individuals in the performing arts, especially Golboo Fiuzi and Amin Miri, gave me their time, allowed me to tag along in their meetings and rehearsals, and invited me to performances.

Many lawyers and legal scholars, especially Mohammad Ali Jedari Foroughi, were helpful in directing me to cases, key legal issues, and strategies. I also thank lawyers who shared their legal strategies with me, including Mojtaba Farabakhsh, Mohammad Moghimi, Mohammad Mostafaei, and Nasrin Sotoudeh. Judge Eftekhari, the head of the Criminal Court for Tehran, gave me permission to sit in on cases. Judge Maliki facilitated my permissions and provided explanation on legal codes, rationales, and procedures. He further directed me to cases that were important to my research questions and sent me reports of cases of forbearance over the many years I was collecting them. Judge Ghorbanzadeh allowed me a seat in his courtroom, took time to explain legal issues and procedures, and facilitated my interviews with other judicial officials, as well as prosecutors and defense lawyers, litigants, and social workers. Mohammad Khaki and Ataollah Roudgar answered many legal questions and facilitated meetings with officials and lawyers. Other judges gave me access to their courtrooms, offered explanations, and sat down for interviews. I do not have the names of every individual but wish to acknowledge the significance of the access that the judiciary allowed in order for me to pursue this project. Many officials were curious about the US criminal justice system and posed questions to me, as well.

My ideas for the manuscript began to take shape during a sabbatical year (2011–12) at Princeton's Program in Law and Public Affairs. I am grateful to then-director Kim Lane Scheppele, associate director, Leslie Gerwin, and the staff, who maintained an eclectic and intellectually invigorating atmosphere. In addition, conversations with Princeton anthropologists I met, including Carole Greenhouse, John Borneman, and Lawrence Rosen, deepened my critical investigations. In 2016, I was able to focus on my writing with the support of a year-long Society of Scholars research fellowship at the UW's Simpson Center for the Humanities and receive critical feedback on one of the early chapters in the book.

Additionally, talks I gave on my research findings helped me sketch out this project's key questions, parameters, outline, narrative, and conclusions. I have benefited from presenting papers related to this project at Brown University, McGill University, Michigan State University, New York University, Princeton University, University of Arizona, University of California at Berkeley,

University of Michigan, University of Toronto, and Yale University. I am particularly grateful to the graduate students at McGill, Toronto, and University of Michigan who workshopped individual chapters and gave me detailed feedback.

Colleagues who invited to me to present parts of this work or attended conferences, talks, or workshops, and then discussed ideas or posed key questions that deepened my inquiry include Kathryn Babayan, William Beeman, Yazid Ben Hounet, Anne Betteridge, Marianne Constable, Susanne Dahlgren, David Engel, Narges Erami, Jairan Gahan, Behrooz Ghamari-Tabrizi, Arang Keshavarzian, Stuart Kirsch, Setrag Manoukian, Michael McCann, Nada Moumtaz, and Jonathan Simon. A further note of thanks goes to Behrooz Ghamari-Tabrizi, who kindly sent me a constant stream of newspaper reports of forbearance cases.

A number of colleagues read specific chapters and provided me with sharp comments, including Benjamin Lawrance, Katherine Lemons, Marjan Moosavi, Nada Moumtaz, Michael Peletz, Nova Robinson, and Michele Statz. My gratitude also goes to Michael Fischer, who read the entire manuscript and offered considered, incisive remarks.

Many colleagues at the University of Washington read parts of the work in varying forms and offered invaluable feedback, including Radhika Govindrajan, Danny Hoffman, Selim Kuru, Jamie Mayerfeld, Michael McCann, Vicente Rafael, Cabeiri Robinson, Jane Winn, and Kathleen Woodward. I also thank Felicia Hecker, the Associate Director of the Middle East Center, who ably dealt with day-to-day affairs and allowed me to concentrate on research and writing.

Several colleagues, Selim Kuru and Aradhana Sharma, as well as my sister, Azadeh Osanloo, have been my touchstones, the ones with whom I am in seemingly continual communication on this project, who are always up for engagement and willing to entertain my attempts to try out new and peculiar ideas.

I am grateful to my writing group, Judith Alexander-McGovern, Deepa Bhandaru, Michael Boudreaux, and Kirsten Lunstrum, who read, discussed, and commented on every chapter. In addition, Wendy Call, Kirsten Lunstrum, and Gail Folkins taught wonderful courses at Seattle's writing center, Hugo House, where I workshopped chapters of this manuscript and gained feedback from writerly readers. Their suggestions broadened the audience for this work.

My graduate assistant, Maral Sahebjame, researched a range of topics and helped catalogue the many Persian-sourced stories of forbearance I had accumulated over the years. My undergraduate reader, Katie McConville, read the entire manuscript and offered sharp comments throughout. Iraj Khademi and Maryam Badiee gave discerning commentary and translation of Persian poetry.

I am grateful to my parents, Enayat Osanloo and Parvin Assadi for their support and exemplary forbearance. My sisters, Azadeh and Azita, read chapters and discussed their ideas with me. My cousins, aunts, and uncles in Iran, brought to my attention films, books, and other cultural production relating to forgiveness.

Princeton University Press's Executive Editor, Fred Appel, took on this project, which took longer than we had originally agreed and saw it through with some measure of forbearance. Three anonymous reviewers provided nuanced and detailed comments that improved the manuscript significantly. I am grateful to the press's editorial assistant, Jenny Tan, and production editor, Ali Parrington, and copyeditor, Michelle Hawkins, all of whom have improved this work.

Finally, no work this individualized actually gets finished alone. I reserve my greatest appreciation for my husband, Olivier Martinez, who not only read and commented on every chapter, but provided unmatched love and support during each step of this project, from debut to fin.

FORGIVENESS WORK

Crimtorts and Lifeworlds

Rather than proceed from historical events and figures,
why not locate our thinking in the here and now,
immersing ourselves in the lifeworlds of others
taking our intellectual cues from their concerns,
and conversing on terms that they decide?

MICHAEL JACKSON, *LIFEWORLDS* (2013:254)

Crimtorts: Spectacle and Social Field

Guards brought the young man out from inside the police van. The light and dark blue stripes of his prison uniform hid his thin frame from sight. With hands cuffed, he was made to stand on a chair. A noose, attached to a crane mounted on an open-bed truck, came down around his neck. In the rare public setting, the very square in which the killing took place, guards readied the perpetrator for execution. As the mask came down over his eyes, he began to weep loudly and beg for mercy and for forgiveness.

Moments before the public execution of this young man sentenced to death for murder, the victim's father stood from within a crowd of protestors, raised his arm to stop the proceeding, and declared, "I forgive him." With this act, the father of the victim signaled *gozasht* (forbearance) of his right to seek *qisas* (retribution) for his son's killer, as the law affords.

In the early days of the new millennium, I witnessed this rather stunning episode of Iran's criminal justice system unfold on a nationally-televised broadcast. This action by a private citizen came after much domestic and international advocacy on behalf of the perpetrator, whose deeds, many individuals believed, did not warrant such severe punishment.[1] While activists abroad advocated for the perpetrator's human rights, others, including Iran's judiciary, defended the rights of the victims and their families to justice.

When the father of the victim signaled his last-minute reprieve of the perpetrator, both sides claimed victory—and a triumph for human rights. Secular
human rights protestors, citing the rights of prisoners, noted that his being
spared was a consequence of their advocacy against the death penalty. Advocates of Iran's victim-centered justice system argued that the forbearance afforded to victims' families served the greater cause of justice—peace and
security.

The "spectacle" of a private act of mercy, as I have described it elsewhere,
betrayed these simple binaries (Osanloo 2006). The facts of the case, its coverage by extant media outlets, and the overall legal proceedings conveyed a complex story about injury and punishment, mercy and retaliation, forbearance
and retribution, forgiveness and justice, and ultimately, life and death, as articulated through the multiple valences of ritual, faith, law, social relations, and
politics. In Iran, the codification of forbearance emerges from a hybrid crimtort justice system, complete with its own conditions of possibility. Sociolegal
scholars Thomas Koenig and Michael Rustad coined the term "crimtort" to
refer to the state's amplification of private remedies to fill a void in criminal law
(1998). In such cases, the state allows private plaintiffs to employ civil lawsuits
to punish corporations through remedies that include increased monetary
damages as well as prison sentences. In Iran, the blending of criminal law with
tort law has had the opposite effect. The state has created a public sanction for
the private harm of murder. However, it did not amplify the punishment. The
public sanction for the private harm of murder and other torts is secondary
and limited to a maximum prison sentence of three to ten years. The determination of life and death remains the unalterable right of the private plaintiffs.

What most observers of Iran's criminal justice system know about it is that
sanctioning is severe. Amnesty International has noted that Iran has the
world's highest rate of capital punishment per capita.[2] After the 1979 Revolution, Iran's religious leaders rewrote the national laws to conform with Islamic
principles as they saw them. Major revisions to the criminal laws reinstituted
severe retributive sanctioning but also codified the possibility of the plaintiff's
forbearance, derived from the Muslim mandate to be merciful and compassionate. One element of the system of criminal sanctioning that is little known
and under-studied is that in homicide, and numerous other crimes, retribution
is literally the right of victims. That is, victims, as plaintiffs in crimtort cases,
can demand that the state carry out retributive sanctioning or forgo it and
forgive their perpetrators. Iran's *Law of Criminal Procedure* also codifies the
religious obligation to be merciful and compassionate as an imperfect duty on
the part of government officials to bring about reconciliation whenever possible. Thus, the penal code (the substantive law) recognizes forbearance as a
right of victims, and the code of criminal procedure demands that government

agents tasked with carrying out the substantive law do so with an eye towards the greater goal of achieving reconciliation.

Since the publication of my first essay on this topic in 2006, I have studied the work of forbearance in Iran's criminal justice system, especially as it pertains to murder in the first degree, that is, with intent. The result is the following work in which I explore Iran's victim-centered approach to criminal justice with a view to unpacking the logic of a system that arguably places the rights of victims before those of the state. As such, I seek to better understand the state's interests in apparently handing over the fundamental power of determining life and death to private parties. Beyond investigating how the private right of forbearance operates within the criminal justice system, my primary interest is to understand how aggrieved individuals reach the decision to forgo retributive sanctioning when the state guarantees their right to it.[3]

In the years since I started this project, Iran's criminal laws and procedures have been finalized. Accordingly, they have been revised, expanded, and "colored in," as my interlocutors referred to the code's more robust character. As we see in the pages that follow, the laws are clear in defining certain categories of punishment as a consequence of specific injuries. The laws also stipulate the conditions for forbearance. However, the penal code is silent with respect to *how* parties should arrive at reconciliation. That is, the state encourages settlement, but for all intents and purposes, leaves to the parties themselves to determine what the substance and process of that settlement might be. The conjuncture of a clear legal and moral duty to seek reconciliation alongside the absence of specific guidelines on how to do so has a generative quality and produces an arena outside of the state's judicial apparatus, yet still of it, for bringing about a settlement short of retribution or, as I will refer to it, for *forgiveness work*.[4] Over the years, this critical combination of duty with an absence of guidelines has engendered unique spaces for negotiation, bargaining, and indeed, reconciliation. Thus, the manifest moral and legal compulsion to forgive without meaningful guidelines on how to do so has produced an informal cottage industry of advocacy, one that is populated by diverse actors and which produces numerous avenues for negotiating forbearance by forging reconciliation and settlement.

With the term cottage industry, I seek to highlight the informality (small, concentrated, loosely organized) as well as the ritual forms that engage in what is a flourishing complex of activity and industry around forgiveness, especially when it comes to capital punishment cases. The activities and actors within the cottage industry of forgiveness work animate and give meaning to the moral and legal duty to forgo retribution and forge reconciliation. This cottage industry is unregulated, informal, and often rife with contests as different actors vie for power, influence, renowned, and sometimes even monetary reward. Over the years, this flurry of activity has generated some rules of engagement, leading to increased professionalization, expertise, and government involvement and oversight. At the same time, the ad-hoc nature of forgiveness work continually invites new actors who have less regard for observed practices and who forge new rules of engagement.

Indeed, as one social worker told me, she operates in a "*hayaat khalvat az qanun*," literally, a field devoid of law. "What do you mean by that?" I asked. My friend explained that the work she does is neither with nor without the government's express consent. While the law "creates this field, there isn't much law managing the work that goes on within it." As she saw it, "the field is open." "Open to what?" I asked. She responded that the field is open to norms and rituals that are specific to the people in the regions where they work. "We use their own practices," she said, referring to the various local mechanisms for conflict resolution.

In this way, in the four decades since the revolution, numerous groups and individuals, political and nongovernmental, have intervened in murder (and other) cases to which they are not parties. Sometimes working together, other times in conflict or at cross-purposes, these actors labor towards the overarching goals of sparing an individual from the death sentence and bringing about reconciliation between victims and their perpetrators—or at least a settlement short of the retaliatory punishment to which victims are legally entitled. Notably, the activities that take place in this space are also both ad-hoc and ritualistic. Over the years, state and civil society actors involved in reconciliation efforts have become more professionalized in their methods of securing victims' forbearance. Few of the approaches, however, are independent of broader social, cultural, and even economic considerations, and are thus subject to the fluctuating zeitgeist of life in Iran.

Building on my friend's perceptive description of this extra-judicial arena where negotiations take place, this cottage industry forged through forgiveness work, I find it helpful to take up Sally Falk Moore's concept of the "semi-autonomous social field" (1973). In proposing an approach for studying extra-legal arrangements, Moore was responding to Schapera (1972) and Malinowski's (1959) calls for scholars to move beyond formal law to understand the informal orders that bind tribal societies. Moore advanced a methodology for examining how groups within larger, more complex societies operate internally. She proposed that semi-autonomous fields can generate their own "rules and customs and symbols" (720). However, such fields are also subject to the directives of higher powers that can force compliance.

In offering a way to study the ties that bind certain groups living within more complex societies, Moore guided researchers to heed the capacity of formal laws and other larger social and economic forces to infiltrate and influence decision-making inside groups, despite those other forces—the *cohesive forces*, so to speak.[5] Moore's approach is useful in shedding light on the processes that shape forgiveness work and create the conditions through which victims' families consent to forgo their right of retribution.

In complex societies, Moore observed, legislation handed down by centralized governments encroaches on or burdens social fields that already possess rules and customs. I am suggesting something slightly different. In this case, the legislation itself is productive; it generates the social field of forgiveness work. Thus, far from being solely a constraint, the law actually produces and preserves the partial autonomy of the social field—those localized rules and customs. I came to see this not as an inadvertent consequence of the law, but as its intent. In this context, the law is both a coercive and cohesive force. The state law codifies with the aim of maintaining the spirit of cohesive force as well.

This book, then, is my attempt to excavate, narrate, and analyze distinct spaces of this cottage industry drawing from stories I have been collecting on annual research trips to Iran since I began working on this project in 2007. Through an ethnographic foray into the different sites where forbearance may come about, I have attempted to sketch the parameters of Iran's intensely victim-centered criminal justice system while also providing a portrait of forgiveness work by diverse actors. Although every case I have encountered is unique, the processing of such cases through Iran's legal system provides some pattern of practice and an outline of stages in which different actors converge and sometimes compete in their forgiveness work.

To be sure, forgiveness work takes place through the state's legal apparatus. The state corrals and constrains the field, but social workers and other actors draw from a broad lexicon that includes rituals, religion, rights, and reason to appeal to their subjects and to forge their own practices dedicated to cultivating what my interlocutors referred to as "a feeling of forgiveness."[6] Thus, inasmuch as this project grew out of the legal considerations raised by the story above, there is an affective dimension to it as well. Understanding the affective component of forgiveness work helps to shed light on social actors' motivations.

Affective Lifeworlds: A Plea for Mercy

Hushed voices from the foyer drew the attention of the old woman, Nayereh. She sat on a petite settee at the far end of the large sitting room, a mere outline in silhouette. A glass filled with tea sat idle on one knee. Behind her, drawn curtains prevented the bright daylight from showering through the windows, darkening the already somber mood in the room. Nayereh was in mourning. This was the seventh day since her husband's death and she had already begun to receive the morning's visitors.[7] Family, friends, and neighbors filed in to sit with her and to remember her husband, the kindly gentleman who left the house with only his dog before dawn most mornings for a hike in the foothills of the Alborz Mountains just beyond their house. He started the samovar before leaving so as to return to his wife, son, and daughter-in-law sitting around the kitchen table sipping freshly brewed tea. His sudden death had brought an abrupt end to their morning routine.

Three of Nayereh's grown children had gotten up to answer the doorbell, a high-pitched whistling cuckoo. Its festive tone belied the ritual at hand. Gradually but heatedly, her two sons and daughter began to chide the person at the door.

"No, you can't," said the oldest son.

"It's not necessary," stated the daughter disdainfully.

"Why did you come?" exclaimed the exasperated youngest son.

At this point, Nayereh, sitting beside her adolescent granddaughter, looked up. Through grief-stricken eyes she saw the commotion and realized who was at the door. She wrested the attention away from the visitor when she spoke out, "It's fine. Let him in." Her words were met with a chorus of outrage.

"Do you know who it is?" asked her eldest.

"Did you tell him to come?" probed her daughter.

Only the youngest son, by virtue of sharing the household with his mother for many years, had determined that, in fact, it was she who had told the man that he could pay his respects. And so, the son relented. He pushed his siblings out of way and let the visitor in. He called out to the kitchen and asked his wife to bring out some tea. As the visitor gingerly removed his shoes, the rest of the household steeled their nerves to hear what he, the man who had killed their father, had come to say.

The man, just twenty-four, had not come alone. He was accompanied by his uncle, who came as an apparent character witness, a moral adjunct, with prayer beads in hand. The men had come from the southernmost part of Tehran, known for its poverty and the urban blight associated with economic disadvantage, a sign of the city's increasingly unrestrained inequality. The young man had been employed by the company for only a few months, and now, likely, would be relieved. His father was dead. He was his mother's sole support. It was a difficult world from which he hailed. Prison and a fine could irredeemably alter his path. The family's forbearance could factor into a reduced sentence, possibly dismiss the monetary penalty for this unintentional killing, and even persuade his employer to give him another chance.

Besides the accident, the young man had no previous entanglements with the law. He worked hard, lived at home, and helped his family. He was engaged and planned to marry within the year. He said his prayers and fasted during Ramadan. He did not drink or gamble. He was a good person. His mistake was only that he had been driving too fast. In the unbounded traffic of Tehran, his driving was not unusual. Instead, what was odd was the wholly unexpected sight of an elderly man crossing the four-lane highway without due consideration of his age or pace.

As the young man approached Nayereh, both began to cry. Then weeping took over the room in bursts as tears engulfed the onlookers. Besides her immediate family, a handful of Nayereh's neighbors and friends sat in the various sofas and chairs that outlined the carpeted room. All looked on as the young man fell to his knees before Nayereh, lowered his head, and cried for her forgiveness, "*marro-bebakhsh*," and her mercy, "*rahm kon.*"

In January 1999, I was preparing to go to Iran for the first time since my family had moved to the United States in 1970. My maternal grandfather, whom I had seen only once since then, was excitedly preparing his house in Tehran for the visit. One morning, several weeks before my arrival, he went out to buy paint. Upon crossing a busy thoroughfare, his seventy-nine-year-old body, albeit fit from daily treks through the outlying mountains, did not carry him as quickly as he had perhaps expected. A speeding minibus hit him. An ambulance rushed my grandfather to the hospital, where he died hours later in the arms of one of his sons. My return to Iran, then, was marked by grief and mourning, and the rituals associated with it, rather than with the celebration my grandfather had intended. Among those rituals, however, was one that I had not expected: the visit by the bus driver to my grandmother, down on one knee, head bowed, full of remorse, asking for forgiveness.

By describing how the law forges a social field of forgiveness work, I provide a sense of how the judicial process operates and gives way to the field's semi-autonomy. That is one aim of this book; another is to mine what goes on inside the field. That is, if the notion of a semi-autonomous social field helps to decipher some of the contours of forgiveness work and the forces that give shape to it, then the second aim is to observe the "form-of-life" to which this semi-autonomous social field gives rise (Agamben 2000:3–4; Das 2006; Fischer 2003).[8] In order to do that, I look for insight into how individuals come to the decision to forgo retributive punishment when they, and they alone, can choose otherwise. For those involved, forgiveness work becomes a world unto itself, a lifeworld comprised of its own affective realm. As such, I examine how and why people who are not parties get involved, what their motivations are, and how that involvement ultimately shapes their subjectivities throughout the decision-making process and possibly beyond it.

In legal terms, my grandmother's forbearance did not carry the same significance as in the first story I recounted. The bus driver had not committed an intentional killing. The victim's family did not possess any power over his life, even if they could slightly influence the length of his confinement. The accident was just that, a negligent homicide, for which the driver's automobile insurance paid a pre-determined *diya*, a compensation fixed annually by the judiciary.

Rather, the bus driver's calling on my grandmother held a more ritualistic place in the meeting between offender and aggrieved and spoke to a socio-cultural dialectic of redemption-seeking and pardon that, if not expected, is highly valued for ending conflict and sowing peace and reconciliation.[9]

Not only was the visit to the aggrieved an expected precursor to forgiveness, it was also a highly stylized and choreographed performance, enacted from a socially-recognized script that Iranians have practiced for millennia. The rehearsed nature of the actions, far from suggesting disingenuousness, provided the common elements through which families, neighbors, and others assess such situations and make determinations about the perpetrator's sincerity, remorse, admission of wrongdoing, and acceptance of responsibility. The script also prescribes face-saving actions for the aggrieved, ensuring their positions as dignified and righteous victims. My grandmother forgave the young bus driver. "What else I could do?" she told me. "He was just a boy. He didn't know what he was doing." It is perhaps worth noting, at this early juncture, that such practices are not solely religious, that is, based on Muslim scriptures, but also reside in rich cultural traditions that predate Islam, and yet, are incorporated into the scriptures and ethico-religious practices that came later.

Momentarily setting aside the sources of such practices and the ethical issues surrounding them, a broad array of forgiveness-seeking rituals operates in these contexts and plays an important role both in acknowledging and quieting the grief associated with homicides, accidental or otherwise. Such ritual practices also undergird a vast affective dimension of the crimtort justice system and make possible the legal act of forbearance, and more broadly, reconciliation and forgiveness, terms I define and distinguish below. Far from serving as independent signifiers, such rituals are woven subtly into the laws to serve the state's logics of maintaining safety and security by preserving the victim's right to retaliation. Such retaliation, moreover, includes victims' emotional validation and their financial compensation.

Anthropologist Michael Jackson employs the concept of lifeworlds to emphasize that human existence is a relational existence, that speech and action are intersubjective ways of being (2013:xii). For Jackson, agency constitutes a person's "capacity to generate, perpetuate, and celebrate life *as well as one's ability to stoically endure its hardships*" (Ibid.) (emphasis in original). Jackson notes the fluidity of relational human experience, while observing that relational experiences are not solely between humans, but include humans with other species, things, and even imaginary actors. In this manner, he signals an interpsychic quality to our understanding of and ability to describe human experience—that is, we can never fully do so. Thus, the social field as lifeworld is a "force field, a constellation of both ideas and passions, moral norms and ethical dilemmas, the tried and true, as well as the unprecedented, a field charged with vitality and animated by struggle" (Jackson 2013:7). Jackson's lifeworlds aptly captures the networks and negotiations I encountered within the semi-autonomous social field that exists for victims in the process of deciding how to dispose of their right to retribution. Crucially, the idea of lifeworlds alludes to the affective dimensions present in this field. My grandmother Nayereh's experience hints at affect's generative power and fluidity in the forbearance process.

Yael Navaro-Yashin extends scholarship on affect to the material environment, suggesting that it exists *not only* in pre-personal psychic states, but also in the hazy and atmospheric spaces of the exterior world.[10] Material environments contain "affective energies" that are transmitted to and between human subjects (Navaro-Yashin 2012:18). Affect in this context is a non-discursive sensation generated by a space, consisting of "charges emanating from the natural and built environment" existing between, through, and around human and non-human worlds (2012:21). Such spaces are brimming with mood and sensation (Behrouzan 2016:9). Physical environments, built or natural, discharge affect; they are populated with both meaning-laden objects and psychically-informed subjectivities. Thus, the environment and items arranged in them invoke affect and act on the interiority of the subject (subjectivity). Among them are legal spaces and records of bureaucratic administration (Stoler 2009). While bureaucracies serve as rationalizing and disciplining apparatuses of governance, they are also domains that conjure and release emotion.

I draw from the co-implication of interior and exterior realms of affect to make sense of how my interlocutors bring themselves to forbearance when the law permits them to exact equal justice. Thus, in making sense of victims' families' decisions to forgo retribution, I explore the legal bureaucracy as part of this affective lifeworld. By doing so, I underscore the emotive domain that emerges through my interlocutors' active interior lives, sometimes brought about by prayer, contemplation, and meditation, but also through their exterior surroundings where reconciliation meetings call upon passionate performances of remorse, pain, suffering, honor, and even pride. Such performative exercises, however, operate through the multiple registers of *Shi'i* sentiment as well as other cultural practices.

In the absence of legal guidelines, forgiveness work comes to be regulated through long-held ritual practices that take place between victims' families and numerous other actors who prevail upon families' faith and their feelings of loss and injury, and appeal to them to cultivate grace and magnanimity with forbearance. Through the course of negotiations, victims' families frequently engage in such rituals, and often come to expect them as a condition of forgiveness, itself. In my grandmother's case, the materiality that I gesture to is not the mere description of the space. Rather, with the physical description, I aim to give readers a sense of the affective environment—the atmospheric quality—on that particular day of mourning that made the exchange between victim and perpetrator possible.

Such processes draw upon and incorporate wider Persian cultural practices, such as *qahr va ashti* (conflict and resolution). Parents or other social actors teach *qahr va ashti*, a socially-recognized "emotional-cognitive-behavioral cultural script," to children who then internalize it in their own social interactions into adulthood (Behzadi 1994:322). *Qahr* begins with a social rupture, and silence signals feelings of hurt by the victims. It evokes the compassion and love of others, including family members, friends, and neighbors, and motivates them to get involved in resolving the conflict and to arrive at reconciliation. In one case where I interviewed family members who had agreed to relinquish their right of retribution, they did so only after meetings with the family of the perpetrator, especially the family matriarch. Originally steadfast in their decision to seek retribution, the victim's family members told social workers and faith leaders that they were surprised and offended by the failure of the perpetrator's family to visit them. Upon hearing this complaint, social workers arranged a meeting between the two families. The perpetrator's relatives, who had originally kept their distance out of a desire not to upset the grieving family, met with them and paid their respects to the family's deceased son, while also listening to bitter complaints about their own son, the perpetrator.

Forbearance: A Gendered Social Ritual and Cultural Trope

The large colorful display caught my eye while I rode the bus line that cuts through the heart of Tehran. On the high traffic bus route on *Vali Asr* Street, *Sabk-e Zendegi* (Lifestyle), a *Bassij* operated website and news service, had posted a vibrant visual depiction of a key moral value: forbearance.[11] The bright, almost fluorescent green of the background expressed the color that honors the *Sayyed*s, the descendants of the Prophet Mohammad. In the center of the drawing sat the ideal family, consisting of a mother, father, and two children—a boy and a girl. All were seated, cross-legged around a tablecloth laid on the ground. The simplicity of the mealtime layout hailed unpretentious, non-materialistic working-class Iranians. In front of the father and two children sat platefuls of rice and hearty stew, the traditional bountiful meal served at midday or the end of a long workday. Before the mother, the cartoon depicted a bowl of yogurt. The caption bubble from the son read, "Mother, why aren't you eating?" The mother's reply, "Today I really crave bread and yogurt," captured the gendered dimension of forbearance. The visual depiction worked so well because the act of a mother's forbearance, unlike that of the heroic and noble fighter of the masculine perspective, is so subtle, so delicate and elusive, that it easily escapes naming. The use of words—the

FIGURE 1. Image from 2015, *Bassiji Lifestyle Magazine*, entitled "Patience and Forbearance," showing a mother eating bread and yogurt while the others have a stew.

enunciation of the depiction—is a violence, itself. The title of the cartoon reads, "Forbearance and Patience," but as the cartoon depicts, a mother's forbearance goes without saying.

In the four decades of Islamic governance in Iran, a cottage industry has emerged that fills the regulatory void produced by the forbearance provisions in the penal code. This industry is shaped by secular and religious persons, government officials, quasi-state entities, like the *Bassij*, as well as anti-death penalty activists working in numerous social, legal, and political arenas to attempt to moderate the effect of death sentences in homicide cases in Iran. Besides social workers, this field includes lawyers, judges, and families of victims, and also celebrities, athletes, politicians, and well-respected members of the community, including the members of the *'ulama* (community of religious scholars), *darvish* (Sufi mystics), and *riche sefeed* (elder sages, *lit.* white beards). The latter convene ritualized ceremonies of *solh va sauzesh* (reconciliation and settlement) or even rework kinship-based practices, such as the *khoon bas* (blood stop) or *khoon solh* (blood peace).

Calls for compassion and forbearance pervade daily public life. State-run television and radio routinely recount true stories of forgiveness. Newspapers and magazines provide gripping tales of loss followed by forbearance. Some highlight stories of forgiveness among the Prophet and his family, while others relate true stories of forbearance in local cases of homicide. Television shows query scholars of Muslim thought about the sources of forgiveness; others talk to other experts, such as scientists and legal scholars, on their respective dimensions of forgiveness. For instance, one day, while flipping through television channels, I caught a segment on the program, *Emrooz Hanooz Tamoom Nashodeh* (*Today Is Not Yet Over*), in which a psychologist was invited to address the positive health effects on those who forgive.[12] She explained, "Forgiveness is hard, but refusing it is much harder. If we don't forgive, it is harder on ourselves. Not only do we deny ourselves peace and serenity, but we become hardened and irritable. Just as we ask for God's forgiveness, we should be forgiving too."

Stories often hail forbearance as a triumph of Islamic values, while some emphasize that forbearance, like *qisas*, is a right.[13] The various media outlets reveal a pedagogical aim to influence everyday social interactions by displaying the language and embodiment of compassion, mercy, and forbearance, in a sense, to show viewers how it works. Academic conferences feature forbearance as a site of social scientific inquiry, as do legal textbooks. In the creative arts, local theater and cinema destined for international audiences ponder questions around forbearance. All of this results in an attempt at a moral (re)making of society, what my interlocutors referred to as *farhang-sazi* (culture-building). In this context, the high-minded civilizational narrative serves as a kind of social engineering aimed at cultivating and strengthening the social conditions for greater forbearance both in public and private relations.[14]

The rise of a forgiveness cottage industry allows for the cultivation of new ethical relations that work to induce new practices of *gozasht* (forbearance), *solh* (reconciliation), and even *bakhshesh* (forgiveness). These terms possess qualitatively (and legally) different meanings, but my interlocutors used them interchangeably. The negotiations conducted inside this cottage industry emerge through the very logics of criminal sanctioning and create the conditions of possibility for forbearance and, to an extent, forgiveness. They are enmeshed and intermingled with everyday life in particular ways. Accordingly, they draw upon specific dimensions of Islam, especially as they are attuned to the ritualized and embodied aspects of Iranian Twelver *Shi'ism*, which include *mazlumiyyat* (grace in suffering), *rahmat* (compassion), *aql* (reason), and *hekmat* (inspiration derived from God's divine wisdom), all of which are expressions of 'true' faith (Momen 1985). Reconciliation practices are embedded in the distinct histories and the semantic webs of signification peculiar to Iranian *Shi'ism*, one which sees the ideal version of itself as both seeker of justice and righteous victim (Fischer 1980). While the stories circulate across time and space, people in different social and economic milieu, faith groups, and regions may attribute different meanings and value to them. Even as parties' embodied practices accord with exalted *Shi'i* attributes, they also reflect pre-Islamic Persian traits of *javanmardi* (chivalry) (Corbin 1973) and *ashti* (resolution or peacemaking).[15]

In these stories of forbearance and forgiveness, we see that, in this victim-centered approach to sanctioning, offenders' actions and emotions, beyond just motives, bear on whether injured parties will even consider forbearance.

Victims' actions, too, are scrutinized by negotiators and the public for their appropriate expressions of grief and ethical handling of sanctioning. In this semi-autonomous social field, which law shapes but from which it retreats, and in which social practices meet, spar, and mix, lies the space where forbearance decisions are mulled over and emotions are performed and spent. These decision processes can go on, quite literally, for years, while defendants are in prison. Throughout this period, victims' and defendants' families are in protracted agony. For injured parties, there is the double agony of loss and decision-making. As time stretches on, the emotional path to healing may begin, first with heated anguish reflected in indecision, then anger, despair, and helplessness, all of which appeal to revenge or at least retribution. For some, however, the distress may dissipate to allow for tranquility accompanied by resignation, perhaps forbearance, and possibly, forgiveness.

The most intense period of social attention to forbearance comes during the month of Ramadan, a holy month for Muslims to set aside physical needs for deep spiritual introspection. This month, best known for fasting, is also the month when Muslims revisit their spirit of generosity and compassion. During Ramadan, forbearance appears as a ubiquitous trope, especially visible under Tehran's urban skies. Throughout the month, decorative street signs in eye-catching calligraphic script, quote the Qur'an, the sayings of the Prophet Mohammad or of *Shi'ism*'s venerated Imam 'Ali, the Prophet's successor. Such messages can be found on highway billboards, placards on busses, and in metro stations. On the popular television program, *Mahe Asal* (*lit.* honeymoon), broadcast live every night during Ramadan, the charismatic host, Ehsan Alikhani, dedicates at least one episode each season to featuring families who have exercised forbearance.[16]

As a cultural trope, forbearance circulates its own social meanings as well. Forbearance is one of the important and distinguishing qualities of the *javanmard* (chivalrous man), exemplified in the person of Imam 'Ali, who is the embodiment of justice comprised of compassion, mercy, humility, selflessness, as well as courage, intellect, and strength. Stories of 'Ali's justice and justness circulate in private conversations, as well as in the mass-media culture. 'Ali's paradigmatic chivalry is folded into Persianate values, as depicted by the mythologies of the great kings of pre-Islamic Persia in Ferdowsi's epic poem, *Shahnameh*. The Iranian national epic in turn highlights the figure of the *pahlavan* (hero), noble fighter and justice warrior. This image is most poignantly represented through the figure of the wrestler.[17] In *zurkhaneh* (gymnasium, *lit.* house of strength), wrestlers foster long-held ethical values, which include both spiritual and physical fortitude (Rochard 2002). Trainees cultivate purity of the heart, honesty, and good temper, alongside physical prowess. Today the broad spirit of the *pahlavan* is signified by athletes, whether it be members of the national wrestling, volleyball, or soccer teams, whose celebrated players are often called upon to engage in forgiveness work. Athleticism and justice are intermingled with the idea of forbearance—a sensibility of magnanimity. There is perhaps some basis in this collusion between athletic prowess, justice, and magnanimity to denote a deeply masculinist persona for the notion of chivalry, perhaps as a counterpoise to the feminine quality that forbearance exudes by itself, best depicted by the image I saw on a public bus during Ramadan in the summer of 2015.

Historically, the female figures from the immediate family of the Prophet, especially the Prophet's daughter (and wife of 'Ali), Fatemeh, as well as Maryam (Mary), the only female to be mentioned by name in the Qur'an, are held in special reverence in *Shi'i* Islam. The lives these women led are considered to be exemplary. Among her qualities, Fatemeh is held out for piety, and also for suffering death, poverty, and injustice with grace. Maryam, also known for her piety, is esteemed as mother to Jesus and for the qualities of purity, sincerity, loyalty, honesty, nurturing, and compassion.[18] In both female figures, the trope of self-sacrifice figures strongly.

The depiction of mothers as forbearing subjects is not unique to the context of retributive sanctioning. In my earlier work, I had many discussions with women about the importance of cultivating forbearance as an attribute of piety (Osanloo 2009). In that project on women's rights discourses, the significance of forbearance played out in the context of marital disputes and women's initiatives to seek divorce. In such cases, my interlocutors, from judges to the women themselves, frequently articulated the need for women's patience and forbearance. While some were deeply critical, the expression of women's forbearance, often in the context of hardship and suffering, was considered an important adjunct to her moral character. Thus, it seems, based on my previous project, women's evident forbearance in suffering projected onto them a moral attribute and thus more credible legal standing before judges when seeking separation.

In cases of homicide, however, a woman's forbearance takes on an even greater significance. Her moral weight—as mother, nurturer, and the relational glue that holds the family together—gains increased importance in the eyes of the law, the state, and often, the family. By law, each immediate relative of a murder victim possesses an individual right of retribution. As a result, forbearance may come only after every member of the family who is accorded the right of retributive sanctioning consents to forgo it. Although the right of retribution belongs to each family member equally and individually, in most of the cases I encountered, one family member, usually the mother, became the proxy decision-maker for everyone. In the context of criminal sanctioning, the moral quality associated with forbearance that mothers of victims possess earns them the stature to handle the weighty decision of how to punish their relative's murderer.

The intensified attention to women's roles as nurturers and comforters has also lent itself to a perception of the gender of forbearance as feminine.[19] But being compassionate and forbearing is not without costs. Some of my interlocutors complained that it was a way that women were made to be less equal, that the societal expectation of forbearance pressured women to make choices against their self-interest.

The figure of the mother is crucial in such decisions because of her *mazlum-iyyat* (grace in suffering), as the earlier cartoon depicts. She is the one who has borne children. Even in the case of the mother's absence, I saw sisters, particularly those who had married and had children, step in to make the key decision. Similarly, in my family's case, my grandmother was tasked with making the decision, even though spouses do not possess the same legal standing as immediate blood relatives. Even in that case, however, my grandmother was not only a figure embodying the loss of her husband, but also one who expressed the collective grief of her children. As the family's designated decision-maker, she was representing and assuring the sense of loss her children felt. In this way, forbearance emphasizes the position of the mother in particular, not women in general, in their different social roles.

Of course, possessing the moral attribute of forbearance does not guarantee an outcome of forbearance. That is, just because a mother is forbearing, it does not mean that she will forgo retributive sanctioning. It means, instead, that she is the one who exudes the grace in suffering that is expected of her station. Other family members look to her to handle the difficult decision; it is up to her to determine what action would right the wrong committed against the beloved.

The Slap Heard Around the World:
Forbearance as Ordinary and Exceptional

In April 2014, Iranian media outlets reported a last-minute act of forbearance in Mazandaran, a province in northern Iran. Western news services picked up the story and highlighted the extraordinary nature of the process (Dehghan 2014). In the rare spectacle of a public execution, the mother of the victim approached the perpetrator, who stood on a chair with his hands tied behind his back, his head shrouded in a black hood, and his neck bound by a noose. This mother stepped on the chair, removed the perpetrator's hood, and then delivered an open-handed slap to the side of his face before removing the noose from his neck, signaling her consent to forgo retribution. Photographers captured the potent blow and published video and still images from the event.

Newspapers followed up with interviews and back-story: The mother had lost another son some years earlier; she was still angry, but, in the end, felt that executing her son's killer would not alleviate her pain.[20]

Over the months that followed, a spate of Iranian newspapers published commentaries about this extraordinary act and others that followed in its wake. Several referred to these acts of forbearance as the beginning of a new movement. One author, a lawyer, wrote of an apparent spike in forbearance, calling it a "wave of forgiveness."[21] Another, a professor and then-President of the Iranian Sociological Association, explained the groundswell as part of the social capital arising from a new administration's investment in hope and reform.[22] A third piece, by a criminal lawyer and law professor, addressed the marketization of forgiveness, and argued that the rise in forgiveness showed that the business of life is more valuable than that of death.[23]

These articles were published after the finalization of the post-revolutionary criminal codes that emphasized reconciliation in criminal procedures. As the writers noted, each in their own way, the extraordinary act of forbearance is ordinary inasmuch as it is a right of every individual victim. Each author also argued that forbearance was becoming a norm, taking precedence over the revenge instinct that the decision, left in the hands of victims, might otherwise foster. The accounting of forbearance in the news goes beyond mere description, however. Forbearance stories become part of a broader socio-cultural landscape in which experts and interested parties express a prescriptive purpose and produce the reality they name. To be sure, some media outlets seek to change the nature of the debate and the on-the-ground culture.

While the individual act of forbearance is extraordinary, practice designates its everyday quality and imbues it with a quotidian sensibility deriving from ordinary ethics. Part of the ordinariness of forbearance is the commonplace occurrence of such extraordinary acts. Champions of forbearance seek to induce or cultivate a change on the ground in the everydayness of forbearance. They note that forbearance exists in everyday life in the most mundane ways. They emphasize how natural or ingrained forbearance is, expressing it as an authentic part of Iranian or Persian culture, emphasizing its Muslim and non-Muslim origins. All this is part of a sensibility of benevolence associated with civilizational values rooted in a take-your-pick array of sources: secular, faith-based, mystical, ancient, classical, modern, western, eastern, ethnic, tribal, and humanistic, including poetry, literature, and folklore. These values, along with their associated morality tales, then become the vehicles for persuasion, depending, of course, on the victim's family's own religious, political, and social sensibilities.

These advocates of forbearance attempt to advance a prescriptive agenda (culture-building) by noting the routine existence of forbearance in everyday life and seeking to normalize its place as a social practice and legal principle, suggesting that this is how people should behave in the extraordinary circumstance of a murder. They contend that while the act of forbearance in such a circumstance *is* extraordinary, forbearance itself is commonplace in Iranian cultural practices and daily life, and so, extending its application to homicide, albeit an extraordinary circumstance, is conceivable.

The process of seeking forbearance is further complicated by the tense nature of the relationships between the perpetrator and their families, victims' next-of-kin, and judicial officials. Activists sometimes falter and offend the victim's family, a big risk in such a high-stakes endeavor. In some cases, state officials intervene in order to prevent the public shaming of the victim or their family, thus stoking the revenge impulse. In other cases, offenders' families tread carefully to evade "*majazee-kardan*" (virtualizing) or publicizing cases on social media, so as to avoid offending the victim's family, who holds the power to kill or let live. These complexities have led to professionalization on both sides. Judicial officials have moved to intervene in and regulate reconciliation efforts, while social workers and other activists increasingly formalize their craft into best practices.[24]

As we will see, state officials take issue with advocacy efforts when they see them shift from forgiveness work to a condemnation of the system of criminal justice. This is not to say that there is no debate on the death penalty within Iran. On the contrary, scholars of Islam, both within the seminaries of Qom and the universities, engage in just such debates with dozens of journals publishing critical inquiries into such issues. It is when a particular publication or speech takes on the tone of denouncing the scripture-based mode of accountability, one through which the state consolidates and justifies its own authority, that leads to censure and sometimes arrest and imprisonment.

Modes of Accountability

Political debates and high-stakes risks notwithstanding, the aim of the cultural work was, as several of my interlocutors told me, to change the conditions on the ground. That is, to shift how people think about accountability for homicide. One general aim of the law—giving victims the right to retribution—is to preserve the broader peace. As one young lawyer explained it to me, "Look, for centuries, this is how people resolved their disputes. Do you think that if the government now came and took away this right, it would work? No. It would force people to take action on their own." Another interlocutor, a social worker fervently committed to ending the death penalty, noted, "I am totally against execution. I think it should not be allowed, but we have to work incrementally to change the culture on the ground." Still another anti-death penalty actor told me, "We work to change the underlying culture. People in some parts of Iran, especially in rural villages, still hang on to the old tribal practices of washing blood with blood. We try to change that way of thinking. We say [to the victim's family], 'Washing blood with blood does not solve anything. You will not feel better, nothing is resolved. But, if you receive compensation, that could help your family live better.' In some regions, however, victims' families view this as an insult. They complain, 'People will say we washed our son's blood with money.'" Victims often feel indignant about the idea of accepting money for their loss. They lament that by putting up funds, perpetrators avoid deserved punishment. Indeed, individuals want to "settle accounts" (Borneman 1997), "get even" (Miller 2006), and have the law hold offenders accountable for wrongs they have committed. Avenging victims' rights is not only just, according to one legal scholar, but is an area in which Iran "comes closest to getting it right" (Rosenbaum 2013:174).

Martha Minow (1998) has explored notions of accountability on a spectrum from forgiveness to revenge. She considers forgiveness at one end of that continuum where revenge, the excess of punishment, is at the other. Forgiveness in most scholarly studies involves an exploration of healing in post-conflict societies in which people on different sides did terrible things to each other. The violence, while perhaps not balanced by the various parties to the conflict, must be addressed so that society can move forward. Forgiveness efforts appear to be more prominent when the different partisans remain in the country after the conflict. In such contexts, forgiveness is often the term used for private or interpersonal disputes, even in post-conflict societies.[25] The much wider society-driven mechanism for accountability is a truth commission, which allows parties to reconcile and the society at-large to move past the conflict. In such contexts, truth commissions serve at least three purposes: establish a record of what happened so that it cannot be contested by future generations; offer survivors a chance to learn what happened to their loved ones; and permit offenders to seek psychic healing by revealing the truth, showing remorse, and possibly apologizing.[26] Public commissions for post-conflict atrocity often serve the purpose of societal reconciliation.

Whether personal forgiveness comes before or after reconciliation is a much-discussed topic in post-conflict studies. For some, the mechanics of reconciliation processes may lead to personal forgiveness (Tutu 2000); for others, personal forgiveness may lead to broader societal reconciliation. The answer lies in how we define forgiveness.[27] For many, forgiveness is interpersonal, outside of the state, and often faith-based (Griswold 2007).[28] Forgiveness that results from outside pressures may bear resentments along the way (Murphy 1988). Forgiveness could be an act of strength or weakness. For some, forgiveness is an unreciprocated gift that provides the grantor with an emotional release that ultimately allows her to reclaim her life.

However, when forgiveness is understood as mercy or clemency coming from the sovereign, it is a "moderation that diminishes a due and deserved punishment to some degree" (Seneca 2010:172). This curbing of a due punishment is appropriate for reasons of equity and fairness (Nussbaum 1993; Meyer 2010). Seen in this way, Derrida (2001b) finds that mercy "seasons justice"; that is, mercy (1) eases justice, (2) elevates it, and (3) gives coherence to the "economy of good grounds" (it replaces justice with goodness, and in doing so, preserves it).[29]

Clemency can be distinguished from mercy in that the former is a reduction of punishment authorized by law, providing relief from legal justice (Sarat 2005:19). Mercy is part of a larger notion of charity and is motivated by a moral sentiment, such as compassion (2005:20). Both have the outcome of forgoing a deserved punishment, but mercy involves some orientation by the grantor towards the grantee. Once considered an important constituent of justice, mercy has fallen in decline in contemporary practice (Tuckness and Parrish 2014).

While the literature on accountability is vast, western scholarship takes as a settled matter that it is the sovereign who accords mercy. Studies of so-called "modern law" take for granted that the sovereign has power over the life of its subjects, that it is not delegated to a private individual. Sociolegal scholars have defined *precisely* this arrogation of the private right of retribution by the state from the individual as a hallmark, indeed, the decisive moment of the break from pre-modern, status-based societies to those of so-called "modern" and contract-based ones (Redfield 1964; Foucault 1996). The fact remains, however, that numerous modes of accountability continue to exist.[30]

Borneman (2011) attempts to systematize theoretically four different kinds of responses or redress for injuries. These distinct modes of accountability exist, with each serving a particular logic and aim: retribution; restitution or compensation; performative redress, including public apologies and requests or demands for forgiveness; and rites of commemoration.[31] The first three modes are singular or unique "events" and are directed towards closure, while the last is intended to be repeated and serves to memorialize.

Modes of accountability also service different ideas about what accountability achieves. Some address calculability and explanation, while others assess responsibility and "being answerable or liable" (Borneman 2011:3). However, both ideas of accountability concern themselves with the redress of social relationships and of reckoning with loss. For Borneman, the state is involved in the different modes to varying degrees. He considers that in the adjudication for punishment or compensation, the state is integral, whereas in the context of performative redress or rituals of commemoration, it may be less so.

Borneman's analytical framework is a useful starting point for organizing how to think about responses to harm or injury. In the Iranian context, the law's retributive logic articulates with appeals for forgiveness alongside a distinct rationale for compensation that is deployed to bring about forbearance, often through some kind of performative redress. That is to say, the different modes of accountability blend into each other analytically, and the state is never fully disassociated from them. Yet, as in other contexts, in the Iranian one, victims' families must constantly contend with the tension between calculating personal harm and seeing that someone is held responsible. The modes of accountability respond to this tension; in different societies these tensions play out differently, both through the accountability mechanisms that the state provides and through the customary practices that societies have created. Here is where the relationship between private and public law emerges and, again, where that of tort and criminal responsibility lie. The areas of law are not distinct categories, but rather related, as are notions of individual liability and collective responsibility. Thus, how the four modes of accountability operate and interrelate, and the extent to which states employ them to prevent extra-judicial violence, is distinct in societies around the world. Even while observing an association between modes of accountability, their outcomes, and the relation between individual and collective responsibility, Borneman contends that "modes of accountability are used more frequently in sequence and not simultaneously" (2011:5). Yet the Iranian example suggests a blended sociolegal system of criminal justice and tort liability in which the four modes of accountability work in tandem.

Accountability and payback, however, have numerous meanings. Philosopher Jean Hampton distinguishes retributive justice from what she refers to as "corrective justice." In the former, the perpetrator receives punishment for wrongful *acts*; in the latter, the perpetrator pays compensation for *harms* (1992a). Hampton considers the compensatory component not to be concerned with the wrongful act itself. This is a distinction that provides expression for the concerns of some victims' families in Iran, particularly when the prison sentence will not exceed ten years. But from where does Iran's system of accountability emerge?

Scriptural Sources: Mercy in Islam[32]

As my interlocutors told me repeatedly, "Forgiveness is in our religion and our laws." Of course, these interlocutors were referring to their religion as Islam and their laws as those codified in the Islamic republic. An estimated 99 percent of Iranians are said to be Muslim (irrespective of levels of piety), and between 90 and 95 percent are *Shiʿi*.[33] These numbers do not account for those who are not practicing or consider themselves to be secular or atheist, and who, nevertheless, are subject to the laws codified by state interpreters of *Shiʿi*

FIGURE 2. Government-issued banner posted over a bridge in Tehran during Ramadan 2019, with the phrase, "I Forgive," then referencing the Qur'an, Chapter 42 (*Shora* [Consultation]:37): "Thee Chivalrous Man, in the Face of Anger, Forgives."

jurisprudence. What I have pointed to in the above sections—sources and motivations for forbearance—however, extend well beyond the tenets of *Shi'i* Islam, even if the laws are ostensibly codified through the state's version of it. Given these numbers and the state's formation, it bears examining the Qur'anic sources of this victim-centered law and forbearance.

For pious Muslims, two of God's primary qualities come from the word for mercy—*Ar-Rahman* and *Ar-Rahim*, meaning "The Most Gracious" and "The Most Merciful." These two attributes are recorded in the phrase recited at the beginning of 113 out of 114 chapters of the Qur'an: "In the name of God, the Most Gracious, the Most Merciful." Through their daily prayers, practicing Muslims repeat the phrase, known as the *bismillah*, over seventeen times each day. The *bismillah* serves as a persistent reminder of God's never-ending mercy and the rewards awaiting followers of the "right path." The *bismillah* makes up the first verse of the Qur'an, starting the first chapter, *Sura al-Fatiheh*, The Opening Chapter, believed to be the first couplet revealed by God through the angel Gabriel to the Prophet Mohammad around 610 CE.[34] Muslims take this phrase to be an opening and invocation to live according to the grace offered by God and to pursue peace and harmony in all relations—with others and with God.[35] Aside from daily prayers, the phrase, *bismillah ar-rahman ar-rahim*, is repeated throughout the day, before every meal, the daily trek to the office, meetings, ceremonies, court, the start of a film, and various other activities. It acts as a reminder to Muslims of the obligation to be just and compassionate in their dealings with one another. The first term, *Bismillah* means "In the Name of God," signifying that the speaker begins all actions with God and invokes Him before all acts (al-Tabari 1987:54).[36]

While definitions of the terms *ar-rahman* and *ar-rahim* derive from a common source as "one who has mercy," the terms do not have the same meanings.

The distinction is best explained by the 10ᵗʰ-century scholar Abu Ja'far Muhammad b. Jarir al-Tabari (838–923) in his authoritative commentary, which notes that *ar-rahman* is broader, larger in scope, both temporally and physically (1987:55–6). *Ar-Rahman* encompasses all creatures in this world and the next. *Ar-Rahim* denotes mercy to believers in the next world. Al-Tabari further offers the distinction between the terms in suggesting that the broader term, *ar-rahman*, offers the idea of the "One Who Feels Compassion," while the latter, *ar-rahim*, refers to the "One Who Treats Gently." Taken together, this indicates that God is compassionate towards all, but singles out believers with kindness in the next world.

Mercy is sanctified in multiple forms and deeply rooted as a core principle in the sacred texts. At least thirty-five Qur'anic verses counsel forgiveness over vengeance or retribution (Nateri 2006:404n22). Shah-Kazemi highlights over one hundred verses that demonstrate the preference for mercy, and particularly emphasizes verses, "*My mercy encompasses all things,*" Chapter 7 (*A'raf* [The Heights]):156, and "*God has prescribed mercy to Himself,*" Chapter 6 (*An'am* [The Cattle]):12.[37] These two verses highlight the breadth of mercy. The former suggests that mercy is defined expansively and is to be incorporated in other modes of being, ways of thinking. The latter conveys that mercy is an obligation. As God has prescribed it for Himself, it is also how Believers should behave towards themselves and others. For Shah-Kazemi, mercy is built-in to justice; it also encompasses forgiveness (Abou El Fadl 2004).

Shah-Kazemi also draws from a "*hadith qudsi,*" which is a divine utterance of the Prophet, "*My mercy takes precedence over my wrath,*" to show that while the Qur'an recognizes that anger is present when one has been wronged, a person, especially a leader, must master that fury in order to achieve the higher purpose of justice: "The wrathful side of the nature of things is not denied here, but it is clearly subordinate to the higher ontological purpose of mercy" (2006:83).[38] Shah-Kazemi continues:

> One is therefore more 'real' insofar as mercy predominates over wrath, spiritually, within one's own soul and morally, in one's conduct; and it is in the very nature of justice, conceived in this sacred manner, to tend towards compassion wherever possible, even though there must also be a place for rigorous application of corrective penalty where this is unavoidable (Ibid.).

Thus, to be just, a leader must incorporate compassion. Corrective penalty is reminiscent of Hampton's inclination towards corrective punishment. Of course, retribution is a principle unambiguously afforded to injured parties; it is often, but not always, accompanied by the complement and commendation of forbearance. In that vein, Chapter 5 (*Maedeh* [The Table Spread]):45 is the single most significant verse of the Qur'an upon which jurists base their interpretations of the retribution and forbearance provisions in the criminal code:

> We ordained therein for them: 'Life for life, eye for eye, nose for nose, ear for ear, tooth for tooth, and wounds equal for equal.' But if any one remits the retaliation by way of charity, it is an act of atonement for himself. And if any fail to judge by (the light of) what Allah hath revealed, they are (no better than) wrong-doers.

The first sentence recognizes the harm done and that the penalty is retaliatory punishment. If, however, the person wronged remits, this will itself be a form of reparation for the injured party. In the last lines of the verse, the injured party is admonished not to go too far astray of exact punishment, as this would render the injured party an offender as well. Thus, the point of this verse is to show that there is a limit on punishment—it must never exceed the harm done. By not exacting in-kind punishment, there are rewards as well. Chapter 2 (Baqarah [The Cow]):178 references another of the most oft-quoted Qur'anic verses associated with retribution and forbearance:

> O ye who believe! The law of equality is prescribed to you in cases of murder: the free for the free, the slave for the slave, the woman for the woman. But if any remission is made by the brother of the slain, then grant any reasonable demand, and compensate him with handsome gratitude, this is a concession and a Mercy from your Lord. After this whoever exceeds the limits shall be in grave penalty.

In this verse as well, the right of in-kind punishment is confirmed, but again with the encouragement of forbearance. It is also here, in this verse, that the wrong-doer is encouraged to seek reconciliation with reparation and appreciation. In the final line, again the Qur'an warns against punishment or compensation that exceeds limits. Scholars who have studied this verse, taking it together with the whole of the Qur'an, have suggested a deeper meaning. Indeed, the verse references a period in which tribal warfare induced a never-ending cycle of violence. In such contexts, where one act of injustice was met with another, often greater act, the response was never in-kind, but exceeded it. Religious scholar Abdulaziz Sachedina suggests that, when taken in its context, this verse compels a remission of violence and counsels proportionality with an aim towards stopping the cycle of violence. In his interpretation of 2:178, Sachedina states:

> Reconciliation flows from forgiveness and willingness on the part of the victim to forgo retribution as an end in itself. From the Koranic admonition

to forgive and accept compensation, it seems retributive punishment is worth pursuing only to the extent that it leads to reconciling (*shifa' al-sudur* = 'healing of the hearts') the victim and wrongdoer, and rehabilitating the latter after his or her acknowledgement of responsibility (2001:111–112).

Taken together, these, as well as numerous other verses, compel Muslims to forgo the right of exact punishment. Throughout the Qur'an, believers are compelled to forgive others for transgressions—even the ultimate one, the killing of a loved one.

The issue of forbearance in such contexts cannot be separated from the relationship between compassion, mercy, and the highest value in Islam—justice.[39] Shah-Kazemi links the values of compassion and mercy with justice: "[T]he capacity to act with compassion in no way conflicts with the demands of justice; rather it is an intrinsic aspect of justice, conceived ontologically" (2006:83). He conceives of the ontological relationship between compassion, mercy, and justice in his reading of the compiled works of 'Ali ibn Abi Talib, whose words and letters were collected in the 10th century CE by Sayyid Sharif al-Radi in one volume entitled, *Nahj al-Balaghah* (Peaks of Eloquence).[40] Among the hundreds of letters and writings that make up the *Nahj al-Balaghah*, one letter stands out for its contemplation on justice—the letter 'Ali ibn Talib wrote to Malik al-Ashtar appointing him governor of Egypt. This epistle, number 52, is regarded by Muslim scholars as a source of inspiration for ideal Islamic governance and ethical principles, not only ideal for a ruler, but for all Muslims. The letter expounds on the nature of justice and governance in Islam. In it, 'Ali appeals to al-Ashtar as a compassionate leader by prescribing forgiveness, "they may act wrongly, wilfully or by neglect. So, extend to them your forgiveness and pardon, in the same way as you would like God to extend His forgiveness and pardon to you" (Ibn Abi Talib 2005:566).[41] 'Ali's writings thus validate the notion that compassion is inherent to justice.

Building on Imam 'Ali as a source of understanding, justice, and mercy, Leonard Lewisohn focuses on forbearance.[42] Lewisohn finds that forbearance has deep roots in the Persian *Sufi* tradition related to the Persian spiritual *futuwwat* (chivalric tradition) for whom 'Ali is the founding father.[43] In the *futuwwat*, 'Ali is "celebrated as being the incarnation of God's attributes of mercy, tolerance, forgiveness, and generosity" and "the epitome of courage, generosity and selflessness" (2006:117–118).

The *futuwwat* were not a mere sect, however; the *futuwwat* were an indivisible feature of the sociocultural history of the *Sufis* throughout the Middle East. Numerous stories from the Persian chivalric tradition feature 'Ali as "an expert in conflict resolution" (Lewisohn 2006:120). A difference of opinion existed between chevaliers of the *Sufi* order and Muslim jurists, especially on the application of the laws of retribution, in which the chevaliers held a more "relaxed attitude towards" its application (Ibid.). 'Ali's moral qualities are highlighted as virtues worthy of emulation because his conduct reflects "a finer justice based on love" (2006:126). Lewisohn recounts several stories of how 'Ali forgave offenders and granted mercy over punishment. These anecdotes of a higher justice, Lewisohn suggests, are stressed by Persian *Sufi* scholars. Citing a set of anecdotes by one such scholar, Suhrawardi, Lewisohn examines 'Ali's ethics of justice, focusing on verse 2:178 and notes that, for 'Ali, the verse advises a "'healing of the heart' rather than a lust for punishment" (2006:127). In Iran, thus, we can trace the lineage of the legal formulation of *gozasht*, which takes its modern form through a legal mechanism in the penal code not only to the sacred text of the Qur'an, but also to Imam 'Ali and the Persian *Sufi* tradition.

In Terms of Mercy: Forbearance, Forgiveness, and Pardon

Iran provides a specific and unique setting in which to consider the Islamic mandate of mercy and a criminal justice system that emphasizes victims' rights. Because Iran is one of the few Muslim-majority countries to have integrated *shari'a* (Islamic principles) into the state form, an Islamic republic, tangible qualities of this religious compulsion exist in civil and legal institutions.

As I have noted, throughout the book, I will explore forgiveness work, but as I do, I am careful not to suggest that forgiveness and mercy are interchangeable. To the contrary, I trace the law back to the Islamic mandate of mercy to understand how in Iran's Islamic republic, specific Qur'anic verses are codified as positive law in the penal code as a state enforced mode of accountability. At the same time, these terms are distinct, even within the Iranian legal system. And, while this work starts with what I see as codified scriptural principles, it is limited neither to legal interpretations nor to religious sources.

I take mercy or *rahmat* to be the guiding scriptural and jurisprudential principle and foundation; forgiveness or *bakhshesh* derives from the scriptural compulsion to be merciful and compassionate. While numerous Qur'anic verses entreat forgiveness, in the Muslim context, mercy, as I noted earlier, includes much more than forgiveness; indeed, mercy encompasses forgiveness (Abou El Fadl 2004; Shah-Kazemi 2007). Thus, to be merciful, one must be forgiving, but a person must be more than just forgiving in order to be merciful. In the context of my study, mercy takes shape partly through acts of forgiveness.

Lastly, we come to forbearance or *gozasht*, which in the case at hand refers to forgoing a recognized right—that of *qisas*. As we will see, the term *gozasht* is codified as exception. However, in Persian, the term is employed colloquially as well, referring to a similar idea—that of taking exception or letting go, say, of a grudge. A person can show forbearance (used as a verb), but one can also be forbearing (as an adjective), and thus self-excepting or self-sacrificing or *khod-gozasht*, literally taking exception to oneself. As discussed previously, these terms carry gendered associations; they are frequently asked of and applied to women, and, in many cases, carry feminine connotations.

Although *bakhshesh* and *gozasht* possess distinct meanings, in daily use and in legal application, my interlocutors often used the terms interchangeably. In legal settings, the term my interlocutors employed is *gozasht*, signifying forgoing a right that they possessed, that of retribution. *Bakhshesh*, however, is the term my interlocutors used more colloquially, in interviews, for instance. The one qualification to this point is that one forgives *a person*, while one forgoes *a right*. Thus, the terms are used to express the ideas in the following way: *forgive him/her* and *forgo it*. In practical terms, forbearance involves giving up a claim, while forgiveness requires giving up a resentment.

My interlocutors distinguished *gozasht* as a legal term with instrumental, not emotional, meaning. However, in interviews, I posed clarifying questions to ascertain if and how my interlocutors distinguished the terms outside of the legal context and what it meant to them to forgive someone (versus forgo retribution). It was not always the case that someone who agreed to forgo retribution also personally or emotionally forgave a perpetrator.

Finally, the Qur'anic, and thus Arabic, term that is often expressed in the context of forbearance or pardon is *afv*. *Afv* is the term employed in the Qur'anic verses I discussed above—5:45 and 2:178. Iranians also employ this term in common parlance, albeit less frequently. However, in Iran, *afv* is used more regularly by state actors to signify a pardon by the sovereign. For example, Iran's Supreme Leader, Ayatollah Ali Khamenei'i, annually announces a certain number of prisoners to whom he has granted *afv*. Thus, I distinguish the term *afv* from *gozasht* as they are so differentiated in the law, with the former referring to state pardons, while the latter refers to individual forbearance of a private right.

In addition to the terms above, in the context of my study, I have encountered the term *solh*, which refers to peace, resolution, settlement, reconciliation, or conciliation. The aim of *solh* is to avert violence and revenge. Iranians often use the term with another, *sauzesh*, also connoting settlement or compromise. Together, the terms form an idiomatic expression, *solh va sauzesh*, which I translate as "reconciliation and settlement." The former term, *solh*, which is also found in the Qur'an, is likewise employed in Iran's penal code.

As *solh* has Arabic roots, Iranians more colloquially use the term *ashti* to refer to the same idea. *Ashti* is often expressed as one half of an idiomatic expression, *qahr va ashti*, signifying conflict and resolution, a phrase that has its own vernacular lineage.

Trends: Is the Extraordinary Act a(n) (Ordinary) Thing?

Religious compulsion, legal obligation, cultural cajoling, and media coaxing aside, the question of the frequency of forbearance remains. While this is not a work of quantifying forbearance numbers, the question of its regularity is worth considering. In other words, is the forbearance afforded in Iran's criminal justice system a common practice? Does it actually happen and, if so, what is the rate of occurrence? And, as some journalists have observed, is there a trend towards forbearance?

Judicial authorities do not readily disclose statistics on forbearance. Some of this has to do with the potentially political uses of statistics related to capital punishment in Iran. Human rights organizations have roundly criticized Iran's record on executions, the majority of which are for offenses other than murder.[44]

In my search for statistics to answer these questions, however, I encountered another, more mundane problem: how do we account for the number of forbearances in any given year and what do they tell us? That is, can one really calculate the ordinariness of such an extraordinary act? Families of victims have few time constraints on their ruminations and frequently take upwards of ten years to decide whether or not to seek retributive action. Thus, a forbearance decision in one instance may date back to a homicide committed many years prior. Similarly, executions for homicide are carried out once all appellate and procedural petitions are completed and the head of the judiciary's Implementations Unit has reached the decision that the victim's family could not be persuaded to forgo retribution. Thus, what I sought to determine, as a marker of frequency of forbearance, was some indication of the incidents of forbearance versus executions for homicide in a given year.

When I broached this subject with members of the judiciary, many agreed that it would be good to know, but stated that their offices kept no such statistics; others said the Office of the Prosecutor holds them. This was the one office I was not able to access, with the exception of one division, the Implementations Unit for Tehran. I met with the supervisor of this office in 2016, and, among other issues, asked about the statistics, making it clear that I was interested in understanding whether this was a trend. He asserted that it was, then called down to each of the five branch offices and asked for their

TABLE 1. Annual *Qisas* Adjudications in Iran: Execution and Forbearance Ratios

Year	*Qisas* Sentences Adjudicated	Executions	Forbearances	Rate of Forbearance
2018	460	188	272	59%
2017	461	240	221	48%
2016	393	142	251	64%
2015	469	207	262	54%

Source: Compiled from Iran Human Rights Annual Reports, 2015–2018.

annual figures. Shortly thereafter, a representative from each of the branch offices arrived, presented a file, and handed it to the supervisor. As the reports filed in one-by-one, he silently read the papers, made notes, and added up the numbers on a piece of paper. When the last report arrived, he held them in his hands and said, "I cannot give you these, but I can tell you that for the previous year and for the first half of this year [2015 and 2016], in Tehran province, in two-thirds of cases, families consented to forbearance, 66 percent." That is, among the murder cases that had reached the point of implementation that year, two-thirds of families elected to forgo retaliatory punishment.

Looking to the country as a whole, in their annual report for 2016, Iran Human Rights (IHR), a Norway-based organization, estimated that of the 530 executions that took place in Iran that year, approximately 27 percent (142) were for murder.[45] In that same year, they report, 251 murderers received a reprieve of their execution by the victim's family. So, out of a total of 393 (142 plus 251) potential executions for murder, 64 percent (251) were spared as a result of forbearance. In the previous year, the IHR report found that some 969 executions took place and approximately 21 percent (207) were for murder. That same year, they found 262 murderers received a reprieve. Thus in 2015, the rate of forbearance was about 54 percent. Table 1 shows the annual rates of forbearance in relation to total *qisas* sentences adjudicated in the year since my conversation with the supervisor until the most recently available.[46]

Determining the frequency is important in gaining a sense of the regularity of such acts. However, the statistics do not tell us why some families ultimately decide to forgo retribution when the law gives them the right to seek equal punishment. The goal is not to seek some general truths about victims' rights, retribution, or mercy and forgiveness. Instead, by highlighting the distinctive qualities and effects of a criminal justice system that privileges victims' rights, we observe an enlightening contrast (Taylor 2007) to western legal systems, in which victims have no such rights.

Methodology: Up-close, near, and far

The tension between the legal and moral compulsion to forgive alongside an absence of rules and regulations about how to do so is productive. It is this productive tension that this book addresses. Anthropological fieldwork methods offer particularly powerful lenses through which to examine the stories and then to assemble the larger and more complex picture of how others make sense of their lives. My approach is an on-the-ground and longitudinal study of crime and forgiveness in Iran that allows for reflection on internal debates and grassroots efforts for penal reform and eradication of the death penalty. I have also aimed to get close enough to individuals who are making such decisions about life and death—people whose practices we might otherwise find inscrutable—to form an empathetical stance.

In doing so, I have explored modes of social organization and accountability for how they inspire and arrange both public and private commitments. An ethical stance about retribution or even the death penalty may grow out of a sense of an inviolate duty to act. Such a sense of duty may emerge from or be informed by other aspects of life (spiritual, political, social) and comes with an affective stance and a sense of ethical self-formation (Asad 1986). Ethical selves are fashioned through hyper-structured ritual practices and embodied and performed—at times consciously and at others not (Manoukian 2011). Politics, too, is performed through such rituals. Social activists with whom I worked followed specific social and cultural rituals. At the same time, class and demographic antagonisms get played out in these affective and ritualized practices—this forgiveness work.

To make sense of the world of forgiveness work and to better understand the factors that lead to forbearance, I draw from archival and ethnographic research, participant-observation, interviews, and life histories conducted with over fifty families of victims, as well as numerous other interested parties, who make up this cottage industry of forgiveness work. These include judges, prosecutors, defense lawyers, NGO actors, social workers, community elders, and members of the 'ulama, involved at various stages of the criminal process. I gathered this data on annual research trips from between one and four months long over a period of ten years, during the latter half of which I maintained my relationships through Skype meetings and almost daily communications through social media applications, especially What's App and Telegram. The advent of social media applications has changed the nature of research; it is no more a "zip in and zip out" affair (Hegland 2004). Contact with interlocutors meant never falling out of touch and being able to plan on-site trips for specific events. It also meant that the period necessary for re-kindling ethnographic intimacy and restoring trust was either shorter or unnecessary.

To gain access to the members of the judiciary who allowed me to conduct fieldwork in Tehran's criminal courts, I met a friend who knew one of the judges in the criminal courts. That judge escorted me to the head of Tehran Municipality's Provincial Criminal Court. In his sweeping top floor office, the head of the court asked about the nature and aims of my research and whether I was an activist. After introducing myself, I explained that my project aimed to explore the unexamined aspect of the criminal justice system, forbearance. I stated that Iran's rate of executions is well-known, but that we did not know about forbearance. I also noted that forbearance does not exist in U.S. criminal law. The latter point surprised him as it would others. The head of the court provided me with a document that allowed me access to courtrooms. His only caution was: "Tell the truth. Tell the good, tell the bad, but just tell the truth." I responded that my project was not about evaluating the good and the bad, but that I would relate and record my findings. I had no "minder," and no one ever asked to see what I wrote.

From that point on, the summer of 2012, I had mostly unfettered access to the courts and over the years have sat in on trials in over eighty cases, most, but not all of them, intentional murder cases. Several judges came to be my most important interlocutors, sitting down and going through the new laws with me, even before they were finalized and implemented. We also had conversations about the substance and procedures of criminal law in the U.S. They directed me to trials that were relevant to my study—"go to branch so-and-so; there is a good case today." The judges spoke to me about the cases, the laws, and often facilitated interviews for me with victims' families, social workers, journalists, and others, with a simple phone call. Over the years, I came to know several of the judges well enough that they sent me stories of forbearance, changes in the laws, or other items of interest. I, too, posed questions of law and process from afar. The judges in criminal court facilitated meetings for me to which I would not otherwise have had access; this includes the elusive Implementations Unit, in the Office of the Prosecutor—the division in charge of carrying out sentences. My sustained research in the courts led only to one dispute, with a female guard at the entrance, who chastised me for a *manteau* (overcoat) that was too short, "What will the judge think?" she said, letting me pass after I promised to wear a longer one the next day.

Phones, computers, and recording devices were not allowed in the courts. As a result, I recorded all of my notes by hand and returned to my apartment to write up my notes in the afternoons. This way, I was able to ask follow-up questions about law and procedure that came up later. One judge told me he would arrange it so that I could come with my phone or other devices. I declined, not wanting to strain the privileged access I had already attained.

The other side of my research had to do with forgiveness work. Although these two sides were not mutually exclusive, I made my entrée into this field through an introduction to social workers and victims' families by several defense lawyers I had met over the years. These individuals, in turn, introduced me to others. They allowed me to accompany them on their activities, interview them, and follow their forgiveness work over the years.

Forgiveness work was emotionally charged, intimate, erratic, and intense. The news was not always good; at times it was brutal. At other times, I felt I came close to sensing the feeling of joy and elation when victims' families decided to let someone live. That feeling was always haunted, for me, at least, by an accompanying reaction: What just happened? I never became comfortable with the idea that individuals held such power over the life of another person, but it did make me question why, then, when the state holds such power, as in the U.S., I do not have the same level of discomfort.

My aims in doing this work have not been fueled by a preconceived moral judgment on the legal system or the choices that my interlocutors make. I have sought, rather, to unpack and open up how a victim-centered approach to punishment operates in one specific legal context and to examine the challenges alongside its appeal. In the broader social and political context, the social activists' impulse to change the conditions on-the-ground also resonates with the deeper politicization of anti-death penalty activism in Iran today. I found it striking to see so many activists, from a broad range of political camps, working on this issue: from those deeply enmeshed within the judicial system, some even working at judicial officials' urgings, to secular human rights activists. I wondered what conditions came to bear on one subset of anti-death penalty activists, whose work was deemed political and a challenge to the Islamic republic, and other advocates, who worked hand-in-hand with judicial officials to help perpetrators evade the death penalty, and yet avoided political persecution.

My exploration of the discursive work of the *kind* of activism, anti-death penalty or forgiveness work, as the case may be, sheds light on these questions, as well. Through the slow work that this project has entailed, what we might call, *anthropology in the meantime*, the course of time allowed me to observe social activists move their own individual consciences by their personal experiences in advocating, at first, only on behalf of convicted youth (under the age of eighteen) to renouncing execution under any circumstances whatsoever.[47] I found it even more striking to meet judges with such personal opinions. These are among the stories offered in the following pages.

Arc, Exposition, and Writerly Affect

Over the years of conducting research, this project has intellectually shifted from my attempting to understand how Iran's criminal justice system's forbearance mechanism operates—and how individuals caught up in it must come to a decision about their personal right of retribution—to one in which I attempt to unpack the many complex aspects of having to make such a decision. During years of writing, a key concern has been to try to do justice to the stories I have gathered.

While setting out the legal dimensions of the story is one part of my project, another more challenging one has been to convey its affective registers. That is, trying to convey, through words on a page the emotional conditions of possibility that this system produces. Following Kathleen Stewart (2007) in writing about "ordinary affects," my goal is not simply to know-and-tell or to impart knowledge about the system. Rather, I aim to hold my writing up to the intensities—physical and emotional—that my interlocutors experienced and expressed.

Capturing affect in a writing voice is a challenge. Affect, comprised of a composite of forces, operates at once at the gut and in the moment, but it also occurs as the result of complicated relations across time and space. That is to say, affect works in nuanced and embedded ways through bureaucracies, objects, and the architecture of space. It is ubiquitous, and yet its lineages and genealogies are difficult to trace. The way I have sought to do this is by storytelling with what I refer to as a writerly affect. The voice is affective because of the theory that calls for paying careful attention to the ephemera of experience—sounds, colors, patterns, materials, who can see what, when, and whom—and an analysis of how material forms invoke and make affect. I share paradigmatic scenes, settling-in on a moment or event and going deep into its workings. I highlight intensities through attention to detail, to dicta, and sometimes even background noises, scents, or seeming dalliances and divergences. These minutiae, however, are part of the larger project of conveying the atmosphere, sensations, feelings, and emotions of the affective spaces I travelled through—the semi-autonomous social field of forgiveness work.

While adhering to a narrative approach that reflects affect, I do not mean to romanticize or sentimentalize forgiveness or mercy, but rather to place it within its conditions of possibility in the context of Iran's criminal justice system. In this way, it is a narrow exploration of the operations of mercy and forgiveness, limited to its sociolegal conditioning through the mechanism of *gozasht* as it operates and circulates in Iran presently. I show what is at stake for the victims, for the system as it stands, and where the expectations, especially of retribution, come from; they are not simply isolated as legal or religious expectations. Indeed, part of my argument is to show that the provisions derived from the sacred texts set a limit on the practice of seeking revenge, again, the excess of punishment, by limiting it to *equal* or *exact* retribution. My findings, I think, lead us to ask whether there really can be such a thing in homicide as equal punishment.

Writing about Iran is always a tricky endeavor. Scholars who attempt to make sense of people's everyday lives amidst the conditions shaped by living in the Islamic Republic of Iran risk critiques of being state-directed apologists or anti-state agitators.[48] Despite the challenges, I think a study of the legal and social conditions of Iran's criminal justice system allows us to reflect, not only on a victim-centered criminal justice system, but on that of our own and to ponder whether there are aspects of attention to victims that are worthy of consideration. At the same time, extra-legally, the issue of resolving disputes, forgiveness, and mercy can have application in all of our lives.

To speak to what some readers might regard as the sheer exoticism of this book's subject matter, I want to address what I see as the stakes of this book: forgiveness by the victim's family and state killing that is not grounded in the history of incarceration. I hope to move beyond an understanding of the death penalty as merely a binary debate: good (modern) states do not possess it versus bad (backward) ones retain it. Rather, I seek to unravel the complex landscape upon which it rests in one context in order to consider deeper questions having to do with the expectations of victims that have emerged through generations of practice. I give nuance to the question of why the death penalty exists in its current form in a country in which the state implements it frequently in comparison with other countries that also employ such a law, hoping perhaps to arrive at better arguments against the death penalty or finding more efficacious ways of involving victims' families in our own system. The theoretical insights from which I draw lay the groundwork for a different approach to the death penalty, seeking to accommodate the deeper histories embedded in the complex dimensions of crime, loss, and the expectation of payback. Ultimately, the broader goal is to challenge unexamined tenets of our own ways of thinking (Bromberger 2009).

This work, then, is divided into two parts that entail and detail forgiveness work. In the first section of the book, I explore Iran's criminal laws—the legal mechanisms and processes—as well as the social conditions which confer substance and form to forbearance, and create the conditions that produce the semi-autonomous social field of forgiveness work. Second, I enter into the affective lifeworld of various agents doing forgiveness work, involved in its processes, and finally, burdened with the decision to determine whether another human being lives or dies.

Chapter 1 begins with an analysis of the victim-centered criminal justice system through the opening of a murder trial. Through it, I examine the foundational aspects of Iran's victim-centered justice system. Chapter 2 explores the final version of the penal code, passed only in 2013. Since just after the Iranian Revolution, this is the first set of transformative revisions in substantive criminal law. I lay out how the "coloring in" of the code compels judicial officials to consider alternative approaches to sanctioning. Chapter 3 embarks on a study of the operations of the criminal law and analyzes how the procedural administration of the law animates the *shari'a*. I consider the role of judges and examine how the laws (substantive and procedural) shape their reasoning and discretion in both sentencing and encouraging forbearance. Chapter 4 explores how the new provisions in the laws that encourage forbearance shape legal practices around post-sentence forgiveness work on the part of judges. Here, I analyze judges' motivations to work for forbearance by looking at the exigencies of the law, as well as spiritual and pragmatic reasons. In doing so, I highlight the consequential aspects of time in forgiveness work.

Building on time and motivations, in the second part of the book I enter into the lifeworld of forgiveness work. I begin by exploring the heavy burden of the decision that is placed on victims' families in Chapter 5. While such decisions might appear as sudden "road to Damascus" moments, they emerge, rather, from a charged atmosphere saturated with the intensities, sensations, and emotions born of the burden of that decision.

In the following chapters, I look more closely at the work of the social activists engaged in forgiveness work. Chapter 6 examines social workers' diverse approaches to the affective labor that forgiveness work entails. I consider the impact this work has on the social workers' own subjectivities, their ethical self-formation. Chapter 7 follows a group of performing artists who attempt to emotionally stir an entire village, including one particular family, in their efforts to change the social meaning of forbearance—from a pejorative act of taking money to "wash away the blood" of a loved one to a celebrated act of humanity. Building on the previous chapter's idea of ethical self-fashioning, I explore what my interlocutors referred to as *farhang-sazi* or the building-up of culture.

Lastly, Chapter 8 reflects on the work of criminal defense lawyers. Although engaged in forgiveness work, particularly post-sentencing, lawyers occupy a distinct position in relation to other actors. Lawyers who take up *qisas* cases, like anti-death penalty lawyers elsewhere, often possess a deeper agenda and, as cause lawyers, go beyond ethical self-fashioning or culture-building. They seek to enforce the rule of law. They work with and within the laws, but their ethically-grounded advocacy risks placing them in the precarious space of apparent opposition to the system itself. The position of defense lawyers, whose rights-based advocacy sits in uncomfortable opposition to the gift economy of forgiveness, ultimately highlights the tensions of human rights advocacy in this climate. I close the book with some reflections on the modern bureaucratic state. I consider what it means for a state's regulatory scheme to be comprised of such a range of free-roaming and diverse actors who operate in a semi-autonomous social field and participate in shaping and regulating its operations. Consequently, I ponder what forgiveness work means for rights, law, and the higher aims of the Qur'anic mandate of mercy.

PART I

Crimtorts

1

Legal Foundations

VICTIMS' RIGHTS AND RETRIBUTION

"WHAT WOULD YOU LIKE TO DO?" The chief judge posed the question to the victim's family, plaintiffs in the criminal case before him.

In the murder trial taking place in Iran's capital, Tehran, a grieving mother rose from her front-row seat and stepped towards the podium in the Grand Courtroom—one of two such courtrooms that hear major murder cases in Iran's most populous province. Deep red curtains lined the walls of the large assembly room, while dozens of rows of plush, plum-colored theater seats accommodated family members of the deceased, journalists, and law students sitting in on a trial deemed by the head of Tehran Municipality's Provincial Criminal Court as instructive for observers of various disciplines. Everyone present knew that the victim's family possessed the right of *qisas* (retribution), but that they could also *gozasht* (forgo) it. In Iran's victim-centered approach to criminal justice, the law recognizes the rights of injured parties ahead of those of the public. In this case, the parents of a deceased young woman were the parties granted the right to settle a score with the alleged perpetrator.

Minutes earlier, the judges had entered the room and all present had risen in a show of respect. The judges took their seats behind desks that sat atop an elevated platform. The chief judge on the case, a forty-year veteran of the court, was positioned in the middle of the stage-like dais at one end of the courtroom. An aisle in the middle of the room divided the rows of seats. On the right side of the room, the defendant, the man accused of murdering the woman, sat in the front row with his attorney beside him. Across the aisle, on the left, sat the deceased's parents, her next-of-kin, and as such, the plaintiffs in the case. A wooden podium equipped with a microphone was mounted at the center of the aisle between the opposing parties, about twenty feet from the judicial panel. Behind a second podium, this one positioned to the left, the assistant prosecutor stood, poised to read the indictment.

The chief judge opened the hearing with a brief case summary and acknowledged the many students and observers present. He turned to the assistant prosecutor, a man in his early thirties, to present the state's case against
the accused. The courtroom remained silent as the prosecutor read the lengthy
indictment, detailed the events leading up to the young woman's death, the
manner and findings of the investigation, and the charge: intentional murder.
The prosecutor then told the court that, on behalf of the people of the province of Tehran, his office sought the maximum penalty for the alleged crime:
a ten-year prison sentence.[1]

The chief judge next turned to the victim's aggrieved parents and identified
them as the private plaintiffs in the case. He asked them to approach the podium. Wearily, they came forward. The mother towered several inches over
her husband. At the lectern, the parents stood a mere foot from the man accused of murdering their daughter. Although there had yet to be a finding of
guilt, the judge, who now spoke in a soothing tone, asked the parents to articulate to the court the relief that they sought for their daughter's death—
retribution or forbearance. As Iran's criminal laws permit, it was the parents
who would determine the fate of their daughter's alleged murderer. However,
first, there had to be a finding of guilt.

Opening the questioning with the relief sought by the victim's next-of-kin
served as a dramatic overture—shining a light on the rights of the injured,
underscoring their centrality to the process, and offering them the courtroom
as a space in which to voice their grievances. And, technically, in order for the
case to proceed, the plaintiffs needed to file their demand. If plaintiffs opted
to forgo retribution, which they could at any time, the accused would face only
the prison sentence sought by the state in a secondary hearing for disrupting
public peace and security. Their demand for retribution would set into motion
a process leading to the defendant's execution, but would not foreclose the
possibly of forbearance prior to it.

The victim's mother, her husband silent by her side, drew the microphone to
her lips and audibly inhaled a mouthful of air before uttering her response.

Iran's Criminal Laws

Although Iran witnessed some codification of positive law (*qanun*) in the mid-
nineteenth century, most scholars reference the Constitutional Revolution of
1906–11 as the pivotal era in which a new parliament set out to draft centralized
statutory laws aimed at state-building and centralizing power (Enayat 2013).[2]
To construct an integrated body of law, over the following decades, legislators
drafted civil and penal codes drawn from French and Belgian laws. At the same
time, the drafters asserted the law's conformity with *Shi'i* Islamic principles

(Banani 1961; Gholami 1998–1999; Mohammadi 2007). Although a protracted affair, the drafting of the penal code was a paramount concern. Law served as a technique of power for the new government, whose prerogative as sovereign was to assert control over the body politic and to maintain order.

Reforming the criminal codes required some finesse, as some statesmen and members of the *'ulama* argued that *shari'a*-based punishments were sacred and thus impervious to codification.[3] Others felt that *shari'a*-based punishments did not adequately address the concerns of the times and that public spectacles of corporal punishment and execution were unnecessary for deterrence. The latter groups of statemen argued that social order could best be achieved through a legal system that adhered to a transparent structure of sanctions imposed through predictable legal procedures. To avoid breaching the sanctity of the *shari'a*, lawmakers framed their pursuit of a codified criminal justice system as a modification of the *'orfi* (customary) laws that left the *shari'a* intact (Enayat 2013:106). The first version, then, of the *Qanun-e Jaza'i-ye 'Orfi* (The Customary Penal Code), adopted in 1917, was modeled on the French Penal Code of 1810 and its 1858 Ottoman adaptation (Enayat 2013:107). That penal code, however, distinguished penalties issued for the preservation of public order from those of felonies (Enayat 2013:108). The latter would be the sole province of the *shari'a* and would be adjudicated in the Special Criminal Courts by a "*shari'a* judge." The classification of crimes had been established in 1912 with promulgation of the Code of Criminal Procedures, also adopted from the French.

Upon Reza Pahlavi's ascension as the Shah (King) of the new Pahlavi dynasty, on December 12, 1925, legislators were already working on drafting a revision to the penal code, fueled by the reformist energies of the previous era. Spurred by the Shah's drive for an Ataturk-style of modernization, reformists were more openly critical of *shari'a* and advocated for Western legal codes. Others, such as Mohammad Mossadeq, who would become Prime Minister in 1951, took a more conciliatory approach, focusing on necessity and reason. Mossadeq, who taught law early in his career, argued in his 1914 doctoral thesis, published in Iran in 1923, that reason is the most important source of Islamic law and that when positive law is based on reason, it is also in conformity with the *shari'a* (Dahlén 2003:147).[4]

The 1926 penal code went further in secularizing the law by making murder a public offense; it would not be adjudicated through *qisas*. Although a provision in the penal code appeared to preserve violations of the *shari'a*, jurists of the time considered it to be a tactic to mollify the *'ulama*. The standards of evidence were set too high to prove *shari'a* offenses and, since *shari'a* courts did not accept forensic or circumstantial evidence, the *shari'a* was rendered ineffectual for the state's criminal justice purposes (Enayat 2013:109). Ultimately, the Special Criminal Court was eliminated.

Despite continued debates over the source of law and jurisdiction for punishing infractions, in the almost seventy years between the constitutional period and the 1979 Revolution, Iran's criminal codes went through a series of secularizing reforms that systematized offenses and punishments while establishing a hierarchy of courts to investigate and adjudicate allegedly criminal behavior and to arbitrate over disputes. Already by 1939 the civil and criminal codes no longer contained references to the *shari'a* (Mohammadi 2007:230).

In 1979, when a popular revolution removed the monarchy, a coalition of leaders, including religious and secular nationalists, established a new system of governance: an Islamic Republic. A referendum vested the *'ulama* with immense political authority through the power of the *Velayat-e Faqih* (Guardianship of the Jurisprudent).[5] In this newly constituted branch of government, the religious leadership consolidated power by supervising judicial, military, and other matters deemed important to the political organization of the state. When Ayatollah Khomeini was elected as the country's highest authority, *Vali-ye Faqih* (Ruling Jurist), he was empowered to determine the conformity of all the nation's laws with Islamic principles. He quickly moved to dissolve the existing judicial apparatus and renewed his call to integrate *shari'a* into state law.[6] This was a substantive shift from the previous era in which laws were not to conflict with *shari'a* (Gholami 1998–1999:214).

The newly-formed Islamic Republic of Iran made interpreting the *shari'a* a project of the central government and gave that authority to a few jurists over legislators or even other qualified jurists.[7] Article 167 of Iran's postrevolutionary constitution limited the sources of law and legal reasoning to *Shi'i* jurisprudence.[8] As a result, many post-revolutionary revisions to the laws arose from the leadership's goal of grounding the institutions of government in *Shi'i* Islamic traditions. Khomeini considered Iran's penal codes, along with its family laws, to fall under the authority of such jurisprudence. Thus, after the 1979 Revolution, the newly formed judiciary began to rewrite the country's legal codes, with the aim of bringing them into conformity with the new leaders' interpretations of the *shari'a*.

Initially, the notion of codification proved to be controversial. Ayatollah Khomeini had stated that there would be no need for legal codes, which he had deemed a western mechanism. Instead, Khomeini was intent on drawing directly from clear religious prescriptions. Thus, the government dismantled much of the systematization of the previous era. For instance, municipal courts that handled a wide range of disputes were initially replaced by revolutionary *shariat* (Islamic) courts that gave judges broad jurisdiction over the kinds of cases they heard, with marked attention to crimes against the state and the aims of the revolution.[9] Shortly thereafter the *shariat* courts proved ill-equipped to interpret loose and malleable scriptural principles, and different jurisdictions issued divergent rulings.

In the immediate post-revolutionary period, the repeal of laws and the closure of courts without institutions to replace them made it difficult for the judiciary to process legal complaints. In an effort to rehabilitate the poor standing and inefficiency of the courts, the judiciary increased the use of alternative dispute resolution practices. Drawing upon what it felt were principles of *shora* (consultation) rooted in Islam, the judiciary created various councils to house alternative dispute resolution practices (Jalali-Karveh 2006). One of the effects of the new councils was the judiciary's decentralization (Mahmoudi 2006a:426). This shift towards conflict resolution outside of the courts led to certain procedural changes, including a mandate to judges to encourage negotiation in disputes.

Nonetheless, this inefficacy necessitated renewed labors to codify and, thus standardize, the laws, but now included an effort to Islamicize them as well. Seeking to rein in the wide-ranging sanctioning practices by judges poorly trained to construe the *shari'a*, in the early 1980s, Iran's parliament, the judiciary, and the Council of Guardians reintroduced criminal codes derived from classical *Shi'i fiqh* (jurisprudence), in accordance with how the state's religious leaders interpreted them. In doing so, the government also asserted a monopoly on exegesis, historically the domain of any qualified jurist, not state leaders or functionaries. Another problem with codification was that the *shari'a*, which had historically been open to debate, interpretation, and contextualization by trained jurists seeking to achieve the *maqasid* (paramount objective) of justice, would now be uncharacteristically fixed, leaving less room for the discretion, prudence, or pragmatism that are hallmarks of the *shari'a*.

With regard to criminal codes, the post-revolutionary government initially presented the new measures as temporary efforts to introduce Islamic jurisprudence into the statutory laws on a trial basis and extended them every five years. These temporary changes were not finalized until June 12, 2013, and constituted a major undertaking that increased the number of provisions in the penal code by one-third. With the passage of the 2013 law, the judiciary finalized the Islamic penal code for the first time since the revolution (Tavana 2014). The laws of criminal procedure were similarly revised and went into effect on June 22, 2015. The laws, albeit modified to better accommodate principles of *Shi'i* Islam as interpreted by the leaders of the revolution, remain codified. Codification has implications for the procedural administration and thus meaning and effect of the laws, even in the context where the laws are derived from Islamic principles.

Laws of Islamic Punishment

The first post-revolutionary criminal codes of 1982 and 1983 reintroduced provisions that, according to some, aimed to bring the Iranian laws in line with classical *Shi'i fiqh*. Accordingly, Iran's penal code—the *Law of Islamic Punishment*—divides crimes into three categories according to the punishment believed to be prescribed by the scriptures: *hudud* (sing. *hadd*; crimes against God), *qisas* (retribution), and *diyat* (sing. *diya*; compensation). *Hudud*, which literally means limits, deal with offenses that have violated the laws of God or the laws of nature. *Hudud* punishments are deemed by many jurists to be fixed by the scriptural sources and, thus, are mandatory and unalterable.[10]

Qisas, as in the case above, applies to injuries to persons (Sadeghi 2016). The punishment permits the injured party or, in cases of death, the immediate next-of-kin, to exact a punishment equal to the injury incurred. Historically, the focus of *qisas*, which literally means equivalence, was on matching the punishment with the crime. That is, this principle aimed to limit the victim's response to the equivalent of the injury incurred and no more. In this sense, *qisas* is a private punishment that materializes as a property right; it can only be exercised by the victim or, in the case of the victim's death, (it is inherited by) his/her closest relatives, against the perpetrator. *Qisas* is divided between *qisas-e nafs* (the taking of a life) and *qisas-e ozv* (the taking of an organ or limb). *Qisas* punishments for personal injuries require a finding of intent.[11] A pamphlet published by the judiciary, one among over a hundred such pamphlets that explain the laws in plain language, lays out the definition of intentional murder:

a) The murderer had the intent to kill another person, whether it was a specific individual or an unspecified individual or individuals from a group.

b) The murderer does not have the intent to kill another person but commits an act which is typically lethal.

c) In this case, as opposed to the prior case, the murderer has no intent to kill and his action is also not fatal, however, his action, due to the adversary's disease, youth, etc., is lethal, and the murderer was also aware of it.[12]

The finding of intent notwithstanding, *qisas* as codified, is a broad category absent any additional sorting by degrees, as in other jurisdictions. Where injury or death is determined to be the result of an unintentional act, then the punishment is not *qisas*, but *diya*.

Diyat consist of crimes for which a compensatory payment for damages may be prescribed.[13] In the penal code *diya* is prescribed for unintentional injuries. There is, however, a relationship between *diya* and *qisas* because the former may replace the latter. That is, in any *qisas* crime, a compensatory payment may replace the taking of the life or limb, but such payments can only happen if the next-of-kin forgo their rights of retribution. In such cases, *diyat* payments are extra-judicial agreements between the parties. They are signed and notarized by the parties, then approved, but not negotiated, by the court.[14]

Between 1982 and 1983, the Council of Guardians reintroduced the penal codes through four laws: (1) the Law Concerning *Hudud* and *Qisas* and Other Relevant Provisions; (2) the Law Concerning *Diyat*; (3) the Law Concerning Islamic Punishments; and (4) the Law Concerning Provisions on the Strength of *Ta'zir*. *Ta'zirat* (pl.) are discretionary punishments that serve a deterrent purpose in criminal sanctioning. In theory, they are corrective punishments intended to reform the offender. Included under *ta'zirat* provisions are sanctions for public offenses of immoral behavior and threats to security and order.

Thus, *hudud, qisas,* and *diyat* are punishments prescribed in scripture as sanctions for specific offenses. *Ta'zirat*, however, are sanctions for offenses that are not specified in the sacred texts.[15] The vast majority of the laws in Iran's penal code are *ta'zirat*, which carry a broader range of sanctions and permit judges greater discretion.

By the early 1990s, Iran's Islamic criminal justice system was structured and organized through a reintroduction of the criminal procedures.[16] In 1991, lawmakers assembled the first three laws under one common penal code, followed in 1996 by the introduction of a revised chapter on *ta'zir.* A 1991 amendment to the penal code created a *ta'zir* offense of public harm for what were until then regarded solely as private torts, punishable only by retribution. These new *ta'zirat* provisions made homicide and other injuries to persons both a public matter for prosecution and, at the same time, a tort with a private plaintiff. Accordingly, in murder cases, personal and criminal liability are assessed by the same court. First, under a theory of tort, the plaintiff or the victim's next-of-kin files a complaint for *qisas.* Then the state uses its discretion under the code's *ta'zirat* provisions to assess the nature of the public harm. As a result, in every murder case, there are two categories of claimants: the next-of-kin and the public. In such cases, only the former possesses the right to retribution. If the victim's family agrees to forgo it, then a second hearing will assess the *ta'zir* sentence. The state's prosecutor makes a case for punishment based on public interest and deterrence, with sentencing ranging from a minimum of three years up to a maximum of ten years imprisonment. Because the offenses for the tort are classified according to punishment, the guilt and sentencing phase of the first hearing (*qisas*) are consolidated.

Processing Retribution: The Enduring Quality of Honor

"*Qisas.*" The mother's voice was as strong as it was defiant. Her guttural pronouncement filled the room as she called out for justice—retributive justice—to avenge her daughter's mysterious and untimely death.

"My daughter was a good girl." She continued through sniffles, as tears lined her face, "She went to college. She would never do the things he says." The 'he' to whom she was referring was the twenty-five-year-old defendant, Hamid, who claimed that the death of the young woman was an accident or suicide after a night of consensual intercourse and drugged debauchery. In his written affidavit, Hamid had stated that the twenty-two-year-old student had been pursuing him and that they had been together before. He claimed that she had called him that night and had gone over to his apartment, where they drank alcohol, smoked crack, and then ended up in bed together. According to the defendant, while he was in the kitchen making drinks, the young woman, in a fit of drugged or suicidal passion, flung herself off his fifth-floor balcony to her death.

The judge looked at the aggrieved mother, and in a tone respectful of her anguish, stated the law: "You are aware that you will have to pay one half of the *diya*." This payment, most everyone in the room knew, would be paid directly to the defendant and was intended to compensate his family should the plaintiffs obtain a guilty verdict and exercise their right to retribution. The reason for having to pay half the *diya* was that the gender of the deceased was female while that of the defendant was male. The law stipulates that the *diya* of a man is twice that of a woman. Because of this, the victim's family would be liable to pay half the *diya* should they seek the execution of the male defendant in order to avenge their daughter's death—only, of course, if the judges found the man guilty of intentional murder.

The father, by now openly sobbing, cried out, "I would sell my house if I need to in order to seek justice for the murder of my daughter." The mother then took over from her husband. She spoke of her daughter, as she supported the indictment and refuted the defendant's claims that the young woman was previously engaged in a relationship with him, was sexually promiscuous, did not attend university, stayed out at night, drank, and took drugs. In disputing those assertions, the aggrieved mother explicitly affirmed her daughter's honor, her irrefutable moral character.

The judge then took a different tack. He told the parents that justice also permitted them to forgo retribution. He explained that intentional murder is a "forgivable crime" and instead of paying compensation (to the accused) in order to carry out retribution, the parents could consider the "magnanimous" route of forbearance. The mother resisted the judge's appeal and instead reiterated her stance on *qisas*. As she did, she vowed to reclaim her daughter's honor by punishing the person who had twice dishonored her family, first by taking her daughter's life, and then by maligning her character.

Forgivable and Unforgivable Crimes

In addition to the categorization of punishment discussed above, the laws are divided into "forgivable" and "non-forgivable" offenses. Iran's criminal laws provide avenues for forgiveness in a variety of legal arenas and are codified as forbearance in various judicial contexts. In *qisas* crimes, plaintiffs may forgo their right to seek in-kind punishment, but in other types of offenses, the plaintiff's forbearance of the right to seek a sanction may have different consequences for the defendant. The stage in the process during which the plaintiff decides to forgo the sanction is also significant. Forbearance before the indictment may halt the investigation, if granted after the indictment, forbearance may stop the case from going to trial, and if granted after the ruling, forbearance may stay implementation of the legal sanction. Forbearance may also affect the investigation or reduce the sanction of the public *ta'zir* offense. Forgivable crimes include murder and torts that include aggravated assaults.

In the scriptural sources, only *qisas* and *diyat* categories of punishment permit the plaintiff to forgo the prescribed sanction.[17] Not all *ta'zirat* offenses have a private plaintiff, but those that do also permit forbearance. In the case of *qisas*, which also prescribes a *ta'zir* punishment, as I described above, the plaintiff's forbearance of retaliation may have the effect of softening the severity of the *ta'zir* sanction.

Unforgivable crimes, or offenses for which forbearance is not available, are those that the state does not consider to be private, even though they might have private plaintiff, such as rape, which falls under *hudud* punishments as a *zina* offense.[18] A gesture of forgiveness by a private plaintiff in non-forgivable offenses may nonetheless have an effect of curbing the punishment.[19] For instance, forbearance in such cases could affect the investigation or issuance of the indictment. However, after the final ruling has been issued by the court, the plaintiff's forbearance in a non-forgivable crime is thought to have no effect on the implementation of the sentence. For instance, *hudud* punish individuals who have violated God's prescribed laws. Sexual assault is classified under *hudud* and the sanction is death. Thus, in such cases, the plaintiff, *by law* cannot forgo sanctioning once the state proves the charge and the court issues its final ruling. In an unusual twist, however, the judiciary has found a way to quash the ruling in cases where the plaintiff forgives the complaint.

One ruling that the judges gave me showed that, after a sentence of rape had been issued, the plaintiff in the case submitted a notarized statement stating that she forgave the defendant. This was a strategic move on her part as well—had she petitioned to retract her accusation, she could have been liable for *qazf*, the crime of making a false accusation of *zina*, a violation also classified under *hudud*, for which an offender could face flogging. Instead, she stated that she forgave her assailant. Since rape is classified as a *hudud* offense, the plaintiff's forgiveness technically could not alter the ruling. When the case went to the Supreme Court for reconsideration, the highest court returned the judgment for resentencing. The Court reasoned that the plaintiff's change of heart added an element of doubt to her claim of rape. Drawing from the jurisprudential maxim, *Qaedeh Dar'eh* (*Principle of Doubt*), the court ruled that the rape charge had not been proven (Osanloo 2017).

The findings of this case and others like it were instrumental in codifying the *Principle of Doubt* in the final version of the penal code. This provision, found in Articles 120 and 121 of the *Law of Islamic Punishment*, and previously applicable only to *hudud*, is crucially important because it expands the application of this principle to all cases and areas of criminal proof, not just rape or *hudud* crimes. With its codification, the *Principle of Doubt* is no longer simply a source of *fiqh* to be applied in the absence of other proof. Now, as codified law, it can be applied in any case where the standard of proof is compromised by evidence that suggests doubt.[20]

The expanded application of the doubt principle alongside the earlier classification of crimes as forgivable and unforgivable are part of the judiciary's broader attempt to institutionalize and standardize a methodology of judicial inquiry as an approach to fact-finding. To be sure, this methodology emerges from the truth-seeking purpose of the judicial process. This aim is also informed by the "ethico-religious" concepts rooted in the Qur'an (Izutsu 2002[1959]).[21] These concerns shape not only the substantive law, but also inform how investigations into crimes involving reputation or honor, including illicit sexual relations, are to be carried out. The system of social ethics that the Qur'an is said to transmit gives meaning and purpose to the penal code and the criminal procedures. As such, the system also informs the habitus of individuals who make decisions about forgiving offenders, like the parents of the deceased young woman in the case mentioned previously. In other words, this system structures the dialogical call and response of mercy—as forbearance in *qisas* cases between the victim's next-of-kin and the alleged perpetrator. The legal system structures a hierarchical power relationship between the grantor of forbearance and its aspirant. In this context, how the plea is made, what facts emerge, and how they are revealed and made public matter. This is all the more so in a system built on codes that value reputation and honor.

Judicial Method and Righteous Restraint

After the parents' testimony, the court turned its attention to the defense. The chief judge called the defendant to the stand. Hamid, dressed from head to toe in the prison attire of alternating light and dark blue stripes, rose and took his place behind the lectern. He stated his name, age, and other personal information for the record. Then, by answering the succession of questions posed by all five of the judges, Hamid slowly laid out his version of the events. Although the question-and-answer between the judges and the defendant seemed relaxed, at times almost convivial, the judges followed a methodology that hewed closely to that of the investigative judge in the European assize tradition, from which Iranian laws are in part derived. The chief judge posed pointed questions to the defendant, his lawyer, and the two eyewitnesses who testified that day. The judges interjected queries about the night in question, including the defendant's behavior, his relationship with the deceased, and her cause of death. The defendant stated that she was depressed and suicidal and, while under the influence of crack cocaine, had climbed outside of the balcony and dangled from a railing. The judges avoided questions about the more puerile details of the case. When Hamid began to speak about the sexual nature of their relationship, he was ostensibly establishing their pre-existing relationship, consent, and perhaps disentangling their sexual relations from a motivation to kill the young woman. At the same time, he was saying something about her moral character in public. Notably, the chief judge swiftly issued the defendant a warning, reminding him of the prohibition on testifying to such details out of respect for the court.

Throughout the course of his testimony, the defendant maintained a calm demeanor. His responses were straightforward and seemingly candid. He said that he had gone into the kitchen and did not actually see what happened to the young woman. He explained that he thought that she must have let go of the railing, perhaps intentionally, or perhaps due to the influence of drugs, because when he came out from the kitchen, she was gone, having fallen five stories to her death. Since the investigation disputed this accounting of the facts, the judges probed much further into these aspects of the events of the young woman's death, including questioning two eye-witnesses.

Finally, with a view to the defendant's lawyer, the judges asked the attorney to approach the podium in the center of the room and present his defense on behalf of his client. In a rare show of courtroom theatrics, the attorney produced a handcrafted wooden scaffold that depicted the side of the building from which the defendant was to have allegedly thrown the young woman. During his testimony in open court, the defendant's lawyer provided details of the defendant's sexual relationship, citing their previous trysts, the sexual nature of texts messages she had sent the defendant, the condom the police found in the apartment, and the young woman's soiled undergarments. Several times the chief judge admonished the lawyer for veering into the salacious details of the case, saying, "Mind your statements." Another time, he cut off the lawyer, stating, "We have reviewed the pathologist's report."

Here the judge warned the lawyer of entering into an inappropriate discussion, one which offended the sanctity of the court and was impermissible during the public session. With such evidence, however, the lawyer was trying to convince the judges that the young woman had initiated the entire relationship, including the ill-fated rendezvous that night. Through such factual details, the attorney may have been aiming to abnegate the requisite motive in the case—that the defendant had planned to kill her. The tawdry details, however, also seemed to attend to another aim—that of suggesting that a young man did not deserve to die for the death of such a shameless woman. The lawyer's testimony, more than any other, highlights the complex public dance that a murder trial entails.

The judge's admonition served the purpose of maintaining a cover on the lewd matters in the case—improprieties considered offensive to the morals of the public present that day and to the stature of the judiciary. The hushing of the defense lawyer was also aimed at keeping the parents' anger and pain at bay. That is, the order that the court maintains is also a demand for restraint from provocation. The lawyer must use every fact at his disposal to achieve a verdict of not guilty; yet, he must be wary of upsetting the victim's family in case he does not achieve the desired outcome of acquittal. Thus, although the state convenes and carries out the proceeding as a criminal trial, its emphasis on the case's relational nature, with its central focus on the victim's next-of-kin, underscores that the trial is primarily a transaction between the adverse parties.

In the end, the lawyer succeeded in convincing the judges that there was an alternate explanation from that produced by the state's investigators to make sense of the young woman's death. The judges, having found none of the additional testimony to be dispositive, decided to continue the case. Prior to adjourning for the day, the chief judge announced that, before they could issue a ruling, they would seek additional evidence, including a personal visit to the scene of the alleged crime.

Discover but Cover and the Virtue of Courts

After the hearing concluded, the journalists sitting next to me began to discuss the detailed testimony about the taboo subjects of sex and drugs. They told me that, despite the judge's reproach and interruption of the lawyer, it was unusual to have such open discussion about sex during the public portion of the trial. This sort of testimony flew in the face of the prevailing standard for cases involving morality issues, one which required judges to clear the courtroom of all observers. The judges strive to maintain the court as a space of virtue, which is part of its justice-seeking mission. In this sense, justice and righteousness are interrelated (Izutsu 2002[1959]:37).[22] The court's responsibility in modeling a virtuous public space stems from this historic and fundamental role in maintaining the social decorum of public spaces and adjudicating questions of social morality well before they became law.[23] Such issues encompass the broader ethical concerns of how members of the community are to relate to and treat one another, what Toshihiko Izutsu called, "the basic ethical attitude of a man to his brethren" (2002[1959]:17). Thus, a key feature of the court's role has been the preservation and recalibration of social order and harmony (Hallaq 2009:166).[24] The constraints of morality, as defined by the sacred texts, clarify the parameters for individual conduct in the public space and cite the foundational events that established the scope and nature of public comportment. Many of the laws emerged in direct relation to the ethical and moral concerns from the time of the Prophet, as codifications of social decrees on morality and virtue in public spaces.[25]

These provisions confirm the well-established notion that *zina* crimes are intentionally difficult to prove.[26] The law operates so as to pursue the most serious cases, particularly those in which the alleged acts invert the social ideal of heteronormative marriage as the foundation of a healthy society. For the state, that might mean cases in which it possesses a strong (sovereign) interest, such as in controlling violence, resolving property disputes, and maintaining public morality. Practically speaking, then, the types of cases that the state most often adjudicates are those in which the mutual consent of the parties is lacking (violence), those in which paternity issues might emerge (property), or those which challenge public values of chastity and virtue.

Of course, Hamid's case was not being prosecuted as a *zina* crime, but what the judge's admonitions and the substance of the procedural laws share is a concern with the publication of overt displays of immodesty in the public sphere. As such, here the court operates as a public arena which allows disputants to express their discord with one another, as Wael Hallaq notes, in defending their honor and reputation (2009:166).[27] Indeed, the court is an arena for the airing out of views, but it is also the judge's role to keep the court's integrity clear of moral taint. In *qisas* cases that involve unlawful sex, however, the proscription on immodesty has consequences for the *qisas* versus forbearance dialogic that is part of the larger process. That is, in cases like the one above, if the parents of the victim feel their honor must be avenged in light of claims against their daughter's sexual behavior, they may see *qisas* as their only choice for clearing their family name or shame, and that forgiveness would be too weak a response—or even a vindication of the perpetrator's story. It is for this reason that a judge, with regard to another case, said to me, "We try to avoid riling the victim's family or enflaming their anger. We don't want to provoke them." He was expressing a moral reticence with regard to highlighting the particularly salacious details of cases that he found to incite or provoke the victim to use *qisas* as an act of reprisal.

In some cases, the court's stature as a moral space guards against public divulgence of certain details that could provoke the anger of the victim's family.[28] However, a problem arises from this protection within other cases, for instance, a claim of self-defense against rape, in which such details could provide important context that would avoid the *qisas* ruling in the first place. Thus, whether or not to allow oral evidence about sexual conduct was often a strategic choice for judges, prosecutors, and defense lawyers.

Covering as Protection of Reputation or Honor

The laws against immoral public behavior emerged in part from concerns with propriety and other "honor-linked values," including a concern for communal modesty (Abu-Lughod 1986:86). These underlying values continue to shape social concerns about public conduct. Insofar as law is a reflection of those values and concerns, they permeate both the substantive law that defines what is being regulated, *as well as* the procedural law that outlines how to conduct investigations of alleged violations of modesty, reputation, and honor. Consequently, it is with an eye towards reticence and restraint that such crimes are investigated only in a modest fashion, or what I have termed above, a righteous restraint on the part of judges. As an extension of this righteous restraint, the act of covering—hiding from view, either physically or verbally, whether from the public eye or in the court—may provide sufficient 'cover' to allow such an act to escape the severe sanction it would otherwise merit under this law.

Covering operates in two forms, both as a defensive shield to an actor and as an admonition against the viewer's intrusiveness. It can serve as a guard of one's honor or reputation, but it can also signal caution to the observer or investigator, to look away or disregard the matter that is none of his/her business. This is a fine line, both ethically and juridically, to know when to look away from or conceal a matter involving sexual relations.[29] Numerous *ahadith* recount variations of a story of the Prophet turning away when a confessor of adultery appears before him. In some stories, the confessor is a woman, in others, it is a man. In most versions, however, the Prophet turns away from the male confessor and does not order punishment until the confessor insists four times. In another story, it is a woman whom the Prophet sends away, but who returns four times to confess to him.[30]

The Islamic system of social ethics came into existence when divine revelations to the Prophet Mohammad rejected some of the beliefs and social practices of the time known as the *jahiliyyah* (the age of ignorance). However, the Qur'an adapted a significant portion of those practices as part of a new code of Islamic ethics (Izutsu 2002[1959]:16).[31] What I underscore here is that the ethico-religious system incorporates pre-existing local norms and ritual procedures and, as such, builds on what were deemed their positive attributes and rejects or revises others. Whatever the case, local norms are intrinsic to this new ethico-religious system; their underlying moral logic is never too far behind.

Often the cases which adjudicate alleged offenses to public morality result in an emphasis on women's sexuality. Indeed, the way personal status laws are structured—allowing men to marry up to four wives and to engage in temporary marriage, the latter having weak registration requirements—provides men with a great deal more autonomy in their sex lives and results in a disparate system or culture of surveillance, scrutiny, and ultimately, control over women's sexual lives. As many scholars have shown, the emphasis on women's sexuality lies with their status as the potential bearers of shame, a living vestige of the communal social values that seek honor and avenge shame. The relationship between honor and gender is important for the structure of the Islamic laws pertaining to punishment and relevant to the discussion of forbearance.

Gender and Honor: From Custom to Tort Law

As we saw in Hamid's case, the private complaint allows the right of retribution to play on the concerns that the victim's next-of-kin has with honor. The concerns of the victim's parents, especially as articulated by her mother, were the family's dignity and the rehabilitation of their daughter's reputation through proper sanctioning of the accused.[32] Far from appealing to the call for Muslims to forgive, the parents in this case were concerned more with avenging their honor. In this way, retribution resonates with *orf* (customary practices), although its operations are not the same.

Women, who have historically borne the weight of maintaining the honor of their kin folk, are here also liable for upholding the honor of the family (Black-Michaud 1975).[33] The case at hand shows that women are also its modern-day enforcers. It was hardly a rare scene inside the courtroom where the female kin of the victim's family sought retribution as the only sanction that could possibly restore the family's honor. In Iran's hybrid courtroom setting, the crimtort context still allows for the avenging of honor by permitting the family members to speak and to partake in the determination of punishment, even before the court issues its final decision.

The persistent concern with honor can be illustrated through proceedings in other cases as well. For instance, in the summer of 2007, a disturbing murder rattled the residents of an upscale neighborhood in Tehran. The case was recounted to me by a social worker attempting to negotiate with the victim's family for the life of a young woman, the alleged murderess.

The victim, a wealthy elderly widower, was bludgeoned to death by his housekeeper. In a gruesome unfolding of details in the press, the young woman had been subjected to years of beatings and sexual abuse and killed the man only after numerous attempts to flee had failed. When social workers prevailed upon the family members of the deceased to consider forbearance, and spare the life of the young woman, who had no substantial kin relations, it was his daughters who objected. They, and not his sons, sought *qisas* and told the court and the social workers that it was important for avenging their father's death and restoring his reputation and, thus, the family's honor. As this anecdote suggests, women have been more concerned with reputation. Historically women, as matriarchs, have been tasked with defending the family's honor, and gendered social and legal standards have placed them in the position of carrying and defending that honor.

Up until now, my discussion of Islamic criminal sanctioning in Iran's hybrid legal system has focused on an intentional murder for which the victim's family can make a legal claim for *qisas* or forgo retributive punishment. In another context, however—that of unintentional death—the law sanctions the defendant to pay *diya* to the victim's family, the plaintiffs. By contrast, in intentional crimes, including murder, *diya* serves as a vital tool for the defendant to negotiate a settlement in lieu of retribution. Although the practice of paying *diya* to the victim's family is common in intentional homicide cases, it is technically not a form of relief in such cases because intentional murder is categorized under the punishment of *qisas*. When such transactions occur, it is as though such cases are pled down to a lesser crime. The resulting settlement, whatever it may be, arises out of extralegal negotiations carried out between the private plaintiff and defendant—although the court must approve the settlement, it is not part of the actual judicial ruling.

In such cases, the judiciary's role is one of harnessing and regulating the space for settling accounts (Borneman 1997). In this way, the state claims its monopoly on legitimate violence by requiring that payback take place within its process. By giving private citizens the right to decide on the exercise of violence, the state implicates its citizens in its logic for settling disputes, regardless of whether they exercise the right or forgo it; the state is never completely absent from extra-judicial modes of accountability, such as performative re-dress or commemorations of loss (Borneman 2011).

Legally, the term *awliya-ye dam* refers to the next-of-kin (*lit.* custodians of the blood) and includes the blood relatives who may inherit from the deceased.[34] While the next-of-kin may be understood as the victim's closest family members, in practice, women's voices are critical. Women's position in the family, as aggrieved mothers, wives, and sometimes even sisters, often lead other family members to defer to their decisions or even delegate them entirely to the women in the family. In such cases, family members frequently told me that, if the family was to forgive the right of retribution, it was their mother who had to find peace with the decision. She was the one who suffered the most, they said, because she carried the child for nine months in her womb, gave birth, and raised the now-deceased offspring.[35] Also, as in the cases above, mothers, daughters, and sisters, acting as the custodians of the family's reputation, will speak out to absolve the deceased of defamatory claims against his/her moral character. Of course, cases involving honor present the greatest challenge to forbearance. In such cases, the offender's life literally lies with the victim's family, but the family may turn away from forbearance if the defendant divulges information about the deceased that would damage his or her reputation and, by extension, the family's.[36]

In other contexts, female matriarchs play another important role, not as the keepers of the moral order and family honor, but as the putative recipients of compensation. This is partly because males have legal obligations to be financially accountable to the women in the family. As a result, a family that has lost its male breadwinner will often have a woman whose voice will figure prominently in the disposition of the case, even if it is not legally stated as such. Women are often the decision makers in questions of compensation when it comes to the loss of the male head of household because it is the women who are left, in effect, with having to provide for the family. For instance, in the fall of 2007, I interviewed Esmat, a woman whose husband had been killed by an automobile while riding his bike in their small village on the outskirts of Tehran. Since the driver of the car was negligent, the state-mandated driver's insurance (which pays the *diya*) refused to compensate (or pay out on an insurance policy) to the wife of the deceased biker. The only path for Esmat to obtain damages was to sue the driver for the compensation. She had the legal right to forgo damages and knew that the settlement would likely force the young driver into debt or worse.[37] When I spoke with her, however, she explained that she was left a widow with two children, so to forgo the lawsuit, and thus the *diya*, would leave her without means to provide for her family. In this unintentional death suit, it was Esmat's decision whether or not to forgo legal action.

As we shall see, women are often entrusted to make life and death decisions in such cases. Women gain a certain privileged position in the family during these times, especially as the economic consequences of the death, along with those of lost honor, affect women more directly and materially.

Closing the gender diya disparity

In order to understand how the law of retribution operates, it is necessary to say a few words about *diya* because it is through such payments that forgiveness is often, though not always, mediated. As such, in this section, I explore contemporary debates about the gendered disparity in valuing compensation for a life and the state's attempts to close this gap.

For decades, a hallmark of discrimination in Iran's laws was the gender disparity in *diya*. Based on Islamic principles derived from the *ahadith*, though not the Qur'an, Iran's criminal code states that in the event a woman is killed, her *diya* is half that of a man's.[38]

In some rural communities, women may not be considered decision-makers because male kin are expected to step in to provide for the female family members. Building on such practices, Iran's civil laws require as much. However, in Iran's family structures, especially prevalent in urban areas, male kin cannot be expected to uphold the local practices of an earlier era, even with laws requiring them to do so. Thus, today's Iranian women are not defined solely as grieving widows, but as de-facto heads of households. They are the primary recipients of *diya* and contemplate the financial and economic issues associated with *diya* in decisions about forbearance.

Thus, observing *diya* through tort law, one can see the development of a different kind of logic, one that is familiar to anyone with knowledge of personal injury laws. In Iran, the state-determined basis of the gender disparity in *diya* rests on an increasingly fictitious world view in which men are the sole breadwinners and women do not contribute financially to the household. This logic, flawed though it may be, is not, however, based on an intractable belief in women's biological inferiority; rather, it is founded on an assumption that women's contribution to household expenses is nonexistent, incalculable, extraneous, or not essential and, therefore, irrelevant.

The underlying basis for the gender disparity in *diya* has its roots in the logic that an injury necessitates in-kind compensation and is based on the idea that the death of a man places a greater financial burden on the family. In 2004, Fatemeh Rakei, then-head of parliament's Committee for Women's Issues, stated, "This argument is invalid. Today you need two incomes to support a family, and all over Iran women are having to work."[39] Determined to align the realities of life in Iran with the law, in 2004, Rakei led the drafting of a bill that proposed gender parity in *diya*, arguing its passage would reflect contemporary social practices. Although Iran's parliament approved the bill, the Council of Guardians denied its conformity to Islamic principles and rejected it.

Iran's legislature, however, seemed to have understood the need for gender parity in *diya* when, in September 2008, the Insurance Ministry's Bodily Indemnification Fund announced it would pay the remaining half of *diya* to families whose female kin were killed in automobile accidents. In this way the government thus closed the gender gap in *diya*, as far as insurance pay outs were concerned. The government developed a sort of work-around in the existing the law.[40] This was an important development for gender equality in Iran and was hailed as a success by religious groups and women's rights advocates.[41] It was even more significant in light of the Council of Guardians' rejection of the 2004 law.

Then, in 2016, as the judiciary announced the rate of *diya* for the year, it also declared that it had, by law and thus with the approval of the Council of Guardians, closed the gender disparity for automobile accidents, stating that there would now be two separate rates of *diya*: one gender-neutral for automobile accidents and the other gender-specific for all other unintentional deaths.[42]

Similarly, by 2012, lawmakers had developed a sort of work-around for the gender disparity in tortious homicide, not unlike that found in accident cases like Esmat's. In such cases, in which the victim's family would have to pay the remaining half of the *diya*—referred to in the law as the *tafazol* (difference)— in order to compensate for the fact that the defendant was male and his victim was female, families could now access state resources to pay the *tafazol*. Thus, though technically the gendered disparity in these cases remains (Article 550), a provision in the new penal code (a note to Article 551) allows victims' families to apply to the national treasury to remit the *tafazol*, provided they can establish economic need. While this work-around may also be viewed as a victory for gender equality, the result does not necessarily bode well for anti-death penalty activists. In this context, closing the gender differential in *diya*, which once operated as a barrier to retribution, now facilitates a family's exercise of it.[43]

Diya as compensation rather than punishment is relevant in all deaths and injuries, not just in intentional murder. The broader significance of *diya*, as it plays out in these cases—both as punishment and as compensation in extrajudicial negotiations—is that it perpetuates the concern with honor. This, of course, persists in all societies which have a personal injury and compensatory component to their justice systems, not just in Iran or other societies in the Middle East. Thus, the gendered logics around *diya* perpetuate concerns with honor, which, as we have seen, remain relevant in negotiations around forbearance today.

Compensatory Diya: From Blood Feuds
to Scriptural Principles to Tort Law

For at least a century, scholars have studied the values that tribes and families sought to protect and regulate through so-called blood feuds.[44] For my purposes, I explore how studies of disputes among groups presage the emergence of tort law and the complex legal institutions of the contemporary period. This attention to the common history of the development of tort law helps to shed light on Iran's criminal justice system, which centers, first and foremost, on preserving the victim's rights and, to a lesser extent, on punishing the harm that the transgressor has caused society.

Earlier studies relayed various findings about the nature of feuds that have, in some ways, persisted in the realm of ethnographic thinking: that the central motive was pride or the restoration of honor, while the failure to retaliate or the taking of pecuniary compensation as a substitute would be considered a disgrace.[45] Scholars of Iran have presented similar practices as custom, arguing that the normative expectations of appropriate behavior eventually transformed into informal systems of social control (Kusha 2002:264).[46] The practice of using *diya* as a means of settling conflicts is the scriptural descendent of these customary practices, which, while still practiced in some form in Iran's tribal areas today, actually predate Islam (Petrushevsky 1985:136).

In Muslim-majority societies, *diya* validated the earlier codes of conduct and became a mechanism for mediating disputes and ending perpetual cycles of retaliatory violence.[47] The Qur'anic source from which *diya* is thought to stem is a verse interpreted to encourage Muslims to forgo their right of lethal retribution: "In the law of retaliation there is life for you—O you who are endowed with intelligence so you may restrain yourselves" (2:178–179).[48] Like blood money, *diya* emerged not to encourage or structure the retaliatory aspects of punishment or the blood feud, but rather to restrict and end it. Earlier scholars sometimes used the terms *diya* and blood money interchangeably.[49] *Diya*, however, is not the same as blood money; it is better understood as compensation and is more closely related to damages for tortious injuries. Both *diya* and torts grew out of the practices of giving blood money, but as correctives to it by placing limits on retribution, constraining it to an equal or equivalent punishment. However, an important way that *diya* differs from blood money is that it grew out of a context in which the retaliatory punishment became an individual right, thereby limiting criminal responsibility to one between individuals, not between tribes (Bassiouni 2014:130). Notably, *diya* limits the sanction as well.

As centralized governments increasingly took on the role of providing security, which had previously been the responsibility of the sub-group—clan,

tribe, family, and so on—informal codes of conduct began to give way to concrete legal codes and systems of adjudication. While this process was uneven,
the dual purposes underlying *diya*—individual punishment and community
protection—were integrated into a broader system of sanctioning that grew
to be a device for discouraging retribution and fostering reconciliation.[50] For
instance, today, victims' families have the right to accept *diya* or other consideration in lieu of retaliation. The codification of forbearance—as a right—
allows the state to encourage and facilitate it (Baderin 2003:73; Nateri
2006:406–407).

In his classic essay, "Primitive Law," Robert Redfield described how simple
societies moved from employing retaliative sanctions to developing proto-
legal institutions. The overall goal of so-called primitive law, Redfield suggested, was to rein in "unlimited revenge" between families or tribes (1964:11).
In line with Redfield's analysis, practices such as the offering of blood money
were mechanisms invoked to limit acts of violent revenge in the wake of social
transgressions. Redfield claimed that the formalization of law occurred over
time through "the development of systems of compensation or of forms of
socially approved retaliation in the development of what might be called a
rudimentary law of torts" (12). This rudimentary tort law included a formal
process and a specific sanction—"a systematization of rules of indemnity"
(Ibid.). Legal process resulted, in effect, when "retaliative force [was] stylized
by custom into a sort of ritualistic revenge" (11).

For Redfield, the critical aspect of this embryonic tort law was that the
harm that the law punished was that which was committed against the society,
not just families. This proto-tort law became "something that we are likely to
think of as criminal law" (12). Referencing Maine's well-known assertion
"from status to contract," Redfield recognized this shift from what he referred
to as "primitive" to "modern" law as a transition in which the legal institutions
recognized their roles as adjudicating both the harm done to the greater society (criminal law) and to the individual victim (tort law) as opposed to just
mediating between disputing families or tribes.[51] Crucially, the codification
secularized and individuated earlier practices, and ultimately privileged the
harms done to society over those of the next-of-kin. For Redfield, this was best
evidenced in the development of a body of criminal law. Thus, what he termed
"modern laws" emerged not only because of codification, but also by distinguishing criminal law from tort, giving crimes against the state the higher privilege and harsher punishment—whether a perpetrator lives or dies is the sovereign's decision.[52] However, as these laws privilege crimes against the public, they
also move away from the restorative aims of sanctioning (Braithwaite 2002:7).[53]

English legal historian J.H. Baker contends that "Anglo-Saxon codes did
not 'codify' existing tribal laws, let alone make new law" (2002:3). Instead,

Baker notes, the new codes were "directed at readers who could be presumed to know the customs already, and offered fixed rules to govern situations which must previously have rested on discretion."[54] Thus, codification limited discretion, but still sought to repair loss or injury based on the customs of the times. Nevertheless, the codification of tort laws, not just in Iran but in western societies, too, is bound up with customs that sought to extract damages incurred from the staining of honor, albeit now limited in most societies to monetary damages.

The rule-making quality of law, which defines behaviors that belong inside and outside of public and private spheres, is what ultimately facilitates the idea of the individuated plaintiff-victim who possesses the right of retribution. As Iranian officials often explained to me, "*qisas* is an individual right," and article 419 of the penal code expressly states as much. Thus, one of the rule-making effects of codification is to limit the violence enacted in punishment as a response to crime. To that end, there are three kinds of limitations: the amount of violence that can be used, who has the right to seek retribution, and finally, against whom the retribution can be directed.

One of the primary roles of a strong state is to mediate over disputes and prevent never-ending cycles of conflict. States do that, in part, by creating a judiciary with a legal system that determines rules for social conduct and punishes transgressions. The Iranian state possesses a formalized arrangement of rules that define violations and corresponding sanctions. The system is different from many others, however, in that, while the state is concerned with people taking the law into their own hands, it does not take the retribution decision away from the victim's family. It preserves and sustains it, thus preserving and sustaining the values underlying the logic of status relationships, along with their ready concern with honor.

Uniquely, while Iran's judiciary carries out the sovereign's roles, in the context of punishment, that role includes privileging the right of the victim to exact retribution. By ensuring the primacy of *qisas*, the state defines its role as the sole arbiter of peace and security. That is to say, the state does not want people to take justice into their own hands by exacting revenge rather than retribution. To that end, the penal code states that someone with the right of *qisas* who carries out the killing of a perpetrator outside of the judiciary's regulations will be punished (with a *ta'zir* punishment), and someone who carries out the *qisas* without the express permission of the victim's next-of-kin is him/herself guilty of murder—for which the punishment is *qisas*.[55]

Not only does the Iranian system emphasize the injury to the victim's family by permitting a private plaintiff to seek retaliation, but, as many judges and legal scholars indicated to me during the course of my research, the principal goal of the law is to uphold the victims' rights. Yet, in giving the victim's family the paramount decision over life and death, the system is still more focused on family relationships and perceived kinship structures, and thus, to some extent, on status over contract. In this sense, too, the Iranian system is dual; it possesses elements that sociolegal scholars would attribute to modern and pre-modern legal institutions. One of the effects of this dual system is that the emphasis on honor is more overt than implicit, as it is in contemporary western contexts.

Thus, contemporary legal systems, regardless of geography, shape the persistence and circulation of discourses of honor and shame in different social contexts. This includes Iran, but also the U.S., where the public discourse on gender-based violence mobilizes shame of both perpetrators and victims alike.[56] Shame, in the former context, is raw and in the open, an affective register that individuals reference as an important regulator of both public and private behavior. It is an important element in the wider ethico-religious landscape, which includes law. In the U.S., individuals refer less to honor or shame as forces structuring their behavior, nor is it a dominant fixture of the legal system. In the recent spate of public accusations of sexual predation made by women against powerful men, however, both accusers and perpetrators regularly cited shame as important factors governing their actions. In the case of the accusers, it prevented them from coming forward sooner; with the accused, it was a dominant feature of their public expressions of remorse.[57] In redressing the harms of gender-based violence, such offenses are so shot through with shame, it raises the question: what does it mean for victims that the criminal justice system subordinates restorative sanctions, the only legal means that might rehabilitate the honor of victims?

The Iranian system's emphasis on the injury to the victim's family not only has the effect of accentuating the social importance of the family's honor, but it also serves to entrench the perceptions of gender roles that emerge from them. This is why, in the cases above, the concern with punishment is deeply ingrained in a justice response that rehabilitates the family's honor. There is even a deeply performative action on the part of the aggrieved family members who are permitted to announce their decision in an open courtroom, publicly reclaiming their honor by disavowing the shame brought onto them by the defendant's adversarial claims. In such contexts, the work that the punishment does—to rehabilitate family honor—is significant and makes the curbing of punishment through forbearance that much more challenging. The family that forgoes punishment risks losing the anticipated repair that retribution might provide. In short, the question emerges—what family would forgo retribution when its honor is at stake? In these contexts, then, what conditions would allow a family to forgo retribution?

Conclusion

Iran's criminal justice system allows a privileging of victims' rights over those of the state, even as the state's delegation of the right of life and death both legitimizes the system and makes the plaintiffs complicit in that system. It is, above all, a victim-centered system. In Hamid's case, the judges returned after a brief recess and determined that they needed to visit the murder scene to assess the probability that the victim fell on her own. Some months later, after a tour of the site, the judges reached a decision on the case. They determined that the defendant's theory was implausible and sentenced Hamid to *qisas*. Hamid appealed his verdict to the nation's highest court, which upheld the trial court's finding, deferring to the fact-finders.

In the end, however, Hamid did not hang for murder. Some years later, I asked the chief judge about Hamid's case. The victim's family, the plaintiffs, he said, gave up their right of retributive sanctioning. According to the judge, over a course of some five years, Hamid, through family, friends, acquaintances, and social workers, lobbied the victim's family to forgo their right to retributive sentencing and accept *diya* in exchange for granting Hamid his life. Hamid's case, although unique in its facts and detail, is among the thousands of murder cases that are resolved through the unique grass-roots activism that is part and parcel of Iran's retributive sanctioning system, one that is modern in its codified form and partly grounded in Islamic principles.

The provisions in the penal code draw from other customs that aim to restore the broken peace. Although codification yields greater power to the sovereign, it limits the discretion possible in a situation that requires it. With the revised codes, the judiciary appears to address this puzzle by allowing judges to reclaim some of the discretionary aspects of the customary practices through provisions that compel judges to work towards reconciliation. The new codes demand that judicial officials seek to reconcile and mediate between the parties, while also allowing them time to determine the conditions of their forbearance. One of the residual effects of customary practices on the codified system is the greater entrenchment of gender roles and the explicit concern with honor. Another trace of the *orfi* system, however, is that parties are not limited to seeking damages prescribed in the laws. The mechanisms for forging resolution are similarly unconstrained. In the context of resolving the dispute, there is a permeability of the border between judicial and extra-judicial remedies. The laws provide for, even prescribe, extra-judicial processes to unfold in the name of restorative justice, and directly charge judicial officials to seek as much through mediation and reconciliation.

2

Codifying Mercy

JUDICIAL REFORM, AFFECTIVE PROCESS,
AND JUDGE'S KNOWLEDGE

I ENTERED the newly renamed "Branch 10" of the Criminal Court of Tehran Province to see painters putting the finishing touches on the walls of the courtroom. In the small inter-chamber, two clerks, working behind desks piled high with thick manila files, greeted me cordially.

"Is this the old Branch 84?" I asked.

"Yes, but now it's Branch 10," the younger of the two explained. "And the old 71 is 2, 74 is 4, and 84 is 10." Assuming I was there to inquire about a case, the older man asked for my file number. When I clarified that the purpose of my visit was observation, the clerks invited me to wait in their small office until the judges arrived. In the quiet of the morning, before plaintiffs, witnesses, defendants, and lawyers started crowding their office with interminable questions about cases, clients, and loved ones, the clerks found some time to chat.

"Among the 10 branches in Tehran's criminal court," the younger clerk explained, "only these three—2, 4, and 10—deal with murder and other serious cases." And he noted another significant change to the laws, "Instead of a five-judge panel, now only three judges—a chief judge and two associates—try these cases."[1]

"Really? Why?" I asked.

"This way, the court can get through the cases faster."

"Do you think that's a good change?"

"It's more efficient. There are so many files."

"That's a big change," I noted.

"Since the first of *Teer* 1394 (June 22, 2015)," the clerk said, "*Everything* has changed." On his desk, beneath the protective glass sheath, lay a crib-sheet diagraming the judicial process after the court obtains the file. For the young clerk, a government functionary working towards his Master's degree in law, indeed much had changed. The date he mentioned, just a month before my visit, signaled when the country's new criminal procedures took effect. Change was afoot and certainly in the air, but it was many years in the making and continues to be reworked.

Judicial Reform and the "Coloring in" of Restorative Justice[2]

As the judiciary worked with Iran's parliament and Council of Guardians to finalize the revised penal code (from 2007 to 2015), it held trainings for its employees, including, of course, judges. Both the penal code and the criminal procedures went through several draft revisions before being finalized and implemented in 2013 and 2015, respectively. This period also coincided with the more sustained fieldwork I conducted in the criminal court. The additional period between the final revisions and their implementation did not alter the efforts of the judges I encountered to learn the new laws and, in turn, to tell me about them. And there were a lot of them. The previous criminal codes consisted of 497 articles, while the new ones contained about one-third more—738 articles in all. Most of the new provisions were *ta'zirat*, discretionary laws that gave judges more leeway in sentencing, and allowed offenders the possibility of sanctions in lieu of prison and corporal punishment.

One judge pointed out to me that the new laws added another set of provisions to the penal codes. He said, "On top of the additional discretionary sanctions, the new laws also '*colored in*' the provisions with respect to arbitration and reconciliation." He used a common quasi-legal idiom "colored in" to convey a sense of the increased fullness of the criminal codes, a phrase often repeated by legal practitioners with whom I spoke. In addition to the added discretionary sanctions, the revised code also "colored in" some of the existing provisions, including those pertaining to reconciliation and arbitration. These changes are significant, too, because many Islamic jurists and the Council of Guardians, the legal vetting body, believe that the laws codifying *hudud*, *qisas*, and *diyat* have emerged from the sacred sources and cannot be removed from the penal code.[3] Thus, in those contexts, new revisions elaborate, restrict, or refine the *shari'a*-based provisions (Osanloo 2016).

Consequently, the "coloring in" of the law can become an important vehicle for its application and practice, particularly with respect to the restorative properties within a penal code that privileges the protection of victims' rights. That is, if the central feature of Iran's criminal laws is to enable the state to maintain its authority (and monopoly on legitimate violence) by claiming to protect victims, as I argued in the previous chapter, then, until now that feature consisted primarily of punishing perpetrators. However, another goal, which

for some believers is the true aim and broader meaning of the Islamic principles upon which these laws are based, is restorative justice (Bassiouni 2014;
Gholami 2006; Hallaq 2009; Hascall 2011; Kamali 2008; Mahmoudi 2006b).[4]
Towards that end, the new code offers alternative sanctioning tools that curb
the severity of punishment and allow it to be tailored to the offender's rehabilitation.[5] For some, the new penal code provisions construe *shari'a*-based
principles pertaining to restorative justice because that, rather than retribution, is the broader aim of the *shari'a*. It was because of this restorative dimension of the *shari'a* that many officials with whom I spoke referred to the new
provisions as "completing" the penal code.

Thus, if, after the revolution, the state modified the laws in order to reinstate
the principle that the victim's next-of-kin possesses the right to seek *qisas*,
then, in the revised provisions, they developed and promoted the complement
to that right—that the victim's family may also *forgo* retribution. One way of
looking at the new provisions of the penal code, then, is that the emphasis is on
cultivating or otherwise "coloring in" the restorative aspects of the law, those
that might create the conditions through which victims may be persuaded to
opt for forbearance. Thus, it is this "coloring in" of restorative justice mechanisms, including alternative sanctioning and conditional punishment provisions of the *Law of Islamic Punishment*, that in this chapter, I seek to explore.

In what follows, I examine how legal reforms of the substantive law and
criminal procedure create a more robust justice system, enhancing the possibilities for forbearance. I consider how the substantive law operates and how
the criminal process authorizes and animates the forbearance that ultimately
shapes the forgiveness work I explore in Section II of this book. The cases
I explore allow me to highlight how judicial actors, the parties, and their representatives engage the court procedures. I show how forbearance as a legal
mechanism intervenes in the court's inquisitorial process and contributes to
the formation of judges' subjectivities. As I do, I pay heed to how criminal
procedures facilitate the bureaucratic layering of instruments (Ho 2006) and
forge "bureaucratic intimacies" (Babul 2016).

During my summers of fieldwork, early each morning, I made my way
through Tehran's busy central district and its Great Bazaar to the Provincial
Criminal Court I, more closely related to a French assize court than a U.S.
criminal court. The court's territorial jurisdiction covered Iran's largest province (Tehran), not just the capital city.[6] On such mornings, as I arrived at the
courthouse, I handed over my phone at the kiosk just outside the court and
made my way through the covered entrance for female security where the
women attendants checked my bags and person. Soon the soldiers sitting as
guards at the front of the court's entrance got to know me. One day, a young
guard quipped, "You come every day." To allay any concern that I had a case

pending, I replied that I was a researcher. A couple of summers later, the same guard stated, "You come every year." When I replied that he was there every year, too, he responded, "But my term is ending in a few weeks," referring to his mandatory military service. The criminal court, an important site of field-work for me, was, however, a space steeped in stories of violence and pain, where distraught families and alleged murderers came face-to-face. It was also a place where perpetrators' families could glimpse and momentarily reunite with an incarcerated relative.

The halls of the court often rattled with the shackles of prisoners who were led into the court with chains on their feet. Weary family members met their fallen ones there. Victims' families, too, with righteous grief, came to testify, tell their stories, and ultimately hope to gain some justice. The court, its clerks' offices, corridors, and courtroom, in this sense became the enclosed space in which accounts would be settled, yet contained, and cyclical violence brought to an end once and for all. Judges, clerks, journalists, social workers, lawyers, law students, and others served both as witnesses and comforters. When it came to forbearance, these actors also played the roles of arbiters, if not also sometimes cajolers.

Inside courtrooms, I met with judges, sat in on trials, and sometimes met other interlocutors, including prosecutors, defense lawyers, witnesses, social workers, family members of victims, and journalists. Only on rare occasions was I able to speak with defendants directly; they were brought in by guards and then escorted out immediately after hearings. Sometimes in passing, a defendant, thinking I was a journalist, would make a comment; other times, the judges, who knew the scope of my interest, would direct a question at the defendant and after his/her response, would look my way and say, "Is that what you wanted to know?" or "Did you get that?"

In the summer of 2012, I met with a judge who was in charge of the court's research committee. The court had composed a research committee, I gath-ered, for learning and disseminating to the other judges the new substantive criminal laws that they would soon be implementing. This judge met me each morning and directed me to a courtroom with cases related to my interest in forbearance, to a meeting with a judge, or sometimes to law professors, jurists, lawyers, or even social workers whom he thought could help me. The most delicate part of the project for me was meeting the victim's next-of-kin and broaching the subject of their forbearance. This, too, was something that many of the judges facilitated. Often, after a trial, the judges would guide the next-of-kin over to me, indicating that it would be fine for them to speak with me. When I was not sitting in on a trial or conducting interviews, this judge, and later others, went over provisions of the revised penal code and attended to my constant stream of questions.

One relatively quiet July morning, I sat with the judge at the back of an empty courtroom. With both hands, he had carried in his heavy, annotated two-volume set of the *Law of Islamic Punishment*. The judge began by explaining that the revised criminal code included new provisions for *edalat-e tarmimi* (restorative justice), a term with which few non-jurists I queried at the time were familiar. He opened the criminal code to the section entitled, "Part Two: Punishments," and added, "These include alternative sanctioning provisions." He began reciting the new provisions aloud and directed me to follow along in my copy. After we examined the provisions, the judge explained, "Now we have many more sanctions to choose from and to apply towards the defendant's reform. We can use alternative sanctions instead of prison, such as prohibiting the offenders from leaving the house or the city. We also have the opposite; we can prohibit the defendant from entering a town, or driving a car, and others."

The *Complementary and Supplementary Sanctions* are possibly the most consequential because they are the only ones that the court may apply in lieu of or in addition to *hudud*, *qisas*, and *ta'zirat* offenses. The court may also apply other provisions, in lieu of or in addition to various *ta'zirat* offenses. These provisions include *Reduction and Exemption from Sanctions* (Art. 37–39), *Deferred Judgment* (Art. 40–45), *Suspended Sentencing* (Art. 46–55), *Half Release* (Art. 56–57), *Conditional Release* (Art. 58–63), and *Substitution for Prison Sanctions* (Art. 64–85).

In addition to these provisions, the judge told me about increased monetary penalties that could replace corporal punishments. He then added, "Corporal punishments have a very negative effect on the defendant. Doctors have testified that the effect can be much worse than previously thought, causing damage to the internal organs."[7]

Thus, the new penal code established additional and alternative provisions which aimed, seemingly, not only to punish, but also to reform offenders. As one law professor explained it to me, the new provisions "provide a new generation of communitarian sanctions, such as public service."[8] When conditions warrant it, the court may also tailor restorative and rehabilitative sanctions to the defendant. Thus, the alternative sanctioning provisions provide more choice in the type of sanctioning available, and allow judges to supplement, substitute, and defer sanctioning of defendants in an array of offenses, albeit only for less serious crimes.

For many legal advocates, these provisions do not go far enough because they did not eliminate the most severe sanctions, including capital punishment, in-kind retribution, and corporal punishment. Moreover, much is left to the discretion of the judges themselves, allowing for wide disparities among jurisdictions and offenses.[9] Defense lawyers, in the proverbial trenches, however, found that more options allowed for better bargaining on behalf of their clients, both with judges and private plaintiffs. They also understood that it is difficult to discuss repealing the laws that the current government believes are the basis upon which the entire system of justice lies. The new punishments, albeit discretionary, offer the possibility of tempering more severe "foundational" punishments—*hudud, qisas, diyat,* and the most serious *ta'zirat*—provided that offenders meet certain conditions, judges are just and well-trained, and next-of-kin are charitable through forbearance.[10]

As our session came to a close, the judge noted that the addition of alternative sanctioning provisions to the *Law of Islamic Punishment* gave it a greater sense of "completeness" because it allowed judges the discretion to formulate suitable sentences that may permit rehabilitation.[11] This became evident as I began to sit in on cases after the new sanctions became law and judges began to implement them.

Judges employing these instruments are also the judiciary's agents of expertise, knowledge, and harmony. Through their judicial performativity they sustain the state's legitimacy and power, while curtailing extra-judicial revenge. The Persian word for procedure, *ayeen,* is also the word for ritual. Criminal procedures, in a sense, represent a certain ritualization through processes that are formalized using familiar cultural practices as methods of reconciliation. Cultural rituals connect religious edicts to legal practices and make them feel familiar and authentic. Law is a daily practice imbued in social relations (Dupret 2011).

Through this examination of the court's processes, I also underscore the affective quality of the space in which judging—and much more—takes place. Court processes exude affects that shape both judging and judgment as well as the kinds of sentiment and reasoning that are to be expressed. Forging an "affect-subjectivity continuum," such spaces profoundly condition a person's capacity to think, feel, and act (Navaro-Yashin 2012:24). That is, inner and outer worlds are constantly shaping one another, and ultimately shaping how individuals experience their reality. Sentiment and affect, moreover, are not synonymous. The former relates to a subjective experience while the latter suggests a sensation that moves through the person.[12] That is to say, sentiment is an attitude, a thought, or judgment prompted by feeling; it is exterior.[13] Feelings are the sensations that register stimuli, in a sense, rendering affective charges psychically intelligible (Brennan 2004:5).

As I explore the court's processes before, during, and after trials, I consider how judges and clerks, along with the constant flows of essential actors (defense lawyers and defendants, prosecutors and private plaintiffs, witnesses and family members on both sides), as well as an assortment of peripheral individuals (such as prison guards, reporters, social workers, law students, and researchers like myself), together populate and shape the affective courtroom space, giving it ambiance, discharging sensations, and conjuring up feelings. As I do, I also attend to the materiality of the space— the architecture—as well as the objects that fill it and contribute to making the court's atmosphere.

Courts are state instruments of hegemony and even overt tactics of social control. In asserting social control, the state's courts allow disputants a sanctioned space for airing grievances, producing an atmosphere of fairness, establishing a public record, and producing a sense of accountability (Minow 1998:50). They also act on individuals to shape legal consciousness and inflect subjectivity—that of an individuated rights-holder (McCann 1994; Merry 2003; Osanloo 2009). Islamic courts are sites of conflict resolution, reconciliation, and compromise (Hirsch 1998; Peletz 2002). They offer a space for public reasoning in which the state asserts its power to interpret the laws and establish norms (Bowen 2003).

In Iran, the moral and legal obligation on the part of state officials to work towards reconciliation contributes to a more complex affective space composed of what I term "sentimental reasoning," by judges and other judicial officials, a way of thinking, acting, and judging, that draws from cognitive associations with *Shi'i* sentiment such as grace in suffering, remorse, and feeling the pain of others. Beyond asserting the normative capacity of the laws and their sanctioned authority to interpret them, judicial officials also display a kind of affected reasoning in which they also embody the qualities of learned and sage advisers. Here, courts are places in which individuals can seek justice, narrate accounts, and create formal records.

Yet, they also serve some of the purposes Minow (1998) has laid out with regard to truth commissions. The criminal courts are affirming to private plaintiffs in permitting them to narrate their truth before judges and many others who witness their grievances. The courts validate, not just the plaintiffs' stories, but also their feelings of loss and pain, and the sense of injustice that needs to be set aright. Often the interrogative method of questioning, at times resembling a therapeutic conversation, allows plaintiffs to unload their grief. It affords plaintiffs a meaningful opportunity to situate their version of events in a wider context, which may mean discharging their own feelings of guilt surrounding the events that led to the death of their loved one. Finally, the criminal court process permits a recalibration of the power hierarchy between victims and perpetrators. The plaintiff's petition, testimony, and public display of righteousness reverts the victim to a higher social standing in the sense that she is no longer degraded by the violence committed (Hampton 1992b).[14]

Next, I examine what this process entails, how it operates. Then through several trials, I show how judges perform their duties as officers of the court and as Islamic legal jurists, tasked at once with issuing just rulings and with bringing parties to settlement. Judges in these circumstances exercise discretion, but they are also constrained by the substantive definitions of the crime of intentional murder. Once the elements of the crime have been met, judges have no discretion with respect to the (*qisas*) ruling.[15]

Processing Retribution

While its substantive laws are in large part drawn from Islamic principles, the form and process of Iran's judicial system follows the French prosecutorial approach. The prosecutor's office employs *bazpors* (interrogators) who collect and examine evidence in collaboration with the police investigators. The *bazpors* interrogate the defendant and witnesses, ultimately building the case against the defendant. In most cases, they provide the evidence that the prosecutors then use to prepare the indictment. Once the defendant is indicted, the case is transferred from the prosecutor's office to the provincial criminal court, a branch of the judiciary.

The new code elaborated the system of process, revised the structure of the courts, and, as the clerk above noted, separated them into specialized divisions (see Table 2). The criminal courts are divided into Criminal Courts I and II.[16] Criminal Court I handles cases for which the punishment is *hudud, qisas,* and *diyat* as well as crimes that are political, press-related, or serious *ta'zirat* offenses.[17] These cases involve the most serious crimes and are those I explore in this work; for them, it is the court, not the prosecutor, that directs the preliminary investigation.[18] The crimes, outlined in the code by punishment, include those that would result in the defendant's loss of life or limb and lifetime incarceration.[19]

Criminal Court II deals with other, less serious, infractions, including offences against persons or property. Except in the most serious crimes, the *dadsara* (office of the public prosecutor), in cooperation with the police, initiates a preliminary investigation and issues the indictment. Once the investigation is complete, the prosecutor's office sends the file to the appropriate criminal trial court. Judges review the indictment and summon the parties to hear the case.

In their roles as officers of the judiciary, judges serve as interrogators as well, checking the facts as presented in the indictment and interrogating witnesses and parties. Thus, the judges direct both the investigation and the trial. In this sense, judges also play a significant role as *investigators* in determining the guilt of the accused. The three-judge panel is composed of two types of officials.[20] First is the *rais* (chief judge), who is the head of the branch and works only on the files for his branch. Then there is the *mostashaar* (associate judge), two of

TABLE 2. System of Criminal Procedure

Public Prosecutor, Investigations Unit	☐ Investigates the allegations (except for the most serious crimes) ☐ Prepares indictment ☐ Represents the public interest during trial
↓	

Criminal Court I/II	☐ Investigatory court
	  o Rules on charges in indictment
	  o Initiates investigation for the most serious crimes (Crim Ct I)
	☐ Holds hearing with parties present
	  o Lawyer required (Crim Ct I)
	☐ Delivers ruling
	  o Three judge panel (Crim Ct I)
	  o Delivers ruling in five days; twenty days to appeal
	  o Decision of majority stands

↓	

Supreme Court or Court of Appeals	☐ Three judge panel
	☐ Supreme Court (Crim Ct I)
	  o No oral arguments
	  o Rules on procedural questions only
	  o Overrules and remands to lower court OR confirms and returns to Public Prosecutor for implementation
	☐ Court of Appeals (Crim Ct II)
	  o Holds a hearing with parties present
	  o Reviews issues of law only, not facts
	  o May issue new ruling

↓	
Public Prosecutor, Implementations Unit	☐ Oversees prisoner while awaiting implementation (during appeal or reconciliation discussions) ☐ Charged with implementing the sentence ☐ Private plaintiff must petition for implementation of sentence
↓	
Head of Judiciary	☐ Petition for Permission (*Estizan*) ☐ Every ruling involving sanction of life or limb must be reviewed and approved by the Head of the Judiciary before being carried out ☐ Sent back to Public Prosecutor, Implementations Unit

which are assigned to each branch, but may be temporarily reassigned to another.[21]

After the trial, the chief judge has one week to render the court's decision.[22] The court is required to send the written judgment within three days of its issuance.[23] Parties have twenty days to appeal from the date the decision is issued.[24] The defendant, private plaintiff, and the prosecutor all have the right to ask for a review of the ruling.[25] The request for appeal may be based on claims that: (a) the ruling lacks credible reasoning or evidence; (b) the ruling is not in accordance with the law; (c) the court lacks jurisdiction; or (d) the court fails to consider manifest evidence.[26]

Not all matters can be appealed. Sanctions that are less than one-tenth of a full *diya* or a prison sentence of less than three months are final and cannot be appealed.[27] Most appeals are heard by the Court of Review.[28] Cases in which the sanction is the loss of life, limb, or organ of the perpetrator, life in prison, *ta'zirat* crimes that are fourth degree or higher, and intentional crimes for which the *diya* is one-third or more of a full *diya*, as well as political and press-related crimes, are appealed directly to the Supreme Court.[29] After the review of an appeal and the issuance of a decision by either the Court of Review or the Supreme Court, there is no mechanism for further appeal. In cases where the sanction is *qisas*, in addition to the Supreme Court's review, the head of the Judiciary must confirm the sanction by issuing a permission (*estizan*), the last step before the sentence can be implemented.[30]

The criminal procedures provide that, upon arrest or detention, the accused must be made aware of the charges and the right to an attorney "as soon as possible."[31] Those unable to afford an attorney will be provided one appointed by the court.[32] One new provision mandates clearer warnings to defendants.[33] Another new provision allows lawyers access to case files while the case is still pending or under investigation.[34] This represents an important shift from the previous procedural rules, where lawyers could only access files after the indictment was issued and the case sent to the criminal court. In another change, lawyers can petition to reopen a case when new information emerges.[35]

Courtroom, Process, and the Making of an Affective Space

Soon after my conversation with the clerk, Judge Maliki arrived, his composure serious but cordial, and greeted me, "Welcome." He invited me into the courtroom; judges do not have separate chambers. By that time, Maliki had been with the court for four years, having been sent to Tehran from the northern city of Ardebil.[36] A transfer to the capital was a commendation and a promotion. As an associate judge, Maliki asked questions, advised, debated, and voted, but generally did not issue rulings.[37]

When a tall older man entered the room, Maliki introduced him as Chief Judge Ghorbanzadeh. The men greeted each other and exchanged pleasantries. Maliki informed me that the chief judge taught criminal law and *fiqh* at a local university, having been trained in both law and *shari'a* in both university

and an Islamic seminary (*howzeh-e elmee-e*). The three-judge panel was complete moments later when the third judge arrived. Like Maliki, he had recently
transferred from another jurisdiction.

Typical of my introductory conversations, I found myself explaining my
research and focus on forbearance. Judge Maliki added, "She comes every
year." Then, looking at me, he asked, "When was the first time you came?"
"2007," I reminded him. Maliki joked, referencing the eight years in between,
"That's right. By now you know the laws as well as we do. You're a colleague."

"Oh no, I couldn't be and so much has changed," I echoed the clerk in referencing the newly implemented laws and procedures. My demurral also referenced the fact that women were not permitted to serve as judges in these
courts. The chief judge weighed in, "It's new for us, too," and thereby affirmed
my presence as an observer in his courtroom.

As our small talk became more substantive, the judges took their places
behind three large desks that sat upon a raised platform. The clerks entered
the courtroom from the ante-chamber carrying case files or presenting documents for signature. Sitting at one end of the room, the judges had their backs
to the wall of newly painted windows. Through them, the day's bright sunlight
seeped in, and neither the open windows nor the temporary fans brought in
to disperse the air could eliminate the strong odor of the paint. Facing the
center of the room, the judges looked at a podium and a dozen rows of red
velvet chairs, which, for the moment, were empty of the complaints, tears,
fears, and reprisals that filled that room several days each week.

Before calling in the parties to the first hearing, the judges reviewed the
cases for the day. Judge Ghorbanzadeh briefed the facts and legal issues aloud
to the associate judges, who posed questions while reviewing the documents
in the fat bundle of files. When I was there, the judges gave me background on
cases, sat for interviews, or answered follow-up questions. So that I could hear
their preliminary discussions, the judges invited me to sit at the small desk
adjacent their seats, the prosecutor's station. Once the prosecutor arrived and
the day's hearings were to proceed, I would move to the wall of tan leather
seats reserved for journalists. The weightiness of a trial was often suggested by
the number of journalists covering it. In such cases, their presence, including
moving about the room to snap photos, often created an air of urgency or
sharpened the significance of a case for all present.

In addition to those participating directly in the hearing, legal interns came
to the court. Sharply-dressed interns set themselves apart from parties to cases,
witnesses, and even, for better or worse, the less smartly-attired lawyers. At the
end of each session, interns handed the chief judge their recordkeeping books
for his signature, affirming that they had completed a portion of their mandatory courtroom observation.[38] The presence of law students often added to

the court's seriousness; it was a place where apprentices come to observe and learn how justice is meted out. Often, not unlike myself, after a trial, they approached the judges for clarification and explanation.

Court was in session from about eight in the morning until the early afternoon, Saturdays through Wednesdays. Some judges taught classes at universities around town; some were also studying for advanced degrees. Ghorbanzadeh's court heard cases on Saturdays, Mondays, and Wednesdays, reserving the rest of the workweek for administrative work and pre- or post-trial meetings that served as a sort of judicial 'office hours' for parties who had cases with the court. In this way, the courtroom is more than a place where judgment is passed and verdicts handed-down.

One morning I entered the chambers to hear the extensive protestations of a woman whose mother had been murdered by her neighbor—a renter and sometimes friend. Over their children's objections, the parents had rented a room to a man recently released from prison for a petty crime. They helped him out financially, shared meals, and generally looked after him. However, the man had unpaid debts and needed cash. Apparently, he decided to rob the couple. Since he knew their daily routine, he had entered the couple's home while the husband took an afternoon walk and the wife napped. He took their hidden cash, but then the jewelry she was wearing caught the perpetrator's eye. As he began removing her bangles and necklace, the old woman was startled awake. The man, himself surprised, didn't know what to do and, in a panic, grabbed a nearby pillow and suffocated the woman. Initially, he said, he wanted only to muffle her screams, but ultimately, she died.

The daughter, incensed by the man's behavior after her parents had supported and helped him, wanted justice for her mother. The daughter wanted to know whether, if they executed the perpetrator, they would have to pay half of the compensation for the gender of the deceased. She had heard, she said, that the new law provided a work-around for this gender incompatibility. The judge informed her of the new provision through which she could petition the state treasury to pay the difference in *diya* for the execution of a male who had killed a female.[39] He explained to her how the process worked and the filings it required to show proof of the family's financial need. The woman, pleased with what she heard, was emboldened to speak more expressively about the details of her mother's death. She began gesticulating and carrying on about the thankless perpetrator who had made so many people suffer with the murder of such a beloved old woman. The judges listened and nodded as she went on. Finally, she thanked the judges, gathered her possessions, and left.

One of the judges turned to me and said, "You see. In some cases, there is nothing we can do. For some, the pain is too much." Then the chief judge interrupted, "With these cases, too, though, sometimes we see that time allows

for their passions to subside and for forbearance to become conceivable. Forbearance in these cases is difficult, and" he added, "children are very protective of their elderly parents, especially daughters." Indeed, judges were aware that
victims' families often did not appreciate the pressures put on them to forgo
their right of retribution and calibrated their coaxing to when they saw it as
appropriate.

In another case, during office hours, a woman came to protest a perpetrator's acquittal. She approached the bench and went on to berate the court and
the entire system that freed a defiant murderer. The judge listened and after
she finished, advised her of her right to appeal the verdict. When she continued to remonstrate, he interrupted and repeated that her complaints could be
heard on appeal. He explained the process, reminding her of the twenty-day
window to file.

Even though this project's focus was on those who agreed to forgo retribution, I also amassed a number of stories of others who lamented the pressures
put on them to forgo retribution when they did not want to. Some cases, it
seemed, were too starkly egregious, too violent, or too disturbing of social
norms for such discussions to take place in the court. In such cases, however,
judges still used their influence and broad networks to contact social workers,
sages, and others to meet with victims' families.

In one case, even a female magistrate from the prosecutor's office, the only
person in all my years of research who asked that I not use her name, worked
to gain families' forbearance. A pious woman, who unabashedly stated that
females should be admitted into the judiciary as full-fledged judges, boasted
to me that she had never failed to achieve forbearance. The reason she did not
want her name published, she told me, was because she did not want to give
victims' families any indication that she, or any other part of the judiciary, was
partisan. In pressing families to forgive, however, she felt that she abided by
both her legal and religious duty.

The duality of this duty—the aim of securing forbearance even while ad-
ministering justice—was neither uncommon nor was it perceived as a contradiction. Some of the reason for this has to do with how crimes are codified,
which is according to punishment. It bears recalling here that cases dealing
with *shari'a*-based punishments, such as *qisas*, leave judges with no discretion
in sentencing. Once the elements of the crime are established, then the non-
discretionary sentence of *qisas* is awarded to the plaintiff(s). Where, or rather
when, judges do have discretion in such cases is after sentencing. This is when
the coaxing of victims' families starts in earnest. In their roles as arbiters of
judgment, prior to the verdict, judges entertain the idea of forbearance or, at
minimum, pose the possibility to victims' families as another form of relief,
but are unable to require it.

The Briefing

"Come in, we have an interesting case today," Judge Maliki said to me as I entered the courtroom one morning. The morning pre-trial briefing was about to begin. All three judges had reviewed the file. The chief judge was about to introduce the case orally to the two associate judges, and now to me as well. The case revolved around a defendant accused of the gruesome murder of his childhood friend. The defendant had confessed. Judge Ghorbanzadeh began: "The defendant is Hadi S. He is from Peshva, Varamin," he said, referring to a neighborhood in a disadvantaged suburb of Tehran. "He is on trial for intentional murder. Both victim and perpetrator were addicts, on *sheesheh* (crystal methamphetamine)." The judge read from the dense file, which contained the indictment, the police report, and the defendant's written confession detailing the events of the night of the murder.

> The defendant goes to the victim's house. They smoke through a pen that's rigged as a pipe. It breaks. Then the defendant leaves. The victim calls the defendant and says that he knows someone who works at Varamin Hospital, where they can get a pipe. The victim tells the defendant that he has to get gas and to meet him at the station. They put a jug of gas in the car. The victim goes into the hospital to get the pipe, while the defendant waits. The victim is gone for a long time. The defendant calls, but the victim doesn't answer. Finally, the defendant flags a taxi and goes home. Then, at one [in the morning], the victim calls the defendant and says that he got the stuff. The defendant goes to the victim's house. They smoke for about twenty minutes. The defendant notices that the victim's house is a total mess; one of the windows is broken, and things are strewn about. He doesn't like how it looks.

The judge turned to me, "Are you getting all this?" opening up the chance for me to ask questions. I replied that I followed as I wrote down his words. Although I would ask for clarifications later, I avoided interrupting the flow of cases as they were in progress. The judge's comments reminded me that he was aware of my presence throughout the session: "All right, don't hesitate if you do," and he continued.

> The victim's mother calls. She tells her son, 'I'll kill myself if I know you are smoking [drugs].' The defendant gets on the phone and tells her not to worry, that he will watch over her son, and hangs up. A few minutes later, the defendant takes a knife that was lying by the couch and stabs the victim. The victim remains alive but has a deep wound in his right side. The

defendant drags the victim into the kitchen, where he stabs him eight or nine more times; so much so that he breaks the knife's handle.

The defendant is bloody and decides to change out of his clothes. He takes off the victim's pants and attempts to put them on, but they are too small. He changes back into his own clothes and leaves to return home on foot. He takes the victim's phone. As he is walking, he realizes he has left his keys in the victim's pants while changing and returns.

When he returns to the house, he sees that the victim had gotten up and walked out of the kitchen. The defendant then takes the handle of a vacuum and strikes him on the head. Then he gets the jug of gasoline that the victim had purchased earlier and pours it over the victim and the interior of the house. The defendant lights the house on fire and leaves. He still forgets his keys, so he goes to his sister's house. It is around five in the morning. He showers and changes, then calls a friend, Dariush, to bring him clean clothes, using the victim's phone.

When investigators went to the scene of the crime, they found the keys and *sheesheh*. There are three charges: intentional murder, desecration of a corpse, and destruction of property. The pathologist's report stated that cause of death was stab wounds.

Also included in the file were the investigator's findings, the pathologist's report, and a list of plaintiffs:

> The victim's family consists of one young son (b.1378/1999), but since he was over fifteen, by seven months and twenty-one days, he is qualified to be a plaintiff. The other family members are the victim's mother and his wife.

The wife's legal standing was different. Although not eligible for *qisas*, she could be eligible for other damages. However, she was not on the complaint. Getting her on the complaint would be important when settling the deceased's estate and determining settlement from the other charges.

Judge Maliki interrupted, "Was there any motivation?"

"No motivation is stated. The indictment only indicates that the defendant stated how much it bothered him that the house was in disarray."

Judge Maliki, turning to me, said, "Understanding the motivation is important in order for the victim's family to be able to forgo retribution."

With this case history, the judges were apprised of the situation before the court—a grisly murder with no clear motive. The chief judge turned to his associates, "Are we ready to call them in?" Noting their nodding agreement, he called the clerk to proceed with the first case of the day.

The Trial

The parties, who had been waiting outside the courtroom, entered. The proximity between them was notable. Grieving family members whisked past the defendant and his mother, his sole family member present. For a split-second, before the parties branched out to their designated sides of the room—the defendant on the right, the victim's family to the left—their physical closeness simulated the warmth of past relations.

The defendant was dressed in a prison uniform—striped long-sleeved shirt and pants and rubber slippers. His hands were shackled in front. A chain between his feet reduced his stride to a noisy slither. A guard escorted the defendant into the courtroom. His lawyer was by his side. Before commencing, the chief judge spoke addressed the guard, "Undo his chains," and exclaimed, "This is the third time I am seeing this. The defendant has a right to be free to express himself during his defense." The statement drew attention to the object restraining the defendant, simultaneously highlighting the state's power over him and the way procedures can be adapted to give the sensorial effect of freedom even in constraint. The judge also asserted his authority over the room and the institutions that controlled the defendant.

Judge Ghorbanzadeh began the session with the invocation, "In the Name of God, the Merciful, the Beneficent" and introduced everyone present. The clerk-stenographer assiduously wrote down the judge's words in clear, legible script. His writing would create an object that would circulate and through which the law (state institutions) would decide and later confirm the defendant's fate. Throughout the session, the judge would pause to let the stenographer catch up, sometimes asking, "Did you get that?" before moving on or repeating his words. The document would comprise the authoritative record of the case. At the end of the hearing, as the parties filed out, everyone who testified would sign their transcribed statements.[40]

The chief judge acknowledged that the defendant had been in prison for the past year and a half and announced the charges against him, along with his confession. The judge noted that the defendant worked in construction, was recently divorced, and had two children.

By offering some background about the defendant, the judge presented the human side of a man whose execution would leave two minor children fatherless. He bridged that degree of humanization with the bald allegations of his crimes. The judge called on the prosecutor to read the indictment. A youthful prosecutor rose and read the findings of the investigation that her office had carried out. The state, however, was just one of the petitioners, and the secondary one, at that.

The primary plaintiffs were the victim's family members. The judge's commanding tone emphasized that his attention was focused on their complaint, "The petitioners are the victim's mother and son." He noted that the victim's wife was not named in the complaint, "but she would like to amend it to add her name." He named the parties to the complaint, slowly spelling out their names. The judge then announced to all that the parties were to attend to their speech and to avoid saying anything that was untrue or against their conscience, law, or decency.[41] He asked the victim's mother to stand at the podium. Weeping, she answered his questions. First about her background: She had a sixth-grade education, was married, her husband deceased. She had eight children, including the victim. She gave her address. Then the judge asked her specific questions based on her petition, "What is your complaint?" But before letting her respond, he began to explain, "You have choices, *qisas*, *diya* . . ." The victim's mother, wiping her tears with her chador, interrupted:

MOTHER: No, that one—*qisas*. I raised these children without a father . . .
J1: So your petition is for *qisas*?
M: He killed my child in a very bad way.

Her voice cracked while uttering the following words:

M: First with a knife, then he burned the body, and then he burned the house to the ground. Why did he have to burn his body?
J1: Did you know him?
M: Yes, he was my son's childhood friend.
J1: Did he ever come to your house?
M: No, no. He killed him in a bad way, stabbed him so many times, then tried to put on his clothes.

The mother did not want to engage the judge's attempt to personalize the issue. She waved the questions away and repeated her previous point as a way of justifying her decision.

J1: Yes, I read the indictment. So, you request *qisas*?
M: Yes.

The judge noted the decision for the record and invited her to return to her seat. He then called the victim's fifteen-year-old son to the podium, addressing him by his first name, "Sadegh, please come to stand. Now, introduce yourself." The slight young man spoke with a soft voice, "Sadegh."

J1: Are you Mohammad's son?
S: Yes.

The judge continued to collect his vitals: date of birth, address, and education.

J1: Do you work?
s: Yes.

Sadegh's face contorted with each response, reflecting a deep psychic wound.

J1: You live with your mother?
s: Yes.

The judge explained for the record, "Originally, his mother was *qayem-e saghir* (guardian of the minor) and had filed a complaint on his behalf." Then looking at the plaintiff, "Now, it looks as though you have reached the age of majority. You can file your own complaint. What do you say in your complaint?"

s: *Qisas.*
J1: Only *qisas*? Nothing other than that?
s: Definitely. It must be *qisas.*
J1: Okay. In your opinion why?
s: I don't know.
J1: Do you have a reason?
s: That night, my father called me and forgot to hang up and I heard him (the defendant) fighting with my father. And two hours later, the incident took place.
JUDGE MALIKI INTERVENED: Do you know what *qisas* is?
s: Execution.
MALIKI: You can ask for *diya.*
s: No.
THE CHIEF JUDGE ADDED: You can have *qisas, diya.* What would you like?
s: *Qisas.*

The judge nodded, made a note in the file, and excused Sadegh. He next asked the victim's wife to rise. A heavy air swept the courtroom as she sighed and sniffled, then stood. Before settling in front of the podium, the victim's wife turned to glare at the defendant. Standing just inches from the man whom she believed had killed her husband, she hissed, "[You piece of] Shit!" The wife composed herself, then turned to the judge, prefacing her response with the loss of her records. "He burned everything when he burned down the house. I have a copy of my identification papers, that's all."

The judge ascertained that she and the deceased were married, lived together, and had no intention to divorce. "Why was her name not on the complaint?" He asked aloud, noting a problem. "You were not divorced. Do you have your marriage certificate?"

"It was burned. I went to Records Office and will get a copy for the court."

Stating for the record, the judge noted, "We need to revise the complaint. In order to do that, we need the marriage certificate."

The judge explained the issue. "The wife has no right to *qisas*, but can file a complaint." Then turning to the wife, "Do you want to file a complaint?"

"Yes."

The petitioners had appeared in court without a lawyer and the judge was helping to preserve the wife's rights for property damages and inheritance. The judge then questioned the victim's wife to determine the nature of the two men's relationship. She acknowledged that they were friends but asserted that her husband had cut off relations because of the defendant's drug problem. She maintained that the two had started to hang out again after many years, just weeks before her husband's death.

Having identified the petitioners and their demands, the chief judge then asked the defendant to rise. The guard stood as well, remaining directly behind him throughout the testimony. The judge repeated the required warning that he be wary of his language when testifying and asked the defendant preliminary questions for the record.

The defendant stated his name and date of birth.

The judge affirmed his age: thirty-six; education: middle school; and occupation: construction worker. The defendant stated that he was married but had gotten divorced six months before the "accident." He had two daughters, aged thirteen and eight, who lived with their mother. The defendant had difficulty stating his address. Since he had been in prison, he had no dwelling, and his mother had moved to a new construction. He did not know where. The house was so new, it did not have a street number. Nor did he have a telephone number. The defendant's mother, sitting several rows back, reluctantly provided hers.

Finally, the judge read the charges and reviewed the facts, citing the defendant's confession. Looking up from the file, the judge said, "You have been charged with these three crimes. How do you defend yourself?"

> D: I don't accept the report [indictment]. I didn't have money for a
>   lawyer. No, I do not accept any of the charges.
> J1: Are you saying you are innocent of the charges of . . . ?
> D: speaking over the judge: I . . .
> J1: Listen to me one second. Are you listening?
> D: Yes.

The judge began reading the defendant's confession aloud, "I put on his pants . . ." He looked up from the file, and asked the defendant, "Are you following?" The defendant nodded. The victim's wife quietly wept as the judge continued:

> Mohammad was moving, getting up. I picked up the vacuum rod and hit him on the head. I went to get the gasoline and poured it in the house and on Mohammad. I lit the house on fire. I took his mobile and left on foot. On my way home, I realized I'd forgotten my keys, but since the house was burning, I could not go back. I went to my sister's house. I showered and washed my clothes. I called Dariush and asked for clothes. He said, 'What are you doing calling me at five in the morning?'

JI: Do you accept that this is your statement?
D: I said these things. Some are correct. I called his mother; I called Dariush, but the rest is not correct. I was tortured.
JI: Where?
D: By the investigator and the interrogator.
JI: So, you are saying that your confession was given under duress?

The judge, contesting the defendant's claim of forced confession, said, "If the investigator tortured you, why did you repeat what you said to the interrogator? You said the same things before you were in custody as well. It was only after you went to prison that you said you no longer accept the confession."

D: Mohammad and I were friends from childhood.
JI: You repeated this same set of facts to the interrogator. The investigation was first.

The judge continued with the torture defense. The defendant had made the same statement to the investigator, before he was taken into custody. The judge noted that he had repeated the same set of facts to the interrogator after his arrest, while incarcerated, but that it was only after that that he stated that his confession had been made under duress. The defendant mumbled something inaudible. Then the judge repeated, "One more time: you told the interrogator . . ."

D: I can't explain it well. I can't speak . . .
JI: In going through your statement, you said that you left the keys in the home of the victim. Using your statements, the inquiry found the keys and confirmed what you said.
D: I went to the house. I did have a relationship with Mohammad.
JI: You accept that?
D: Yes.

The judge went through the defendant's confession, line by line, to determine which parts the defendant agreed with and which he did not. The defendant made new assertions, not recorded in his interrogation or confessions. He shifted the blame to others, alleging that three perpetrators unknown to him had entered, killed Mohammad, and also mistreated him.

J1: Did you go to your sister's house after you left?
D: Yes, because I left my keys when I left.
J1: Why didn't you go back to his house?
D: I knew this accident had happened.
J1: You said you were together, but you left. How did you know about the accident?
D: Some people arrived after me. I knew some people would come and take me to the *camp* [drug rehab]. When I got there, the window of the house was broken. It looked to me like someone was looking for something. The house was a mess.
J1: So how did you know he was killed?
D: I was in the house.
J1: If you were there, then who killed him?
D: I don't know.
J1: If they killed Mohammad, then why not you?
D: They didn't have a problem with me.
J1: You were a witness.
D: I ran away.
J1: Why did you not state this before?
D1: I told the investigator.
J1: What were they doing there?
D: They were looking for money or something. They struck me and tied my hands and feet.

As the testimony continued, it proved to be lengthy and discordant. The other judges began to enter into the exchange, posing their own questions and receiving often contradictory or improbable answers.

J2: The three men also attacked you?
D: They hit me in the face and hung me upside down.
J2: Why didn't you say this in your confession?
D: I said those [other] things because they [the interrogators] tortured me.
J1: When a person is being tortured, he cannot give such details. But you did so, a clear, detailed confession.
D: I was inside the house. They killed him before my own eyes.
J2: Who is the murderer?
D: Some people.

J2: Who are they?

D: I don't know them. From the instant they entered the home, they hit my knees. I said, 'At least let me put my pants on.' [Since] I had spoken to his [Mohammad's] mother, I thought they were from the *camp* [drug rehab].

J2: Did Mohammad know them?

D: He . . . They had come before. This wasn't the first time. Three people came to the house. They came after I spoke to Mohammad's mother. They arrived around eleven [p.m.]

J2: If they wanted to talk to Mohammad, why did you stay? Could you have left?

D: I told Mohammad's mother I'd take care of him.

J2: to the victim's mother: Did you hear from the defendant?

MOTHER: Yes. He's lying. It's all lies. He called. He said, 'Mohammad isn't well. I'm with him.' That's all.

J3: What time did you leave?

D: Around two-thirty in the morning.

The judges questioned the defendant's mother and Dariush, the friend who had brought him clothes. Then they returned to asking about the scene of the crime:

J3: How did you leave Mohammad's house?

D: I got out by myself. My hands and feet were tied.

J2: How did you get free?

D: I spread and spread my hands and got free. They lit the house on fire while I was in it. I was able to escape in just twenty seconds.

J2: How big was the house?

D: Fifty meters squared.

J2: How did you escape?

D: They were leaving, and as they left, I escaped.

J1: How come they did not see you?

D: I went a different way. They had a Peugeot and the alleyway was very narrow.

The defendant changed the subject, stating he wanted to change his attorney, from the court-appointed one to hire a private lawyer. The defendant's lawyer interjected:

L: I am sorry, but you can't expect the defendant to know the laws. When I asked if he wanted my representation, he said he didn't know. I can defend him or not here today.

J1: As long as he doesn't have a lawyer, the court appoints one.

L: Legally, there are lots of issues here. The defendant removed me. Give him the right to hire his own lawyer. I've met with him for only ten minutes. We were supposed to meet on four other occasions, but each time, I was not able. Once I had a flat tire, another time it was a snow storm, and . . .

J2: He is going to need at least 50 million *toman* (about $17,000 at the time).

L: If they execute him now, an innocent man will be dragged up the scaffold. Sometimes the interrogators do things they aren't supposed to do. They slap around . . .

J1: Okay, I am going to ask everyone to step out.

The chief judge cleared the courtroom so that they could discuss the procedural issue of the right to choose counsel. The judges discussed the right to an attorney, the defendant's failure to procure or submit the name of a private lawyer, as required, and when such an attorney would be appointed.[42] The judges were trying to determine whether the defendant's concern was legitimate or a delaying tactic.

J3: If he doesn't vacillate, he should be allowed to select his own lawyer.

J1: He needs to introduce the [name of a] lawyer . . .

J2: No law can do everything, we have to establish some rules . . .

J3: But the punishment is very severe, *qisas*.

J2: He can't decide the time; he's had over six months.

J1: He still hasn't introduced any names.

J2: It's a procedural question about choosing a lawyer. One month to find a lawyer . . .

J3: refers to Article 348.2: *"Any time the defendant determines . . ."*

J1: As of now, he still had not introduced a lawyer.

Given the defendant's failure to name a private attorney and having already been appointed an attorney by the court, two of the three judges ruled that the proceeding could continue with the court-appointed attorney. The chief judge called the parties back and stated for the record that the request was denied. The in-camera discussion of the issue of representation is an instance of how the courts are contending with new procedures that have no established norms, here, how much time the defendant is given to select his own attorney.

In response, the lawyer raised another procedural point—the Principle of Lenity, "When the law is unclear, then it should be interpreted to the advantage of the defendant (148.2, 48)." The judge noted that the lawyer's protest was reserved and explained to the defendant that he could appeal. He then asked the lawyer to present his arguments.

The lawyer opened, "The respectful court could have permitted a delay in the proceedings to permit the defendant to obtain a lawyer," and proceeded with three substantive arguments on behalf of the defendant. "One, the defendant's confession is not valid [it was taken under duress]. Two, the victim's wife admitted to breaking the window herself and that there were three people there the morning after, which confirms that there were three people looking for the victim and those three people were the ones who my client saw while at the victim's house. Three, the defendant denies that he committed any murder and requests that the court follow-up with a competent investigation worthy of this court."

Without pause, the chief judge called the defendant to the podium one last time and asked, "What is your last defense?"

"I did not do it. He was my childhood friend. I have nothing to lose. I did not do this."

The parties filed in a line to sign their statements. As she approached the defendant, the victim's wife jeered, "Only the smell of your blood will bring me peace. Rest assured."

The case was finished. The ruling would be in the plaintiffs' favor. The judgment—*qisas*. The defendant would appeal. The procedural issues of the defendant's choice of lawyer and his claim of forced confession had been reserved for appeal.

Elm-e Qazi (Judge's Knowledge)

The case above is not about forgiveness, per se. In depicting this trial, my aim was to emphasize legal procedures, interrogatory methods, and how judges use them and other evidence to formulate their opinions. The judges were aware of the defendant's intent to withdraw or undermine the authority of his written confession. During the trial, the judges pursued another angle for delivering their ruling—the judge's knowledge.

Judge's knowledge is a form of evidentiary proof in *Shi'ism*.[43] The criminal code classifies evidentiary requirements needed to prove criminal cases. Drawn from *Shi'i* jurisprudence, the four bases of proof include confession (*eqrar*), witness testimony (*shahadat*), sworn oaths (*qassameh* and *sogand*), and, finally, judge's knowledge (*elm-e qazi*).[44] With regard to the last method, *Shi'i fiqh* permits a judge in certain "fixed punishments [*hudud*] and death sentences by-way-of-retaliation [*qisas*]" to sentence offenders on the basis of "his own knowledge" (Peters 2005:163).

Judge's knowledge rests uneasily on judges' own perceptions of the elements that make up the crime. In murder, this includes the *actus reus*, or the commission of the physical act that constitutes the crime, and the *mens rea*, or the possession of the requisite intent to commit the act. These elements are necessary for proving the crime of intentional murder. Beyond this, when judge's knowledge is the form of proof that determines the defendant's guilt, judges must demonstrate that they possess this knowledge with certainty. Such explanations often rest on oral testimonies of the victims, the accused, witnesses, and experts.

Iran's penal code construes judge's knowledge as "the certainty that the judge attains from clear evidence presented in a matter brought before him."[45] This provision further obligates judges to state the source of evidence that serves as the basis of their knowledge in making the decision. The penal code adds a note to this provision listing the acceptable forms of evidence that can comprise the judge's knowledge: expert opinions, site inspection, local investigation, witness statements, and reports by law enforcement officers. Judge's knowledge cannot be derived from a generic perception. This footnote, elaborating the requirement (and forms) of documentary evidence, is a check on judges' claims of certainty.

Another provision explains that if the judge arrives at a decision based on his knowledge and that it contradicts other lawful evidence, then the judge may disregard that other evidence.[46] The judge must, however, explain the basis of his findings and justify his rejection of the other evidence.

The penal code also develops a hierarchy of evidentiary forms. Where there is conflicting evidence, confession has priority over testimony and sworn oaths. Testimony is given priority over sworn oath.[47] Since judge's knowledge is one of the primary evidentiary bases of legal rulings, its elaboration in the new penal code has significant consequences for rulings and the stated logic behind them.

The elaboration of judge's knowledge in the new codes suggests a drawing of boundaries around or imposing a limit on what can comprise the basis of a judge's decision, particularly in capital cases. These provisions in the penal code suggest increased attention by Iran's legislative and judicial bodies to the development of parameters guiding judges in their legal rulings. At the same time, the elaboration of judge's knowledge as a form of evidence signals an attempt to preserve the historical openness that the *shari'a* ideally possesses. This ideal allows judges the necessary discretion to tailor decisions to the exigencies of individual cases. However, it could also leave judges with too much individual authority and lead to uneven applications of the law.[48]

This case is also an illustration of an issue that a number of jurists have pointed out to me as the basis for many of the challenges in Iran's criminal laws which I have earlier noted—the definition of intent is very broad. The breadth of the definition has significant consequences for perpetrators. Once there is a finding of intent, judges possess no discretion in sentencing as judges cannot alter *shari'a*-prescribed punishments, such as *qisas*, once they have deemed that the actions of the defendant meet the elements of the crime.

Much of the legal process, including judges' interrogations of parties, aims to establish intent. As Messick noted, finding intent is essential and yet, it is by nature "inward and inaccessible." Islamic jurists seek to uncover intent by examining "manifest signs and forms of legal expression, including, but not limited to, individuals' spoken words and writings" (2001:153). Through *elm*, judges assess intent by observing linguistic expressions and performative signs. Judges consider the circumstances and context of the alleged crime through the testimonies and attempt to establish an account of the incident with certainty.

Scholars of Islamic law have cited important tensions between interpreting and adjudicating the law. Historically, the administration of Islamic law has resided with jurists educated in the science of jurisprudence. That is, only those trained in the broad moral issues involved in carrying out justice could be allowed to administer the *shari'a*. For this reason, Schacht (1964) referred to Islamic law as "jurist's" rather than "judge's" law, noting the concern with ethical issues inherent in the *shari'a*. Jurists trained in *fiqh* were averse to a codified system of process that could be carried out by mere judges simply enforcing rules without adequate knowledge of their underlying principles, what scholars refer to as *usul*, shorthand for *usul-e fiqh* (principles of jurisprudence).[49] Thus, the administration of justice was characterized by a lack of procedural uniformity, recognized as "*qadi-justice*" by Max Weber (1978). Moral considerations and a personalized style of process were characteristic traits of Weber's *qadi-justice*.

On the other hand, contemporary scholars of Islamic law argue that, while codification gives the *shari'a* unambiguous legal force, it disrupts the power of Islamic jurists to use their discretion in assessing cases. Their concern is that justice should be composed of fairness and equivalence rather than equal application of the law (Rosen 2018).

Iran's hybrid criminal justice system codifies laws that are to be implemented by judges serving as functionaries and provides a legal framework for those judges to act as Islamic jurists in certain cases and in some categories of crime. Codification, derived from western law, presides over an ossification of the more fluid jurist's system, where Islamic scholars make decisions based on study and knowledge of the jurisprudential logics of the *shari'a*. If this system is to work, however, it places a burden on the state to train jurisprudents at the bench. For advocates of this system, codification provides a basis for transparency and predictability, markers of a fair legal system.[50]

Conclusion

As part of the broader "coloring in" of the criminal laws that I wrote about in the previous chapter, the procedures that I have been exploring in this chapter give greater definition to judges' duties, both to seek reconciliation, as I have noted, but also, to render decisions which state their reasoning, including the finding of intent. In this way, despite the lack of discretion with regard to principles said to be based squarely on the *shari'a*, by construing judge's reasoning in this way, the laws permit some latitude with regard to *shari'a*-based non-discretionary punishments. And it is for this reason that the post-verdict emphasis on reconciliation extends to judges.

Thus far I have sought to illustrate how the courtroom serves as a space in which the state, through its judicial officials, corrals victims' instincts for revenge. As an affective space, the courtroom also conditions how judges reason and inflects subjectivities of all the parties in the courtroom. By serving in the role of arbiter in the ultimate settling of accounts, the state's aim is to contain extrajudicial violence. It does this, in part, by attending to the victim's need for justice, or rather, through providing an outlet for a "healthy" emotional response to an injury—the desire for retaliation (Rosenbaum 2013). Judges attempt to make victims whole and reestablish their sense of lost dignity.[51]

These cases also illustrate how selective and deliberate judges are in emphasizing reconciliation. Of the most violent cases, one judge told me, "there is little we can do . . . there is too much hatred, anger." This is especially so when emotional or kinship connections between parties are absent and when underlying factors continue to fuel the enmity. Such factors range from ethnic tensions to personal grudges. In the case outlined previously, during the wife's testimony, additional, personal reasons for her disdain for the defendant were revealed—he had stolen nude photos of her.

Finally, members of the judiciary are aware of the risk to the foundational impartiality of the system and the stature of the judges should they press victims' families too hard, particularly during the merits phase of the case. For this reason, the judges' behavior and demeanor is a shifting amalgamation of jurist, judge, officer of the state, but also, at times, stern father, compassionate compatriot, and reasonable arbiter. These roles are not always complementary. Sometimes, only when one ends can another begin.

3

Seeking Reconciliation

SENTIMENTAL REASONING
AND RECONCILED DUTIES

WHAT DOES it look like when, on the one hand, state officials are required to enforce the law of *lex talionis* and, at the same time, that law also asks of them to act as brokers for reconciliation between parties? My courtroom observations of the sanctioning hearings add to the robust scholarly discussion about reasoning and judging in Islamic jurisprudence (Bowen 2003; Feener 2014; Hirsch 1998; Peletz 2002; Rosen 1989; Stiles 2009; Vogel 2000). I argue that the panel of adjudicators in Tehran's criminal courts are something of a cross between judges and jurists (jurisprudential scholars) and employ both emotion and reason in their decision-making process.

The deliberations of these jurisprudential scholars take place in the affective space of the courts, and include attention to the defendants' demeanor and emotion, such as expressions of remorse and piety. Notwithstanding the decision of the victim's family to forgo retribution, the judges are tasked with considering the nature of the crime and gathering information. To do so, they often invite emotional testimonials. Judges will also contemplate the broad context in which the crime was committed to determine the length and breadth of the sanctions *after* the plaintiff's forbearance. While they can include measures such as probation, expulsion from a city or village, and prison, such sanctions do not include capital punishment.

The courtroom, with its fixtures and furnishings, rows of red velvet chairs, austere brown wooden desks placed on the raised platform, produces the conditions through which both plaintiffs and defendants carry out—and sometimes, expel—pain, suffering, regret, honor, and even pride. The space of the court, its physical trimmings, and even actors, such as the prosecutor, the judges, officers, and spectators, such as myself, witness and authenticate passionate performances. Individuals' courtroom statements as evocative and performative exercises often rely on implicit and sometimes explicit registers of *Shi'i* sentiment.

Take, for example, a mother who had lost her son and spoke only of *qisas* during the murder trial. She expressed a desire to recuperate her son's good name. He was not a thug or a drug dealer, as the defendant had alleged. In that case, the chief judge, seeing the elderly mother leaning heavily on her cane asked one of the clerks to pull up a chair for her to sit in, "Right here," he pointed to the floor just in front of his desk. The elderly woman took the weight off her feet and relaxed into the chair. From there, the judge, who referred to her endearingly as "Mother," asked her again, "What do you want?" She told the court that she wanted *qisas* because her son's reputation was tarnished when the defendant stated that he sold drugs. The mother's logic stressed that forbearance would be akin to accepting the defendant's side of the story. For her, *qisas* was an important vehicle through which she could redeem her son's damaged reputation. The chief judge, however, wanted her to see things differently; he wanted to show her that there, seated in the court, she could find repose and the stillness and comfort she had lost with her son's death. It was in occupying that space that serenity could come, not through the decision to seek retribution.

As the judge saw it, he could offer up the courtroom and the proceedings to these beleaguered families as a space in which to perform, but it is a space that also generates these performances of sentiment through specific affective registers. In previous chapters, I explored the court as a performative space for petitioners and respondents, but it is also important to explore the work of judging in this space. In addition to passing judgment, judges also attempt to bring about reconciliation, as the law compels. During hearings, they speak to the families of victims, through questions, statements of fact and law, and they coax, as well. The way the judges talk to defendants, often in the tripartite roles of stern fathers, wise jurists, and enforcing judges, also reveals a logic of sentencing. In an interview in the summer of 2012, one judge explained how he approaches victims' families:

I say to them, 'Yes this offender killed your (X).' Perhaps it was violent or not, a young or old person, whatever. I say to them, 'You have this right, but with the death of this person, will it be compensated? Will it bring X back?' They reflect and, after some time, they accept. If they are balanced, logical, then they go and think and come to the conclusion, that X will not be brought back. They decide how to consent—they may do it for God, they may get compensation—but that is their prerogative. It's a private contract. They write a formal contract with a notary. Those who are more pious will forgive, unless the murder is very harsh, then they need to take time to think, to decide. They will wait two to three years to forgo retribution.

The judge's reasoning is crucial in Islamic sanctioning and an element of proof in the *Shi'i mazhab* (school of thought). Moreover, while judges have no discretion upon a finding of intentional liability for *qisas*, appeals to emotion and even reconciliation, nonetheless, remain important components of both judgment and sentencing. This can be seen in a case for *qisas* that came before the court in July 2012. Through a lawyer, the plaintiff filed a complaint for proportionate punishment for loss of eyesight.

Forbearance in Sight

After convening the hearing, the chief judge turned to the prosecutor to state the charges. The prosecutor admitted into evidence the legal physician's report finding loss of eyesight in the plaintiff's right eye.[1] The judge then turned to the slender young man seated in the front and asked him to come forward. The plaintiff, wearing glasses with a thick lens on the right side stood before the judges with his arms folded in front of his chest. The judge asked, "Can you see anything?

"No. Nothing" replied the plaintiff with evident anger.

"Given your situation, there cannot be *qisas*," stated the judge. And then began to question the plaintiff. "Who did this? Were you friends?"

"No, I was a customer. He is a painter [in an auto repair shop] and didn't do the job."

The plaintiff then went on to tell the court what happened. He had gone to the shop that day to contest charges for a repair that had never materialized. He and the defendant had words that led to a dispute. According to the plaintiff, as he turned to walk away, the defendant hit the back of his head. When he turned around to see what it was, the defendant struck him again, this time in the face. The plaintiff stated that he ran to his car, bleeding from his head and face, and drove away.

"We asked people there and no one saw him hit you. The witnesses said that several people broke out into a fight. Did they lie?"

The plaintiff repeated his allegations. "I fell from the blow. I know it was him with an iron rod."

"What do you want?"

"*Qisas*."

"I can't give you that."

"Why not? I lost my eyesight. Two years of work!"

"Listen, why not *diya*? Why don't you talk to each other? Try to come to an agreement about compensation. I can't give you *qisas*."

"Can I go again, to the legal physician?"

"We have the legal physician's report, and it's final."

The judge dismissed the plaintiff and called on the defendant. From the other side of the room, a stout man with reddish-brown hair and an unkempt beard rose. He spoke with a thick regional accent that required the judges to intervene frequently and ask for clarification. The defendant's vocation, demeanor, and accent revealed a class difference between him and the other men in the room. The defendant stated a completely different version of the story. He contended that the plaintiff appeared in the garage while he was working, and insisted he look at the car immediately. The defendant added that he said he would repair the car, but that he needed to finish something else first. He also alleged that the plaintiff came with a group of six men who had surrounded him. He said that they threw the first punches, then struck him with pipes and tools they had picked up in the shop. He claimed he was defending his life, that he did not hit the plaintiff, and that it was likely one of the other men who hit the plaintiff during the brawl. The man looked down at the podium and quietly wept as he asserted his innocence.

Next was the plaintiff's lawyer, who restated his client's allegations and dismissed the defendant's story. The judges listened while passing the file between them.

The judge recalled the plaintiff and asked about his eye. "So, what can you see?" The plaintiff attempted to refute the defendant's statements, but the judge interrupted, insisting he only answer his question. The plaintiff responded with a pained expression. He said he could not see, that he was unable to continue his employment or complete his studies, and that his future was ruined. He would be disabled for the rest of his life, and wanted the defendant to experience the same.

The judge looked up from his notes and spoke earnestly to the plaintiff, "The legal physician's report says you've lost eighty-seven percent of your vision, but you still have thirteen percent."

"But I can't see!" exclaimed the plaintiff.

"We cannot order *qisas* for eighty-seven percent. It is impossible to achieve." The judge turned to the defendant. "Look, he has an argument with you. You two should come together and reach a settlement. No one else was involved or saw what happened. I advise . . ."

"I swear I didn't do it."

"What is your last defense?"

"I can only say that I did not do it. They were six or seven other people."

A second judge addressed the defendant, "You can't compare yourself with him. His eye is damaged. Tell the truth."

"I've been in prison for the last year and a half. He brought others."

The chief judge offered further consideration, "Look, you two should make an arrangement and move on. It's only going to hurt you further. I can't order *qisas*."

The implication was that he would rule it an unintentional tort, for which the defendant would be ordered to pay *diya*. He would also sentence the defendant to two years in prison for the crime of disturbing public safety. The judge used the courtroom as a space to deliver a coherent, if not consistent narrative about the incident. Having read the file prior to the hearing, he seemed to have been aware that the plaintiff's complaint would not meet the elements for *qisas*. In the absence of clear procedures to settle conflicts, he used his discretion in the process to push the parties to reconciliation. But there was also a hidden message to the plaintiff, one perhaps he did not realize. If the court determined the amount of compensation, it would be set according to the regulations for unintentional loss of an organ (one-third of a full *diya*). However, parties can come to their own agreements, which usually work out better for the plaintiff. This is what the judge was getting at.

Bureaucratic Subjectivities

When I asked Judge Aziz-Mohammadi if he held any special memories of particular cases, he said, "I remember all of them. I have handed down over four thousand sentences. They call me 'the most experienced criminal judge in Iran.'" Judge Noorallah Aziz-Mohammadi was given this title by the newspapers.[2] By the time he retired in 2015, he had presided over the courts for more than forty-four years, longer than the Islamic Republic had been in existence. He took pride in his role as the most experienced judge in the criminal court in all of Iran. The judges I had come to know held him in great esteem for his judgments and his work ethic. "You must talk to Aziz-Mohammadi, he is *bee-nazir* [without equal]," I was told more than once.

I first met Aziz-Mohammadi in 2007, when he presided over the first murder trial I ever attended. At that initial encounter, I entered his chambers to greet him before we moved to the rarely-used salon reserved for high profile cases. He gave me a brief summary of what I was about the see, asked if I had any questions, and answered them before moving into the courtroom. On the bench he was serious, if not stern, but at times, if circumstances permitted, he could also be warm, even jocular, to opposing parties. He had already become a well-known legal expert in Tehran, if not the country, teaching in law schools around the city, and he had written several textbooks on judging and criminal law.[3]

But it was not until years later that I learned of another, more critical, reason to interview the judge. At the end of 2014, Aziz-Mohammadi chose to forgive a young man who, four years earlier, had murdered his eighty-eight-year-old father. That is to say, he, Aziz-Mohammadi, had given up his right to retaliation or, said differently, he exercised his right of forbearance in a case involving the murder of his father.

That summer (2014), I sat down with Aziz-Mohammadi to conduct a series of interviews to better understand his decision to forgo retribution. At the time, he was preparing to retire and was in the midst of writing his memoir. I went to his courtroom with a few judges from the branch I had been in that morning. As we entered Branch 71, Aziz-Mohammadi looked up from the file he was reading and, though he knew of me and my research, looked surprised. Judge Maliki, who had arranged the meeting, did the explaining on my behalf, telling Aziz-Mohammadi that I wanted to interview him because he had forgone his right to retribution. Then, from behind the raised podium where he sat every day, Aziz-Mohammadi moved to the chairs alongside the wall on his left, seats reserved for journalists, to create a space for our interview. The other judges gathered around, forming a large circle. With Aziz-Mohammadi to my right, I began asking questions, hoping to gain insight into his role as a judge, the place of forbearance in the criminal justice system, and his decision to forgo sanctioning when he had presided over many cases and had issued thousands of sentences.

In order to gain insight into his interpretation of the incident and to pave a way to discuss the broader issues, I first asked what had happened to his father—the facts of the case. Aziz-Mohammadi responded in a low, slightly wounded tone, different from the firm, assured voice I knew from the bench.

> A boy, about sixteen, choked him to death. It was for a robbery. He came to my father's house, knocked and, when my father opened the door, he pushed his way in. He already knew that an old man lived alone there. He was an addict and was looking to rob someone, to get money or goods to use to get his drugs. My father was an easy target. I didn't even file a complaint. I have seven brothers and a sister, who all filed complaints. They wanted *qisas*.

By not filing a complaint, the judge sought to convey his determination *not* to exercise retribution. In a sense, he emphasized his remission of punishment well before the case went forward. His resolute stance against *qisas* in his father's case led me to asked about his motivations—"How did you come to the decision to forgo *qisas* when everyone else wanted it?" His response was quick and matter-of-fact, "I don't believe in *qisas.*"

I looked up. The other judges looked up. Aziz-Mohammadi was looking down pensively. The most experienced criminal judge in Iran, the one who has delivered four thousand sentences, does not believe in *qisas*? My first reaction was to think that they were probably addressing me as a naïve American, someone who would go back to the U.S. and send a facile message about *qisas*, the court, and the humanity of the judges. But, in fact, that was not their concern at all. After Aziz-Mohammadi stated his beliefs about *qisas*, another judge interrupted, "Let me explain what the judge means when he says he doesn't believe in *qisas*. He is a man of the law. *Qisas* is effective; it's our law and comes from our religion. When he says he doesn't believe in it, he is speaking about his personal belief towards *qisas*, not about the law."

Indeed, this judge wanted to address an important concern of the judiciary, that *qisas* is the law and that it based on the Qur'an, and thus not subject to change or criticism, and not open to debate. Far from wanting to make me look naïve, as I had initially thought, this judge's explanation, it now seemed, was intended to establish the adherence of the judiciary to the state's interpretation of the religious laws, obedience, thus, to the judiciary and Iran's Supreme Leader.

Aziz-Mohammadi added his own clarification:

As long as I worked in the courts, I believed I had to follow the law. If the victim's family wants *qisas* and the law is met, we can't deny them unless there is a legal issue that would allow us to dispense with *qisas*. I am always looking for one [legal issue] in these files. I look for a direction. If not, then we have to give the victim's family their rights. If there is even a ten percent chance [of doubt], we won't give *qisas*, even with *elm* [*-e qazi*] we won't. In court, I try to make the victim's family consider forgoing *qisas*. I tell them, "forgo it and take compensation." I say, "*Qisas* won't resolve your problems, nor those of society." Since I don't believe in *qisas*, as a son, when I saw that my father had been killed, I knew that it would not help to kill another person's son. It would not bring my father back. And this person was very young. He was not fully mature. How would people take me seriously as a judge when I tell them to forgo [*qisas*], if I could not? They would say, "He tells us to forgo, but he didn't. So why should we?"

Echoing his colleague, Aziz-Mohammadi emphasized the personal aspect of the decision to forgo retribution. He distinguished his role as a state administrator—judge—from that of a member of a kin group. He did not challenge the system that gives the right to the victims' families; instead, he focused on his individual beliefs. Like anyone might, he drew from his experiences. In his case, it happened to be in the capacity of a judge in criminal court.

Aziz-Mohammadi also elaborated on his efforts to convince his siblings to forgo their right to retribution. "I always said, 'Yes, *qisas* is our right, but so, too, is forbearance. We won't gain anything by doing this.'" Aziz-Mohammadi's stature and experience helped convince his siblings to forgo retribution. In the end, the family also declined to ask for financial or other compensation from the perpetrator's family to make up for their injury.

Through Judge Aziz-Mohammadi's subjectivity we see what Engseng Ho (2006) has referred to as the layering effect of modern bureaucratic administration as it is grafted onto Islamic jurisprudence. With layering effect, I refer to the bureaucratic network that is comprised of key *Shi'i* principles and modern state technologies to which I have elsewhere referred as Islamico-civil law. I have argued that this blending produces liberal subjectivities, even if the substance of claims is based on principles found in Muslim scriptures (Osanloo 2009). Although based on Islamic principles, many of the substantive claims, especially in criminal law, are themselves derived from, or rather built upon, many centuries of pre-Islamic and Islamic juridical practices that continue today, through the judge's *elm*.[4]

Through this process of layering, Iran's religious leaders sought to rewrite Iranian laws as a response to the Shah's levelling reforms wrought by the 1960s White Revolution, the purpose of which was to breakdown non-state hierarchies, such as the *'ulama*, within the monarchy. The resulting post-revolutionary Islamico-civil laws maintained and recreated a federal bureaucracy, only now with the religious leaders at the center. These leaders now receive monetary support through alms (religious), taxes, and rents (oil) as the resulting bureaucratic system builds on both *patronage*—the hierarchical system from which the religious elites emerged and justified their claim to authority—and *rights*—the populist discourses that the left and religious groups employed to join forces, mount a revolution, and depose Iran's monarchy. One effect of this layered bureaucratic network, which Ho has found as resulting from administrative state power, is that it "imparts a schizophrenic quality" to the state's bureaucracy (2006:296).[5] With the example of Aziz-Mohammadi, I highlight the confusion that ensued with the judge saying that he did not believe in *qisas*. Rather than confusion, however, the complexity in the judge's thinking personally and professionally is perhaps better understood as an effect of this bureaucratic layering, of the plural legal system itself. However, Iran is not unlike other contemporary bureaucratic states, which in one way or another bear the effects of this administrative layering.

In a following one-on-one meeting with Aziz-Mohammadi, I addressed the issue about his belief in *qisas* by asking the question in a different way, "Why do you give so many *qisas* sentences, when you do not believe in *qisas*?" He responded, "It's the law. I have to follow the law. I try, when it is possible, to advise reconciliation."[6] In this context, Judge Aziz-Mohammadi's position corresponds with the German term *Rechtsstaat*, which loosely translates as "rule of law." In such contexts, civil servants must abide by bureaucratic rules and rule-governed decision-making even if, as individuals, they nonetheless have their own conscience and hold opinions that diverge from the requirements of their office, such as enforcing the law.

When I discussed this interview with a social worker, she was unsettled by the judge's comments and remarked, "They give them [sentences of *qisas*] so readily, and then call on us [social workers] to get the victim's family to forgive. Why do they do that?"

Returning to the laws for a moment, as I noted previously, the religious obligation to be merciful and compassionate is codified, not just in Iran's substantive criminal laws, but also in Iran's laws of criminal procedure (Articles 1 and 192), which create an imperfect duty on the part of government officials to bring about reconciliation and to avoid *qisas* whenever possible. Thus, the penal code (the substantive law) recognizes forbearance as a right and the code of criminal procedure calls on government agents tasked with carrying out the substantive law to do so with an eye towards achieving reconciliation. However, procedurally, this can happen only after the sentence has been handed down, although we have seen some slight nudging by judges in the merits phase in some cases mentioned previously.

In spite of the legal and moral obligations, there are few, if any, guidelines regulating how forbearance should be brought about or by whom. So, the right to forbearance is weakly defined procedurally, yet, the unconstrained right of victims to retaliation is clear and well-delineated, both substantively and procedurally. In the context of sentencing, the judges' issuance of *qisas* may be more straightforward, protecting them on appeal, and allowing for swifter disposition of cases. With *qisas*, moreover, judges appear to be tough on crime, serving up the deterrent purpose that *qisas* is said to be performing. At the same time, perpetrators still possess a possible route to saving themselves, through forbearance, which gives victims' families significant authority, not to mention complicity, with the state. Several judges with whom I spoke also believed that recognizing the centrality of victims' rights, both in *qisas* and forbearance, helped prevent revenge crimes that prolong the cycle of violence.

As I explore the work of bureaucrats who participate in this system, I am attentive to the fact that, unlike the other agents I worked with (social workers, activists, and defense lawyers), government officials are not only working in the system, but they comprise it. When there are few if any guidelines governing their forgiveness work, then the actions, practices, or rituals they introduce *are* the system.

Duty to Seek Reconciliation:
Conditioning Judgment, Discretion, and Reason

When I posed the question of why people, including judges, perform the role of conciliator when they have no legal obligation to do so to Judge Ghorban-zadeh that first day, he casually nodded and said, "There is a duty of mediation [*mianjigari*]." Judge Ghorbanzadeh cited the first article of the new laws of

criminal procedure as proof of a clarified and specified affirmative responsibility on the part of members of the justice system to oversee reconciliation efforts. From his desk drawer, he pulled out a worn paperback edition of the new
code of criminal procedure. I was pleased that for the first time in all my years
of research, I was not the only person carrying around the codes. Every court
clerk and judge I saw that summer (2015) had copies readily at hand. The laws
were new, not only to me, but to everyone encountering them, and they were
constantly consulting them during the proceedings and discussions. The
judges were often helpful in explaining the law, even looking up the references
when I asked, "What article of the code is that?" and, increasingly, I gave myself license to ask questions.

As if announcing his response to my question to all present, including the
two associate judges and the clerks, the chief judge read aloud from the code
of criminal procedure:

> Article one sets rules and regulations for the discovery of crimes, the pros-
> ecution of the accused, the preliminary investigation, mediation, reconcili-
> ation between the parties, manner of investigation, issuance of the judg-
> ment, manner of appealing the judgment, implementation of the judgment,
> assigns duties and powers of the judicial authorities and officers of the
> court, and compliance with the rights of the accused, the victim, and the
> public.

The judge then looked up and declared, "This is both in our religion and our
laws." The phrase "in our religion and our laws" is one I often heard in the process of carrying out this research. The distinction, frequently made to me by
state officials, raised an important question about the relationship between
the two: What does it mean in an Islamic republic that bureaucrats make a
distinction between religion and law? In Iran's Islamic Republic it is government representatives who have the final and definitive word on state laws, but
it is based on their readings of religious principles. The distinction between
religion and law is important because, in the final analysis, law is a question of
state sovereignty. Ultimately, the state's monopoly on law and its interpretation
overtake the heated debates and nuances found in Islamic jurisprudence (*fiqh*)
and which take place in the religious schools in Qom.

Indeed, the fact that the judge points out his religious duty has significance.
Such an obligation suggests a concern with ethics, derived from a duty towards
God, which is not sublimated by or reduced to worldly concerns of the state's
monopoly on violence, in other words, law. It remains, however, that what is
being adjudicated in the criminal court is law (*qanun*) and not Islamic principles (*shari'a*) per se, but rather a state-administered and distilled interpretation
of it. The distillation freezes what were broad guidelines into legal codes.

The court's processes reveal how law conceals, by its very codification, the ethical attributes, room for nuance, and space for debate implicit in *shari'a*, while at the same time securing the state's sovereign authority over the people. While the scholarly debates in the seminaries in Qom and Najaf highlight the changing, fluid, and evolving nature of the *shari'a*, its codification as law solidifies and fixes principles while disassociating them from their ethical underpinnings, the very basis of their fluidity. It is thus left up to individual judges, the better among them trained both in *shari'a* and its ethical foundations, to apply skilled ethical discretion in reconciliation, but they do so selectively, as the earlier case shows, perhaps to preserve the state's role as the ultimate arbiter of justice—and thus not taking sides in any case, despite a growing procedural preference for reconciliation.

As one defense lawyer told me, "This is a big problem in the law. Judges are forced to give the ruling for intentional murder when it is not always so." He was referring to the broad definition of intentional murder, arguing that it tied the hands of judges because few exceptions exist when the elements of intentional murder are met. The revisions to the law permit some argument on the part of lawyers that there were circumstances that mitigate a sentence of intentional murder, the case of the "noble" cause being one of them.

Conditioning Retribution in Law and Practice

The judges continually emphasized that whether the victim's family decided to forgo retribution often rested on the reasons the murder occurred in the first place. As Judge Maliki had noted, understanding the motivations for a murder is very important. The judge was alluding to the fact that, depending on the motivations, the penal code could actually provide relief for the alleged perpetrators. For instance, in a trial I attended, a father confessed that he killed the person who had raped his daughter. In the case, the father had proof that the person he killed had raped his daughter. In addition to his daughter's statement, the rapist had boasted to his friends about it and one of them had informed the father. When the father held a birthday party for his daughter, he invited the alleged rapist. There, he took the young man aside and confronted him. Words were exchanged, a fight ensued, and the defendant-father killed his daughter's rapist. During the trial, several witnesses testified, confirming that the man had told them about assaulting the defendant's daughter. In such cases, the defendant may file a petition arguing that the killing was in the service of a noble cause (Article 302.2).[7] Clearly, this provision reinforces the importance of honor in dispute resolution. If the court accepts the argument that the murder was committed in the furtherance of such a cause, then the defendant would be spared *qisas*, but would still be liable for *ta'zir* sanctions. Thus, the commission of a "noble offense" serves as an affirmative defense in this context and could also be the basis for a reduced prison sentence or other alternative sanctions, but the defendant must petition for and prove it. Nevertheless, this new provision in the penal code emphasizes the relationship between the motivations for the murder and the possible curbing of sanctions or a reduction in the severity of punishment. This, indeed, is one context in which the judges appear to have discretion in intentional murder.

One day, the chief judge spoke to me of the numerous provisions in the new laws that confirm the rights of victims or their families as being the cornerstone of Iran's criminal justice system. He emphasized how the penal code was founded on a logic that aimed to satisfy victims' next-of-kin. He stated, "Even after our ruling is issued, the sentence will not be carried out until the family of the victim requests its implementation. They must follow up at every stage in the process. If they do not petition to have the sentence implemented, then it will not be carried out." To emphasize this point, the judge pointed out a new provision in the revised *Law of Islamic Punishment* that permits the perpetrator to petition the court for release if, after having served ten years, the victim's family still has not requested the court to implement the *qisas* sentence. The judge explained the logic of the new provision, "Since the maximum sentence the court can issue for a homicide is ten years, once the perpetrator has served it, the state has no justification for continuing to hold the person." The new provision permits the perpetrator to petition the court for release upon the deposit of a security.[8]

"Wait." I said, trying to understand. "You mean with this new provision, after an offender has spent ten years in prison, he/she can post bond and go free?"

> Well, technically. But it doesn't work like that. There are offenders in prison now who have served many years—some more than ten, but the victim's family will not petition to have the *qisas* implemented. They just cannot bring themselves to do it, but they also are not willing to forgo retribution. At the same time, the state cannot keep these people in prison indefinitely. So, this new provision requires the judge of the Implementations Unit to summon the next-of-kin. If they don't come, and many don't, or if they cannot make a decision, then the judge will give them a reasonable amount of time to decide, maybe even call them again, [and] if they still do not make a decision, then the perpetrator may go free after leaving a security.

The reason for the security is that in this victim-centered criminal justice system, the victim's family never loses its right of retribution. As in other jurisdictions, there is no statute of limitations on murder. So, with this in mind, I asked the judge, "If the victim's next-of-kin finally decides they want the offender executed, then the person would supposedly present himself or herself to be executed?"

"Yes, in principle," the judge conceded, "But this doesn't happen. When the victim's family doesn't pursue *qisas* after so much time has passed, they will let it go."

I envisioned a number of scenarios in which this would not be the case and voiced them to the judge. "But what if the victim's next-of-kin was away or living abroad and finally returned to seek retribution? What if the perpetrator's release reignites the family's anger?"

The judge, circumspect, observed that various scenarios were possible, but that the new provision was based on the court's experiences. It was more a way to relieve the state of having to confine the perpetrator after he/she was deemed to have served his/her time. He again reminded me that in spirit and practice, *qisas* is the private right of each individual plaintiff, and the state's primary role is to preserve and maintain that right, even while encouraging forbearance. The judge noted that forbearance must be unanimous, but with *qisas*, "even if only one member of the victim's family seeks it, *qisas* will be carried out."

The work of the state in encouraging forbearance while preserving *qisas* leads to seemingly competing agendas and practices. State officials charged with carrying out *qisas* are increasingly tasked with seeking a substitute punishment or alternative arrangement. This is all done, ostensibly, in view of the preservation of victims' rights. Such actions may, perhaps, be understood in light of the expression "the exception swallows the rule." In the *Law of Islamic Punishment, qisas* is the rule, but there are provisions that make it less appealing or necessary to carry out, as well.

In cases in which one family member is a sole hold-out for *qisas*, the law requires that the family member pay a portion of compensation to the others who seek forbearance.[9] For instance, if there are two family members who want *qisas*, but four who do not, then the two who seek retribution must each pay a one-sixth share of the *diya* to the four family members who do not (because there are six total next-of-kin). Moreover, if the family members who forgo retribution do not wish to receive any compensation, then the law requires the family members who seek *qisas* to pay the *diya* share to the defendant before executing him/her.[10]

This emphasis, of course, raises the question of what happens when the murder victim has no family members, the state is unable to locate any members of the victim's family, the family member is incapacitated, or the only member of the family is a minor. For instance, one case the judge directed me to that summer was a murder of an Afghan citizen. The deceased was a single man who worked in construction. He was killed during a fight. When the prosecutor's office tried to locate the man's family, they learned that all of his kin lived in Afghanistan.

In such cases, the law recognizes the Supreme Leader as the *qayem* (guardian). Technically, the Leader delegates the right of the victim to the judiciary, whose delegate is the state's Public Prosecutor (Article 356). In that case, the Public Prosecutor contacted the Afghan Embassy in Iran and proceeded to seek a resolution from the family in Afghanistan. When no family members could be located, the case was sent to the Public Prosecutor's Implementations Unit (*Ejra Ahkam*), which issued a document indicating that the claim to *qisas* was relinquished. The document was sent to the Embassy for signature and returned to the court. The defendant then was tried on the Article 612 charge of public harm and sentenced to six years. As the Leader's delegated *qayem*, the prosecutor could have also pursued *qisas*.

In cases where the next-of-kin is a minor, the prosecutor and the court usually wait until he/she reaches the age of majority to determine the course of action.[11] Similarly, in cases where the next-of-kin is missing, the prosecutor is charged with locating the missing family member(s), but may be urged by the defense to take action after the passage of time, usually when the defendant has served ten years, thus completing the maximum sanction for public harm. Here is where the new provision that permits defendants who have served the full sentence for the public offense to petition the court for release (Art. 429) is useful. If several family members insist on execution while one is missing or incapacitated, the law requires those family members who want *qisas* to pay *diya* to those who are unable to exercise their rights (Articles 421 and 423).

"I have something to say," Judge Maliki intervened, "The point is, the judge's hands are not closed. You see, before, the court had only *hadd*, *qisas*, and *diyat*, but now, these other provisions can be useful."

Judge Maliki gave me a run-down of possible dispositions. "There are four choices for the settlement of intentional murder cases—retribution [*qisas*]; compensation [*diya*], acceptance of compensatory damages, set annually by the state, in lieu of retribution; conciliation [*mosalehe*] more or less same as *diya*, but here they set their own conditions; and forbearance without any compensation or conditions [*gozasht bella avaz*]."

Judge Maliki went on to explain how it is that the laws possess some constraints embedded in them that facilitate the victim's family's choosing forbearance over retribution. "There are many ways in which the laws make retribution a less attractive choice for the victim's family or where the law creates the conditions that make it next to impossible to implement *qisas* ['*adam-e ejra ye qisas*']." These instances, he continued, "create cases of 'compelled forbearance' ['*gozasht-e na'char*'] because the constraints in the laws make it difficult for plaintiffs to have *qisas* implemented." Then he enumerated such

TABLE 3. Situations that Serve as Legal Barriers to *Qisas*.

Situation		Barrier to *Qisas*		Logic
Two (male) defendants murder one (male) victim	→	Family of victim must pay one full *diya*	→	Two defendants killed one person
Victim has minor children	→	Victim's family members must pay "minor's share" to victim's children	→	When the children grow up, they might not have chosen retribution[a]
Victim is female; defendant is male	→	Victim's family must pay a male murderer's family half of the *diya*	→	Surviving family-members of male defendant, if executed, lose breadwinner[b]
One of two defendants flees	→	Victim's family must pay *diya*	→	Payment covers one who fled
One member of victim's family chooses forbearance	→	The other family members must pay *diya* to that family member	→	Family members compensate those who do not seek *qisas*[c]
Victim's family is not found	→	No complaint or petition to carry out *qisas* is filed	→	Only victim's closest relatives can exercise right of *qisas*[d]
Court issues *qisas* sentence	→	Victim's family does not petition to have sentence implemented	→	Only victim's closest relatives can exercise right of *qisas*

[a.] The payment is made into a trust created for the children and released when they reach majority. In an interesting twist, if the victim does not have minor children, but the defendant does, then the payment would be made to the defendant's minor children.

[b.] By law, male family members must support female kin. In reality, this is rarely the case. I discuss this controversial gendered inequity in Chapter 1.

[c.] If that family member forgoes retribution and does not seek any compensation (*bella avaz*), then the remaining family members would pay a *diya* to the defendant—before executing him/her.

[d.] In a case where the state cannot locate the victim's next-of-kin, the law delegates the right to *qisas* to the public prosecutor. In only very rare cases would it be exercised, as was depicted in Pouran Derakhshandeh's 2013 film, *Hush, Girls Don't Scream*. During my research, legal practitioners, including defense lawyers, pointed out to me the anomalous outcome in the film's denouement.

situations (see Table 3) and added, "Of course, many families have financial difficulties and prefer compensation."

The judge concluded by emphasizing the goal of deterrence. "These are in Islam, in the *ahadith*," he said, stressing that constraints embedded in the system exist, "so that *qisas* will be carried out less frequently. The *damaneh-ye* [domain of] *qisas* is *mahdood* [restricted]. Its value lies in the quality of deterrence."

As a fuller response to my serial questioning of potential scenarios, the judge emailed me a handout entitled, simply, *Answers to Questions* which, while not exhaustive, reveals the regulations in place that shape the broader substantive laws. At the top of the message, he wrote, "Murder is considered one of the greatest sins."

This pamphlet, like others I received, explained in plain language the meaning of the law. It was another means through which the state gave attention and precedence to victims' rights, even while encouraging forbearance. Of course, the prioritizing of victims is also a means of state control.

Again and again, judges and jurists I encountered emphasized the private nature of murder, its corresponding punishment—*qisas*—and the system that results from it. "*Qisas* is *talions*," explained one law professor, citing the Latin term. "It is not a state punishment, but a private sanction afforded by the Qur'an when there is a taking of life [*nafs*], because life is private property."[12] Thus, the sanctioning process revolves around the logic that a murder creates a private right of retaliation. The state's role is to preserve the right of the victim and to serve as the arbiter in the adjudication of that right. By institutionalizing violence in the form of private retribution, the state does not delegate authority as much as it manages agents who partake in and legitimize its system of justice.

The law professor then turned to a foundational basis for restorative justice, adding, "Reconciliation, too, is private, between the victim and offender, and it comes from the Qur'anic provisions, as well." By way of example, he continued, "*Diya* is pecuniary compensation. One can bargain with it. It paves a way for horizontal justice or *edalat-e tarmimi* [restorative justice]." He added, "*Qisas* is the response to private crimes, the judiciary institutionalizes it, but the victim's family may forgo *qisas* at any time, even up until the last moment." Through its penal code, the state creates parameters for how *qisas* may be exercised, but resists determining the *terms* of forbearance. Technically, such forbearance agreements are extra-judicial and between the two adverse parties. Until the provisions of the penal code were implemented, there was little-to-no formal regulation of the terms of the extra-judicial negotiations between opposing parties. But the new penal code emphasizes *mianjigari* and the role of judiciary officials in seeking reconciliation and settlement (*solh va sauzesh*).

A first-year criminal law textbook introduces the section on *qisas* with an Arabic idiom, "*Qes Asreh*." The author, a legal scholar, Shambayati, states, "The term, *qisas*, originates from '*qas*' or '*yeqas*' and comes from the source '*qes asreh*' ([in Arabic] meaning 'to cut the impact of' or 'the following up on something or someone.')" Thus, Shambayati notes, "It is from here that it can be said that the figure of the narrator and story-teller relates *qisas* by following up on the traditions of the forbearers and then describes and analyzes them for others" (1997:227).

While the state has codified *qisas* as retribution, debates about what it means do exist, mostly in law schools and Islamic seminaries. A meeting I had with Grand Ayatollah Bayat-Zanjani in the summer of 2016 illustrates those debates.[13] In that meeting, he first asked me what I knew about the Qur'anic sources of forbearance. I quoted him the passages that I have mentioned thus far (5:45 and 2:178). He took me on an hour-long foray into the meaning of the term *qisas* and ended with the same conclusion as Shambayati. The verse (5:45) means that "there must be a *process*—follow the story—find out what happened." I interrupted, "But what about the state's codification of *qisas* as retribution?" "Well," he said, with a wave and a shrug, "They do their own thing. They make the law." He inserted the distinction I have been emphasizing all along—the *qanun* (law) as the state's distillation of the sources. State officials make sense of the sources in a way that secures their power over the people.

The result of the state's reform of the penal code includes increased discretion and a changing role on the part of judges. The new provisions require better trained judges, those who are not simply state functionaries applying the provisions, but rather who have a deep appreciation for the aims and spirit of both the law and the sacred sources upon which it is based. Consequently, the state's new emphasis on restorative justice mechanisms becomes part of the larger aim of maintaining social control.

While forgiveness work has been occurring on an ad hoc basis for years, Iran's new code of criminal procedure validates the judges' role as mediator and even compels them to seek reconciliation between the parties. Thus, while the discretion in punishment of *qisas* is significantly constrained by the broad definition of intent, the legal process allows for a "flexible uncertainty" (Gluckman 1955:24).[14] That is, the judges, the better among them, can make use of the ambiguities in the law—the unstated—to modify the process. Certainly, in other contexts, as we saw, judges now increasingly have alternative or discretionary sanctions, but, in the non-discretionary context of *qisas*, sometimes they are able to make use of procedures as well. Gluckman's statement emphasizes that judges need to know how to use the laws effectively and be willing to do so.[15]

Making Room for Forgiveness

In a criminal trial that took place in Tehran's provincial criminal court in late August 2016, a wife and two daughters accepted the charges of having murdered their husband and father and of dismembering the body with an electric saw. At the end of the nearly three-hour hearing, the chief judge brought the trial to a close by having the plaintiffs—the victim's brother and two sisters—and the defendants sign their testimonies. He then looked at the parties on both sides and said, "I think you need to talk."

He proposed clearing the court room of spectators, leaving only the victim's nearest relatives and the defendants so that the parties could discuss their conflict—at that very moment. With the parties' agreement, the chief judge, along with his two associate judges, stepped out of his role as fact finder to that of *mianjigar* (mediator), holding a reconciliation meeting between the parties that would avoid the imposition of the harshest sentence the plaintiffs could demand—*qisas* of the victim's two daughters and wife.

In a final admonition, the chief judge noted, "I'm not taking any side in this hearing. Your right of retribution is preserved by law. But I want you to consider this: every murder has its reason." To those in the courtroom, this was a reference to the notarized letters the defendants had submitted alleging years of violent behavior consisting of beatings and both verbal and sexual abuse. "I recommend that you read the letters your nieces have written," he said to the victim's brother and two sisters.

The problem with the letters was that they were allegations unsupported by any other evidence besides the defendants' own assertions. During the trial, one of the judges noted that they had read the letters in the file, but added, "Give us something that can prove your claims. Did you ever tell anyone about this abuse?" Over the decades of alleged abuse, the women in the family had never reported the violence, never filed a police report, never confided in any member of the family. Given this society's grave concerns with propriety and *aberu* (saving face), it surprised no one when the defendants responded with an unequivocal, "No." One of the daughters testified, "Our mother told us that what he did to us should never leave this house."

Such testimony may have been useful in making a claim that the killing was in self-defense. Without corroborating evidence, however, there was little that the judges could do to avoid a finding of intentional murder, the sentence for which was *qisas*, but a sentence that only the victim's nearest relatives could exercise or forgive.

And so, the judges convened a reconciliation meeting between the parties. The tête-à-tête provided the victim's family a forum in which to air the anger and hurt they felt. It also allowed a non-official, non-recorded, and thus face-saving venue in which the defendants could speak of the violence and abuse, not as justification for the murder, but as factors contributing to the defendants' state of mind.

Reconciliation and Settlement Meeting

With the room cleared, there remained the parties, the judges, the prison guards, the psychologists from the Juvenile Correction and Rehabilitation Center, two social workers present at the request of the defendants, a couple of journalists, and myself, the researcher. To assure the propriety of what was about to take place, the chief judge reiterated at the end of the hearing, "Everything is over. This is the start of the reconciliation and settlement meeting."

As though taking those words as a cue to step away from the role of impartial trier of fact to sage adviser, one of the associate judges stepped off the raised platform to begin the unofficial meeting between the opposing parties. He walked over to the parties holding his arms out and aloft, as though willing them to come together. Notably, the associate judge had some clout in this context; although a younger man, he was a son of a *shaheed* (martyr) in the war with Iraq and was well-regarded in the Criminal Court as a fair and principled judge. As he approached the family members of the victim, the associate judge said, "There is room for forgiveness in this case."

Having read their detailed letters of abuse, the judges were apparently swayed by the pleas on the part of the perpetrators. The letters, however, carried no legal weight, even if they were telling and sympathy-bearing.

"I am not ready to execute them, but right now I am exploding with grief," cried the uncle, who had been awaiting this day of reckoning for three years. "So many times I told them, 'Come tell me . . .' but they never did. The other time, I said, 'If you don't like my brother, then divorce.' All these people are getting divorced."

Still up on his perch, the chief judge spoke, "We don't want to hear this now." And then, more softly than when he was acting as the trier-of-truth, "Our duty for all our files is to arrive at reconciliation. I want to ask this of you: that you try to come to a solution between you."

Then one of the aunt's answered, "They don't pray," as a way of undercutting the young women's character and credibility. She was looking directly at her two nieces who were hesitantly walking towards her. "If my brother was so bad, then why not tell me?"

The young women were shepherded by the social workers and prison guards who guided them towards their aunts and uncle. The social workers, the guards, and others admonished the young women, "Plead with them. Go!"

When the aunts stood and also approached, the guards interjected with their hands and told the aunts to refrain from touching the girls. The aunts began loudly castigating the young women. The guards stood closely by to protect the girls from any physical attack by their relatives. The journalists hung back, taking in the situation.

The girls then fell to their knees at the feet of their aunts. The uncle sat several seats away and spoke to one of the judges. The girls pulled their chadors well below their foreheads and then lowered their heads at the floor. They begged for their lives and through their tears they repeatedly whimpered, "Forgive us. Please. Please, forgive us." Their mother lingered behind, seated in a nearby chair, head bowed. Slightly weeping into her chest, she appeared to be making herself so small as to be unseen.

With the girls' heads bowed at their feet, the aunts looked away, their arms folded at their chests. Instead of looking at their nieces, the women looked up at the crowd of mostly women gathered around them. "Why should we forgive? Why should we be merciful when they were not?"

Now, everyone, including the prison guards and journalists, were advocating to spare the lives of the women. Different women spoke with varying degrees of rapidity, and some in Azeri Turkic, the language the family spoke. "They did wrong, but you do right!"

"I will not consent [to forgo retribution]."

"By killing them, you won't receive God's mercy."

The youngest of the two nieces now had her head in her now-seated aunt's lap and was wailing.

The chief judge, while tidying his desk and packing his briefcase, looked at the aunts and spoke over the others, "With your mercy, you will be helping them to become better [people]."

"They said those things about him! No, I will not consent."

The younger associate judge shooed the social workers away from the aunts. He leaned towards them and said, "You saw that we did not accept the things that they said about your brother." He drew the defendants in, forming a circle, "but they are his family. His children. Do this act of kindness on your brother's behalf. Do it for him. For his memory. It will bring you peace and rewards from God."

The associate judge was aware that the young women's testimonies of abuse by their father had had an effect on the victim's family and, as a consequence, on their willingness to forgive their nieces. That testimony, although providing context and motive in the defendants' case, elicited anger and additional grief in the siblings. In such contexts, victims' families suffered a double injury. First, they had to contend with the physical loss of their loved one. On top of that harm, they had to endure the desecration of his/her reputation. Here, the legal process of truth-seeking clashed with the culture of face-saving. This particular tension arose frequently as a delicate conundrum in the context of forgiveness work. How could the victim's family forgo retribution after hurtful or disparaging claims that the defendant made, even if only as a legal defense? In such contexts, families feared that others would see their forbearance as a validation of the defendants' claims. On the other hand, carrying out retribution, some felt, would prove and punish what the family saw as lies and provide relief to the surviving kin and redeem the deceased's reputation.

Most hearings that deal with questions around morality and chastity, such as rape, are held in-camera, without the public in attendance. Even when just one of the charges deals with sexual conduct, the judges will clear the courtroom for testimony on that particular issue.

In this case, the testimony was more difficult to avoid discussing because it was presented as part of a defense, an explanation of the defendants' underlying motives. Sensitive to this particular challenge, at several intervals during the hearing the judges had invited the aunts or uncle to leave the courtroom. The judges further admonished the defendants to avoid graphic sexual testimony that would possibly harm them and reiterated throughout the trial that they had read the file, a less than subtle reference to the fact that they were aware of the defendants' sexual abuse allegations.[16]

"But my brother did not do those things. He did not . . ."

The associate judge turned to the older daughter, "Say you made a mistake."

Through her sobs, she repeatedly cried out, "I made a mistake." Her younger sister, too, repeated the statement. By then, their mother had left her seat on the other side of the room and joined her daughters, kneeling before the aunts and begging for life.

The associate judge, apparently seeing an opening, called for the clerk to bring him the court's official forms. He looked at the sisters and said, "They admitted they were wrong to have done that, to have said those things about him. Now have mercy. You'll see, you'll find peace." Then he dictated the contents of the forbearance statement as the clerk wrote it out in long-hand.

He called over a journalist and told him to do an interview with the uncle and aunts, to clarify for the record that their brother was not an immoral person—to be published in the next day's paper. The journalist stepped forward, knelt in front of the uncle and began writing in his notepad. Suddenly, the significance of the journalist's role became intelligible. Beyond simply documenting the proceeding, the reporter could help assuage the family's concerns with the testimony, providing a compensation of sorts to restore their reputation.

Other witnesses who had been allowed to remain in the courtroom also stepped in to play a role in encouraging reconciliation. As they approached the sisters, hugged, and kissed them, they assured the women that they did the

FIGURE 3. Image accompanying the article about the case in the next day's paper, *E'temaad*, August 30, 2016/*Shahrivar* 9, 1395; illustration credit: Fatemeh Jafari.

right thing. While the associate judge went to work on the forbearance affidavit, the social workers stepped in. One clarified what appeared to be a point of confusion for the aunts, "No, they will not be freed if you forgo retribution. They will go to prison—for ten years." A prison guard added, "Even after being released, they will be on parole." Another prison guard noted, "They won't get prison release, either." A social worker then chimed in, "You can also receive compensation."

The uncle expressed uncertainty about taking any compensation. The associate judge came back over to the family and explained, "You can keep the compensation, or, if you don't need it, then give it away to charity." One of the social workers added, "But let them pay something for what they did."

The statement of forbearance had legal effect and the agreement between the parties would be approved by the court; none of the assurances of the social workers and prison guards held that same official force. Upon the approval of forbearance, the case would be remanded back to that same court for sentencing for the public offense of disturbing peace and security. While the maximum sentence for such an offense was indeed ten years (minus time served), there was no guarantee that the women would receive it or any of the supplementary (and new) sanctions the prison guards and social workers referenced.

Nevertheless, the time had come to sign. The judge offered the aunts the document that had just been prepared and in which, individually, each of the members of the victim's family attested to forgo of their right of retribution, "without doubt or reservation," a legal term of art that would not invalidate other extra-judicial agreements between the parties, including that of compensation, except what the new law provided.[17]

The associate judge extended the document to the aunts, "Do it for God. Sign."

The first aunt, the quieter one, signed.

Then to the other aunt, the associate judge handed over the document, "Sign."

"I am asking this of you. Sign," the chief judge called over to them.

The judges were aware that their words held tremendous weight. Besides having judicial authority, the stature of many judges carried moral rectitude, as well.

Meanwhile the young women remained on their knees—wailing now out of a cautious relief. Besides the women, others in the room, social workers, prison guards, and even the journalists, had trouble holding back tears.

Upon obtaining the final signature, that of the uncle, the associate judge victoriously proclaimed, "With largesse and chivalry, you have forgone your right of retribution."

Everyone in the room sent *salavat* (greetings to the Prophet Mohammad and his descendants).[18] People congratulated one another. The perpetrators gathered themselves and stood up, still grateful and still crying. They were herded away by the prison guards, who did not bother to place them in handcuffs, "Time to go back." Even if the women were still going to see some prison time, the absence of restraint, the shackles, reflected that they had passed into a new period, one of life.

The social workers congratulated the family members of the victim—telling them how big what they had just done was, how happy they would feel, how God would reward them, how the perpetrators would not escape God's judgment. "You did well to leave it to God. Now you will feel peace." The social workers took down the siblings' numbers, promising to visit and see to their needs, both emotionally and materially.

As we filed out of the courtroom, others congratulated the judges for how well they presided over the hearing and how well they handled the reconciliation and settlement meeting. The judges seemed unaffected by it all. I met the chief judge in the elevator. I noted how rare it was to hold such a meeting before even the ruling on the case had been officially issued. I asked, "How did you know to hold the meeting right away?"

"Forty-three years of experience," he replied.

A few days later, the associate judge was a bit more forthcoming. "I knew by their hesitation. When I asked them what they wanted to do, the uncle, especially, did not want retribution. I knew these were not the type of people to carry out *qisas*. Since I knew they would eventually forgo retribution, I thought we could just finish it right then and there." And they did. This case exemplifies the strategies that experienced judges, who know how to deploy *elm* and discretion, use to navigate through procedural and cultural constraints. The judges brought the parties to mediation and settlement in the face of the broad definition of intentional murder, strong codes of gendered family honor underlying the system, and weak gender-based violence protections.

After Forbearance: Article 612 hearings

Until 1991, the law operated in such a way that, if the victim's family forgave, there was no further sanction. In a change of laws meant to reflect the harm that a murder does to social welfare, the legislature enacted a revision to the relevant section of law, under the discretionary laws of *ta'zir*, which are not derived from scriptures, per se, but of broader social concerns, such as public welfare or security. This new law created a social harm in murder and allowed for the public prosecutor to adjudicate the murder through a logic of harm to public safety and security on behalf of society at large. As a result, murder now has two plaintiffs, public and private. The important qualification to make here is that the public prosecutor does not possess the right of retributive sanctioning; it is not *qisas*. It is a discretionary law, invoked to penalize transgressions of public order and the maximum sentence the state can prescribe is between three and ten years of imprisonment. Article 612 hearings, as they are colloquially called, take place only if the victim's family forgoes its right of retribution. Often, such hearings are held after the convicted has already spent some years in prison.

While scholars have historically analyzed bureaucracy as a rationalizing and disciplining apparatus of governance, bureaucracies are also producers of a complex mix of emotions induced by bureaucratic effects, including documents, personnel, and the physical landscapes. The Article 612 hearing is one of the best venues to illustrate how regulation and the lack of it shape the court as an affective space of forgiveness work. The anticipation of forgiveness work conditions the atmosphere of the court to be responsive to sentimental reasoning. In what follows, I draw a portrait of how these judicial processes operate.

Just before entering the courtroom one day, I asked the judge how the court determines the sentence for public harm. I wanted to know what issues the judges consider in sentencing for the lesser offense of public harm in comparison with that of intentional murder. "We look at the crime, the physical,

mental, and emotional state of the defendant, whether there has been rehabilitation, if he/she shows remorse, and how likely the defendant might be to
repeat this or other crimes. And, we consider the defendant's moral character."
I asked if forbearance (of the underlying murder) carried any weight. The
judge replied, "We like to talk to the defendant's family members and, if possible, to the victim's." The last, of course, helps the defendant's case, but the
victim's family is not required to testify. "The plaintiff's forbearance can be a
mitigating factor in sentencing for the *ta'zir* offense."[19]

Affecting States of Mind

In a case of a young man who had killed his father and was granted forbearance
by his grandmother and aunt (his father's next-of-kin), the man then had to
appear before the court for the second phase of sentencing, the state's sanctioning arm. A panel of judges would decide the punishment that ranged from
three to ten years imprisonment; a series of additional tools—alternative
sanctions—allowed probation, suspended sentences, and banishment. In this
process, the defendant, who was already in prison, would learn for how long
his sentence would continue.

The chief judge read the charging document and stated the facts of the case:
"The defendant killed his father. The next-of-kin, the mother and sister [of the
deceased], have agreed to forgo *qisas*." He stated for the record all who were
present: the defendant, his lawyer, five judges, and a researcher.[20]

The prosecutor then read the indictment and requested the maximum
prison sentence of ten years, plus banishment from Tehran after the defendant
was released. The chief judge called the defendant to the stand and began
questioning him. The defendant claimed that his mental illness and drug abuse
led to the incident.

> JUDGE 1 (CHIEF JUDGE): How do you defend yourself?
> D: At that time, I did not have a normal state. I was another person. My
>   head was telling me to do things. I used to take drugs. I am bipolar,
>   mentally ill.
> J3: I have never heard of this; what's this?
> D: I don't know. Something comes into my head.
> J2: It's not an issue. He does not regret [what he did]. *Looks to* D: One
>   year, I won't even give you one year [reduction from the maximum
>   sentence].

The affective space releases intensities, charges, which then act as stimuli,
prompting the interior mind, the individual's subjectivity, to react. Even as the
defendant spoke of his state of mind, some judges challenged him, shaking up

his statements; others would take up the mantle of earnest advisor. In this way, the judges also affect one another, and play off each other. They communicate scorn, annoyance, distrust, doubt, pity, or even reason, logic, and sincerity. These sentiments are the effects the atmosphere rouses.

D: I'm ill; I take drugs.

J1: What happened?

D: My father was a security guard in Tehran. We lived outside the city. He wanted to be closer to his job and moved. I didn't. My mother and I stayed in our village [three hours away].

J1: Even though you say you're bipolar, you got the deed for the house from your father. Your mother said you made him put the house in your name.

The judge was referencing the fact that the defendant forced the title to be put in his name and then committed the murder, implying that, despite his claims of illness, the defendant's mental state at the time of the murder was intact.

D: Then why did she [grandmother] consent [to forbearance]?

J1: Because she is your grandmother.

D: I regret it; it shouldn't have happened. My mother was living with me, but then she left and went to Tehran. I was alone for six months. I got sick. I went to my father and said, "Tell me what I am supposed to do." My father beat me, and I lost control. It was a nightmare. I was in prison, and for six months, I didn't even know why.

J3: You say you're ill, how did you choose, plan, to do this? You took your mother and sister in a room, locked the door and threatened to kill them. Then, before killing him, you made your father sign over title to the house. You have none of these illnesses you claim. The doctors don't confirm them. Your reason and conscience are intact.

D: I swear to God I . . .

J1: Don't swear to God.

J3: Did the judges [adjudicating the murder case] make a mistake?

D: Send me to the doctor.

J3: From night to morning, you tortured your father.

D: I don't remember.

J2: We can't help you if you lie.

D: I'm not lying. [Names his doctors who can attest to his illness].

J3: We don't have any reports from the legal physician.

J2: Before this, did you ever go to the doctor?

D: Yes.

J4: This is the worst crime to commit in our religion, patricide. In Islam, one must show kindness, respect, and devotion to one's father.

Unlike some of his colleagues, this judge was soft-spoken. His graying hair and finely-lined face suggested he was around the age the defendant's father would have been. Sitting with an enormous Qur'an before him, he spoke to the defendant while flipping through it. He read aloud verses on respect for parents.[21]

J4: Given your illness, did you ever do anything like this to anyone else?
D: I swear to God, no.
J5: Do not swear to God.
J1: [Reviewing the file. Looks at D] Were you an addict? Opium, heroin, crack?
J4: Did you quit?

Judge four's prompting questions sought to induce mitigating evidence.

D: [I quit] with six years in jail.
J2: Do you have any family visits?
D: Only my mother and sister.
J2: Did you have any problems in jail?
D: No.
J5: So, you locked you sister and mother in a room while you killed your father?
D: No, they felt it was necessary to say that.
J3: Now you're lying.
J5: You asked for forgiveness before, but now you're repeating the lies.
D: From the first instance, I've regretted it. I'm no different from anyone else.
J1: What is your last defense?
D: I regret what I did.
J5: If you have remorse, then tell the truth.
D: It wasn't in my hands.
J4: So, it's drugs, not illness.
D: Yes, but I was ill, too.
J4: Explain how this is.
D: When the police came, they saw me; I was ill.
J4: But you have no documents to prove this.
D: I am a miserable wretch.

The judges were focused on the defendant's duel claims of illness and addiction, which made it seem as if he was trying to cover his bases: he regretted what he did, but, at the same time, claimed illness and addiction. The judges wanted him to take responsibility, a necessary admission to reduce his sentence. The defendant seemed to avoid responsibility yet expressed remorse. This led some judges to doubt the sincerity of his remorse and rehabilitation.

J3: We think your family agreed to forbearance because you threatened them.

D: No. I have no problems with them. If I'm freed, I would live a quiet life and help my mother.

J3: I wish they had come to speak for themselves.

D: You could call them.

J2: Even if we free you, you will never find happiness because you killed your father.

J1: I read the file; it's very painful. I wouldn't give you even a one-year reduction [of the maximum ten-year prison sentence].

J4: Are you being treated in prison?

D: They give me medication and I have no problems.

The end of the hearing had approached. The judges were talking over one another. They had many questions and reactions. They excused the defendant and began a lively debate to determine their ruling.

J2: The grandmother and aunt agreed to forbearance because they are scared.

J3: Scared of what? To *qisas*?

J1: This is becoming a discussion of spirituality.

J2: The fact that they didn't come is troubling.

J4: The law doesn't require them to appear.

J2: He made his father put the family home in his name.

J1: Then he strangled him.

J4: But what if he's sick?

J2: The legal physician's report says he's not.

J3: His actions have an impact on society, as well. And usually the next-of-kin does consent.

The judge was pointing out that the family's forbearance should not be grounds to compromise the public sanction.

J1: There was planning and deliberation.

J5: When that's the case, usually they don't consent.

J2: They are emotional.

J5: Since they didn't come, it shows that they consented, but they leave the decision [for civil punishment] in the hands of the law.

J1: The father was only fifty-three years old.

J3: He strangled his father with a rope. That requires five minutes, and you need to hold with a really tight grip. You have to get very close to the victim. It was a whole-hearted decision.

The judges ultimately sentenced the defendant to the full ten years in prison. He had already served six, so he would remain imprisoned for another four years. However, the absence of the defendant's family from the hearing had left an impression on the judges, who saw it as a signal that they may have some reservations, despite their forbearance. As a result of this concern, though the judges did not speak to them, they added the additional sanction of banishing the defendant from Tehran for ten years after his release.

The Rehabilitated Defendant

In the summer of 2013, several months after the new penal codes were implemented, the judge from the research committee directed me to a case involving alternative sanctions. "The defendant killed his grandmother. He was an addict [of] *sheesheh* [crystal methamphetamine]." According to his confession, he had intended to frighten her into giving him money, but in a drug-addled rage, he ended up stabbing her sixteen times with a butcher knife. Six of his relatives, including his own mother, were the victim's next-of-kin, the plaintiffs who would determine his fate.

The defendant's mother figured out that her son was the perpetrator when she learned that he had used his grandmother's ATM card to withdraw funds from her account hours after her death. She turned her son over to the police and he confessed. All but two of the victim's next-of-kin consented to forgo *qisas*. Those two, the defendant's cousins (the children of a deceased aunt), demanded retribution.[22] *Qisas* is an individual right belonging to the victim's immediate next-of-kin.[23] In order for the defendant to be spared, every *qisas* rights-holders must forgo it. Since this was not the case, the court sentenced the defendant to *qisas*. The defendant appealed. While the case was pending, the other two family members agreed to forgo retribution. The defendant's lawyer amended his appeal. The Supreme Court accepted it and returned the file to the lower court with an order approving the family's forbearance. In light of this, the trial court held an Article 612 hearing for the defendant's *ta'zir* offense of disrupting public order. His parents, anxious and grief-stricken, sat in the row behind their son. Aside from the defendant's lawyer, no one else was present.

The chief judge called the defendant to approach and asked if he understood the reason for the hearing. The defendant's slender frame was turned towards the judges, but, as it would be throughout the testimony, his head was bowed down. In response to the judge, he simply nodded. The judge said, "I need to hear your response" and repeated the question, "Do you understand?" The answer was audible and clear, "Yes." Then, through a series of questions posed to the defendant, the judges elicited responses that revisited the incident, explored the defendant's state of mind at the time of the murder, and inquired into his recovery from addiction.

The defendant's case rested on his addiction and his drugged state of mind during the incident. He was soft-spoken as he recounted his youth, his family life, how he got involved in drugs—"it was just something to do"—and, finally, related the events of the night of the crime—at least what he said he could remember, given his state of mind at the time. Through tears, he expressed sorrow for having killed his grandmother. He explained how, shortly after arriving in prison, he had enrolled in an addiction recovery program and got clean. By taking responsibility for his actions, he guarded against the maximum sentence. He expressed remorse and demonstrated rehabilitation, two key requirements necessary for alternative sanctions.

Once the judges had finished questioning the defendant, they invited his lawyer to make a statement, reminding him that they had read his brief. The lawyer emphasized his client's rehabilitation and addressed other conditions necessary to mitigate the sentence. The judges listened while flipping through various filings, including an assessment from the psychologist at the hospital's addiction clinic. The lawyer stated that the defendant, who was only nineteen when he committed the crime, had fallen in with a bad crowd, made mistakes, and unwittingly became an addict. He explained that during the year and a half that his client was in prison, he sought treatment, and was quickly and without incident rehabilitated. The lawyer added that his client attended Qur'an classes and prayed regularly. He explained that these measures had helped the defendant find his way. The defendant wanted to reenter society, the lawyer added, and become a mentor to troubled youth like himself.

Once the lawyer had completed his statement, one of the associate judges recalled the defendant and asked him whether the two family members who had consented to forgo *qisas* had received any compensation. The defendant said, "No, they just felt sorry for me." He suddenly exploded in grief and began to cry. His parents, too, were quietly weeping. The defendant's father spoke from his seat, "I will keep him with me; I will put him to work."

The chief judge asked his mother to approach. He acknowledged that she occupied the unenviable position of being both the deceased's next-of-kin and the offender's mother. The judge asked her to speak about her son and his life before the incident, what she knew of his addiction to drugs, and how he seemed to her now. The mother composed herself and recounted her son's carefree youth, his talent for math, and his jovial demeanor. When their son was ten-years-old, she said, her husband had lost his job. They no longer had funds to enroll him in sports; he began slipping in his studies. As the family's economic situation deteriorated, a deep depression took hold of her husband. The family was forced to move into a small two-bedroom apartment in a less affluent neighborhood. While the new residence was in a less prosperous district, it was near her family, which the defendant's mother had hoped would temper the disruption to their lives. The changes in neighborhood, school, friends, and, ultimately, her husband's demeanor, however, caused her son to buckle. Instead of the happy child he had been, he became morose and withdrawn.

The chief judge interrupted the mother's wistful narrative with pointed questions about the defendant's development and character. She answered succinctly, then added, "My son did a terrible thing, but he loved his grandmother. He didn't mean to do it. He was very sick."

The chief judge seemed persuaded by the testimony and the filings. The judges concluded the hearing and, after briefly conferring, the chief judge announced the decision. They sentenced the defendant to a four-year suspended sentence; the year-and-a-half he had already spent in prison would be timeserved. For the remaining two-and-half years, the judges decided to use the alternative sanctions and permit the defendant to remain free on bond, pursuant to certain conditions: that he live with his parents, study or work, and report to an addiction counselor. The judge spoke firmly as he cautioned the defendant to stay away from drugs. He encouraged his parents to help him. He added, "If, for any reason, he ceases his recovery and causes trouble, then he will go back to prison."

As with the first case mentioned where the defendant had killed his father, this defendant's contrition and apparent rehabilitation carried significant weight with the judges. Their questions were designed to elicit responses that would address these very issues. Along with his remorse, the judges were swayed by the fact that the defendant had turned himself in and confessed his crime. The confession aided the investigation and resulting prosecution. All of the above factors, in addition to the plaintiffs' forbearance and his parents' statements, served to justify mitigating the sentence.[24]

Securing the State: Punishing Private Harms Versus Public Injuries

After the session ended, the judge emphasized the importance of the victim's rights in the sanctioning process. He confirmed that the possibility of additional sanctions—complementary, reduced, suspended—could only arise after the victim's family's forbearance. I understood, of course, that the purpose of this second hearing was to punish the defendant's harm to public safety and security, and it could only happen once the victim's family had agreed to forgo retribution. However, the judge was advancing a different implication for the hearing concerning victims' rights. He was suggesting that the additional sanctioning provisions also serve as an important vehicle for convincing victims' families that the state would punish offenders appropriately. This, he implied, would increase the likelihood that victims' families would forgo retribution, particularly if they saw that the defendant would face a punishment that was more severe, more appropriate, or perhaps more rehabilitating, than a prison sentence. With the additional sanctioning provisions, judges, then, are increasingly seeing their roles expanded, representing the state, and at the same time, negotiating between opposing parties.

While the supplemental measures are intended to be applied to the discretionary portion of sentencing, the existence of such provisions serves another purpose as well. Knowing that judges may sanction offenders through supplemental measures could offer some relief to victims' families, who, as plaintiffs, possess the right to demand *qisas*. In such cases, the private plaintiffs may be convinced to forgo their complaint and allow the court to issue supplemental sanctions, either in addition to or in lieu of those prescribed by the *ta'zirat* punishments.[25] In a sense, the additional measures can serve as tools for saving the defendant's life, as might monetary compensation.

I had many conversations with lawyers, social workers, and victims' family members who lamented the fact that, if the next-of-kin forgoes retributive sanctioning, then the maximum sentence the perpetrator can receive is only between three and ten years. One defense lawyer, whose client killed an elderly neighbor and then burned down his family's home, had already met with the victim's grieving family—just months after the murder. He spoke with incredulity about how the victim's wife and children had been dignified and gracious in their meeting and, while they did not greet the possibility of the perpetrator's execution with joy, they were not willing to forgo retribution. The lawyer commented that one of the issues that the family raised was that they could not reconcile themselves with the fact that the perpetrator would serve only a maximum of ten years in prison. The brevity of the sentence was even more troubling to them because the perpetrator was twenty-years old at the time of the homicide. After his confinement, which would include time-served prior to the sentence, the perpetrator would be out of prison and would be able to live a full life. For the victim's family, this punishment of a mere ten years, in view of forbearance, did not seem adequate given the gravity of the crime. "Since life imprisonment does not exist [in such contexts]," the defense lawyer said, "the family will likely seek *qisas*."

The issue remains that a sentence of ten years for the death of a loved one is troubling for most families, even if, strictly speaking, the sanction is for a separate offense. Scholars, jurists, and even defense lawyers with whom I spoke pointed out the difficulty for victims' families to forgo retribution when the perpetrator could be released after what they believed was a short time for having killed their loved one, sometimes in a rather brutal fashion.

Nonetheless, several judges with whom I spoke emphasized the logic behind this proposition. One judge, who also taught law, explained it this way: "The maximum of ten years is for the public harm. We are not punishing the perpetrator for murder at this point. Only the victim's family holds that right. If they forgo it, then we judge the harm to the public. When the perpetrator has completed the sentence and is no longer a harm to the public, the state has no justifiable reason for holding him/her." To emphasize the distinct logics of retributive and public sanctions, the judge explained, "After the victim's family has consented to forbearance and the defendant has completed his/her prison sentence, justice has been restored. The defendant has been rehabilitated."

The judge reminded me that when the laws were promulgated just after the revolution (1361/1982), there was no public offense to be prosecuted whatsoever. The only punishment for murder was *qisas*. If the victim's next-of-kin agreed to forgo retribution, the defendant was allowed to go free. A decade later (1370/1991), the judiciary added the provision for harm to society, resulting in the additional *ta'zir* sentence of three to ten years. While an accumulation of complaints about injustices prompted the revision, one story—a triple murder of a mother and her two daughters—recounted in law school textbooks, stands out as the trigger incident for the revision to the homicide law. The 1986 murder of Azita and Rozita, along with their mother, remains an exemplar of the need for the state to sanction the public harms caused by murder. In his criminal law textbook, Professor Shambayati recounts the story in this way:

> A young mother, twice married and divorced, gave birth to two children from two different men, Azita and Rozita. Despite the laws that award custody of children after divorce to fathers, the girls' mother is their sole custodian, responsible for all of their maintenance and supervision. When Azita was just fourteen years old and over her protests, her mother entered her into a contract for marriage. Because of her desire to continue her studies, Azita decided to ask her husband for a divorce. After a long discussion with him, she attempted to convince him that they amicably go to the notary to dissolve the agreement that she had forcibly and compulsorily entered into. Her husband responded, "Shut up! Stupid idiot! I will cut your tongue out of your throat if you ever repeat this nonsense. Make no mistake (without a shred of a doubt), I will kill you and separate your head from your body."

Finally, one day, Azita's mother tries to act as an intermediary and asks her son-in-law, saying that since from the very beginning her daughter did not want to enter into the union, and it was she who imposed her belief on her daughter, that he agree to divorce her. The son-in-law, instead of agreeing, proceeds to obtain gasoline and blows up the place of residence of his wife, her mother, and his wife's sister and in the process, kills all three in a horrifying manner. Following the explosion, the murderer becomes a fugitive. After many months of searching, with the efforts of police and at great expense, he is arrested and turned over to the justice system.

In this case, the only heirs of the mother were her two daughters, and the two young women's heirs were their fathers. Since the daughters were deceased, their right of retribution for the death of their mother, was, as any property right, to be inherited by their fathers. Since Azita's father had no love lost for his former wife and did not have the slightest bit of affection for his daughter, he easily surrendered his rights of retribution on behalf of both mother and daughter and only petitioned for compensation. The father of the second daughter, Rozita, was a drug addict and had long since been in prison. When he learned about this incident, he cried, "A monstrous crime had occurred! I will file a complaint and seek the most severe punishment for my daughter and her mother." Thus, the indictment was issued, and the case was sent to the Provincial Criminal Court.

After one year, the murderer returned to the office of the public prosecutor and asked the magistrate on the case to return to him the documents from the record of his search and arrest. When he was asked how it was that he was freed, with a smile, he replied, "I'm married and have a child. In the end, how did I obtain Azita and Rozita's fathers' agreement to forgo retribution from *qisas*? I gave 20,000 *toman* to Azita's father and 30,000 *toman* to Rozita's father and got their forbearance!!" Thusly, with the extortion and abuse of two men who bore the name "father," for 50,000 *toman* [about $740 at the time] relinquished the blood of three human beings, the case of three murders concludes (1376/1997:229–231).

This tragic incident was among others that triggered the evolution of new legislation. In 1370/1991 and subsequently in 1375/1996, Iran's legislators established the new *ta'zir* punishment, not only for these sorts of murders that in the face of the next-of-kin's forbearance allowed murderers to walk, but also for the purpose of maintaining public order and protecting against offenses to the social good.

When I mentioned the case to the judges, they agreed that it was influential, but pointedly noted that the main problem with the earlier law was that, in failing to prosecute such cases, the state failed to carry out an important state function: its duty to protect the public. And, one judge emphasized, "If the state fails to do that, people will take violent actions themselves. Revenge."

I encountered others who also pointed out problems with the law before it had the secondary sentencing provision. I met a man whose wife's family had encountered such a situation. His perspective shined a different light on the merciful view of forbearance and the paramount right of victims that had been the narrative of state officials. The gentleman, who lived outside of Iran, but who had at one point held an important governmental post, described with apparent disdain how during the Iran-Iraq war, a veteran from one of the state's armed branches had killed his wife's brother. The family was consumed by grief, having lost their beloved son and brother. The family had to decide whether to demand exact retribution. It was at this point, the man explained, that state forces began showing up regularly at their home. They were not impolite, but, nonetheless, were forceful in demanding that the family find it in themselves to forgo retribution. They wanted to protect their friend. The family, although bereaved, wanted some punishment for the veteran. At that time, their forbearance would have allowed the perpetrator to go completely free. Ultimately, fearing reprisals from government agents, the family was persuaded forgo retribution in exchange for *diya*. At the time, the compensation was nominal, this man explained to me, and did little to soften the double blows of injury and insult the family felt, first at the murder of their loved one and, second, at being pressured to forgo their right to justice, as they saw it.

For the judges I encountered, such stories were anomalies in comparison with the violence they adjudicated regularly. No one ever denied such things happened, but instead of condemning the system, such events confirmed the imperfections of criminal justice systems, which exist everywhere. At times, judges even pointed out similar injustices that occurred in the U.S., such as the 2012 execution of Marvin Lee Wilson in Texas. Wilson's sentence was upheld by the U.S. Supreme Court, even after his lawyers documented their client's inability to appreciate his actions. On the day of Wilson's execution, August 7th, the research judge brought a printout of news of the execution. "What do you think about this?" he asked me that morning. I nodded in agreement and said, "Yes, these things happen in the United States." This was often a shocking discovery for my interlocutors, many of whom were unaware that the death penalty still existed in the U.S.

As we spoke, I reminded the judge that capital punishment was illegal in Europe, but not the U.S. I explained the 1976 "July 2nd cases," in which the Supreme Court effectively ended the de facto moratorium on capital punishment that had resulted from the *Furman v. Georgia* (1972) case. By striking down *Furman*, I noted, the Court allowed states to determine whether to outlaw the death penalty and that different states had different laws. We discussed the states that had outlawed the death penalty—less than half—then those that maintained it, but rarely employed it, and finally, the remaining states that used the death penalty regularly.

The greatest source of incredulity, however, was not the existence of the death penalty in the U.S., but rather how little influence victims' families had in sanctioning the murder. I noted that the distinction emerged from the fact that, in the U.S., executions were the state's sanction and not that of the victim's next-of-kin. In fact, most people I spoke with found that to be an injustice to the victim's family, who, they believed, as the first and immediate victims, should possess the right to determine the perpetrator's fate. Those familiar with Iran's criminal justice system stressed this point.

The broader issue that the conversations about the death penalty in the U.S. raised was about the lack of equal application of the law in both contexts. For the jurists in Iran, this confirmed their belief that a murder is a private matter and the deceased's closest relatives should decide what to do. I argued that that was the very basis of inequality before the law. The judges said their law was applied equally to all, while in the U.S., states give the death sentence to some, highlighting racially and economically disenfranchised groups, and not others. Given the very personalized nature of murder, they could not understand why, even if the state sentenced someone to death, the victim's family could not intervene to forgo retributive sanctioning. The question was not a procedural one; they understood the system. They were puzzled that victims' families had little direct influence in sentencing.[26] For them, victims' rights were paramount for securing the peace in society.

Conclusion

Iran's post-revolutionary laws and these specific regulations produce an affective administration that, in turn, conditions the courtroom as a space responsive to *Shi'i* (subjective and intersubjective) sentiments, values, emotions, and thus inflects subjectivity in specific ways. Objects, such as the Qur'an, prayer beads, and even the courtroom, further generate the hazy atmosphere, the affective space, in which judges, defendants, and other actors attempt to resolve disputes. At the same time, these practices legitimate the state's monopoly on law and the Islamic principles that guide Muslims' ways of being—and this centralization is an important codification, indeed, enunciation, of what had previously been diverse, decentralized practices.

Through a resulting set of pluralistic governance practices and laws, state administrators, including judges, magistrates, and other officials, are implicated in a wider socio-cultural system of Irano-Islamic *qahr va ashti* (conflict and resolution) practices. These practices, in large part, fill-in the regulatory void around the laws that encourage forbearance. It is this layering—of codes, upon principles, on top of customs and rituals—which imparts a schizophrenic quality on the part of individuals working within it that I have highlighted here.

Iranian criminal laws provide many avenues for victims to forgo retributive sanctioning. Such possibilities serve as important tools for the development of informal or extra-legal avenues for alternative dispute resolution in both civil and criminal disputes, and affect verdicts, even in unforgivable crimes. The right of retribution grants to the victim's next-of-kin an extreme right of punishment and introduces a problematic non-neutral arbiter of law into the determination of appropriate punishment

But preserving the right of retribution serves several purposes: maintaining the sovereign's monopoly on legitimate violence, giving victims a sense of power, and halting the cycle of violence. The way Iran achieves this comprises an interesting balancing act between maintaining the monopoly over legitimate violence and granting individual victims the right of retribution, which its leaders believe, through their interpretation of the *shari'a*, cannot be appropriated by the sovereign. The case above provides a good illustration of this balancing act. On the one hand, the judges preserved the right of retribution, but there were clear problems, even though the girls confessed to intentionally killing their father. Alluding to those issues, the judges stressed the "room" the case had for forgiveness.

Since the law categorizes intentional murder as *qisas* and leaves judges with no discretion in sentencing, the judges may use their considerable influence to pressure the family to forgo retribution. Thus, judges apply discretion in the post-sentencing process. The codes also suggest that the sanction that is conferred to the victim's family is not *qisas*, but the *right to it*, an intimation that the victim's family does not have to exercise it. The new penal codes, moreover, provide guidance on conditions that the victim's family may place on forbearance and the enforceability of the right of *qisas*, should the perpetrator not follow through with extra-judicial agreements between parties in forbearance. Together, these provisions in the new legal code add emphasis, or color in, as my interlocutors put it, the vague and imperfect duty to seek reconciliation into, arguably, an affirmative one.

4

Judicial Forbearance Advocacy

MOTIVATIONS, POTENTIALITIES, AND THE INTERSTICES OF TIME

I WENT to the top floor of Tehran Municipality's Prosecutor's Criminal Tribunal, an agency within the Office of the Prosecutor. This governmental institution houses the Implementations Unit. I entered the front office to wait for my appointment with Mohammad Shahriyari, the Supervisor of Tehran Municipality's office, who oversees the implementations of sanctions. Government officials, lawyers, private individuals, often perpetrators' family members, and sometimes even individuals held in custody, came and went, always introduced by Shahriyari's assistant, who occupied the front office. Although forbearance can and does take place at any stage of the criminal proceeding (after the indictment, during the trial, after sentencing), forbearance most often takes place at the implementations stage of a case. That is, during the often-protracted period between the issuance of the ruling and the implementation of the sentence, while the offender is waiting.

My wait alternated between extracts of commotion and silence, scenes of the excess of tragedy—the distraught outbursts of a wife decrying the injustice of her husband's arrest were suddenly brought closer as officials escorted her up to the top floor office for a stern warning for her public disturbance; the stooped silence of the Afghan prisoner ushered in by soldiers who stood by while the assistant did the illiterate young man's intake. People entered, obtained signatures, retrieved files, and then returned to drop them off.

At one point, I found myself sitting next to a woman whose story I had heard about. She had come to request an official letter confirming that the family of her daughter's victim had agreed to forgo retribution. She needed the document to take to the prison where her daughter was being held. In turn, she had come with receipts, showing her family had deposited the agreed upon compensation into the accounts of the victim's next-of-kin. The assistant reviewed her papers and asked several questions, before stepping into his boss's office. When she sat next to me, I asked about her daughter. She took me in with an inquiring look before responding in a whisper, "Are you a journalist? I don't want to talk to journalists. We have tried to keep this quiet. We don't want it to go viral." I assured her that I was a researcher. The woman added, "There was that case a few years ago," referring to Reyhaneh Jabbari, "when it went viral, the victim's family refused to forgive."[1] I told that I knew about her daughter's case: she had worked in the railway and was said to have killed a co-worker during an altercation.

I was intentionally vague on details to avoid repeating rumors. What interested me, instead, was that this was one of the few cases of forbearance that I had encountered in which the victim's family had agreed to forgo retribution despite having no kin relationship with the perpetrator. "Yes," she finally opened up. "I came to get an official letter." The letter, from Implementations, would confirm that the defendant was no longer subject to *qisas*. The mother adjusted her chador by pulling one side, the side closer to the office, over her mouth, and said, "We had to do so much running here and there. So many people intervened, but whatever we did, they [the victim's family] insisted on *qisas*. Finally, last week, they held a meeting right here in this office and they finally agreed to forgo retribution." Our conversation was interrupted when the assistant reemerged and told the mother she could return the next day to pick up the letter.

At times, the waiting room emptied of this energetic activity and I was alone. At these junctures, the assistant would look at me and offer a note of acknowledgment, "It won't be much longer now" or "He knows you're here." Of course, I, unlike the others who came to see him, possessed none of the exigencies that that waiting room held.

States of Waiting

The state of awaiting execution, in any context, is a complex one in which time is "frozen, infinite, torturous" (Othman 2018). For offenders on death row, the wait is itself a punishment, set into motion by the state as a technology of governance, one that draws on the human panic and anxiety originating from the anticipation of death. The experience of state-imposed forms of waiting, in any context, are techniques through which governments enact power over populations. The way a government structures time is one of the ways of dominating the life of the incarcerated (Foucault 1977).

Waiting, however, is also a generative temporal condition, fraught and troubled though it is, "agency oozes out of waiting" (Hage 2009:2). As the state acts to prescribe docility on incarcerated bodies, its techniques also generate subjectivities (Auyero 2012). As Amira Othman (2018) argues in her exploration of the death penalty in Egypt, the state sets the "life rhythms" of the perpetrator by organizing his/her time both for its minutiae and significant events: for visits, to know about developments in the case, for the ultimate day or moment of reckoning. The constant negotiation of waiting's duality— languishing stasis versus dynamic mobilization—in the space of death row's waiting time is a "temporary agony," which has also been called "death row phenomenon" and "death row syndrome."[2]

In the Iranian judicial system, the perpetrator's temporal agony is one that officials and victims' families are aware of and of which they take advantage, sometimes to extend the perpetrator's punishment, other times to substitute it for *qisas*. The uncertainty of *when* execution will be carried out is accompanied by that of *whether* relief will come, either in the form of appeal or forbearance, for both are often in play simultaneously. These manifold layers of uncertainty add to the punishment, beyond the incarceration.[3] Prisoners or their families described the heightened period of liminality to me as a feeling of a protracted limbo. They described it as being *belataklif* or without a sense of what to do.[4]

This feeling notwithstanding, it is also a time of intense mobilizations (Jeffrey 2010). In Iran's victim-centered criminal justice system, the waiting techniques of the state also empower non-state actors to set into motion intense activity.[5] Such mobilizations often affect state power and may even influence its actions. The question I pose in this chapter is what motivates judicial actors to forge ahead, themselves instituting increasingly defined practices, within this previously unregulated space. What motivates the shift of forgiveness work from one of mere urging to that of an increasingly expected, accepted, and regulated practice?

When my turn arrived, the assistant led me into the large office where Shahriyari was in the midst of business with several others. His duties as supervisor covered all operations after the verdict of guilt had been issued; implementation was just one of them. As I entered, I saw a tall man, dressed in a gray suit and white shirt, leaning over a desk. Shahriyari was engaged in several different conversations at once, addressing a handful of people who had brought individual matters to him. A couple was trying to get information of the whereabouts of their imprisoned son. A lawyer had a question about his client's file. Several subordinates were requesting instructions on cases.

Shahriyari, who was quick and to the point, worked to address their concerns. With a kind of buck-stops-here attitude, he directed them to subsidiary offices, made phone calls of introduction, asked follow-up questions, and signed paperwork. I stood by the door, thinking, erroneously, in a linear fashion, that once he had finished with the others, he would address me—as if the flow of inquiries had an end point. Instead, he just looked past the others, greeted me by checking my name, and invited me to approach, even while continuing to address the continuous stream of people entering and leaving.

The large rectangular office was divided in half through carefully arranged furniture. At the far-right corner, farthest from the door, lay a desk with a computer workstation. Closer to me, on that side, was a large conference table with a dozen high-backed yellow chairs. On the left side of the room, a large writing table without electronic trappings was positioned in front of a series of dark cushioned armchairs and glass coffee tables. Since Shahriyari was seated behind the desk on the right, I chose a yellow chair on that same side and positioned myself to face him. Throughout our four-hour meeting, he bounced from desk to desk, looking for information, answering questions, and searching through materials. As he did, I, too, switched seats in order to be positioned across from him. We were frequently interrupted, as he took queries from his assistant, his employees, and others.

At the time of our meeting, Shahriyari had been in the supervisory position for about a year and a half, since January 2014. I had heard from friends who had had experiences with him that he was tough, but that he allowed social workers to engage in forgiveness work.[6] I also knew from my interlocutors that Shahriyari held reconciliation meetings in his office. As his attention turned to me, I quickly got to the point of my visit—I wanted to understand how forbearance operated at this stage of sanctioning—at the point in which the sentence was to be carried out. I sought to understand Shahriyari's motivations for holding such meetings and how he arranged them. Initially, he was not altogether convinced of my intentions and queried me. "Are you an activist? A journalist? Are you doing human rights work?" I distinguished myself from those more suspect (to him) categories by emphasizing my interests in how forbearance operates.

Only half persuaded, he asked how I knew the people who had set-up our appointment and I offered what amounted to a genealogy of relations that had led me to his office. His concerns seemed only slightly allayed until I offered the final justification for my research. "Look," I said, "Everyone already knows about *qisas*, the death penalty, and the rate of capital punishment in Iran. Amnesty International and other NGOs already report those. So that is not new, and not what I'm researching." He sat still in his chair and listened. "What people don't know about," I insisted, "is what else is going on—the work that many people are engaged in, including yourself, the other side of implementation—forbearance." At last, I had engaged his interest, and continued, "You are not required to do this." He looked at me squarely, registering his understanding, as I added, "It's not part of your job to get people to forgo their right of retribution. There is no official requirement that you hold reconciliation meetings here, in this office. This is *Implementations*," I emphasized, "the place where sentences are carried out. The only thing you *have* to do, it seems to me, is implement punishments. So, I am interested to know why you seek reconciliation when you don't have to; I am interested in your motivations."

I examine motivations around fogiveness work with an eye to time, particularly the waiting time that seeps into the post-conviction operations of the judicial system. This waiting, however, is not only a passing one of languishing (*chronos*) but rather, an active (*kairos*) mode of mobilization (Kermode 1967). The time after the ruling is a specific temporal arrangement, particularly precarious for the offender.[7] If not already underway, forgiveness work intensifies in this period. Through an exploration of waiting for the possibility of forbearance in this period, I explore the new forms that "action, thought, and social relationships acquire" (Bandak and Janeja 2018:2).

Given the long period of waiting that often follows the issuance of the *qisas* ruling, the temporal relationship between social actors engaging in forbearance work shifts from temporary dealings and associations, to permanent ones with known actors and agents, becoming a form-of-life (Das 2006).[8] A form-of-life around forgiveness work as an everyday practice is forged through mutual agreements by the interested parties around what constitutes and encompasses *form* and *life* in *qisas*. In other words, by living through this social context with a shared language around *qisas*, the community comes to possess mutually conceived ideas about what forms life can take during this time. These concepts, form and life, are mutually reinforcing and dynamic, and together allow for everyday practices of forbearance to emerge and remain, but also to change and accommodate. After the issuance of the verdict, Iran's *qisas*-sentenced perpetrator enters a waiting period that is often bustling with intense negotiations involving numerous parties.

In his reflections on hunger and poverty, Bhrigupati Singh explored what he refers to as "fluctuating vitalities," or changing qualities of what it means to be alive during periods of insecurity and vulnerability (2015). For Singh, during periods of precarity of life, actions and pressures around vivification intensify (2016:584). Singh's reflections address not only the subjective and spoken motivations of judicial or other actors, but also the undeclared pressures that exist in a period when life becomes precarious. Here, the precarious state of living that I explore is the issuance of the death sentence, and the possibility of forbearance rests at the core of its *potentiality* (Agamben 1999).[9]

On the one hand, the state's passing down of a death sentence is a technique of state power, but the legal and moral pressures to forbear are also techniques; they authorize activists, lawyers, and victims' families to maneuver. In this way, time is malleable through dialogical engagements involving numerous interested parties. This period possesses a potential, which then drives the possibilities and motivations for various actors, including judicial, to seek to bring about forbearance. The system, based on Qur'anic verses, *ahadith*, and stories about Imam 'Ali, nonetheless, takes shape through other cultural histories, patterns, and practices to reveal a complexity that is neither fixed nor finished, but rather a patient praxis occurring "in the meantime" where ideas, rules, and practices can be worked out (Fischer 2018).[10] However, the sources as state officials know them, form the basis of what jurists, legislators, and judges understand to be immutable religious prescriptions and, as such, they underly their motivation to urge forbearance.

In this last chapter on judicial practice, through ethnographic portraits of state officials, I explore the deeply interpretive and blended scriptural, legal, historical, mystical, and cultural foundations animating forbearance practices. I return to the Implementations Unit to study the impetus for holding reconciliation meetings. I then explore how the potentiality within the sacred sources works through multiple layers of local practices to provide a foundation for forbearance and, at the same time, to balance, as these interlocutors see it, the ever-present imperative of punishment. Finally, I consider the efforts of the Director of Tehran's Juvenile Correction and Rehabilitation Center to spare the lives of inmates under the age of eighteen. Together, these portraits explore what the judge in the previous chapter left me with: the question of why they do this. What drives state actors to encourage reconciliation?

Mercy Comes After: Informal Judicial Regulation of Forbearance

Back in Shahriyari's office, I persisted in my questions about motivations, his and those of other similarly-situated government officials, especially those whose only required task was to carry out sentences, not to settle differences amicably.[11] At this point, the phone rang and Shahriyari moved to the other desk to take the call and motioned for me to follow. As I walked past the glass coffee tables, several brightly colored paperbacks caught my eye. Between words to the caller, Shahriyari said to me, "Those are my books. Take a look." I noted the titles, *Murder During the Final Visit*, *Crime within Crime*, *Crime at the Notary*, *The Plot*, *Victim of Illusions*, *A Shooting at Night*, and *Bloody Partying on Facebook*." Shahryari hung up the phone and said to me, "You can have those. They are my *romans* [novels]." In fact, they were short story collections he had written based on cases he investigated. "Each one has a moral; it's a warning to the reader. For instance, this story," he flipped through one of the books, "is about how young people get caught up in the virtual world, like Facebook, Viber, and so on. This happened. This was one of the cases we had here." It was a story about a young woman who was slain by a man she had met through the internet. The story ended with a warning to young people to be vigilant and avoid clandestine meetings with people they encounter online.

I attempted to tie my inquiry to his morality tales. "So," I said, holding up one of the books, "what are your motivations for writing morality tales and holding reconciliation and settlement meetings?"

Shahriyari, leaned back in his chair, crossed his legs, and began,

> There are many motivations. They come from our religion and the rituals of our culture. We draw on those resources. It is what we refer to as *edalat-e tarmimi*. Restorative justice is part of what happens in these cases. There are even some who want our current system to be replaced by it. Others say that restorative justice should at least come before retribution. *Qisas* is in the Qur'an; it is also in the *ahadith*, but they state that reconciliation is better. There is also the human perspective. We have to consider the rights and suffering of the victim's family. We, in the judiciary, must be impartial during the proceedings, until the decision is issued. Then, afterwards, we can ask the victim's family to be merciful and consider forbearance.

As Shahriyari noted, the scriptural sources underlying the system at once permit retribution and compel forbearance. The religious sources are not the only forces that influence families tasked with determining the fate of an offender. From the state's perspective, its role consists of enforcing the plaintiff's decision. That does not, however, rule out their efforts to persuade victims' families after the ruling has been issued. Throughout our meeting, Shahriyari emphasized the strict necessity of the judiciary's impartiality during the criminal proceedings, before the sentenced is handed down. Shahriyari stressed:

> Reconciliation is in our religion. We can judge; we can involve ourselves. It's in our criminal procedure, too. But it is very sensitive work. We cannot be or appear to be on the defendant's side. In our law, it is written and implemented—if it is an intentional killing, then the punishment is *qisas* and the right of retribution belongs to the victim's family. As in Kant, it is absolute justice, it is proportionate. Kant's maxim is also found in Islam.

The invocation of Kant's categorical imperative in Shahriyari's understanding of punishment is noteworthy. Kant's notion of absolute justice sought to highlight human equality. From that position, punishment must be individual and deserved; it cannot be collective. Only the guilty should be punished and thus, punishment is delivered by the consent of the punished. This idea is drawn from Kant's categorical imperative or the doctrine of virtue: "Act upon a maxim which can also hold as a universal law." That is to say, where all individuals are equal, they consent to the law, and it must be universally applied.

For Kant, a system of punishment that does not protect the innocent is immoral. Kant clarifies that punishment should be proportionate or like the wrongful act. Thus, for Kant, proportionate punishment is not always exact punishment, but rather allows for substitute punishments, which are often necessary for the aim of equality. For instance, a monetary penalty may not adequately punish a wealthy wrongdoer. Kant is also deeply critical of life in prison as a substitute for capital punishment.[12]

Shahriyari interpreted Kant's maxim as allowing for substitute punishments, which he construed as promoting reconciliation, although like others, Shahriyari saw *qisas* as scriptural and, therefore, immutable. He then explained how his office gets involved:

> We work for reconciliation after the sentence is issued. We are careful to work with both parties and respect their rights. We have a duty to reach a settlement, but if we go about it incorrectly, victims could come to feel injured a second time and then the result could be that they are more convinced of revenge. In this regard, how we work for reconciliation is very delicate.

Following his cue, I asked about the legal sources that prompt the duty towards reconciliation. He flipped through his worn copy of the new criminal procedures and, like Judge Ghorbanzadeh, noted that Article 1 refers to reconciliation and mediation as part of the broad aims of the code. Then he referred me to the specific sections of the law that deal with reconciliation, "Article 93, refers to the interrogators' duties towards mediation; Articles 82–4 deal with mediation of the prosecutor's office, including Implementations." Shahriyari continued:

> I've been here [the criminal tribunal] for fifteen years; I've held all of the posts. In the Implementations Unit, we never advise *qisas*. Never. Not only do we not advise *qisas*, we do the opposite. We do our best to justify forbearance, but only once the trial has ended. We do not want to be perceived as being on any side.

Shahriyari stood up to make some coffee and he explained how they conduct their forgiveness work.

> We have a Reconciliation and Settlement Committee, which consists of magistrates and myself. We invite victims' families here. Sometimes there are actors, athletes, and other well-reputed people. But some have lost confidence in them. Why? Because they don't observe peoples' cultural boundaries. In many cases, their ways of life are too different from those they're trying to persuade.

To emphasize his point, he recited a line from a celebrated twelfth-century Persian writer, and poet, Suhrawardi, "Words that come from the heart, enter the heart but if they come from the tongue, they will not pass beyond the ears." This now-proverbial phrase means that sincere, unassuming, and heartfelt words that come from the depths of one's soul can have a special effect on the listener and sit in his/her heart.[13]

Shahriyari offered some thoughts on the problems associated with a generally unregulated system of mediation that takes place outside of the state's bureaucratic frame. "Some activists get involved and take advantage. They aren't actually humanitarians." He was drawing attention to two well-known problems. The first was that of urbanormativity or privileging urban social values as normative.[14] These social actors, often well-to-do elites, he suggested, did not know how to manage the socio-cultural disparities between themselves and victims' families. Victims' families, who are often pious, working class, poor, or rural, he said, questioned the values of urban sophisticates. The second problem was with the unregulated means of collecting funds for compensation. Sometimes people approached the parties and introduced themselves as humanitarians with the financial means to pay a compensation to the victim's family. They would then seek funds based on those claims and disappear, the collected funds gone as well.

Shahriyari continued, "There are also those from inside the prison, the magistrates there; they also don't work with the necessary sensitivity." He clarified:

> What do the prison magistrates do wrong? They immediately go to their [victims' families'] homes and tell them to forgive straightaway. They work on emotions and it often makes things worse. We realized this was happening and that there was a need for mediation. So now, we do it ourselves.

In this exchange, Shahriyari addressed remarks from a social worker who had observed that the judiciary had lately become more active and simultaneously restrictive of their efforts. In light of this, I asked Shahriyari the specific steps his office took to engage victims' families in reconciliation, while maintaining impartiality.

> I organize meetings. We bring the defendant and she/he asks for forgiveness. They beg, fall on their feet, literally. We tell victims' families, you have three choices: 1) *qisas*, 2) forbearance with compensation, or 3) forbearance without compensation. I work to gain their trust. I don't tell them to forgive. Instead, I say, "*Qisas* is your right, and you can execute this person today. Shall we go? Do you really want to? We can also wait a week. Why not? You can't go back from the decision if you execute. Let's wait and see

how you feel in a week." I tell the families to consider how they will feel if they kill. We have to be good psychologists. The victim's family is very sensitive. We have to be careful not to do something that will make them angry and embolden them [to carry out the punishment] or lead them to say that the judge has committed a breach of his duties.

As Shahriyari continued, he spoke of an incipient methodology, a strategy for remaining impartial, while also encouraging reconciliation.

These are questions of justice. We try to get the families together, let the two sides meet and we, as judges, are present. We engage in *ashti*. They gain confidence in us if they see that we aren't working for one side. Often what happens is that no one from the perpetrator's side has spoken to the victim's family. Sometimes they complain and say, "they didn't come see us." The victim's family wants to know what happened. So, when we invite them and ask the defendant to explain. We say, "Why did you kill this person? What actually happened?" We tell the defendant to try to make amends with the victim's family. Some people have a religious viewpoint and they forgive purely out of their love of God. Some say they want money, so they try to reach a financial settlement. For many in our society, taking money for the loss of a family member has not fallen into place. Many families feel they need to avenge a death with another. We try to show them that there's another way. For the perpetrator, we want them to understand that it's not just about money; it's also about respect for the life taken.

"How do you do that?" I asked, to which he responded:

Our practices are foundational of restorative justice; we draw on our own customs. In addition to the mediation that we carry out here, we [Iranians] have ritual practices, like the *khoon bas* [blood stop]. We also have folktales, classical stories about forgiveness. We have our *riche sefeed* [lit. white beards], the community elders, who engage in *kadkhoda maneshi* [mediation by village-head]. There is also *javanmardi* [chivalric tradition]. Here, we say, "You want to draw blood? Spilling more blood will not wash away the blood that has been spilled." We value *ashti*.

Shahriyari laid out a multi-valenced approach, drawn from pre-Islamic Persian practices, which, while sanctioned by Islamic principles, did, nevertheless, coincide with customary practices that preceded and worked in tandem with practices derived from the scriptural sources. It is difficult to differentiate practices that are deeply culturally-embedded in the society's justice paradigm. This admixture and understanding of ethico-religious principles as having multiple sources supports Rosen's call for understanding Islamic law within a cultural context (2018).

At that moment we were interrupted by several young men, who, dressed in white overalls, caps, and tennis shoes, entered with a ladder and tools. They announced that they were the exterminators and were setting traps for a mouse that had apparently been running amok in the office. A brief conversation between Shahriyari and the exterminators determined the best method for killing the rodent.

Executions usually take place on Wednesday mornings, before dawn. This being Tuesday, one of Shahriyari's associates entered. The gentleman then stood behind me and spoke to Shahriyari in a low but still audible voice. When I turned my head to listen, Shahriyari introduced me, and the associate stepped forward. He stated several names. At first I did not know what they involved, but when I heard one name, just a first name, Sahar, I knew what the subject was. They were determining—perhaps finalizing—the list of offenders to be executed the following morning and coming weeks. Perpetrators' families would be notified and invited to a final meeting with their soon-to-be-executed relative.

Shahriyari paused ever so briefly and then, with an upwards nod, indicating the negative, uttered an airy, "*Noooo*, it looks like they are going to settle." Since I was aware of this case, I asked how much time he allowed for mediation in such cases.

> We don't give it a definitive ending. If they are meeting and talking, we won't set a date. If they can't come to an agreement between them, we ask the families to meet with us. The whole process is informal. We go back and forth. We meet at least three times. If, after those meetings, the victim's family is still not willing to forgo retribution, we then set an implementation date. I call the victim's family in and speak with them personally. I tell them that killing another family's son will not bring back theirs. I say, "The pleasure you'll find in forgiveness is not found in execution." All this is to get them to think. If they insist, then, in the implementation chamber, during the last moments, I bring the defendant in a room and tell the victim's family, "At least listen to what [the offender] has to say" and I make them listen. That person speaks, and often, in those last seconds, they forgive. Some, still, say, "let's take them to implement the sentence." And just to scare them, they put the rope around the offender's neck, but they don't execute. To the last seconds, we try. Even when they want to implement, say there are five people up for execution that day. They [the victim's family] have to do it [the execution]. They must do it. We implement the executions one by one, in the early morning, just before dawn because that is when God is most forgiving. I let the others see what it's like and often some families stop short. They can't go through with it. Those whom I know will not change their minds, I make them go first while the others watch.

Adding emphasis, he repeated, "I make *them* pull the lever. I stand behind them, and even then, I speak in their ears, 'You can still change your mind. You'll regret it. Don't . . .'"

While he was speaking, Shahriyari's assistant escorted a man into his office and introduced him as Siamak Asgarzadeh. The assistant handed Shahriyari a six-inch-thick file. The man approached and, standing beside Shahriyari's desk, asked whether he was in the right place. Shahriyari, perusing the file, looked up and nodded. Asgarzadeh complained that he did not know where the guilty party was and where they were in the proceedings. He lamented, "Why won't they execute him? He killed my father." Asgarzadeh explained that he had travelled through the night just to arrive that morning. He had to miss a day's work. His family, including his mother and five siblings, were in great pain, constantly weeping, he said. "It's been six years. Why is it taking so long? We don't want to forgive. We want *qisas*."

"Are you sure?" Shahriyari said.

"Yes. We are so tired of this. We just want to move on, but we can't. The social workers won't leave us alone. This one, that one, they all come. My sisters are so depressed over this."

"The social workers are just trying to help. How many are in your family?"

"Three sisters and three brothers. He killed our father; he was only fifty-five." The man continued, asking a series of questions. "Is the guilty party in prison? Does he get to leave?"

Shahriyari said, "I know this case. It's not currently in our jurisdiction. It's gone up to have the sentence confirmed. When it comes back to us, I'll give it my attention and see that it's brought to a conclusion. Rest assured, the perpetrator remains in prison. Your right of *qisas* is secure. No one can take it away." With that reassurance, Shahriyari signaled the end of the ad hoc encounter. The man thanked Shahriyari and, as he walked out, exhorted him once more to hurry things up. "We just want this over. It's taking too long!"

Waiting weighs heavily on the victims' families. While time can be deployed as a mechanism to inform reflection, it does not necessarily mean that such deliberation will lead to forbearance. The impatience of victims' families to "get it over with" may also suggest an aversion to reflection and pressures to which they do not want to leave themselves open. Such families often feel that only with execution will they find closure.

Shahriyari signaled that our meeting had come to a close by putting on his jacket and holding his briefcase. He said, "We had a [reconciliation] meeting here last week. It would have been good for you to see." Then, opening the door, he added, "Can you come on Thursday? There will be a good case then."

'Amr be ma'ruf va nahy az monkar' (Commanding Right and Forbidding Wrong)

When I showed up on Thursday, the case turned out to be one I had heard about—the Khalili case. One of my social worker friends had told me about it just days before:

> We have a case in Tehran. It involves an incident that took place three years earlier. The deceased is Ali Khalili and the perpetrator, Ehsan Shah-Ghasemi. The two young men, both in their early twenties started bickering, when, according to Ali, he saw Ehsan bothering two girls. Ali, who is from a *bassiji* family, said he was standing up for the girls. Ehsan denies this version of the story. He says he was with friends and not bothering anyone. Ehsan said he saw Ali come towards him and reach into his pocket. Ehsan said it was dark, so he couldn't see very well. He thought Ali was going for a knife, but it was only his glasses. Ehsan got scared and threw his knife at Ali. He struck him in the neck. Ehsan said he was just trying to protect himself. Ali was seriously injured, but he recovered.

Ehsan was charged for the bodily injuries (assault) and disrupting public order. He was sentenced to *diya* for the assault, plus three years in prison for the public order violation. In court, Ali announced that he forgave Ehsan. Ali's forbearance in this assault had the effect of reducing the amount of *diya* and likely reduced his incarceration. But that is not where the story ended, as my friend continued:

> Ali was very pious and in those three years, he made two trips to Karbala [Iraq] for Arba'een.[15] However, Ali had a genetic blood disease. After his trip, he got very sick, and then, unfortunately, died. It was three years after the incident with Ehsan.

In relating the story of Ali's piety and his travel to the shrine of Imam Hossein, the social worker was relaying an important aspect of the story. Ali's death, possibly a murder, was being compared to the brutal slaying of Imam Hossein, whose suffering and death is a crucial founding moment for *Shi'ism*. Hossein is the embodiment of the one who is sacrificed in the struggle against injustice and oppression. Hossein's martyrdom and the battle signify what Michael Fischer has referred to as the "Karbala paradigm." Thus, the battle is more than simply a politically decisive one; the story behind it relates a "structure of thought full of traditional formulas, standardized metaphors, and implications," that is taught, shared, and understood among the *Shi'i* (1980:7).

Like Hossein, Ali was by then referred to as *shaheed* (martyr). The doctor examining Ali's body reported that the injury was not the direct cause of death, but he could not rule it out as a contributing factor. Based on this assessment, Ehsan, who had just days before been released from prison, was arrested for intentional murder and sentenced to *qisas*.[16] He went to prison and, again, was in need of the family's forgiveness.

When I arrived at the courthouse on the appointed day, I noticed the presence of journalists from at least five different newspapers. I realized that Shahriyari had wanted me to observe a significant development in the Khalili case. The family had arrived at the courthouse to submit their affidavit of forbearance. The Iranian press followed the story, and on August 25, 2015, the headline in *Sharq*, a reformist newspaper, read: "*Khanevadeh 'Amr be Ma'ruf' az Qisas Gozasht Kardan* [Family 'Commanding Right' Forgoes Qisas]." The widely-published statement reproduced an emotional letter by Ali's parents to their deceased son. It offered insight into their decision to forgo retribution:

> Our darling son, dear Ali, now with the blood of your jugular, the scent of defending the space of honor of our Islamic society, once again life has been taken and with the blinding spite of our internal and foreign enemies, the rich Islamic culture and the duty of 'commanding right and forbidding wrong,' you have been damned as an icon of the restoration of this forgotten obligation. What place is there for sorrow and distress of separation from your youthful, beautiful laughing face; what place is there for sadness and grief over not seeing your luminous face that generously gave its blood with sacrifice and forbearance for unforgiveable errors, errors that had as their goal your life, and which you took to the limit of perfection.

The letter continues in this style for some time, the entirety published in the Iranian media. What struck me about this case, however, was the invocation of the Qur'anic principle, '*Amr be ma'ruf va nahy az monkar*' (Commanding Right and Forbidding Wrong).

Michael Cook, in his book of the same name, charts the history, origins, and development of this principle. He explores the question of the duty and character of the individual and the surrounding community. The principle is found in eight Qur'anic verses and the two phrases are rarely found independent of one another. Cook's work is largely a meditation on what scholars have understood this principle to mean, but then he considers: Who performs it? Who is its target, and what is it about?" (2006[2000]:13). Cook concludes that the duty "is an appeal for the community of believers" (Ibid.). Who is the target of the duty? Cook notes, "we are left in the dark" (14). Thus, while there is a discursive compulsion to follow the principle, there is no clear recipient. What is the duty about? "There is no further indication" (Ibid.). This is, then, a broad ethical affirmation to the community, or to the world at large, but it is by no means clear.

To try to illuminate the meaning of the duty being compelled, Cook explores the meaning of the term '*ma'ruf* (what is right or appropriate). Among the first relevant verses is 2:178, which I noted earlier, is used to infer a Qur'anic preference for forbearance. According to Cook, the term *ma'ruf* might refer to acting "in a decent and honoruable fashion" or "with 'kindliness' (*ihsan*)" (15). What exactly constitutes such conduct is never spelled out. Thus, it is a duty that lacks clear formalization.

Nevertheless, the ambiguity that Cook emphasizes has important implications for how Iran's scripture-based laws appear to construe the vague but affirmative religious duty of commanding right. The Khalili family's forbearance comes to exemplify this duty and highlights a modern instance of it. Indeed, Cook cites contemporary *Shi'i* scholar, Ayatollah Mohammad Baqer Hakim's reference to the principle as a demonstration of "the superiority of Islam in providing guarantees of human rights" (532).

Cook's analysis is significant for showing that, while there is a clear obligation to command right and forbid wrong, it is not at all clear what actions are entailed in carrying out those principles. The imperative of the principle alongside its lack of specificity and formalization allows some to displace the obligation onto the state. It can also be an instance of individuals giving shape to unclear religious directives. Indeed, it underlies many of the cottage industry's actions and even fuels forgiveness workers' bold appeals to grieving families.

Kevin Reinhart has written about the meaning of the term *ma'ruf* more recently. He finds that there is an "emphatic suggestion to 'do the *mar'uf*'" (2017:51). The term, which literally means "known" is found in three distinct Qur'anic contexts, each of which exhorts people to do what is good, known, and kindly (64–65). Thus the "Qur'an itself assumes that revelational knowledge is to be supplemented with conventional moral understandings of what is right and wrong" (51) or "ordinary knowledge" (61). Thus, to do the *ma'ruf*, as Reinhart puts it, would include an appreciation of "norms extrinsic" to the text (60). To achieve this, individuals need "to reflect ethically," even as they are grounded in the norms of their society. Here, Reinhart underscores the ethical compulsion to *think* with reference to the commentary of the prominent Iranian *Shi'i* scholar, Allameh Tabataba'i (1903–1981).[17]

Turning to the Qur'anic commentary of another Persian exegete, Nizam al-Din Hasan al-Nishaburi (?-1328/9), Reinhart offers an example that touches on the subject of forbearance.[18] Reinhart quotes Nishaburi's exegesis of 2:183, which refers to the responsibilities of the next-of-kin in the context of forgoing retribution. "It is incumbent on the forgiver to follow *al-ma'ruf* so that he is not severe in his demands. Rather, he should act in the matter according to the familiar custom" (62). Nishaburi adds the consideration of social context: the financial situation of the murderer or his/her family and the need for time to obtain cash (Ibid.). Thus, despite the ambiguous nature of *ma'ruf,* there are social customs from which actors can draw. What those customs are, however, is a point of debate.

The rivalry to which Shahriyari alluded between some social actors and judicial advocates highlights this debate. However, instead of examining it as set practices, the very choice of forbearance strategy sheds light on the nature and meaning of the activism. Even in such highly sensitive contexts, activists are also advocating an agenda, sometimes even an epistemological one—regarding the basis for forbearance: rights advocacy, anti-death penalty activism, and forbearance practices.

Through their act of forbearance, the Khalili family made a statement about the Qur'anic principle. The Khalili family, in a sense, "did the *ma'ruf,*" as "an act of piety" (Cook 2006[2000]:10). They became its exemplars. Their actions were exemplary on at least two levels: first to tell Iran's international adversaries that Islamic Iran has its own norms of humanity; second, to tell internal actors that being merciful is what is right and appropriate, even while maintaining that retribution remains in the hands of the victim.[19] The wide media coverage of this act of forbearance, at least in Iran, served as a pedagogical example of how to do the *ma'ruf.* At the same time, it operated of a piece with the broader forbearance work aiming to change the culture around *qisas*—from a punishment that exists only as a right to retribution to one that includes, indeed exhorts, forbearance. It was, however, methodologically in competition with the more secular approaches to forbearance. Here, an ethics hewn to piety stands out in the face of secular calls for an end to the death penalty. Highlighting the Khalili family's forbearance as *'amr be ma'ruf* was consistent with the judiciary's attempt to step in and regulate forbearance work in the face of competition from human rights or secular activists, or, as Shahriyari noted, "people who don't know what they are doing and make the situation worse."

As Reinhart elaborates, echoing contemporary anthropological work on the subject, Islamic piety is embodied not just by physical actions, but also by a disposition and an attitude that "transcends the act" (Reinhart 2017:58).[20] This is important as it underscores the significance of forbearance work and the approach that judicial officials take. That is, the focus of their work is on a deeper and more long-term shift in the thinking of individuals. From the perspective of the state, it is imperative that the outwardly forbearing victim does not later seek personal revenge. That is, from the state's vantage point, the act of forbearance must be sufficiently sincere in its embodiment that it breaks the cycle of violence. Conscious acts of forbearance, as part of a wider set of ethico-religious principles that compel thinking, speaking, and doing what is *ma'ruf*, are also operational practices of Islamic piety. Talal Asad translates the maxim as "commanding right and opposing wrong," suggesting they are "twin principles" that "capture the complex processes of self-cultivation" (2015). Such practices are what James Laidlaw (2014) calls "the operation of practical reason and judgement in everyday life," underscoring Michael Lambek's notion of "ordinary ethics" (2010) and Veena Das's "experience of the everyday" (2010).[21]

By publicizing the press conference and highlighting forbearance as an act that is *ma'ruf*—good, kindly, and ordinary—the judiciary also emphasized forbearance as a normative value. This normative quality touches on Das's understanding of form-of-life and its naturalness in the everyday (2006; Han and Das 2016). The state actors and the Khalili family, too, perhaps, confirmed that they did what is right and natural. Their action points to the incremental notion of change, one which accompanies reflection, but also an appreciation of current norms and practices. Their act underscores social workers' attempts to make change based on the existing understanding of social norms while also striving to shift the ground of what is right and natural.

Absent the state stepping in and overtaking the retribution right, concerns with honor and face-saving persist in Iran. Judicial actors are attuned to these subtleties. The judge's emphasis on sensitivity to the nuances in families' decisions about *qisas*, combined with the gradual and deliberate nature of change in the societal zeitgeist, help me to contextualize what one lawyer said to me about this victim-centered criminal justice system. One evening, while having dinner in urbane northern Tehran with four lawyers, one stated his stance against the death penalty, "but in this country, right now, they can't eliminate it for murder."

"Why not?" I asked.

"Because people will take the law into their own hands. They will seek revenge." He was referring to what he believed to be a norm in certain parts of the country. "First the *adab-e roosoom* [customs and mores] have to be changed."

"How does that happen?"

"It needs to start from the foundation of society, in the small towns and villages, where people still see the loss of blood as something they have to avenge to save their family honor. They have to change this kind of thinking and realize that killing another person is not going to make them feel better."

"But what if it does, or if they think it will?" I wasn't exactly playing the devil's advocate, just pointing to research emphasizing the human desire for payback.

"That's what I mean," responded the lawyer. "What needs to change is the feeling itself; it's not just intellectual, but emotional and psychological. If we humans could learn to change our thinking such that, in the event of a loss, what actually, physically made us feel better was not retribution, but magnanimity, I think this would be a much better world to live in."

The others nodded in agreement, but we all acknowledged how different it would be if any of us were placed in the position of deciding qisas. One of the other lawyers said, "It's easy to judge when you're not the one making the decision and to say that you'd forgo retribution."

Changing the norms of society in favor of forbearance seemed to be an incremental project, occurring bit by bit. Perhaps the norm is more obviously changing with respect to the execution of juveniles. Certainly, the more concentrated efforts to change the norm, both internationally and domestically, began with forbearance for youth offenders. Possibly this emerging norm is a steppingstone to changing the norm from retribution to forbearance for broader categories of defendants as well.

Forgiving youth offenders

Many of my interlocutors, lawyers and social workers, alike, locate the temporal opening of this "wave of forgiveness" at around the mid-1990s, with the rise of advocacy aimed at ending juvenile executions under Iran's commitments to the Convention on the Rights of the Child (CRC), which it ratified in 1994.[22] For many, that advocacy came to envelop the larger purpose of endorsing an end to the death penalty. For others, it suggested emphasizing forbearance. Strikingly, in the former cases, advocates often stood in opposition to the state, while in the latter, they worked alongside it. What that meant on the ground was that campaigns operated to influence the state and private parties alike. After the finalization of the penal code (2013) and the criminal procedures (2015), actual changes were made to the law to make the sentence of qisas more difficult to enforce, particularly for youth who committed crimes under the age of eighteen. I emphasize, however, that this is neither a ban on capital punishment for such youth nor is it easy to apply; it is an incremental shift. The law has changed only insofar as it creates barriers to enforcing the death penalty for juvenile offenders.

To understand how this incremental change in law impacted youth offenders who would have previously been sentenced to qisas under the old laws, essentially tried as adults, I met with Dr. Ali Rostami, the Director of the Juvenile Correction and Rehabilitation Center in Tehran. Rostami holds a PhD in psychology and, at the time of our interview (the summer of 2015), had been the Center's director for over ten years. The Center housed over two hundred juveniles. Of those, a dozen were sentenced to qisas. Under the new criminal laws, all were entitled to a hearing to determine whether they possessed the mental maturity necessary to be held accountable in the most serious crimes, including intentional murder.

Here again, I explore the potentiality of time and how Rostami uses it during this period of waiting for death after the issuance of the *qisas* verdict. I continue to draw on Agamben's complex exposition on potentiality, for which we can say that the *kairos* of time allows actors to use waiting to the advantage of forbearance over that of the retributive urge (1999). Within the wait emerges a potential—a possibility that can be exposed to nurture an attitude of forbearance.

When we met, Rostami reported that most of the cases in his facility had been converted to *diya*. "Some have already been freed. We are raising money for others to pay *diya*."

Rostami explained the new legal process for juveniles and how he and his colleagues work with victims' families and perpetrators to attempt to reach a settlement short of *qisas*.

> We speak to them [inmates] all the time. Their parents come. We inquire about the situation at home and try to get a complete understanding of their lives in order to better understand how they got to the point of killing someone.

Rostami also served as an expert child psychologist for the court. In that capacity, he used what he described as scientific methods to determine whether the juvenile offenders possessed the legal threshold for responsibility that the new laws required. The laws provided additional guidelines for how judges were to assess whether youth offenders had reached majority through mental maturity. For example, a new provision in the criminal procedures requires the juvenile court to hold a hearing with expert advisors present.[23] During the trial, "we [such psychological experts] do not testify or give an opinion. We provide a report on how the defendant comported him/herself [throughout the proceedings]." As an advisor, Rostami observes how defendants behave in court, including how they respond to questions posed by judges.

> We consider how they [juvenile defendants] answer various questions. For instance, in a recent case, when the judge asked the defendant, "Why did you have a knife," the defendant said, "Because kids in the neighborhood all have knives and if I didn't, they called me a mama's boy." This is an indication that the youth had not reached mental maturity. The mature youth would answer something like, "My father is a fruit vendor and I use a knife for work." We try to determine whether there was deliberation in their actions, whether the act was planned in advance.

Along with the expert evaluators, another new provision compels the court to commission a "character file" on the defendant—a report on the situation that the adolescent was in prior to committing the offense.[24] The idea is that these character files, which are also required for adult defendants, may contain mitigating factors. The reports are evidence meant to guide the judges' ruling. Although the laws affect the foundations of the case, the topic of forbearance was still germane, as youth offenders could still be sentenced to *qisas*.

When I broached the topic of forbearance, Rostami nodded and elaborated on the forgiveness work that he engages in as the Center director, "I hold meetings here in my office." He continued:

> In the ten years I've been here, I've obtained forbearance from nine families. It's a long process and takes one to two years. I meet with victims' families at least six or seven times before they agree to forgo retribution.
>
> For example, there was a murder case around 1387 [2008]. Both the victim and perpetrator were sixteen-years-old. Both came from affluent families in northern Tehran. The two got into a fight; the perpetrator pulled out a knife and stabbed the other. The perpetrator was sentenced to *qisas*. The victim's family wanted *qisas*, but they didn't force it. The perpetrator was brought here. After about two years, I could see that he was really a good kid. By then, he was almost twenty-years-old. I knew that I might be summoned to send him to the adult prison. So we, along with an NGO and an intermediary from their neighborhood, held a meeting.
>
> During that first meeting, we didn't talk about forgoing retribution. We asked family members how they were coping with their loss. We wanted them to know that we were with them, fellow-travelers in their pain and grief. The mother said, "Don't tell me to forgo the blood of my child," and we didn't. Instead, we talked about their situation. The deceased had a twenty-three-year-old sister who was very influential in the family. We invited her to come to the Center to see the youth here.
>
> About three months after that first meeting, they themselves called and came to see us. The mother of the deceased said that she wanted to see the perpetrator. We arranged a meeting in my office. When she saw him, she cried and shouted at him, "How could you?!" She asked him to explain what happened. The young man told her in detail how he came to kill her son. He cried and begged for her forgiveness. He fell on her feet. She was revolted and screamed, "Don't come near me!" That was how the first meeting ended. I saw that the family needed more time.
>
> Then, about three weeks later, the mother came to see me and said she wanted to see the perpetrator's family. I arranged a meeting, again in my

office, between the two families. There were eleven from the perpetrator's family and four from the victim's. That second meeting was very interesting. The victim's family members were yelling at the perpetrator's. Everyone was crying. The victim's family became more adamant about retribution. They said they would petition for implementation, but they didn't.

I asked Rostami whether, after that session, he regretted holding the meeting or was concerned that it had diminished the possibility of forbearance.

No, I wasn't concerned. It was a release, a bursting of their hatred. Each stage in the process is a kind of release. We know they need time. But we were starting to think that they would not consent to forbearance. Then, seven months later, I got a call from the mother. She wanted another meeting. She said that she had consulted her family and that they would forgo *qisas* in exchange for compensation. They wanted 700 million [*toman*]. In 1389 [2010], this was a lot more money than it is today [about $400,000]. I made no promises. I said we were just intermediaries.

However, this phone call indicated to me that they were starting to abandon the idea of *qisas*. I communicated this to the perpetrator and his family. We didn't call the victim's family. One day about five months later, the victim's mother called. I said the family was raising the money. She said that time was just passing and asked what we were going to do. By then, the offender's family had raised about 100 million. I told her that and invited her to my office to discuss it. When she came, I explained that the perpetrator's family couldn't raise 700 million. "The most they could raise was 300," I said, "Could she accept less?" She said that she had to speak with her daughter. A few weeks later, both mother and daughter came. I spoke with them about how the youth had been reformed. If he came out, he would be a good citizen. I showed them his report cards and photos of his activities. I told her that I didn't believe he would repeat his error. Then I said, "It [the decision] makes no difference to us," and asked, "Do you believe I am impartial?" She said, "Not earlier, but now I do." She said she needed to think.

A week later, I went to see her. Before I said anything, she said, "Only because of you we'll do this." She saw that we were totally disinterested. From there, we went straight to a notary. The signed affidavit affirming forbearance became an official document. They could not revoke it. The mother then said that she wanted to help us and the other youth in the Center. In the end, we held around six or seven meetings with this family. With each meeting, we got a little closer and it got easier to speak. With the social workers' help, we raised 300 million, three times the rate of *diya* at the time. Of course, it's not enough. Nothing can replace the loss.

Rostami's account of the case showed his strategy of using time as a mechanism to allow families to grieve and reflect. Grief can be broken down into the exigencies of time: to absorb the loss, which usually involved not having contact with the perpetrator; to find out the details of the incident that led to death; to expel anger directed at the person who caused it; to learn about the perpetrator's circumstances; to see the perpetrator as a human being, after which time, it often becomes impossible to carry out the retribution; and finally, to find a satisfying resolution short of retribution.[25]

The story also raised the question of how Rostami maintains the crucial impartiality.

> Over the years that I have been doing this, I realized that, in order to talk to victims' parents, you have to wait until they are ready. So, the first thing you do is wait. It takes time before they are even ready to talk to anyone. When I meet them, in that first meeting, I express my condolences first and foremost. I want to recognize their profound grief. I also acknowledge that I can never put myself in their place. I ask God to give them patience. I offer to help them by telling them that I am a psychologist. I see if they want to talk. Our position is that we will follow the law. We say, "Whatever the law decides."
>
> To the perpetrator's family, I say, "Put yourself in the place of the victim's family." Then, to the victim's family, I say, "There must be something contributing to the clash between the two." I ask them to imagine that it was their son who was killed. I say, "What would you do?"

The issue that I return to at this point is the one of guidelines. Rostami does not follow any established plan or method for his forgiveness work. The strategies emerge through practice. Thus, I asked what motivated him to convene such meetings and encourage victims' families to forgo retribution.

> I try to help all the youth here. The new laws allow me to make a report to Juvenile Court. I can ask for a modified sentence in *ta'zir* cases.[26] I feel that if I can do something, I must. Given the age of the offenders here, the youth . . . it can be said that they're [the crimes committed] all by accident or happenstance. The problems that lead to these crimes are children's issues. When there is a fight over a bike when a youth was fifteen, that person doesn't understand what she/he is doing. Under the previous law, we had no choice. The new law requires us to use scientific knowledge to determine legal responsibility.[27] This is also in the Qur'an.

Here, Dr. Rostami was referring to the jurisprudential debates on *booloogh* (physical maturity) and *roshd* (intellectual maturity). These debates recognize an important shift in children around the age of seven. From this age, children are understood to have the capacity of discernment—to understand what is happening around them. This is not, however, the same as intellectual maturity, which is the test for *roshd* under the new Art. 91. "Our laws now divide criminal responsibility based on a scientific approach that takes the stages of cognitive development into consideration," Rostami added, referencing Swiss psychologist, Jean Piaget, who found that children begin developing logical thinking around the age of seven. Because children apply their new-found logic to physical objects, Piaget named this stage of cognitive development "the concrete operational stage."[28] To this, Rostami added,

> The new code divides youth criminal responsibility according to age, first three to seven years, then seven to twelve, and then twelve to eighteen. This coincides, by the way, with Piaget, who said that anywhere between the ages of twelve and eighteen adolescents arrive at full cognitive maturity.

Rostami was referring to Piaget's final stage of adolescent development, the "formal operational stage," during which adolescents begin to move into adulthood at roughly between the ages of twelve to approximately fifteen-to-twenty. During this stage—the last of Piaget's stages of cognitive development—youth develop the ability to think in abstract concepts. That is, instead of relying solely on previous experience, adolescents begin to consider the consequences of actions. This type of thinking is important in long-term planning. Youth at this stage of cognitive development also acquire the skills of logical thinking, deductive reasoning, and systematic planning. Rostami then explained, "The average age of arriving at this thinking is eighteen, while only ten to fifteen percent arrive at it by the age of fifteen." And, he added, "Of course many still have not developed this by the age of twenty."[29]

Building on his motivations, he added, "We do a lot of social work. The individuals here are damaged, no matter what they did. Someone who ends up here cannot be otherwise. We work to help them get better psychologically, help them move beyond the murder." He ended with a final, more personal reflection, "We are a religious people. I feel when I help, God will help me. This is my responsibility as a human."

Conclusion

Rostami's motivations, like those of other judicial actors I have explored in this chapter, emerge from the complex interweaving of law, religious duty, scientific or expert knowledge, and sometimes compassion. In some way, time is the other side of the coin of waiting. Drawing from his scientific and professional training to guide such work, Rostami mobilizes his knowledge by utilizing the potentiality of time, which requires engagement and respect for the victims as well as the humanization of the perpetrator. The new laws are not full-proof assurances that adolescent offenders will not be executed. Advocacy and further procedural guidance are still required. The judicial actors are vetted public officials who have a demonstrated allegiance to Iran's criminal justice system, but these stories show that the actors operate within a judiciary that is neither monolithic nor irrationally doctrinaire. Even if individually these judicial actors may disavow *qisas*, in their capacities as officials, they work within it. This is not to suggest, however, that the system is impervious to change or that debates about its efficacy, even within the judiciary, are absent.

I have tried to demonstrate that what is sometimes referred to as "Islamic law" is actually a process of becoming; it is neither singularly 'Islamic,' nor exclusively 'law.' Laws come into being through dynamic and changing interpretations, if not through their substantive form, then through procedural praxis by practitioners, including some activist members of the judiciary. Bureaucratic actors take up, interpret, and give meaning to Islamic principles— *shari'a*—which are better thought of, not just as rules, but as attitudes as well (Reinhart 2017:58). Here we see that, while scriptural principles share qualities with other moral codes, they also take shape through them. Although codified to an extent, the scriptures are further construed, interpreted, and then promulgated both through official and unofficial channels. For many Muslims, the Qur'an is an immutable and unalterable text. The operations and practices to which its verses give rise, however, change and modify through the very human forces whose work both adheres to and animates the sacred texts. Through interviews with *Shi'i* scholars and state bureaucrats charged with implementing this duty, I have shown how these religious prescriptions come to be translated into contemporary socio-cultural and legal praxis in the *Shi'i* context. I have pointed out how the reformed laws are taken up and put into operation by civil bureaucrats. The stories I present offer a perspective on how the legal system is changing over time, incrementally, and, in particular, how the criminal procedures are being regularized and how their subtle interplay with international norms leads to small but significant changes to law over time.

Through these stories, I do not mean to romanticize the judiciary or its officials; the system is different from those in the west. I aim to think about what it means to include victims in the sanctioning process. One of the aims of this project is to examine the views and opinions of those from whom we do not hear, including state officials, in order to understand how forbearance and forgiveness are achieved in Iran, and to have a more informed understanding about the death penalty in Iran's criminal justice system.

PART II

Lifeworlds

5

Forgiveness Sanctioned

AFFECTIVE FAITH IN HEALING

ON A HOT breezy summer day in August 2013, twenty-six-year-old Sogand was scheduled to be hanged, her punishment for having murdered her husband, Hamid, six years earlier. As required by law, the victim's family was in attendance, represented only by the deceased's mother, Mrs. Heydari. Before leading the parties to the gallows, however, the prison magistrate in charge of implementing the death sentence escorted the mother-plaintiff and daughter-in-law-offender to a small windowless room inside the prison. There, she held a reconciliation meeting between the two parties with the aim of gaining Mrs. Heydari's consent to forgo retributive punishment. After several hours of solemn discussion, finally, Hamid's mother, who was meeting her former daughter-in-law for only the second time since the tragic death of her son, agreed to forgo her right of retribution, thus sparing Sogand's life. A month later, a still bereaved Mrs. Heydari confirmed to me that she "forgave Sogand." The tears that filled her eyes and streamed down her joyless face accentuated the words that followed, "with all my heart."

In this chapter, I explore how Mrs. Heydari and others like her who possess a right of retribution come to the decision to forgo it when the law permits them to pursue the ultimate sanction of death. In Mrs. Heydari's case, she went a step further; beyond simply forgoing her right of retribution, she forgave Sogand. One of the questions I pose in this chapter is what conditions need to be present for someone who has been wronged to forgive or remit the right of retaliation. Of course, this depends on what we take forgiveness to mean. There is plenty of debate on the nature of forgiveness, which may be beyond the scope of this chapter. There is, however, some agreement that forgiveness may bring about reconciliation between two parties (Minow 1998). For an individual who forgives, it may further provide the consolation of personal peace.[1]

Philosopher Charles Griswold has considered the depth and breadth of forgiveness and finds it to be an elusive subject. However, Griswold understands forgiveness as a moral relationship between a person wronged and a wrongdoer, but it is "governed by norms" of a society (2007:xv). In some contexts, forgiveness may even possess an official quality, as in a state-sanctioned truth and reconciliation process or perhaps something like the codified forbearance I explore here. For Griswold, forgiveness comes with terms attached; it is not unconditional. As a condition of forgiveness, one gives up the need or urge to seek revenge (2007:20). Although traces of resentment may still remain, they do not hinder or prevent an act of forgiveness. However, forgiveness is not a process easily undertaken. Griswold explores six conditions that make forgiveness possible: (1) acknowledgement of wrongdoing, (2) repudiation of the action, (3) communication of regret or apology, (4) rehabilitation, (5) understanding of wrongdoing, and (6) a narrative explaining the act in question (2007:49–51). I take Griswold's argument to apply in the case at hand. Not all of his conditions need be present for forbearance to occur and certainly forgiveness can take place without all of them, too. Some mix of these condition, however, seems to be present in every case I have explored. Forgiveness may result in the elimination of revenge, or, as in the cases I examine in this book, it may result in forbearance of the right of retaliation.

In what follows, I examine families' stories of forbearance and forgiveness. Driven by the question of how aggrieved family members, who possess a right to retribution, come to the decision to be merciful, I describe the conditions that made forgiveness or forbearance possible and more desirable than retribution. I explore the vast affective space that shapes and conditions the manifestations of forgiveness. In doing so, I consider how time, dreams, gender, and social reputation all play crucial roles in families' decisions to forgo retaliation and, indeed, to forgive.

Affected Time

In this unregulated space between law and social practice lies the neither ossified (as legal codes are) nor fluid (as social practice can be) space of forbearance decisions. These decision processes go on, quite literally, for years, usually while the defendants are in prison. Throughout this period, victims' families and defendants and their families linger in unremitting agony and equivocation; lives are encumbered and in a state of interruption. Perpetrators' families live in constant fear and trepidation—fear for the imminence of a loss they cannot prevent and trepidation around actions that could fail to bridge reconciliation.

One morning, while waiting to interview one of the magistrates at the judiciary's Implementations Unit in Tehran, I met a middle-aged couple who had been summoned by the magistrate. The mother, seated beside me, explained that they were told that they would see their son, Ali, who was in prison for murder. Ali had exhausted his appeals and the only hope left was to procure the forbearance of the victim's family. His parents were trying to raise funds to offer the victim's family as possible compensation, although they had no agreement from the victim's family to accept it. The mother told me, "We don't know what else to do." The parents lived in fear of the day they would be called to see Ali for the last time, to say their final goodbye. As she quietly wept, I realized that the mother was worried that this was exactly the reason that they had been summoned. The couple waited for almost an hour, expecting Ali to be brought in. Instead, after a series of phone calls, one of the clerks looked up from his desk and told them they could leave. They would not see their son that day. They left with a bit of relief that time for Ali had not come to a stop. After they departed, the clerk explained that the magistrate was trying to organize a reconciliation meeting between the offender's parents and the victim's family, but the latter had refused his summons.

For victims' families, there is the double agony of loss and indecision. And even after they have made up their minds to execute their right of retribution, they are often made to wait while the process plays itself out, sometimes to their dismay and indignation. This was the case of Mr. Asgarzadeh, from the previous chapter, who sought to avenge his father's murder. As he walked into the office of Tehran's supervisor of Implementations, Mr. Asgarzadeh bristled impatiently and said, "We just want this over. It's taking too long!"[2]

As we saw in Chapter 4, state officials use time to buy time. Over the years, I conferred with numerous judicial officials, who confirmed that the paramount right of retribution (and forbearance) belongs to the victim's family. In one conversation, a judge from the criminal court told me, "The societal goal in this law is deterrence. Another concern is that people should not take the law into their own hands." This statement confirmed the concern with revenge, a degree of payback that extends beyond in-kind or proportionate retribution. Revenge extracts an excess of punishment. The law of retribution thus provides a limit and, ideally, a constraining effect on punishment.

The judge continued, "But, what this right gives the victim's family, which they lack, is a degree of control over a situation in which they feel they have no power. Sure, it's a difficult decision for the family [of the victim] to make, but the very fact that it is their decision is what is crucial in many cases of forbearance." The judge seemed to be saying that the state's (or public's) recognition that retribution is a right that belongs to the aggrieved, itself, returns to victims' families a degree of control over a situation in which they feel they have none. Thus, the very power to decide affords some reparation. As one judicial official put it, "For some, time is the ultimate healer. If we can convince them to wait, many will change their minds [about execution]; but they need

time. If they have time, their intensity wanes and they can let go of their pain."
The power over life, together with time, which can be carefully managed by
state and other actors, may provide an opening for healing, reflection, and
assuagement, and ultimately pave a path towards forbearance, one that some
just might be willing to take. But to have an exception, the rule must hold.[3]

During another visit to the Implementations Unit, as I sat in a magistrate's
office, an irate middle-aged woman came charging in. "Why won't you carry
out the *qisas*?" she screamed. "It's been eight years since he was convicted. He
killed my son in his sleep." Then turning to me she continued, "My son was
hard-working and decent. He drove a taxi all night to make ends meet for his
wife and newborn. He [the offender] stabbed him in his taxi while he slept!
ELEVEN TIMES!"

"Please, sit, Madam, we are getting your file," the young magistrate said.

"You people think you are doing right by not executing him. You think that
you are doing human rights. But it is *my* right you are preventing me from
exercising. You think that people like this should be spared, but this is not so.
People like him should be executed, for the good of society."

The magistrate assured her that he would look into her file and get in touch
with her. He and several assistants calmed her enough to escort her out of the
office. Once gone, the magistrate confirmed that she had been there before.
He said, "This is an example of someone who will not change her mind even
with the passing of time. She will not rest until she sees him executed." And
she would see him executed. One of the constraints of the retribution law is
that at least one member of the victim's family must be present during the
execution. Although it is unclear whether the law requires it, in some jurisdictions, a family member of the victim even serves as executioner—pulling the
lever or kicking the stool that sets into motion the death sentence.[4]

Time works differently for others; some are sure they cannot go through
with the execution, even from the start, but they are also reluctant to give up
their right to it. It's a time of agony, but it's also an agony of time that isn't moving quickly enough. An emotional journey to reconciliation begins with a
heated anguish characterized by indecision, anger, and helplessness, one
which appeals to revenge or at least retribution. Slowly, ever so slowly, that
angry passion may settle and calm.

Willing Forgiveness

For Mrs. Heydari, whose daughter-in-law, Sogand, had killed her son, Hamid,
healing came gradually, and with prayer. In her supplications to God, she asked
for guidance. Her family, including a husband and four sons, gave her their
power of attorney. She had to decide what to do. "Because you are the mother,"

her husband had said to her. He did not want *qisas*, but she was not sure. So, he said, when she made up her mind, that would be the family's decision. He wanted her to be satisfied and the family would agree with whatever decision she took, he had told her.

Even though she did not believe she could kill Sogand, her reluctance to forgo retribution was couched in two dilemmas. First, Mrs. Heydari believed that she had been left, in a sense, as the sole executor of her son's will, literally. That is, she understood the right to determine the fate of the offender to belong to the deceased. Thus, she believed that she was charged not with carrying out her own will, but that of her deceased son. But how could she be sure about what he would want her to do? Mrs. Heydari said, "Everyone kept asking me what I wanted to do, but I didn't know. How could I know? I didn't know what Hamid would want to do." As Mrs. Heydari understood it, she was acting only as a proxy, on behalf of her deceased son. She had to be sure she would do right by her boy.

The second dilemma Mrs. Heydari grappled with was that her son was dead and, if she forgave, Sogand would be free—free to live her life. At twenty-six, Mrs. Heydari told me, Sogand was still youthful and pretty. "She would get out, get on with her life, maybe even marry again, have children, and live a good life, while Hamid was dead." Mrs. Heydari sensed the injustice too strongly, especially in the early years. At that time, she felt that Sogand was headstrong, unrepentant, and even a little presumptuous. "It's as though they think they can kill someone and then beg for forgiveness," she said, referring to Sogand and others who insist on being forgiven. For Mrs. Heydari, this was just too small a price to pay for having killed someone. Even later, she did not feel that Sogand would be sufficiently punished, since the maximum sentence she could serve, should Mrs. Heydari forgo retribution, was ten years. Even if Sogand were sentenced to the full ten years, the court would count the six that she had spent in prison as time-served and likely reduce the remainder for good behavior. Mrs. Heydari could not permit herself to carry out her son's will in this way.

As the years went by, however, time took its toll. The burden of the decision wore on her. For six years, Mrs. Heydari lived with this misery, she told me. She couldn't sleep through the night. She thought about only this—"what to do about Sogand"—every day. She frequently visited her son at the cemetery. "I would lie on Hamid's grave and cry and ask him, 'What should I do?'" she said.

I asked Mrs. Heydari if she discussed her decision with anyone, whether she sought council. She replied that everyone, including relatives, social workers, judges, lawyers, community elders, and even, especially, Sogand's mother, tried to talk to her. No one told her what to do, she said, but they gave her suggestions. Her husband said, "Don't soil your hands with her tainted blood."

Some people had dreams about it and related them to her. Her cousin told her that Sogand came to her in a dream, repentant, but Mrs. Heydari had replied that if that were true, then why did she not come to her. Her older brother, with whom she was close, was the only person to whom she directly posed the question, "What should I do?" He said, "I can't tell you what to do. You have this right, but forbearance is better." His statement referencing the Qur'an (5:45) affirmed her right while situating it in a moral context in which forbearance is the righteous choice.

Hamid was killed when his wife struck him with a kitchen knife. Sogand, which literally means oath, swore that it was an accident. They had been fighting over money, as young couples do. Their fight became heated and, when she threw the knife, it caught his neck and severed the carotid artery. He bled to death before the ambulance arrived. She was just nineteen. He was twenty-two. Almost seven years later, when Sogand was twenty-six, the Implementations Unit had summoned Mrs. Heydari for the second time. They wanted her to decide. The first time, Mrs. Heydari said she wanted *qisas*. She went to the prison, ready to watch Sogand be executed or so she thought. But the prison magistrate, who had grown to like Sogand, believed that she (Sogand) had made a horrible mistake, but could be, indeed was, redeemed. The first time, it was the prison magistrate who postponed the execution. Another year went by. Now, the prison magistrate called often, and social workers came by. They continued the refrain, "It's your decision." They did not approach the issue directly but talked about Mrs. Heydari's suffering and how she could extinguish it. "You aren't going to feel better by taking another life." Others told her, "It is not in you to do this; you are not this vicious. It takes a brutish heart to do this."

Sogand's mother also called on her. The women cried together. They watched the wedding video together. How could something that started like this end so badly? Over time, the relationships between the women—the social workers, the prison magistrate, the mothers—all strengthened. Mrs. Heydari came to see Sogand's mother as another victim.

On several occasions, I observed victims' families, especially mothers, who asked to see the perpetrator's mother. I came to understand this desire to behold the other as consisting of something greater than simply a visceral pleasure in experiencing others' suffering. When the victim's mother sees that of the perpetrator, whose son or daughter she can have killed, she beholds a face full of remorse and experiences a check on her own reality, often a jarring one. In spite of what the other mother's child did to hers, the victim's mother might now ask herself whether she could do the same. In such a meeting, the victim's mother seeks an affinity with the other. In that exchange, she will ask herself—Could she inflict such pain on another (often) mother? Could she herself become a killer?

Until she started meeting with Sogand's mother, Mrs. Heydari had no interest in seeing Sogand or hearing what she had to say. "She was so obstinate; I didn't want to listen to her." But the years also wore on Sogand; she had appeared to change while in prison. She became repentant. The prison guards spoke well of her. She was reportedly friendly and caring towards the other inmates, and she was well-liked. The prison magistrate wanted her out, not dead. She called Mrs. Heydari in again to meet with Sogand. By the time that call from the prison came, the only thing Mrs. Heydari wanted was to see Sogand—one last time—to witness some pain or regret on her face. If her own attitude exhibited grace in her quiet suffering, Mrs. Heydari sought it in her adversary, too. And so, she agreed to have a meeting with Sogand.

Trauma scholars have noted that victims often express a desire to see whether and how the family of the perpetrator or the perpetrator him/herself is suffering (Gobodo-Madikizela 2008). Victims want the perpetrator to see and respond to their pain and suffering. That is, their grief in this context is interpsychic and healing requires a dialogical encounter. However, immediately after trauma, victims experience a loss of empathy and attachment to their social community. Before they can consider forgiveness, victims need to reengage their capacity for empathy, which happens through intersubjective dialogue between victims and perpetrators or, what Gobodo-Madikizela terms "empathic repair" (2008).[5] Thus, the desire on the part of the victim's family to see the perpetrator's family or their indignation when the latter do not come, suggests the reigniting of a capacity for empathic relations, just the opening or softening that social workers work towards. In the cases I followed, when victims wanted to be seen and heard, and sought to have their suffering witnessed by the perpetrator and his/her family, they were signaling a readiness for empathic repair.

Often in such cases, the victims also needed to see the perpetrators, to learn some details about the death of their loved one, usually involving the truth of what happened. In seeing the perpetrator, victims sought to observe for themselves whether the perpetrator adequately expressed remorse. When victims are able to allow perpetrators to witness their vulnerability in grief and the perpetrator shows remorse, then empathic repair, the path to reconciliation, can proceed. As the two sides come together, a rehumanizing happens on both sides and each sees the other outside of the incident that brought them together. This happens through both the small talk and that thing they share, the incident. Once there is a kind of humanizing of the perpetrator, here through the family members, it is much harder to seek execution. Killing requires the opposite, a dehumanizing.

I asked Mrs. Heydari what she and Sogand talked about during that last reconciliation meeting. "I wanted her to tell me what had happened that night [that Hamid was killed]. The story was the same, but the emphasis was different. This time, Sogand focused on her reaction to the fight. Before the focus was only on Hamid and what he did to her. Where there was anger and justification before, now there was sorrow and grief."

"Were you looking for an apology? Did she say she was sorry?" I asked.

"She did not need to say she was sorry. I don't care if she is sorry. I wanted to see that she, too, had suffered."

As with other victims' families, for Mrs. Heydari, the defendant's remorse was a sentiment crucial to her forgiveness. She was very clear that it was not an apology that she sought. Instead, Mrs. Heydari was looking for signs of genuine remorse. She wanted to see that Sogand felt sorrow and regret for what she had done. For victims' families, remorse was a key element in the decision to forgive. The families were looking for that essential quality that made the offender human and would provide a sign in which their recognition of the defendant's humanity (by virtue of their forgiveness) would be warranted.

The artifice of a regulation of forbearance, thus, emerges through sentimental practices between victims' families and other interlocutors. Through the course of negotiations, certain sentiments come to be expected. Over time, through the cases that make the press and circulate, a loose set of processes for engendering forgiveness emerge. This not only involves sentiment, but also some financial settlement. In Mrs. Heydari's case, this was a problem because she did not want anything in exchange for her son's death. She said, "You can fill a house full of gold and give it to me, but it won't change anything for me." But negotiators, social workers on her behalf, had come up with a sum. Mrs. Heydari gave in, and the prison magistrate enforced it. Otherwise, they argued, Sogand would get off too easily and Hamid's death would be dishonored. The payment of this sum ultimately became a contingency for the defendant's release, even though Mrs. Heydari had forgiven her and hadn't asked for it.[6]

I visited Mrs. Heydari after she had already signed the affidavit consenting to forbearance. Sogand was still in prison, though, and Mrs. Heydari was troubled. She had been to the prison, she told me, to protest Sogand's continued stay there when she was due to be released. The officials told her that Sogand's family had not yet secured the compensation, but it was on the way and Sogand was only days from release, they assured her. Troubled, Mrs. Heydari, along with Sogand's mother, continued to insist that Sogand be released, until she finally was, about one month later.

I asked Mrs. Heydari whether she was satisfied with her decision. She said that she had found relief and tranquility, but she still hurt all the time. The only perceptible regret she expressed was that all the people who had been calling on her no longer did, especially Sogand's mother, which made her think that the relationships she thought she had forged were only instrumental. I invited

Mrs. Heydari to consider whether she forgave Sogand or only consented not to have her executed. Her response was as passionate as it was swift, "I did it from my heart; I forgave her. I entrust her to God. I don't want her death; my son didn't want her death."

Dreaming of Forgiveness

Mrs. Heydari's decision was hastened by a dream. "Hamid came to me in my sleep. He said, 'Mother, forgive her.'" After seeing her son in a dream, Mrs. Heydari was able to end her indecision, her search for a solution. All that time, it was not so much that Mrs. Heydari wanted retributive sanctioning to be carried out, but that she could not bring herself to forgo it, either, on her son's behalf—not until he told her she could. For Mrs. Heydari, coming to this decision did not involve money or other conditions; her will came with Hamid appearing before her in a dream. Dreaming of Hamid, she explained, was *hekmat* (divine wisdom) and "God's wisdom is never without reason."

A number of the people with whom I spoke, those who forgave, came to their ultimate decision through just such a dream. Social workers confirmed to me that this is a common route for the families of victims deciding that they can forgive. One social worker explained why she thought this happens, "The dream tells them that they are not committing an injustice against their loved one by forgoing retributive sanctioning. It shows that they are still seeking justice on behalf of their loved one." It is very difficult to make a decision like this. To be burdened with carrying out justice on behalf of your child, your mother, father, or closest and most beloved relative, and the dream is often a turning point. For Mrs. Heydari, the dream became a "landscape of imagination," where she could be divinely inspired towards forgiveness. As Amira Mittermaier has shown through her study of Muslim dreaming practices in contemporary Egypt, imaginative worlds of dreams address everyday concerns with piety and virtue. Dreams carry significant ethical meanings and "often direct dreamers to concrete action" (2011:50). Mittermaier's excavation of dreams locates a space of imagining that adds an important ethical dimension to the affective world of forgiveness I explore here.

My interlocutors frequently cited dreams of the beloved as the turning point in their decisions to forgive. This was the case in Mrs. Heydari's forgiveness of Sogand and most others that I encountered. In some cases, the dream was important for several family members as an outlet for the feelings of sorrow, a way to communicate the lost chance to say goodbye. This was evident in Mrs. Javanmardi's case. Like Mrs. Heydari, Mrs. Javanmardi had lost her son, Mohsen. In her case, it, too, was the result of a knife fight. This time, however, it was by the hand of his wife's brother, Nader.

I visited with Mr. and Mrs. Javanmardi in the summer of 2014. The couple, a retired policeman and his wife, a homemaker, had recently relocated to the outskirts of town, to the further recesses of Tehran's never-ending urban sprawl, where the pollution was less intense and the cleaner air calmed Mr. Javanmardi's bronchitis. Their three-bedroom apartment was spacious and modern. My hosts led me to their large sitting room. Without asking, they served me blended honeydew melon smoothies, an antidote to the oppressive summer heat. Aware of the reason for my visit, the elderly couple sat next to eachother on the adjacent couch as I drew my notebook out of my purse. Our conversation centered on their decision to forgo sanctioning of their son's murderer by his brother-in-law. Theirs was a story that had circulated broadly, hailed by state-run media outlets. Mrs. Javanmardi had already granted many interviews, had appeared on national television, and was the subject of several newspaper articles.

After learning that I live in Seattle, Mrs. Javanmardi's face lit up as she recounted how her daughter had moved to Vancouver some years earlier. "From the start, she told me to forgive him," she said of her daughter in Canada. Throughout our meeting, the couple's three other children, along with their respective spouses and children, walked in and out of the room, half-listening to our conversations. "The children never said 'you must or must not . . .' They always said that father and mother must decide, but they did say, 'qisas is not worthy of you.'"

Mrs. Javanmardi spoke with ease and affection of her deceased son, who was killed by his wife's brother when he (the deceased) sought to intervene on her behalf in a dispute between her family members. She prefaced her comments with an explanation of her motivations for forbearance. In her explanation of what inspired her forgiveness, Mrs. Javanmardi evoked her faith, "We did it for God, one week before it [the execution] was to take place. At first, we wanted qisas for the murder. Our son was innocent."

I asked her about the incident that led to her son's death. Even though years had passed and they had repeated the story innumerable times, several family members walked out of the room. Those who remained began to weep as Mrs. Javanmardi recounted what had happened to her son:

> Mohsen got a call and went to talk to Nader. He left around six-thirty in the evening and, by midnight, I still hadn't heard from him. "Why didn't he call?" I said. Then, I grew anxious; I began trembling. I sat. I got up. I walked around. I didn't know what to do, but I knew something was wrong. I called his mobile, and their home [Mohsen's father-in-law]. My husband felt sick. At midnight, my daughter got a call. Their daughter-in-law's sister called and told us that he was dead. That midnight was the beginning of our mourning. This was four years ago. Nader is now in prison.

Just like that, Mrs. Javanmardi seemed to be saying, she'd lost her son. The lack of detail and explanation accentuated the senselessness of his passing. Given the family's evident grief, I did not press for particulars about the incident. As Mrs. Javanmardi continued, she focused on her son, "Mohsen came to me in a dream. [In the dream], he covered his eyes. I said, 'Mohsen, Mohsen, look at me.' He said, 'I feel shame because Father told me not to go.' He comes to me in my sleep since the first day we saw him in the morgue."

Mrs. Javanmardi only offered these small hints that the relationship between the two families had not been good. Initially, her dreams of Mohsen were purely a comfort to her. Then, she received a clear signal from her son.

> Wherever we would go, everyone would say, "Forgive; take some compensation or something [i.e. property]." Our children were more open. They wanted their parents to have some peace. But I didn't know what to do. Then, one day when Mohsen came to me and I said, "Mohsen, come sit with me." I asked, "What do I do about Nader?" He said, "Who's he?" I said, "He's the one who killed you with a knife." Then Mohsen said to me, "Oh, let it go, Mother. Let it go. I will always be by your side." When I told my husband that Mohsen came to me while I slept, he, too, was calmed by this. Then, days later, Mohsen came again. He asked me, "Mother, are you pleased with me?" I said, "Mohsen, I am very pleased with you, my son . . ."

I asked Mrs. Javanmardi whether she felt at peace with her decision. She replied, "Yes. I am not so nervous and worried all the time. I have found peace." Then she added that Mr. Javanmardi was even more comforted. She said, "It's a peculiar stress. He would get sick." Then Mr. Javanmardi chimed in to explain his own peculiar stress—or guilt.

> It was around three o'clock in the afternoon. I was at Fatemeh Square to purchase a train ticket. After I got the ticket, I went to the ATM to get some cash and a man [panhandler] appeared. He wanted money. I said, "Wait, I'll give you some money as soon as I go to the ATM." Then the man disappeared. I searched for him. I got annoyed and lost patience, so I went home. Once at home, Mohsen said, "You should have given him some money, but it's okay. Give some to another person." This was a test from God. This was the day Mohsen was killed. God's work is never without wisdom. [*Heeech kare khodah bee hekmat neest*]. I should not have refused the poor man. This scene will never leave my mind. God makes you work. Help others and don't worry about the rest.

I asked Mr. Javanmardi how he now felt about forgoing retribution,

> For one week after, my conscience made me question whether what we did was good or bad, but after one week, I found comfort in the fact that

Mohsen was not the kind to kill others. And, our situation was different [from other murder cases]. Mohsen's murderer is not likely to hurt others.

Here, like Mrs. Heydari, the Javanmardis attribute the right of retribution to the deceased. It was his will they sought to exercise. When Mrs. Javanmardi thought about her decision, her conscience drifted towards her son. His continued affirmations over time led to her decision. Mrs. Javanmardi attributed her dream visions of Mohsen to her faith, "When I prayed, I asked God what to do. God said to me, 'A life is in your hands—forbear.' Then He sent Mohsen to help me decide." Mrs. Javanmardi's dream provided a space for her indecision to become solidified; it supported her inclination towards forbearance.

As with Mrs. Heydari, I asked Mrs. Javanmardi whether she saw her decision of legally consenting to forbearance as something more personal; I asked if she also forgave Nader. She replied, "I forgave in my heart. What happened between the two was an accident. It was unintended." She again emphasized the strength she found in her faith. "It was just for God, to do right by our son. I have to fear God if I am responsible for a decision that leads to a person's death."

Then Mrs. Javanmardi spoke again of dreaming of Mohsen, but with a slightly comical twist, representing a now more pacified quality to her life. "Our other son, Hamid, was very depressed with Mohsen's death." Hamid, who was thirty-six years old, was the closest in age to his brother. He was in the room and cracked a smile as his mother spoke,

> He was always the one who saw Mohsen in his dreams. They were very close. But for one week now, Mohsen doesn't come. Hamid just got engaged. They [the couple] have loved each other for seventeen years, and three months ago, she said yes. Now, Mohsen doesn't come because he knows Hamid is getting on with his life. He's happy for Hamid.

Dream visions provide important encounters with loved ones, and can be the source of enormous relief, especially from pent up guilt about what to do. Those who forgive frequently do not arrive at that decision until the date of the execution draws near, when the realities of retribution envelop and implicate them, and they must face the life they could take and all the responsibility that accompanies such a decision.

Face and Forgiveness

Mahboubeh, the social worker who introduced me to victims' families, including those in the preceding sections, was led into forgiveness work because of her own experience a few years earlier. Like the other women discussed here,

Mahboubeh had to make the decision whether to forgo or exercise retribution after her brother, Behrouz, was killed. A teacher in her mid-thirties, Mahboubeh lived with her husband and three sons in the working-class neighbourhood of Shad Abad, not far from the Tehran's iconic Freedom Square. She was close to her five brothers, especially Behrouz, the youngest, who died when he was just twenty-one. As the only daughter in the family, Mahboubeh had assumed the role of nurturer and mother to her brothers after their mother passed away six years earlier. As Mahboubeh described it, theirs was a "traditional family, but our family is very affectionate, and I took care of my brothers when my mother died."

Having stepped into the role of family matriarch, Mahboubeh also had to decide whether to forgive her brother's assailant. Although the entire family needed to reach an agreement, Mahboubeh explained to me why it was, in the final analysis, up to her, "I am very important in this family. The decision about what to do was mine. To be happy in a family, you have to make the woman *ghaneh* [satisfied]." But it was not just her role in the family that made her the final arbiter of whether the family forgave her brother's assailant. In fact, her father and brothers looked to her for comfort after they had lost their mother. They also looked to Mahboubeh to do what a mother would do in such a situation. Mahboubeh explained as much "because we had lost our mother, this gave me a lot of influence; I was the one who made all the decisions." But because Behrouz was so young when their mother died, Mahboubeh's relationship to her youngest brother took on even more of a mothering role.

Like with the other women's stories I have recounted in this chapter, Mahboubeh's role in the decision to exercise retribution or forgo it figured strongly in the family. Mahboubeh was clear and firm in her explanation of the role she played as mother. "The mother is the one who carries the child," she told me. Mahboubeh's explanation underscored the gendered bond between mercy and motherhood. The Arabic term for mercy, *rahmat*, shares the same linguistic root as that for womb, *rahem* (Chittick 2013). And Mahboubeh felt the pressure, not just from the pain of her own loss, but also that of having to represent their deceased mother's wishes. "I became sick. My father saw that my illness was making me suffer." Initially, the family was in agreement, as Mahboubeh related:

> At first, all of my family wanted execution. We all wanted *qisas* and nothing more because my family is very pious and we believe in God. We believed that the Qur'an stated that, if someone kills, then *qisas* is the just punishment.

Mahboubeh then recounted how little by little, her brothers and father began to change their minds. Members of the community in which they lived, from which both the deceased and the assailant hailed, came to the house. They talked to the family, as did members of the 'ulama. Mahboubeh explained, "over time, my brothers and father began to feel that opting for *qisas* could influence our *ruh* [soul], and make us angry and influence us to teach our children to be vengeful."

Soon, Mahboubeh was the lone holdout in the decision to forgive her brother's murderer. "My father said if Mahboubeh is satisfied, then I forgive." Yet, she could not reconcile herself with the advice and the pleas of their wider relations. At this time, she told me, she hardly went out or spoke with anyone because she felt that everywhere she went, people were trying to get her to change her mind, "They would say, 'your father is satisfied with forgiveness,' and then they would ask me to do the same." She went on:

> Even to our extended family, I would say, "You don't feel the pain and suffering that I do; my brother was about to get married; his voice is still in my head." And it would make me mad—their insistence that I forgive. Then my father saw that I was angry, and would say, "no, I just want the law [*qisas*]."

The case went on this way for years, until the day of the planned execution. Mahboubeh was the sole member of her family who did not agree to forgive, and so the family was going to go ahead with their legal right to seek retributive punishment. Because Mahboubeh was the only person who wanted the death sentence carried out, she played an important role in what was to happen. Before dawn, she awoke, performed her prayers, dressed in her black chador, and went to the prison. Her father was the only family member who would accompany her. The others refused; some were not speaking to her. Mahboubeh told me that the decision was really weighing on her, but at that point, she just wanted it over. She put on a brave face and went to exercise their right of retribution. Executions take place just before dawn, usually with crowds gathered outside the prison gates. This day was no different. "Just outside of Evin [prison], there were many, many people because they were going to execute four people, so about one thousand people were there," Mahboubeh said. She then heard a mother's wails, just beyond the prison's fenced-in yard, which separated the crowd from those entering the secluded inner grounds where executions take place. This gave her pause for the first time since her brother's death:

> I heard the scream of a woman. It is in my ears still. There were many women who were screaming and crying, but one stayed in my mind. It was a high-pitched, ringing scream that just went on and on. I called over to my brother who was also standing outside the prison gates and asked who that was. He said this is someone who is going to lose her son; someone like you is going to execute her son.

As Mahboubeh explained, the mother's wails continued ringing in her ears, even as she entered the prison's private chambers. Mahboubeh then approached four large athletic men. "I asked them, 'Why are you here?' and they said, 'We want to execute the murderer of our brother.'" Mahboubeh responded instinctively, "What? That's so sad! His mother is really crying in a bad way, and they said, 'Our mother is also crying—and the pain really hurts. And a mother is not really like a sister.'"

The grief and raw pain of the woman she had heard was getting to Mahboubeh. Once inside the prison yard, Mahboubeh could still hear the cries. She recounted how she suddenly began thinking about the possibility of relieving that woman of her pain. As they brought out the defendants, she saw how small and youthful they appeared. Ali, her brother's assailant, was crying as he held a picture of Behrouz to his chest. The scene that lay before her became heavy and she was starting to see the scenario differently. Now, when she considered the other families and other defendants, she started to think outside of her own personal desire for revenge. She began to feel a sense of pain for the defendants, too. She went to the brothers and said if they agree to forgive, then she would, as well. At first they were hesitant, but she would not stop pleading with them. She discussed the importance of forgiveness and how she could see that they would never feel ease or calm or peace after killing someone, even if that person had killed their brother. She said that she would forgive and that is what would bring peace, not just to her mind, but to her family and community. In the end, both Mahboubeh and the brothers gave in and decided to forgo retribution. Both families also accepted a financial settlement in exchange for it.

As Mahboubeh described her story, she emphasized that it was in seeing and feeling the humanity of the others, the mothers crying, the perpetrators pleading, that made her question, for the first time in many months, her desire to seek retribution. "She is a mother and I am a mother," Mahboubeh said of the woman she had heard wailing. "Suddenly, I became aware of how she must be suffering, too, maybe even more than me." Mahboubeh's reflection, raised once she faced the suffering of another, made her conscious of the effect her action was going to have. Until then, she did not want to see or think about the pain of others, those whose suffering she would intensify by seeking retaliation. She recalled, "I was in pain. I could not think about them. Not until I heard that mother's screams."

Mahboubeh's sudden reflection of herself in the mother of the man about to be executed signified a sensitivity on her part for the humanity of the other. In order to be able to forgive, the person forgiving needs to be able to imagine him/herself in the place of the other, which is what Griswold states is "the recognition of the shared nature of humanity" (2007:5). Mahboubeh's attitude similarly reinforces what Levinas has referred to as being conscious of the face of the other in your actions, "The face speaks to me and thereby invites me to a relation" (1969:198). For Levinas, it is in the faces of others that humans can see themselves and be compelled into action, "[T]he Other faces me and puts me in question and obliges me" (1969:207). In one relevant passage, Levinas speaks of the religious commandment against murder:

> The first word of the face is the "Thou shalt not kill." It is an order. There is a commandment in the appearance of the face, as if a master spoke to me. However, at the same time, the face of the Other is destitute; it is the poor for whom I can do all and to whom I owe all (1985:89).

For Levinas, the human face encompasses the living presence of the Other. The recognition of a person as a social and ethical being creates a bond with another. This connection is an appeal to a relational ethics; "the face presents itself and demands justice" (1969:294). Given Levinas's contention that the face is a living presence, it is important to consider that Iran's criminal justice system requires the victims' families to be present before the offender whose life they seek to take. Not until Mahboubeh felt the pain of the Other was she able to understand her actions because she was, at that point, enveloped in the totality of another's living presence, one which she had the power to deny.

But Mahboubeh did not actually face the man's mother. The evocation of the feeling it gave her when she heard the screams was enough to inflect an intensity that moved her emotionally. This scene, which Mahboubeh described as pivotal to her forbearance, also provides a clear example of how affect works non-discursively—a physical confrontation was not necessary for 'facing' the other. However, it was not just the mother's screams that created the affective environment. Mahboubeh was deeply moved by the events that followed as she walked towards the gallows, to the enclosed space inside the prison where four executions were to be carried out that day.

One of the other young men to be executed was Sina Paymard, a young down-and-out who had killed a man widely rumored to be his drug dealer during a sale gone wrong. As Mahboubeh described it, on the fateful day of his execution, authorities asked Sina if he had a last request. He asked to play his *ney* (Persian wooden reed flute) for one last time. The story from here is taken up by Mahboubeh who gave me the details of her experience of that morning.

> Four people were to be executed that day. I was there to see Ali, who killed Behrouz, executed. Then, one of the other prisoners, who was very small, started to play his *ney*. He played so beautifully, and it impacted me so

deeply. I was already very emotional, but upon hearing him play, *Mollana* [Rumi], I could no longer control my tears.[7] I said, who is this boy and what did he do for which he deserves to be killed? I saw four men standing not far from me. Someone pointed them out. "They are the victim's family. He killed their brother." I ran to them and said, "Please, don't do this. How could you do this?" One of the brothers looked at me and said, "But you are about to do the same thing." Then, I said, "Look, how about both of us forgive." With this, they agreed. And three of the four were spared that day.

Sina's moving performance also gave his would-be executioners pause. They decided that they would consider payment in exchange for his life and forgo retribution. An Amnesty International report quoted Sina's father as he described what happened when his son asked to play his *ney*.

We . . . asked the officials to allow us to see Sina once more. Nobody listened to us. Then the prison officer said Sina had asked for his instrument. Sina plays the flute. I gave it to him . . . that was Sina's last wish at the gallows . . . He started playing and all the families started crying . . . One of the women, who was apparently one of the [representatives of the murder victim], went to the other party and [agreed to accept blood money]. She then went to the other [members of the victim's family] . . . and they listened to her (Amnesty International 2011, citing, *E'temaad-e Melli*).

Here it was a combination of the face and the affective environment, created by both the mother's screams and the young man's musical performance, that generated and ultimately led to Mahboubeh's feeling of forgiveness. In such cases, seeing can be a witnessing of the other's humanity and a recognizing of oneself as inextricably connected through the shared loss that only they know and feel. This recognition of shared humanity becomes evident through the request, common among my interlocutors who had lost loved ones, to see the family of the perpetrator.

In the stories I have gathered, from both victims' families and those of offenders, the parties attach immense meaning to their face-to-face meetings. Without fail, every family I spoke with talked about the significance of seeing the perpetrator's family, although not necessarily the perpetrator, him/herself. Social, ethical, and religious codes require family members, neighbors, friends, and others to call on the family members of the deceased. What was striking in the conversations I had with victims and their families was the importance they attributed to seeing the perpetrators' family members. A victim of a car accident that had left him with a broken leg and permanent limp spoke disdainfully of the perpetrator's family, "Can you believe they didn't even call to see how I was doing?" In the above cases, Mrs. Heydari was moved by her meetings with Sogand's mother, then hurt, when, after the forgiveness, the latter stopped calling.

Likewise, in Mrs. Javanmardi case, the discussion of meeting the perpetrator's mother conveyed how pivotal it was in her ability to forgo retribution. She said, "Then his [the perpetrator's] mother requested a reconciliation and settlement meeting. [During the meeting] I told her, 'your son killed my son. The world isn't enough to compensate for my son.' Nader's [the perpetrator's] mother had come to see us about six months before the murder. Mohsen had said to her, 'Keep an eye on your son.' She said she would rip him [Mohsen] to pieces. 'Four years ago you said you wanted to do this,' I told her. But in the end, his mother and father sat here next to my husband and me. I looked into her face and recognized that she is a mother, too. I wasn't disrespectful."

In conversations between the mothers of victims and perpetrators, one can unload her grief onto the one person who could really understand it. The perpetrator's mother is the one who can share in the loss and, possibly, experience it as well. It's perhaps her grief that the victim's family wants to see, even more so than that of the perpetrator, whose emotional protestations they cannot trust. Moreover, as in Mrs. Javanmardi's case, the face-to-face meeting can also become a moral lesson to the perpetrator's family, and an exercise of righteousness. Thus appears a gendered mirroring through grief of one mother's forbearance and another's authentic sorrow. In this way, righteous forbearance in the face of genuine sorrow flattens the hierarchy, first created by the homicide, then inverted with the right of retribution.

"After we consented to forbearance, I said to her, 'Do you see this Qur'an? I forgave for this Qur'an, but you wouldn't.' It's okay. I would. She wouldn't." If the right of retribution is a power that the state affords to victims, the right to forgo it, too, can be a demonstration of strength and, in particular, of moral rectitude and, perhaps, superiority.

Given that she had met with the members of the perpetrator's family, I asked Mrs. Javanmardi whether it was important that she meet with the perpetrator himself. She replied:

They [his mother and wife, sister . . .] said, "He's sick. You can go see him for yourself." I didn't care whether he was ill or healthy; I didn't want to see him. We didn't want anything to do with him. Then the prison magistrate told us to come and we said we could not. Our sons and son-in-law would not go either. But other prison officials said he's in bad shape and that we should come. So, we went. When he came out in his prison uniform, with his hands and feet chained, it affected us. He was sick over what he had done. He was gaunt and thin. He looked down at his feet. He cried and begged us to forgive him. I felt sorry for him, for having gotten himself in this situation. I thought to myself, killing him serves no purpose.

As in the case of Mrs. Heydari, Mrs. Javanmardi found peace in facing the perpetrator—seeing the quiet suffering and his remorse. Her prayers, her dreams—encounters with her son—and then the very real encounters with the offender's family and the offender himself, all gave her solace in her decision to forgo retribution. "I don't know if I did the right thing," She said of her decision. "I'm no one special. But I realized that his death would not bring back my child. We did it for God, only God." Mrs. Javanmardi repeated the final sentence several times throughout our conversation. Each time she did, her face came alive. At this last utterance, the corners of her eyes crinkled as she smiled, "God means Love. When you forgive, you become closer to God." Mrs. Javanmardi's remarks signal her attachment to the attainment of mystical or Sufi values in which prayer is a start towards a path in which love for God and others is the goal (Chittick 2000).

Seeing the face of the other has important significance in ways that are particular to Persian rituals of civility and sociability as well.

Aberu: Saving Face, Honor's Corollary

The act of physically regarding the face of the other is not the only consideration of the face in forgiveness stories. While seeing the face of the other may provide an opening for empathic action, the holder of this right—a victim's family member—must also consider her/his own face, or reputation. That is, the rights-holders' concerns of what others in their social or familial networks might think of their decisions highlights just how socially grounded the ethos of the right of retribution or forbearance is. Such concerns derive from kinship or the customary practices of preserving or upholding honor previously discussed. In struggling to determine the decision, family members sometimes worried about losing aberu, which can be loosely defined as reputation or dignity.[8] Thus, concerns with status or social standing in the family's community, village, clan, and so on, often figure prominently in these decisions, particularly when the conflicts take place in small rural communities.

This concern with aberu figured prominently in one family's decision in an ongoing case. The Ghomshayee's son had been stabbed to death in a fight. The man convicted of the crime was in prison awaiting the family's decision of whether to exercise retribution. The family lives in a small rural hamlet in northwestern Iran, in Azerbaijan province. In the summer of 2014, I accompanied two social workers from Tehran to speak with the mother of the deceased. The family had already been courted by the social workers as well as state officials, the family of the perpetrators, village elders, members of the 'ulama, and others who were urging them to forgo the sanction. Still, after seven years, they were not able to decide whether to forgo retribution. When we arrived in the village, we met with the mother and one of her daughters. Mrs. Ghomshayee, a petite woman in a black chador, told us that her youngest son, who was not present, pressed for retribution. The son, she told us, was very 'hot' and angry. He insisted on the execution of the perpetrator to avenge his brother's killing. The son had been very close to his brother and wanted to exhibit his family's *gheyrat* (honor) by seeing the ultimate punishment meted out. The family believed that their son had been wronged and did not feel it right to forgive the perpetrator, a notorious thug, who, they said, drew the eighteen-year-old into a fight as he walked home from work one night. It was unfair from the start, the deceased's sister said, because the thug, an older man of twenty-four, had a knife. The fight started with the men having words over the deceased's promise to sell the perpetrator his motor bike, a promise he did not keep. After they had words, they got into fisticuffs and, finally, the perpetrator drew out a knife and stabbed the unarmed younger man in the chest, killing him on the spot. The perpetrator had been sitting in prison for six years while the family was deciding what to do.

In our meeting, Mrs. Ghomshayee expressed a concern that weighed most heavily on her, "If I forgive him [the perpetrator], then what will people [*mardom*] think? They will say, 'She washed her son's blood with money.'" Mrs. Ghomshayee's use of the term 'money' invoked the idea that she might receive a financial settlement and adjusted the common expression, "blood washes blood." The social workers responded insistently, employing a different idiom, a new expression used in opposition to the classic one. They said, "blood cannot be washed away with more blood."

Mrs. Ghomshayee's preoccupation with what people would think of her figures prominently in many social contexts and is indicative of a desire for conformity. In this context, *mardom* may be her relatives, neighbors, or friends, but the term also serves as a metaphor that signifies the arrangement of social relationships based on the authority of an anonymous social force (Ahmadi and Ahmadi 1998:212). Present in their everyday lives, this social force urges people to adjust their words and deeds to those of some cohesive but amorphous unity.[9]

The direction of Mrs. Ghomshayee's concern about what people would think, however, seemed to me to be counterintuitive. Initially, I thought that the opposite would be true—that if she carried out the execution, *then* people would think ill of her. I said, "But won't your neighbors will be impressed if you forgo *qisas*?" In fact, in this tiny hamlet, the rules of social reputation—the maintenance of *aberu*—reflected long-held clan-based practices that suggest force (or violence) is a driver of social cohesion (Black-Michaud 1975). This approach depended on the social concern of maintaining the group's honor rather than on appealing to the humanity of the other, which relies on individual recognition. The latter, which I described in the earlier section, was more pronounced in the urban contexts in which I was carrying out most of my research. To my question, Mrs. Ghomshayee looked down pensively and said, "Here things are different from Tehran. Here we have to answer for the decisions we make."

"Answer to whom?" I probed.

"To everyone, to our neighbors, to family."

Seeing an opening, one of the social workers then said, "No, the only one to whom you must answer is God." At that point, Mrs. Ghomshayee nodded and spoke directly to God, "God, help us all."

As we discussed the case on the way home, one of the social workers related to me the sensibility she had learned from the work that she did.

> You see, I have had to understand the different social concerns that the families in these small and rural towns have. They are operating through different social matrices and we need to be sensitive to that. We can't just rely on the attitudes we have and take for granted in Tehran. As Mrs. Ghomshayee said, it's very different there. It's not like *aberu* is not a concern for me. Of course it is, but the difference is that the consequences are different. For that family, given where they live, the consequences are very real; they are material. Even if they are not killers, making the wrong decision in their son's case could impact their *aberu* in the village and then that would affect how people treat them, whether people in the town have respect for them, and so on.

My friend was deeply sensitive to the problem of urbanormativity; indeed, many of the Tehran-based social workers whom I encountered were acutely aware of their privileged perspectives. I asked my friend what she meant by the consequences being more real. She replied, "For example, it could affect the choice of husband for their daughter or the kind of job their son might be able to obtain. But it could also have a daily consequence of isolation, where people in the town ignore them and refuse to show them any respect."

The antidote to these concerns becomes a two-pronged approach by groups who work on these cases. On the one hand, they will work individually with the families of victims to try to persuade them to forgo sanctioning by appealing to their beliefs or values and drawing from their own rituals. On the other hand, such groups also work on changing the underlying value system in which concerns with *aberu*, for instance, figure so prominently.

Conclusion

Much has been written about the role of victims in sanctioning processes in legal scholarship and it is important to consider the various roles that victims play in the Iranian sanctioning context as well. As I have noted, few regulations guide how forbearance happens. However, this is no oversight on the part of the state. I suggest that this is a purposeful ambiguity in a system that grows out of a need and desire not only to involve victims' families, but also to make the process emotional and sentimental because it is an important component of the faith, of healing, and of reconstituting a virtuous self-identity—both for victim and offender. Interestingly, the gendered affectations the system produces place the sincere forbearance of the victim's mother in concordance with the authentic grief coming from that of the perpetrator.

The ambiguity in the law, moreover, permits tailoring the world of possibilities to the various situations that individuals encounter. There is no denying that in this system, as in all tort law, we see resonances of a customary system of punishment. We might consider how and if this exploration of sentiment in the criminal sanctioning system of post-revolutionary Iran reproduces customary practices. Muslim forbearance in that context was a form of justice derived from the *shari'a* that aimed to bring an end to local revenge practices. These practices, mediated and bureaucratized by state actors, reproduce and repurpose these practices in novel forms that afford new possibilities for ethical practices.

6

Mediating Mercy

THE AFFECTIVE LIFEWORLDS
OF FORGIVENESS ACTIVISTS

The sons of Adam are limbs of each other,
Having been created of one essence.
When the calamity of time affects one limb
The other limbs cannot remain at rest.
If thou hast no sympathy for the troubles of others,
Thou art unworthy to be called by the name of a Human.

SA'DI SHIRAZI, *GOLESTAN*, CHAPTER 1, STORY 10 (1258)
(TRANSLATED BY RICHARD FRANCIS BURTON)

WHEN THEY SAW us coming, they closed the gate to their house. From behind it, they yelled at us to leave. But we kept talking to them from the other side of the door. Mahboubeh, the social worker I was with, kept repeating that she just wanted to talk. The response came, "Leave us alone." I knew that she wanted to make a connection, after all the distance we'd covered to get there. She asked that they give us a few moments—just to hear what we came to say. Again, they refused. Someone shouted, "We don't want to hear what you have to say." Another voice pleaded, "Go away, please." But we didn't. We stayed and Mahboubeh spoke softly, tenderly. She was respectful and remained calm as she again implored them to open the gate. Then, as if conceding something, Mahboubeh said, almost playfully, "Could you open, just a little bit, to let me see your beautiful face?" She talked like that, through good-natured teasing.

Finally, after about a quarter of an hour of such entreaties to the family of the deceased, the mother opened the door a crack. She didn't appear angry, just tired. Mahboubeh extended her arm through the doorway and placed her hand on the mother's shoulder. She smiled warmly. Her large black eyes took in the grieving mother's unhappy demeanour. Mahboubeh, then holding the mother's gaze in hers, told her that we weren't there to bother her, that we had come only to express our sadness at her loss, and to extend our condolences. The mother looked down and whispered, "Okay, come in," and opened the door more widely than her words had conveyed, and led us down the small path to her home. She invited us into her sitting room and offered tea as we exchanged pleasantries. Mahboubeh explained that she worked alone, did not represent any party, and had no stake in the case or its outcome. She said, as a social worker, her main concern was with the victim's family, to see how they were coping. She asked after the youngest son, who had been close to his brother, the deceased, and had experienced a breakdown after the tragedy. She asked if the mother needed anything, how she could help them.

That day in the summer of 2014, I had travelled with Mahboubeh to visit a family who had lost a loved one in a homicide some months earlier. I observed how she approached families of victims, grieving over the death of a close relative, usually a child or spouse. Mahboubeh would sit with them for hours, cry with them, and tell them her own story of forgiving, even at the cost of reopening the wounds of her brother's death. She would tell them that it would get better, but only if they could let go. "To give *reziat* [consent] is a letting go and, in so doing, you gain something, too," Mahboubeh told them, "peace." In this context, 'letting go' was not only relinquishing the right of retribution, but also an act through which the victims were giving themselves permission to renounce their pain and sorrow. For this reason, Mahboubeh acknowledged, the forgiveness work in which she engages takes years before achieving its goal of forbearance because, in order to forgo retribution, victims' families must be able to put aside their anguish. In this sense, forgiveness work also involves cultivating a new affect and a new way of being. It is slow work that is generously nurtured by numerous social actors, such as Mahboubeh.

In this chapter, I trace the attempts of social workers and members of several nongovernmental organizations (NGOs) to persuade families of victims to forgive. I consider their strategies, the challenges they face, and the greater professionalization of their activities as skilled labor and expertise, both increasingly subject to internal best practices and managerial efficiency. Taken together, these progressively codified practices provide an aura of guidelines and serve as regulatory devices in this otherwise unconstrained social field. Through these practices, experts and expertise emerge among the cadres of social workers and other agents working towards forgiveness.

To be sure, the forgiveness work that I explore in these pages takes place through the state's legal apparatus and is part of its lawfare (Comaroff and Comaroff 2006). Its lawfare, moreover, extends to, includes, and implicates its citizens such that we can say that the state corrals and, in some ways, compels or imposes the social field. At the same time, social workers, like Mahboubeh, draw from a broad lexicon of cultural resources that include rituals, religion, rights, and reason to appeal to their subjects and to forge methods that amount to their own practice, one dedicated to cultivating that feeling of forgiveness. In doing so, these social actors evoke *Shiʻi* attributes that include sentiment and reason as well as local traditions that stress settlement and compromise. Such practices fill the absence of state regulatory mechanisms that are sometimes in place to direct competing parties towards conflict resolution.[1]

Rather than chiding state agents for their rights-based concerns or appealing to human rights discourses that hold little interest for aggrieved families, and indeed pose some risk for the social workers, these activists work through intersubjective, ethical dialogues based on mercy and compassion, which, in *Shiʻism*, are connected to the *maqasid* (higher principles) of justice in Islam. Although the circumstances in which they engage their activities are extraordinary, forgiveness workers like Mahboubeh, nonetheless, draw from disciplines of everyday life (Das 2012; Stewart 2007).[2]

A range of social workers, from pious religious actors to secular anti-death penalty activists, participate in cultivating these affective sociolegal spaces, or a lifeworld, for their ethical practices. Their forgiveness work becomes the site of ethical action through which they, too, fashion new ethical selves (Lambek 2010).[3] By referring to their activities as work, I emphasize the on-going labor entailed in achieving forbearance. Through productive social engagements, these agents draw attention to a metaphysical rapture that forbearance affords, both for themselves and for victims' families. Their engagement with a kind of social work that extends directly from the potentialities made possible through Iran's Islamic justice system also serves to underscore a commitment to Islam publicly, whether intentional or not (Deeb 2006). Social workers' myriad activities also bring attention to and even solidify the rationalization or increased corporatization of otherwise loosely organized local, spiritual, and/or ritual practices (Peletz 2016).[4]

Throughout this chapter, I am mindful that I am exploring my interlocutors' own ethical self-fashioning through the framework of a specific regime of punishment. As such, I am attentive to the idea that punishment entails a process of subjectivization (Butler 2014). In a review of Derrida's writings on the death penalty, Butler underscores Nietzsche's concern with the lack of equivalence between injury and punishment.[5] In retributive punishment, the offender, for having inflicted an injury, has incurred a debt and, from that position, a subject is formed, that of debtor. As Butler notes, guilt is the psychic modality through which the subject-position of the debtor is formed. The victim becomes a creditor whose psychic modality lies in reimbursement or payback. Thus, according to Nietzsche, Derrida, and Butler, retributive justice schemes produce creditor-subjects, the aims of which are not to be whole again, but to profit and punish debtor-subjects more joyfully for an indefinite period. In this chapter focusing on mediators, I consider the novelty of the forgiveness workers that Iran's criminal justice system produces and the subjectivization of those who engage in forgiveness work. Perhaps they are more or less reconcilers and, as such, their psychic modality is neither debtor nor creditor, but rather peacemaker. Ultimately, Iran's retributive justice system subjectivizes through these modalities, which are expressed by the different agents, victims and perpetrators, to be sure, but also, the mediators. Through their performativity, mediators convey discrete forms of corporeal expertise (Boyer 2005).[6]

In thinking about what it means to be working through the modality of the peacemaker, I suggest that activists and social workers strive to move both themselves and the targets of their advocacy (victims' families) away from "a regime of justice" and instead work to get them to see their decision through a "regime of peace" or "love" (Boltanski 2012).[7] Thus, in this chapter, I argue that forgiveness workers' endeavors are what Das refers to as "constitutive moral strivings" or an "adjacent self" (2010:377).[8]

Forgiveness workers engage in this kind of advocacy for their own reasons, conscious and sub-conscious alike perhaps, and their motivations are not unlike those of social workers in other parts of the world. When I asked, most, if not all, gave faith or their desire to improve the lot of those less fortunate as their primary motivations. Given the risks associated with forgiveness work, however, the question of motivation does bear some deeper investigation. If all one wanted was to feel better about the plight of humankind, surely, there are less perilous ways of pursuing it than risking verbal abuse or physical violence, as forgiveness workers often do. Forgiveness workers also risk having legal complaints filed against them for interference into a case or even for trespass. The labor that forgiveness work entails, moreover, is neither insignificant nor remunerated. In fact, Mahboubeh, like many forgiveness workers, engages in it at considerable economic and emotional cost.[9]

Thus, the question about motivations is not immaterial. Returning to Das's notion of moral striving, I consider how forgiveness work allows individuals like Mahboubeh to endeavour to constitute an idealized version of herself. What is significant in Das's attention to the ordinary in individual ethics is her discussion of love. The adjacent self, Das finds, comes into being through love, whose primary task is "embracing the reality of the other as one's own" (2010:397). Accordingly, by loving others, individuals come to realize their adjacent selves—or strive towards some idealized versions of themselves. Ultimately, Das proposes, it is in the "everyday labors of caring for others," that this moral striving comes into view.[10] Given Mahboubeh's own experiences with the system and ultimately having forgiven her brother's killer, she was well-placed to embrace the reality of other victims.[11] Thus, I found that in Mahboubeh's case, as for many social workers, forgiveness work was an opportunity to embrace the reality of others as their own and to strive for the idealized versions of themselves through the everyday labor of caring for and about others.

Cultivating a "Feeling of Forgiveness"

Having finished our tea, Mahboubeh and I got up to leave, with no firm commitment from the mother other than agreeing to see us again. That was just the opening that Mahboubeh had sought. Upon departing, Mahboubeh asked that the mother consider everything she said to her, to think about her health and that of her children, and to be mindful of the peace that forgiveness would bring them. She added that that she would stop by again in a month's time. She would also call and text in the meantime.

In the taxi back to her house, Mahboubeh explained her process, "I want them to think of the feeling that forgiveness brings, as opposed to how they will feel if they execute. The feeling of forgiveness brings *lezat* [joy] to one's life and it's something that only someone who does this great act [of forbearance] can understand. For now, just having her think about it is good; it's a softening." The softening, which Mahboubeh spoke of, reflected a psychic concern with healing as a process. Her work aimed to open the psyche to healing and constitutes part of the broader attempt at reconciliation or a "healing of the heart" (Sachedina 2001:111–12). Such meetings open up a space for the cultivation of another dimension of human relationships, that of empathy, "the intertwining of our lives with those of others" (Merleau-Ponty 1968:49).

Cultivating empathy or the "feeling with" of victims' families towards perpetrators is a key component of the process of bringing about the feeling of forgiveness and an important aspect of social workers' efforts. Social workers' attempts at building relationships with families of victims are part of a broader strategy of creating the conditions for empathy, which require a sustained dialogical engagement with the other. At its core, empathy is a "capacity to feel *with* and to participate in shared reflective engagement with the other's inner life" (Gobodo-Madikizela 2008:344, emphasis in original). For her part, Mahboubeh is conscious of building such relationships with the families she visits. Sometimes, however, the social and economic distance between Mahboubeh and the victim's family could make them distant others, even if geographically they were not. In such an instance, Mahboubeh explained to me how she forged a relationship over a period of years:

Usually it takes several attempts to have the first meeting, but, after that, as time passes, we become friends. They realize that I care about them. That's why it's important that they understand that I am not working for the perpetrator. I am working to help them work through their grief. I see if they need anything. Sometimes, if it's the husband who is killed, then [the widow] might need help with government agencies [to go after pensions]. I visit them if I learn of new information or for an important holiday, such as the anniversary of the death, and, of course, during Ashura or in the month of Ramadan.[12]

Mahboubeh builds relationships over time, gaining the family's trust through a series of meetings and telephone calls, not always on the subject of forbearance. She attends to their needs, both emotional and material, as best as she can, going to birthday parties, accompanying family members to the cemetery, or connecting them to doctors, psychologists, or even potential employers, as their needs require. This is the day-to-day work of changing the attitudes of victims' families, helping them to cultivate a different outlook, while giving time, as well, for grieving and expelling anger. This wider or more comprehensive engagement with the lives of victims' families forges the possibility of empathic repair, which, given her own experiences, is work she is uniquely qualified to undertake.

Through such forgiveness work, Mahboubeh cultivates a feeling in herself, as well, a kind of ethical care for the pain of others. She opens herself to an authentic feeling of caring for strangers, who possess power over another life. While these relationships often take years to forge and are very real, the strength of the bond, like most friendships, is not without limit or complication. In one case, as we were leaving the home of another mother whose forbearance Mahboubeh was trying to realize, the mother asked, "Would you still be my friend if I didn't consent to forbearance?" Mahboubeh smiled broadly while packing her things to leave. "I just know you aren't the type of person who would execute. You aren't that type. I'll call you soon," was all she said. After we left, I pressed Mahboubeh on the question. She hesitated, then gathered her thoughts before responding more fully, "I don't think I could. It would mean that she is such a different person from the one I see her to be now."

Such limitations notwithstanding, the work of cultivating a different outlook in the victim's family, this feeling of forgiveness, comprises an incipient expertise and has, over time, congealed into a professional operation. Forgiveness work has accumulated into discrete skills and corporeal performativity that include eloquence, empathy, and embodiment in ways that are specific to shared dimensions of Irano-*Shi'i* and Persian social and ritual practices. In the sections of this chapter, I explore these qualities, which work in tandem, but

FIGURE 4. Mahboubeh participating in a reconciliation and settlement meeting.
Used with permission.

which I disaggregate for illustrative purposes. Of course, as the specific practices are increasingly recognized as methods for cultivating a feeling of forgiveness, they come to serve as regulatory forces of forgiveness work. Thus, in the absence of legal guidelines, social workers, through patient praxis, develop their own best practices.

Forgiveness Strategies: Intersubjective Dialogue and the Expertise of Eloquence

"There was a young couple who had a lot of disputes from the beginning." We were sitting in a café near the center of town, as Mahboubeh told me about a case where the perpetrator was the brother-in-law of the deceased. (The deceased was married to the perpetrator's sister).

The wife usually called her brother when she had a fight with her husband because he was the family elder. He was also good friends with the husband

and had introduced him to his sister. The perpetrator said his sister had left an urgent message asking him to call. When he did, his sister picked up and said that her husband was saying "bad" things to her. Now she says she did not say this. The parents of the deceased also deny it. She says that her husband placed the call to her brother, and he came over to her house as a result.[13] He rang the doorbell, her husband hid in kitchen, and her brother went inside.

The two men fought, and a gun went off. The husband was shot. They tried to take him to the hospital but, on the way, they got into a car accident. The husband died from loss of blood. At the time I heard this story, the defendant (her brother) had been in prison for four years. The father of the deceased said he was willing to forgive, but the mother wanted *qisas*.[14]

As I noted earlier, when a victim's family members are not in agreement, officials often delay the execution while family members, friends, neighbors, and social workers converge upon the victim's family in hopes of forging a settlement short of retribution. Mahboubeh recounted the contents of her first few meetings with the parents of the deceased, "This is what I told them:"

> *Qisas* is your right, but it is only a right, not an obligation. The plaintiff gets the right of *qisas*. But *gozasht* [forbearance] is the will of God; it is a mercy, and that is better. In mercy, you are not only absolving the perpetrator, but also yourself of having to punish. God has created a way for mediation and settlement. With this, God is saying to you, "Let me punish, so you can be free."

"Free of what?" I asked.

"Free of the anger and violence that accompanies the killing of another person," she replied. "People forget to take God's mediation into account; it's an opportunity to be relieved of having to make such an awful decision." She was referring to how difficult the decision to exercise or forgo retribution was for the victim's family to have to make. "The government tells victims' families that they must make the decision but then God offers to lift the weight of that decision from us."

I was able to see her convey this message when I accompanied her to visit the family. As the lone hold-out, the mother was still not satisfied with forgoing *qisas*. She repeated her grievance, "He took my son to the hospital too late," pointing out what she saw as an element of aggravation in the crime. The offender had shot her son, but he did not have to die. His death was caused by loss of blood due to lack of timely medical attention. Mahboubeh, however, did not rehearse the facts. After so many years of this kind of social work, she had learned that it was not productive to try to change the narrative of the death in the minds of the victim's family. Holding on to or even directing the narrative was partly what made them feel empowered. She was not going to bid for that power. Instead, she looked to the future. "Killing him will not bring back your son; it will not bring you peace. In forbearance, you are not giving up punishing; you are taking the decision to be magnanimous; this is what will bring you peace. Put your faith in God [to punish] and you will find ease and serenity." Then, Mahboubeh made her reference to the Qur'an (2:281) more explicit by reciting the verse in Arabic, then relating its meaning back to the mother.[15]

That day, Mahboubeh progressed further with the mother. Though she was still not ready to forgo her right, the mother said that she would not "insist on *qisas* because she did not want to be responsible for executing someone." However, in order to forgive him, she said, she "needed more time." We took her words as a good sign that served a procedural purpose. As plaintiffs, families of victims must petition to have a sentence carried out. We took this to mean that she would not petition, at least not any time soon.

As we got up to leave, the mother expressed a new frustration. "Why haven't they come?" she complained. She was offended that no one from the defendant's family had followed up to see how she was doing. Mahboubeh reminded her of how, just after the incident, they had gotten in touch to express their remorse and condolences. He was, after all, the brother of their daughter-in-law and had been a friend of their deceased son. Initially, the victim's family was so deeply hurt that they had blocked any communication. Mahboubeh presently assured the mother that they were staying away only to give her space. She told the mother that she would relay a message to them and promised her that they would drop by in a few days.

On the way home, Mahboubeh depicted the mother's current feelings as a beat in the rhythm of forbearance, noting, "She needs time to feel the calm that forgiveness brings." She continued,

> We are waiting for the feeling of forgiveness to come. To consent to forgo *qisas*, they have to arrive at it on their own. Those with whom I speak aren't always ready, but when they say, "Don't come because I don't want you to influence me," that tells me that they are open. In those cases, I try to enter into that small opening of sentiment that is available. It is sensitive work because that feeling could turn into anger, and we don't want to push these decisions too hard or too fast.

The interactions between Mahboubeh and the mother form an intersubjective dialogue in which Mahboubeh invokes specific elements of faith, both subtly and overtly, to arouse a feeling of forgiveness. The elements, including compassion and grace, draw attention to spiritual and metaphysical rewards.[16]

There are two important moves in this part of Mahboubeh's forgiveness work that I seek to underscore. First, Mahboubeh is empowering the mother. Due to the loss, the victim's family initially feels disempowered. The social worker strives to recharacterize what it means to be empowered in this context. As Mahboubeh noted, "It is not taking a life. Rather, her power lies in the fact that she is the decisionmaker." That power is the right to decide over life, and it is emphasized more so in leniency than in its full exercise.[17] In forgiveness, Mahboubeh is also underlining "redemption" for the mother who "reclaims [her] own life," by acknowledging she is not required to love, absolve, or even understand her adversaries (Jackson 2013:213). In forgiveness, she frees herself of the bonds of retribution, of being a creditor, one who must seek payback.

The second element of stirring the feeling of forgiveness that I highlight lies with the mother's concern with the perpetrator's family—why hadn't they come to see her? As we saw in Chapter 5, victims' families are *mazlum*, graceful sufferers, who, upon demanding to see the other side, suggest a softening in their position. In their subject-position as creditors, victims' families may shift from calling in the debt to forgiving the debtor of it. This is the softening that commonly suggests the victim's family has embarked on the path to forgiveness or at least is signaling a tempering of the desire for *qisas*.

About a year later, I followed up with Mahboubeh on the case. She said, "I still see her, but she has not yet decided." When she visited the mother, Mahboubeh told me, they would talk about their families and catch each other up on what had happened since their previous exchange. They discussed the mother's continued struggles with grief and missing her child. They also discussed forbearance but, increasingly, in a light, almost jocular fashion. Mahboubeh said, "I tell her jokes—'*Mordab be rood goft, "Che kardee ke zolalee?" Goft, "Gozashtam."*'" ['The bog said to the stream, "What have you done to be clear?" [The stream] replied, "I flowed [went forward/*gozasht kardam*]".'"][18] Her joke, a play on words, implied that the mother would find peace, purity, even cleansing, if she forgoes; but, if she didn't, her pain would remain, fester, and perhaps even intensify because she would be responsible for the death of another person. "If you *qisas*" (used as a verb here), she said, "then you will never find a release. You will always remain angry and heavy, like that bog."

I thought about how far Mahboubeh had come with the mother. She had gone from speaking gently from behind a closed door to directly confronting her about what she should do. By now Mahboubeh had gained the mother's trust. I marveled at how she could speak frankly of forbearance and its rewards, and even menace the mother with the severe psychological consequences of retribution. The goal, after all, was to help discharge embittering anger and cultivate compassion in order to spare the life of another. "Yes," Mahboubeh replied, "we are friends now. I can to talk with her more openly." Through her acts of friendship, mutual understanding and affection had emerged between the two women. As they did, Mahboubeh intensified her urgings. In observing these interactions over the years, one could easily forget that Mahboubeh had started out as a complete stranger to this mother, who had no reason or requirement to open the door to her, let alone speak with her about the grim, difficult, and deeply personal decision she had to make.

Mahboubeh's success in forging such connections was in large measure characterized by her speaking ability. She possessed an inviting, melodious voice and spoke with a rapid, poetic eloquence that allowed her to connect with the families of victims. She maintained their attention as she spoke breathlessly, reciting Qur'anic verses and Persian idioms as easily as she would punchy anecdotes about other families she had helped. She also spoke Azeri (a Turkic dialect) to foster intimacy through an ethnic or language-based affinity. Eloquence, an important and valued aesthetic feature of Iranians' interpersonal communications, confers status to speakers who possess it. In Iran, artful communicators successfully employ "language in conjunction with their knowledge of society and its dynamics," as Beeman has noted, "to negotiate and even transform an uncertain world with skill and grace" (1986:20). Mahboubeh's eloquence sets her apart from other social workers, who often stressed her distinct speaking ability through expressions like "Mahboubeh can talk." When we went to visit with families of victims, her lyrical voice, often behind a closed gate or an intercom, got her through the doors and eventually allowed her to try to change the world of possibility for the families of victims to whom she spoke.

As a result of her labors throughout the years, Mahboubeh has gained a certain renown. Her number is circulated among prison inmates from all over the country, calling her for help. Working on her own, apart from any official sponsor, government or NGO, moreover, gives her a more principled positionality. That is, by working independently, she avoids subjecting herself to distrust by government officials suspicious of political agitators working against the death penalty or the victims' families who think she is working for perpetrators. She is also often called upon by various groups, and even appeared on national television (once as the subject of a documentary) to discuss both her experiences of forgiving her brother's killer and her subsequent forgiveness work.

In this cottage industry, forgiveness workers like Mahboubeh also cultivate spaces of ethical practice. Through her activities, Mahboubeh became a trusted friend and fellow-traveler to victims' families. In doing so, she engaged in ethical self-fashioning, as well, cultivating her persona as an ethical being in the world. In other words, Mahboubeh's encounters with victims' families also affected her.

Mahboubeh, like many others I met, got her start as a social worker with a clearly bounded view of anti-death penalty activity: working only with under-age offenders. As she explained it:

> When I first started this work, I only wanted to help juvenile offenders. I could not bear to work on behalf of a grown man who [had] killed someone and, sometimes, you know, they did such awful things. People like that, I thought, deserved to die. But since I have been doing this work, I don't know. I have changed. I see things so differently now. I don't think anyone deserves to die. How could I tell one person that she should not kill, even if she lost someone, because killing is not worthy of her and yet, then say that it's okay for someone else?

Thus, inasmuch as these practices are dedicated to cultivating a feeling of forgiveness in families of victims and they define the parameters of this cottage industry, I contend that they also change the forgiveness workers themselves. When I met her in 2010, Mahboubeh was working as an independent social worker. She possessed a unique charisma that, alongside her position as a next-of-kin who forgave retribution, helped her emerge as something of a person-age among forgiveness workers. Having achieved a measure of local celebrity when she forgave her brother's killer, Mahboubeh realized that she had a spe-cial influence on the subject of forbearance. Over the years, Mahbubeh devel-oped her own distinct strategies for her forgiveness work based on families' social, class, religious affiliation, and degree of piety, as well as geographic loca-tion or even profession. She was also acutely aware of how cases came to be politicized through any number of issues and avoided actions that she thought would jeopardize a person's life. As a measure of her own credibility, she was also wary of her persona or her work being exploited for political purposes, even if she, like any other person, appreciated the acknowledgement, both public and private, that she received for her good work. Despite coming to see her work as a kind of profession, she was never paid and, only on some occa-sions where she had to travel long distances, would donors or the family of the perpetrator pay for her transportation and lodging. Because she wanted to maintain the appearance of impartiality, she did not associate with families of perpetrators, even if they were often the first ones to call about a case. These strategies, accompanied by extensive knowledge of the Qur'an and her own humble economic background, gave her credibility and relatability in the eyes of the victims' families she encountered.

Over the years, Mahboubeh's ethical persona became inextricably linked to her own high-mindedness and that which she successfully encouraged in others. She appealed to the *ensaniat* (humanity) of her subjects and advised them that, in their decision, their very essence as humans was at risk—"You will become angry, irascible, and unhappy" or "How will you live your life as a person who committed such violence?"[19] She, like others I encountered, focused on an idea of humanity, both for herself and the families with whom she worked. This focus on humanitarian care, as I term it, distinguished from other approaches that call for attention to individual rights or rights-based discourses, is significant. In the next section, we see the significance of this distinction in the practices of a local NGO that focuses on protecting youth in all areas of life, including sparing juvenile offenders convicted of homicide from the death penalty. Indeed, it was here that I first encountered Mahboubeh, after she gave a speech about her forgiveness work. In exploring the strategies of the NGO, I seek to shine a light on this other dimension of the social field of forgiveness work—that of humanitarian care.

Humanitarian Cares: Forbearance as a Right

"At first they threw stones to keep us from approaching them, but eventually we reached them with appeals to their humanity," Leila recounted.[20] At the time she was a social worker at the Society for Protecting the Rights of the Child (SPRC), a Tehran-based NGO. Leila was describing her attempts to talk to a bereaved family that had lost a loved one through a homicide.

The strategies that SPRC employed were not unlike those of an independent social worker such as Mahboubeh. At the time I saw their tactics as part of a broader overall goal to support youth. And both social workers had initially expressed the limits of their work–to seek only that perpetrators who committed their offenses when they were under the age of eighteen be spared the death penalty. In the SPRC's case, social workers operated within the narrow mandate of supporting Iran's conformity with the Convention on the Rights of the Child (CRC). For that reason, SPRC social workers focused on juveniles in all aspects of their work. For many activists and social workers, however, advocacy for youth within the definition of the convention was just a starting point.

In the politicized context in which Western human rights defenders may be seen as challenging principles grounded in Iranian laws, activists highlighted forbearance as grounded in scriptures and indigenous cultural practices, thus moving away from a discourse of rights towards one that emphasized *ensaniat*.

As Samira, an attorney at the SPRC, told me in November 2007:

> We cannot explicitly talk about ending the death penalty. This is why the CRC has proven useful. We start with juvenile defendants and refer to Iran's own normative legal structure. Its ratification of the CRC is part of this.

Iran's 1994 ratification of the CRC first had to be approved by the Council of Guardians, the governmental body that vets laws for their conformity with Islamic principles.[21] The CRC required Iran to license the operation of organizations to support underage defendants in death penalty cases. Among those receiving approval was the SPRC, which also came into being in 1994. The main goals of the SPRC are to publicize and promote the principles of the CRC by introducing them to the Iranian public while also seeking to improve "the living conditions and the physical, mental, emotional and social growth" of children.[22] The organization operates primarily in three fields of advocacy for children: legislation, enforcement, and social work, and sponsors many activities to foster children's rights.[23] In this section I focus on its advocacy related to protecting juvenile offenders from the death penalty.[24]

As Leila described her advocacy work with the organization whose very title employs the word "rights," she avoided using rights-based language, especially in explaining her approach to speaking with victims' families. When I asked her about this, she reflected on the notion of rights, noting that grieving families are thinking about their own right of retribution. "They are not thinking about the rights the defendant may have." If she started talking about rights in a purely legalistic way, Leila observed, it appeared "to distance the issue at hand." I asked her what she meant by that. In responding, Leila described an approach that focused on the human condition:

> When we talk about rights, we are referencing individuals, but it seems to take them out of the context of their social lives, their problems, and what led to the incident. If we talk instead about how the mother of the victim lost a child and, if she pursues retaliation, that there will be another mother who loses a child, we address the humanity of the other person. For us, this seems to be more persuasive because it shows that this mother has something in common with that other mother.

Leila's description of her efforts at advocacy fit well with SPRC's overall emphasis on the broad goals of child welfare. Her strategy for this advocacy, however, drew from an approach that centered on the human connection between victims' and defendants' mothers and sought to touch upon a specific emotion—a mother's sympathy for another mother. Crucially, such an appeal to human connection and emotion offered more than strategic value.

Social workers and legal practitioners employ the Islamic mandate of forgiveness to address sensitive social and economic problems such as child abuse, abuse in the form of prostitution, domestic and gender-based violence, as well as a range of other social maladies that are difficult to raise in public settings. In cases of this sort, social activists and local leaders use local restorative justice traditions. They are part of a wider trend aimed at reducing over-criminalisation and working towards reconciliation (Gholami 2006). Such alternatives could include informal mediation and negotiating for discretionary remedies, such as financial reparations. Mediators draw from Islamic principles and local customs. In doing so, the language of mediators is laced with "socio-syntax" or common speech variations employed to achieve social ends, such as living peaceably with one another (Beeman 1986:199).

One such linguistic practice is *kutah amadan* (stopping short or acquiescence), a device that mediators use to lessen the heightening volatility of a conflict.[25] In the cases I studied, social workers or mediators used the phrase to ask families of victims to stop short of exercising their right of forbearance. For example, a mediator from the city of Shiraz expressed what might be called a "mixed methods" approach of drawing from principles in Islam, regional or local mechanisms for dispute resolution, and an overall admonition to his interlocutors to stop short. The man, Mr. Saheb, dubbed by many who know him as "the man of forgiveness" due to his successes in getting victims' families to forgo retribution, travels all over the country to obtain families' willingness to forgo retribution.[26] He used the phrase *kutah amadan* in describing how he spoke to a family in a small village in the north of the country, "I told them, 'You could end this conflict forever by stopping short [*ba kutah amadan*]. But if you *qisas*, then they [the offender's family] will always be angry and neither of you will find peace.'"

As a speech mechanism to draw down conflict, *kutah amadan* works best between individuals who are acquainted or who have regular interactions. *Kutah amadan* appeals to an earthly or neighbourly peace, as opposed to the spiritual peace that Mahboubeh earlier invoked when referring to the peace of mind the mother would feel by forgoing retributive sanctioning. The call to *kutah amadan* also signals power in a status relationship by simultaneously confirming and entreating those who hold power in conflict situations.

As with Mahboubeh, gaining access to the families of victims was one of the most difficult aspects of Leila's work. After some time had passed, however, and often after several attempts, she would succeed in meeting with them. "At the beginning, they are too hot," she explained. "So, we have to wait until they have had a chance to grieve." Like others, Leila emphasized grief as a corporeal passion, boiling just beneath the surface of outward pain, a rage in need of an outlet.[27] If this anguish could be expelled and time permitted the hatred to diminish, then the grief-stricken could arrive at a point of clarity. "I want to be an outlet for them. I try to find ways to allow them to expel the heat so that execution does not become their sole means of doing so. And this is what I tell them: 'All I ask is that your decision is made after the anger has passed.' It's also then that they can hear me."

Leila said that once she did meet with the families, she, too, confirmed their right of retribution by the law, but stressed that forgiveness was God's will—"The peacemakers forgive and leave the rest to the judgment of God." She continued, "I tell them that they can be merciful; this is what God asks of you. And being merciful will bring about peace." She observed, "This peace is not just a peace to bring about reconciliation between parties, but peace in the heart of the individuals themselves." Leila's comments resonate with Griswold's consideration of forgiveness as the elimination of revenge (2007). Even while traces of resentment may still be present, they do not prevent an act of forbearance.

Leila pointed out, moreover, that moving away from a rights discourse was necessary because the right at the center of concern, that of retribution, was also that of the victim's family. As I noted earlier, that right produces a debt on the part of the perpetrator, making the victims' families creditors intent upon extracting payback. In other words, the right of retribution preserved by the state was one side of a dialectic, or a sociolegal call and response; it legitimated an expectation of payback.[28] As Leila saw it, her role was to diffuse the expectation of payback on the part of the victims and guide the victim's family towards a different possibility or way of thinking about their right. She did so by attending to their humanity. In forbearance, she found, she could cultivate a sense of the victims' own humanity. Thus, forbearance was not just a giving up of something, but also an affirmative exercise of a right, one focused on rehabilitating both the victim and perpetrator's humanity.

Considering the kinds of appeals social workers made to victims' families—to forgo the very right that the law gave them as a measure of empowerment in the face of loss—it was hardly surprising that social workers such as Leila, who worked for an organization intent on rights-based advocacy, still approached this part of their work through humanitarian appeals by cultivating feelings of kindness and compassion. The aim of cultivating personal peace in aggrieved victims was a tack that social workers had in common, and they drew from a diverse range of tools to engage the families of victims in their work—from pleas to humanism, folkloric traditions, and faith.

Moreover, in presenting this expertise, social workers not only employ cultural references verbally, but their work is also a performative experience embodied through a physical cultivation of virtuous moral agency, sometimes through referents of *Shi'i* piety well-known to their audiences. Social workers, like Mahboubeh and Leila, radiate an embodied expertise through their physical movements. This embodied activism is evident in the way social workers speak and move, as their words recount significant tropes of virtue and their movements embody both piety and sagacity. In the next section, I will examine a third aspect of forgiveness work as embodied expertise through an investigation of the performative encounters of another organization, one which draws from stories from the Qur'an and the Sunnah, but especially, from the figure and personification of Imam 'Ali. The embodiment of this most righteous of *Shi'i* figures indexes moral agency, not only through physical or verbal exhortations on forgiveness and care, as we have seen, but also draws from a rich citational lexicon of pious figures worthy of emulation.

Performing Relief: Embodying Activism

My first occasion to observe the citational performativity that came to be an important brand of forgiveness work occurred while I was attending a reconciliation performance—there can be no other word for it—by Sharmin Meymandi Nejad, the founder of a well-known relief organization, *Jameat-e Emdad Daneshjooyee—Mardoomee Imam 'Ali* (Imam 'Ali's Popular Students Relief Society [*sic*]). The Society's work was modeled on the virtuous qualities of their eponymous namesake, Imam 'Ali.[29] Sharmin Meymandi Nejad had established the Society with his wife, managing director Zahra Rahimi, some fifteen years earlier when they decided to do something about the manifold difficulties faced by the impoverished children in Iran.[30] The work, both relief-oriented and modeled on *Shi'i* Islam's most revered figure, had attracted much positive attention throughout the country and drew scores of volunteers and contributions.[31]

In mid-July 2014, social workers invited me to attend a mourning service held by the Society's student volunteers and hosted by Sharmin. The event commemorated the seventh anniversary of the death of Dr. Morteza Sarbandi. Reyhaneh Jabbari was convicted of his intentional murder and sentenced to *qisas* in 2007. The case, highly publicized and controversial, both for the criminal process that led to the issuance of the *qisas* sentence and for the defendant's claim of self-defense from imminent sexual assault, had deeply embittered the victim's family, the very people who were now being asked to forgo their right of retribution. The Sarbandi family, pious and resolute, had remained quietly unmoved during years of attempts at persuasion by lawyers, social workers, and other advocates, but had agreed to the ceremony and were rumored to attend. The service was held at the cemetery *Behesht-e Zahra* (Zahra's Paradise), on the outer edge of Tehran, where the deceased was buried. To honor the Sarbandi family, the perpetrator's parents attended as well.[32]

Beyond his oratory gift for importuning forgiveness and his organization's efforts at providing humanitarian care for vulnerable populations, Sharmin's performativity stands out for drawing from a corpus of known rituals, serving as a citational index from which he communicates to his audiences (Butler 1993; Derrida 1988).[33] By referencing commonly shared stories, Sharmin evokes the affective qualities that the rituals exude and elicits emotions intended to dissipate anger and arouse compassion.

Amidst the pine, willow, and box trees that surrounded the Sarbandi family plot, some fifty or so of the Society's student volunteers had prepared a program for the occasion and distributed it to the attendees as we entered. Those present included social workers, activists, and journalists covering the event for papers. The volunteers had prepared roles for orphans and other vulnerable children that the Society supports. Among the volunteers were several young women who had been rescued from prostitution and, with the assistance of the Society, lived free from social ills. One woman's arrival drew attention for her face, which was visibly marred from an acid attack. She had forgiven her assailant, a social worker whispered in my ear.

The proceedings began after the honored guest, Jalal Sarbandi, the son of the deceased, pulled up in his white SUV. He was the only member of the victim's family to attend. I asked my friend if that was a bad omen. "Not really. He's an important decision-maker in the family." Among social workers, there was often speculation about the internal workings of the victims' families: which family members were the decision-makers; which held power to sway others; which would be amenable to meeting social workers, and what their beliefs were. The now-deceased Sarbandi was a doctor, but he also had connections to the government, having worked some years in the Interior Ministry. While rumors about links to the deep state swirled, nothing was known for certain except that the family was devout. Sharmin had tried to make a connection with the family by befriending Jalal.

As spectators fidgeted in the late afternoon heat, a faint breeze blew out of the trees, reminding everyone that the sun was close to setting and relief was within sight. Our eyes shifted to crackling speakers; their crunching sounds soon transformed into a permeating religious invocation that signaled the opening ceremony. Then a young man stood and recited a prayer for the deceased. Finally, Sharmin, tall and slender, rose from his center front-row seat and welcomed the attendees. Dressed in muted tones of navy and brown, his attire evoked a somber contrast to Jalal's white dress shirt and sky-blue blazer. Jalal stroked prayer beads between his fingers and thumb as Sharmin picked up the microphone and held it up to his mouth with both hands. He stood on the flat rectangular gravestone, which was now the set and stage for the event.

Sharmin commenced the program with the simple invocation that inaugurated almost every gathering—"In the name of God, the Merciful, the Compassionate"—then, added less audibly, "Grant us forgiveness." Sharmin looked at the crowd around him. Spectators had filled the dozen or so rows of seats, while others stood amidst the foliage. Thoughtful and circumspect, he began, "The story of Man is a very sad one," and he started to narrate the story, also referenced in the Qur'an, relating the first murder, when Cain killed Abel.[34] As Sharmin recounted the brothers' final moments, he cited Abel's words to Cain as: "You did this to me, but I won't do this to you." Then, peering intently at his audience, Sharmin said, "It is from here that our story begins." The story of Cain and Abel, situated just thirteen verses before those which define and characterize the codified law of retribution (5:45), is telling. It is precisely this Biblical story, of a brother killing a brother, that gives context to the prescription for exact justice alongside the compulsion of forbearance.

Sharmin turned his gaze to the gravestone beneath his feet. "I found a connection with this man who is lying here . . . of love and kindness. *Een mard-e paak* [This pure man]." Then, raising his voice, he shouted, "This pure man!" To the audience, the phrase would signify more than moral virtue. Rather, the locutionary phrase summoned the image of the most righteous of all men— Imam 'Ali. He whose death was both untimely and consequential. With those words, Sharmin referenced the injustice of Sarbandi's death and his uprightness, signaling towards a public rehabilitation of his character. Yet, Sharmin also asserted that it was God's will to punish the assailant in the hereafter. In the momentary silence that followed, Sharmin lowered himself to his knees, transferred the microphone to one hand, and he gently stroked the marble gravestone with the other. He looked at Jalal, seated in the first row, and said, "The first time I saw Jalal, when I placed my hand on his knee, I saw the light. I had a beautiful feeling." Sharmin, still on his knees, looked out to the crowd and pleaded, "But I don't see Cain here." His eyes welled up, his voice cracked, and he stammered through tears, "God Damn the Devil who brought so much pain to these two families!"

Continuing with the theme of purity, Sharmin asked, "With all this dirtiness, can it be that a miracle of love can come?" He stood, looked up from the grave and out to the audience, "This man of God who gave me so much strength. I want today, the anniversary of the death of this virtuous man, to be the day of forgiveness. The day of Abel, as opposed to Cain. I don't want my hands to be empty between these families. We have come together three times now." Then Sharmin studied the gravestone and spoke directly to the deceased, calling him by his first name, "Morteza dear, let today be the day of forgiveness, not today per se, but it's the start that, God willing, we move in the direction of love. I wanted today to be the day of forgiveness. I wanted Reyhaneh to know today that she would be freed. But no, it's the day of the start of forgiveness . . ."

A gentle movement from the front disrupted the flow of Sharmin's address. Jalal stood up and took a place beside Sharmin. He removed the microphone from Sharmin's hand and took it into his own. At that point, Sharmin gestured towards Reyhaneh's father, Fereydoun Jabbari, and motioned for him to come forward. As Jalal began to speak, Sharmin brought his arms around the

FIGURE 5. Image of the ceremony—Sharmin (center), Fereydoun Jabbari (left), Jalal Sarbandi (right). Photo credit: Imam 'Ali Students Society.

shoulders of each man and pulled them in, effectively pushing them closer to one another.

Jalal, however, cut through the drama, speaking in a deep tranquil voice, as one in possession of the true righteous credit:

> I thank everyone for being here and for all the troubles the Society has gone to. Because there are reporters here, I want to be clear. We, like all humans, would not like *qisas* and wish to experience the joy of forgiveness. But there is one point I would like to make: We just want the truth. We only want to know what happened. A human can only forgive if he feels the other's sense of sorrow or regret. Until now, we thought we could let the law do its work, but this has not happened. If there is repentance or regret, or if there was a mistake made, we would like to know. We have never made a promise of forgiveness. We have always said, "If we move in the right direction, God will help with forgiveness." It was never planned that today would be the day of forgiveness. So, there is no announcement of forgiveness today. We are all going towards God.

Upon hearing this statement, those in attendance had received their answer. There was to be no forgiveness that day. Jalal, having minced no words, exited the scene, climbed into his car, and drove off.

Sharmin's oratory style suggested an ease with performance. His evocations of love, purity, and God's mercy were attempts at placating Jalal's creditor-subject position, and soothing, dislodging, and, to some extent, perhaps, paying back the debt on Reyhaneh's behalf. Sharmin's tone, while subtle, evinced an effort to rehabilitate the lost honor of the deceased.

Jalal's response, however, showed the difficulties in strategizing such cases, and cued up the disagreements and disputes between social workers and advocates over their efforts at advocacy. This case also shows how the legal tactics that lawyers employ prior to the issuance of the verdict can compromise the defendant's ability to seek forbearance after. As with the earlier case of the young women who killed their father (Chapter 3), here, the legal strategy the lawyers had pursued was one that positioned the defendant, Reyhaneh, not as a perpetrator, but as a victim of sexual violence. Indeed, they claimed that Reyhaneh was asserting her right of self-defense to protect herself, and her (family's) honor, from violation.

This legal strategy had the effect of confirming the defendant's story, giving her the authority to determine the narrative that would shape the parties' reputations. In this case, however, the nature of that defense, protecting herself against sexual assault, would forever compromise the defendant's ability to seek forgiveness. For, if the family were to forgo retribution, it would lead to the suggestion that they had accepted the defendant's claims about their father. Unlike in the previous case, it is worth mentioning, the parties here had no connections, familial or otherwise, that would lean on their emotions.

In this exchange, we also gain insight into the discord between rights-based advocacy and humanitarian sentiment.[35] This tension comes into painful relief when magnified through the self-defense strategy in murder cases litigated in the Iranian justice system. To cultivate a feeling of forgiveness, social workers attempt to evoke the victim-creditors' sympathies. They require a showing of self-deprecation and effacement on the part of the perpetrator-debtor. The self-defense strategy is predicated on just the opposite—a claim of right, effected through self-awareness, outspokenness, and righteousness—said differently, a liberal rights-bearing subject-position. It was precisely the latter, in Reyhaneh's case, that added to the complexity of her situation. Her adamant assertion that she was acting to save herself from certain violence and despoilment was an appropriate defense in the courtroom. But, once her defense was rejected, she was left with the need for mercy from the victim's family. After the verdict, her defense strategy remained and appeared to undermine her chances of securing a reprieve that was wholly dependent on the forbearance of the victim's family. Victim-creditors frequently evaluate whether the perpetrator-debtor deserves mercy by assessing the latter's remorse and suffering.[36] Reyhaneh, both in the substance of her self-defense claim and in her resolute assertion of it, seemed to elude such sympathies from among the victim's family. Reyhaneh's demeanor, her forthrightness, and even her height—since she was tall—seemed to contribute to her seemingly anomic character.[37] Such strategies possess potentially adverse temporal elements, as well. As the earlier chapters showed, the appeal to mercy can arrive at any moment. In most cases, such appeals do not arise until the judges issue a verdict, in which case the defense may weaken the later appeals for mercy.[38]

In his performance, Sharmin seemed to be aware of this conflict—between Reyhaneh's righteous self-defense and her post-verdict need for forbearance— and attuned to the damage that the self-defense claim had done to her chances for mercy. Accordingly, Sharmin played the role of humble self-effacer, while also attempting to rectify the reputation of the deceased. Jalal, however, appeared not to accept Sharmin's narrative. In response, he reiterated a different claim—that Reyhaneh had not expressed sufficient remorse and had maintained her assertions. As long as she declared her actions were in self-defense, it seemed, she would not be able to satisfy the Sarbandi family.

Despite Jalal's departure, the students from the Society soldiered on. The ceremony continued as a group of girls, orphans living under the Society's guidance, dressed in matching green shifts with white blouses, began a dance over the gravestone. Slowly the crowd dissipated, even as the students strove to complete the remaining activities in their program. Little by little, attendees rose from their chairs and passed on pleasantries with acquaintances they had come to know from other such gatherings. One social worker chided a young man, Safar, who had just been released from prison, having received the forbearance of his victim's family. "You know how hard everyone worked to get you out? How much your family suffered; how much your mother cried? Now, you need to find work. You understand?"

"Yes," he replied, smiling at the admonishments.

"And you need to put away the knife. Don't carry the knife around with you."

"It's just for my protection."

Turning to me, she said, "He's right. Where he's from, they all carry them, but it's the source of his problems, too." Turning back to the young man, "I know it's hard to find work that pays and to move on, but you owe it to your family and all of us."

The young man gestured with his hands, "I know, I know. I have found work." He described an apprenticeship at an auto mechanic's shop that social workers had helped him secure.

"Good. I only want to hear good news about you from now on."

As the fading sun cast a shadow on the early evening light, organizers came around like sheepherders trying to gather-in the attendees. There was to be a reading from the Qur'an, they instructed, while handing out copies of the verses. "If everyone could just take their seats."

Sharmin's method of emulating the work of Imam 'Ali, his knowledge of scripture, alongside a background in the performing arts, gave him a unique approach that was often effective for the persuasive impact that forbearance requires, but is sometimes met with suspicion as well. Of the qualities that distinguish Sharmin from others who engage in forgiveness work is the way he embodies his intellectual knowledge of the scriptures and the Sunnah in a pious performativity. That knowledge, alongside his background in performance, converges into a modern form of *Shi'i*-inflected social justice activism and separates him from secular anti-death penalty activists. Through his leadership, the Society aims to emulate the works of Imam 'Ali, who focused on helping the vulnerable, especially women and children. In his performativity, Sharmin ultimately brings together eloquence, care, and an embodiment of piety to make his relief organization one of the few that transcends secular or religious dogmatism. As such, the Society's successes both in culture-building and sparing individuals from the death penalty bears deeper examination.

Stirring Faith in Forgiveness: Imam 'Ali's Popular Students Relief Society

Fereydoun Jabbari picked me up at my apartment in central Tehran. I climbed into the car, a four-door, Iran-assembled Peugeot, its air conditioner blasting. The beige interior, the cigarette butts, and the rearview mirror charms, reminded me of a different era. It was late July 2014 and Jabbari's daughter, Reyhaneh, was still alive. She was still incarcerated, but he thought her case was coming to a close. During the drive, Jabbari explained why he was hopeful that she would be spared. She had so many supporters and was so well-liked. Even inside the prison, the female attendants were advocating that she be spared. They wouldn't execute her, not after eight years, he thought. If they were going to do it, he surmised, they'd have done it by now. Reyhaneh had become friends with many of the inmates, including Sahar Mohabadi, her cellmate, on whose behalf we were now heading to a reconciliation meeting. Just then, Jabbari's phone rang. He glanced down at the screen and took the call. It was Reyhaneh, phoning from prison. He put her on speaker and her voice, strong yet melodious, came through clearly. She gave her father two telephone numbers. He pulled over to jot them down. As Reyhaneh described it, these were the numbers of two women just being released from prison. He was to help them in any way they needed—in finding them a place to live, clothes, even work—anything to help them get settled. The call was short, as calls from prison have to be. He hung up and smiled broadly, "This is my life now." It was a better time.

Reyhaneh's call, like others she'd made before, would start a chain reaction of efficacious involvements between her parents, her lawyers, social activists, and their respective networks and relations. Lives like hers, hanging in the balance, brought together disparate characters and intertwined their lives. They came together around a single cause—sparing a life—while launching divergent and sometimes competing practices, visions, and strategies for how to do that. His daughter's lawyer, Mohammad Ali Jedari Foroughi, who was also Sahar's lawyer—another Reyhaneh connection—had put me in touch with Jabbari.[39] Foroughi, who would not attend, had said to me, "See how others work," referring to the different tactics within the larger forgiveness work cottage industry and arranged for me to accompany Jabbari to a reconciliation meeting between social workers and the family of the man Sahar had killed. Since Sahar had killed her husband, the reconciliation meeting would be with her in-laws, specifically her mother-in-law.

As we drove through the thicket of Tehran's traffic, night fell and, with it, the *azaan* sounded throughout the city. The final days of Ramadan were upon us and in the heat of the long July days, the call to prayer, signaling the setting of the sun, offered a welcome reprieve. After almost two hours of navigating endless circuits of cars, buses, and motorcycles, not to mention pedestrians eager to reach the *iftar* meals that awaited them, we arrived in Varamin, a town located south of Tehran. I learned that our first stop would be inside a small house, where males and females in separate rooms were praying and breaking fast. In the kitchen, the student volunteers of Imam 'Ali's Popular Students Relief Society [*sic*] were at work dividing flour, rice, meat, and other basic provisions into individual sacks. I found a seat next to a young woman who explained what they were up to on those last days of Ramadan. "We distribute food in keeping with 'Ali's directives on orphans and the poor." "*Kuchegardan-e Asheq* [*lit.* Loving Alley-Strollers] is modeled on the life of Imam 'Ali."[40] After packing the sacks, the volunteers would then walk around the neighborhood and deliver them throughout the night to families in need.[41] "There is a story: 'Ali goes to give condolences to the family of a deceased soldier who had died under his command. They don't know it's him. 'Ali arrives; he consoles them, he cries with them, he feeds the children with his own hands, and begs them to forgive 'Ali. Then he tells them that he is 'Ali." This well-known story, *The Unknown*, is passed on in numerous settings, recounted in religious ceremonies, books, and now through electronic resources. The story's allure lies in its vivid depiction of 'Ali's ubiquitous humanity, with the core of his being defined through acts of humility and generosity.[42]

"There are these stories of 'Ali's kindness, service, and his own forgiveness. We reenact these stories in our work," said Sharmin, who had entered the room. He sat on the floor among us, legs crossed, leaning in to speak softly, while others prayed. Sharmin explained that the *Kuchegardan-e Asheq* was a contemporary application of Imam 'Ali's good works, adding, "These rituals are important, especially to traditional families." Even as he spoke to me, Sharmin looked out to the room of women and directed them in a prayer. He evoked the Qur'anic chapter on the *Tawhid* (meaning "Unity" or "Purity"). Espousing monotheism, the chapter consists of just four short verses. The lines comprise the declaration of God's indivisibility and inimitability, His absolute oneness and unity:

Say, "He, God, is One,
God, the Eternally Sufficient unto Himself.
He beget not; nor was He begotten.
And none is like unto Him." [43]

"Say it quietly to yourselves," Sharmin said in a whisper. "You will find sustenance."[44]

The connection to physical and spiritual nourishment is a key theme in the Society's social work, through which it seeks to provide that sustenance for the bereaved and vulnerable, alike, hoping to achieve both renewal and reprieve. The Society's often performative activities, especially those of its founding director, follow from and illustrate yet again forgiveness work conditioned by the state and embodied by specific actors.[45]

Sharmin's performance is also a discipline, an ethical self-fashioning that employs and interprets practices that his colleagues and audiences alike associate with piety. In doing so, his performances, as much as the physical surroundings, cultivate an affective environment of piety, strength, and nourishment for preparing the grounds for forgiveness.

The Society's Good Works

Over several meetings with the Society's social workers, I learned more about their aims, motivations, and principles. Different teams work around specific issues: capital punishment for juveniles, children who have committed serious crimes, ("we have six and seven-year-olds who have been accused of armed robbery"), child labor, addiction, illness, abuse, inability to pursue education, lack of birth certificate, mothers as heads of household, and children in need of organ transplants. "In each of these issues, we focus on prevention," explained Farzad, a social worker who managed the youth programs, as he highlighted the range of the Society's work. "There are children who may not have seen *mahabbat* [loving kindness]," he explained.[46] "That child has a sort of abhorrence towards society. These children need to be seen. No one has seen them. They need people to care about them and to give them attention." Farzad's comments implicitly referenced the Levinasian notion of seeing the face of the other. He was also speaking to the social workers' attempts to make people at the margins of society visible to the broader society, so that the lives of such individuals could be made the subject of social concern and humanitarian endeavors (Osanloo 2019). Through similar means, social workers acted to make the plight of such individuals visible to the state, so that they could be privy to the confluence of its social service regimes as well (Harris 2017).[47]

Beyond legibility, the student volunteers at the Society see themselves engaging in a societal shift, one in which they change the normative perceptions of the people they serve in much the same way as Sharmin did in his appeal for forbearance. The Society works in different contexts to rectify the image of the ne'er-do-well or delinquent as, if not innocent, at least as a product of social conditions in which the state and civil society, not just the individuals themselves, are implicated. As Farzad put it,

> We see women who become [private] surrogates [*notfeh keshee* (*lit.* sperm extraction)]. The woman might have a child; it's unclear how she got pregnant, and then sells it [the child] for anywhere between 30,000–3,000,000 *toman*, depending on her level of desperation.[48] The woman herself was likely abused, fled from home, and got addicted.
>
> One example is Kobra. She was twenty-two-years-old. She had four children, her first child at thirteen, then a second. She never saw them. They went to the Health Department. She had a third child and sold it to traffickers, and sold a fourth to a family. The Health Department returned her first two children; she sold them as well. These kids are called "illegitimate." She's too poor to keep them, and they become cheaper than puppies to sell. We found a family who will raise them, but the children have no birth certificates because families need a father to obtain a birth certificate.
>
> Eventually, these children will be abused; they'll end up in the streets, become slaves for drug gangs. We can say that she's a bad woman and do nothing for her or we can understand her circumstances and try to help.

Farzad's stories, confirmed and repeated by many of my interlocutors, were mobilized by social workers through the craft of storytelling to shed light on the harsh realities of the lives of perpetrators. Such individuals represent a borderland littered by the bodies-in-pain of women, children, and men pushed to society's margins by social and economic hardships they endured and could not escape. The stories, of the past, of 'Ali, and of individual perpetrators inform and shape each other as they are narrated over and again. The narratives circulated among my interlocutors, in the press, in social media, and in art and cultural productions, and ultimately increased the visibility of social suffering. The frequent repetition of such narratives also rendered some perpetrators icons of social suffering, much to the displeasure of victims' families. The larger aim of the circulation of such narrative accounts of individuals in need was to raise awareness of ethical obligations among members of society and to call upon them to act (Laqueur 2009). Diverse forms of storytelling by social activists, including theater, are now popular and used to garner the public's attention for serious and often taboo issues.

One such example of this storytelling was the theatrical production, *Intentionally, Amorously, Murderously*, which played to sold out audiences in the summer of 2015.[49] The play, which featured some of Iran's finest actresses, recounted the lives of three notorious women murderesses, condemned to death, and gave the context of each of their plights. The first was an impoverished female taxi driver who preyed on well-to-do elderly women. She offered her clients a barbiturate laced-tea that knocked them out. She then drove to a clandestine location where she strangled and robbed them. In the play's first-person account, the taxi driver spoke of the injustices throughout her life that led to her eventual execution. The second actress played the role of Shahla Jahed, one of Iran's most well-known and sympathetic condemned. Jahed, a nurse, was condemned for her involvement in the death of the wife of a famous soccer player, Nasser Mohammadkhani, with whom she had been having a secret relationship, albeit a lawful temporary marriage. Stories circulated that Jahed confessed to the crime a year after her arrest, though only after her lover went to see her and asked her to take responsibility. Rumors suggested that Mohammadkhani had convinced her that he would obtain the victim's family's forbearance if she confessed. Once Jahed saw that this would not happen, she repeatedly retracted her confession, but to no avail. Despite public criticisms of the trial and the alleged involvement of Mohammadkhani, Jahed was executed on December 1, 2010.[50]

Once too politicized even to mention, the topics of domestic violence, poverty, addiction, prostitution, trafficking, and sexual abuse were now discussed by society's caretakers: social workers, lawyers, even government officials, who referenced them through the growing list of names of the fallen: Kobra, Gholam-Reza, Shahla, or Soheila. Each name, a speech act citing an otherwise quieted social ailment too impertinent even to acknowledge, was now made legible by its repeated utterance. As illocutionary expressions, the names contain the painful cases that served as the catalysts for the Society's engagement with youth. Like bodies strewn on a bloodied war front, the names frame the boundaries of the Society's humanitarian concerns and forge its paths of strategic action. As Farzad continued, he explained the Society's motivations, as "catalysts" that forced them into action.

Catalysts: Vampire of the Night

We take in kids who come out of the Juvenile Correction and Rehabilitation Center. There, children turn into criminals because there is no education or investigation into their situation. They end up having lots of difficulties. For example, there is the case of Gholam-Reza Khoshroo. At six or seven-years-old, he fled his home; he was homeless, slept in the streets. He had no one to help him. He became a thief and went to the juvenile reform center a number of times. When he turned eighteen, they transferred him to the Big House. Sharmin went to see him and said, "I've come to help you." Khoshroo said, "You can't. You should have come fifteen years ago. Where were you when I was in the streets being raped? Today you come to me?"

At the age of twenty, Khoshroo was freed from prison, alone; no one was waiting for him. He got a car that he drove as a private taxi. Each night he picked up a woman, took her somewhere, where he raped then killed her. He burned the body, cut it into pieces, or left the corpse in the street. He became known as 'Khofash-e Shab,' [Vampire of the Night]. In total, he killed nine women.

Sharmin went to see him just before he was executed. Afterward, there was no one to take down his body from the scaffold. Sharmin said to him [his corpse], "From this moment on, you will rest in peace, but I will not." Khoshroo's death became the catalyst for his [Sharmin's] relief work, with a focus on children. Sharmin thought that if he could have helped Khoshroo as a child, he could have saved him. We don't like capital punishment at all, even in the case of Khoshroo, because we don't see him as responsible, but [rather as] someone who has seen so much pain and who society has hurt.

Farzad reiterated the Society's approach to capital punishment for juveniles. "We think it is inhumane." He elaborated his own position, "Personally, I am against the death penalty in any case." His ethical stance took account of the conditions that produced such an offender. "The person being executed is very important. Who is the defendant? Is he really the only person who is guilty? We see files of robberies, kidnappings, and rape. A harsh society exists out there and, in this kind of society, murder happens."

Offering an example of how harsh the social conditions could be, Farzad referenced another well-known case that had a role in shaping the Society's mission.

There was the case of Soheila, who took her five-day-old child to Department of Health and Welfare because she couldn't take care of it. They said that they couldn't take the child because he was illegitimate. Soheila walked outside and cut the baby into pieces right there, in front of the Health Department. She was in prison for seven years before she was executed. She would wash her hands one hundred times a day. Sharmin asked the question, "Who Is Soheila?" At fifteen she had fled her home, was homeless, and slept in a *carton* [cardboard box] in the cold. In return for refuge from the cold, she sold herself. She was raped and psychologically abused.

The point of Soheila's story was not just to demonstrate how harsh society could be; it also revealed the violence of indifference. For the Society, this indifference was consequential; they saw it as the causal link between the crimes people like Soheila commit and the failure of the state and society to protect the most vulnerable. "As a result of these injustices," Farzad reiterated, "we are against capital punishment. We are all responsible. The sinner is society at-large."

Such experiences led the Society to reach out to people living in the most precarious conditions and to create their trademark children's homes— *Khaneh-ye Irani* (Iranian House). "We went into the margins [of society] and created them." There are twenty-four such homes throughout Iran now, ten in Tehran, seven or eight in the outlying areas, and the rest in regions throughout the country. Farzad continued,

> *Khaneh-ye Irani* are aimed at education and ensuring that children get at least one meal a day. When children are born into a noxious environment, [one] lacking a loving family, they only have one route, and that is to become delinquent. Our goal is to prevent that. We have therapeutic theater for children so that they can discharge their pain and anger. We have lots of programs. We want to create employment and career services, a free health clinic, and an athletic program because playing sports also permits [the children] to expend their frustrations.

Despite such work, which focused on prevention and reduction of suffering, the members of the Society felt they still needed to develop additional strategies to combat urgent and persistent problems.

> Even with all this preventative work, still, a time comes when the child becomes an offender and we must do something. We say, "How can we help? What can we do?" That's what happened with the case of Safar A. He is a former death-row youth. A knife is a like a toy for these kids. They all carry them. They have no real toys. Their brothers are in the juvenile center or in prison or have been executed, and they are falling in line, following the same route. We try to prevent it. We see a child now and think he's like Safar.

As Farzad discussed it, he made the point of noting the precarious situation of such children, who live in economic and social conditions that deprive them of the most basic features of what it means to be a child.

The Society's good works are not solely directed towards charitable aid. Sharmin and his student volunteers are also important agents in the lifeworld of forgiveness work. As with the social workers I had encountered, the Society, with its emphasis on youth as agents and subjects, started out with forgiveness work directed towards offenders who were under eighteen when they committed the crime, but moved to an anti-death penalty position as a result of that work. Activism changes the activists' own positions and thinking. They see the underbelly and work in the "margins," as Farzad called it, and change their own ethical positioning. Doing the work to change the culture on the ground also changes the activists' own ways of thinking, clarifying and sharpening their activism. The motivations to do forgiveness work have roots in compassionate activism following the example of Imam 'Ali. Over time, competition with other organizations and the pressures to demonstrate success has led to greater professionalization and an accounting of their strategies.

Method: Loving Kindness

The sheer physicality of Sharmin's work sets him apart from all other social workers that I encountered. Perhaps because he concentrates on youth, Sharmin displays warmth and affection as much through the language of love as in his physical embraces of the children. He expresses love as an attunement to their needs, an expression of "vigilant attentiveness" (De Vries and Schott 2015:2).[51]

"Sharmin teaches '*deegar-khahee*,'" Farzad related the Society's approach through an invented term-of-art derived from the colloquial word combination, "*khod-khahee*," meaning selfishness or self-centeredness. The pejorative term (consisting of the noun "*khod*," meaning "self," and the verb "*khaastan*," meaning "to want") references an individual's egotism and emphasis on selfish desires. By shifting its subject from "self" to that of *deegar* (other), the Society seeks to convey its aim of placing the needs of others as its central focus. "We establish relationships with families in need, but our help does not stop there. We keep up with them; we follow-up throughout their time of need." Farzad further explained that, "through *mahabbat* [loving kindness] for the children and the families with whom they work," the Society's social workers "build themselves" (*khod-sazi*). Through their acts of *mahabbat*, the social workers' self-building thus also suggests an ethical self-fashioning (Lambek 2010).[52] The result is "the courage to go places where even politicians won't go."

The Society operates a two-track strategy regarding murder cases. First, they pursue the legal track, in which they try to influence changes to the law and legal system. In that capacity, the Society works alongside other advocates, such as the Society for Protecting the Rights of the Child. In addition, the Imam 'Ali Society advocates in individual cases against death sentences for underage youth. They interview defendants and present information about their circumstances to lawyers and sometimes the media, hoping to modify the sentences based on a defendant's lack of mental maturity, applying Article 91 of Iran's penal code.[53]

Farzad, however, was unimpressed by the new provision, which allowed a panel of three judges to consider mental maturity through the testimony and affidavits of psychologists and two social workers. "There was a lot of hoopla about the new law ending execution for youth under eighteen, but it's not true. The judges can avoid the sentence of execution, but don't have to." Although Farzad was not satisfied with this new law, because of it his organization and social workers, like himself, now had an increased role in advocacy. "This [advocacy] is also where the information and communications strategies are very important." In line with the new law, the Society moved to communicate in new ways, using social media to spread the word about sensitive cases and to raise funds for forbearance. Over the years however, the use of social media to expand advocacy communications has become a sensitive and hotly contested issue among social workers, government agents, and defense lawyers, not to mention the families of perpetrators.[54]

Beyond the legal track, the second branch of the Society's forgiveness work involves seeking reconciliation between the parties. Much like the other social actors, Farzad described the need for neutrality, reducing the pain and enmity, and "creating the conditions for peace." The society seeks to build relationships and move towards diffusing enmity. Farzad continued,

> Putting aside hatred is hard. It takes time. Patience is very important to this process. Sharmin has developed a way to talk to people. When he first started [in 2007], Sharmin went to talk with a family and ended up running out of the house with the deceased's brother coming after him with a knife. Today, that person is a good friend. They [the families of victims] need to feel understood. They need a friend, a brother. Otherwise, maybe the only thing they have to grab is that noose.
>
> For example, the Rezaei family, whose son Safar had killed, the [victim's] father sat [as if on a throne]. He had the power of holding someone's life in his hands. That gave him an identity, like he was God. With our help, that family did not execute [Safar]. They found peace in forbearance. The father is very different now. He was playing God, now he's a friend. We can reduce the hatred by a lot, from one-hundred percent, say, to twenty, but not to zero.

Some people, however, try to raise the level of hatred. Some work on a "culture of revenge," many more than on a "culture of forgiveness." For Safar, for example, we made a Facebook page. Many comments said, "Why do you want to help a murderer?" Our society likes revenge more than forgiveness.

Farzad's explanation spoke to his own exploration into what he called a "culture of revenge" over a "culture of forgivenss." Here is where the Society's methods intersected with those of other social actors working in this forgiveness lifeworld. Farzad was not only aware of the methodological and socio-cultural challenges of forgiveness work but was also conscious of the need to change the culture on the ground—what he called the culture of revenge, something he felt that the legal system fostered.

The Society's methods sought not only the reprieve of individual cases, but also broader social changes: to bring about a sense of satisfaction from forbearance rather than retribution. The Society's members attempted, with loving-kindness, to empower their interlocutors with feelings of compassion and to bring them into a social world they were trying to create, out of what they perceived as the perpetrators' anomie and disconnect from both social and spiritual worlds. As Farzad offered more details about the Society's methods he also clarified his earlier assertions of the Society's neutrality. This is to say, the Society, while neutral with regard to the parties involved, was partial with respect to the outcome they sought—the Society clearly advocates forbearance. As Farzad said,

> We see ourselves as representatives of both families, but we attend more to the rights of the victim's family. The relative of that person was killed; you must understand. Our relationship is closer to that of a witness; witnesses don't speak of forgiveness. People want those who are closer to their thinking and ideas. We try to support them by understanding them and their needs. Families from different regions or more traditional backgrounds tend to keep more to their customs. We familiarize ourselves with their rituals and religious ceremonies. We follow their practices, use their language.

Attention to local rituals is another strategy that sets the Society apart from other actors in the forgiveness lifeworld. Rituals are built on a sense of shared symbols and, when effectuated in all of their sensuality, rituals become believable. The shared symbolism alongside their aesthetic performativity bring meaning and emotion together to heighten the persuasive powers of ritual performances.

Farzad recounted how the Society adapted their approach to a victim's family to make use of rituals. "So, for those sentenced to qisas, we use the rituals of Ashura, or other local mourning rituals. We have a case now of two very religious families. In those cases, they feel their father was martyred; they don't want to meet with artists and actors. For them, we had a prayer ceremony." Ritual performativity may very well be the kind of attention to others that constitutes De Vries and Schott's notion of love as attunement (2015). It was there, at the prayer ceremony, that Farzad's depiction of Sharmin's motivations and the Society's methods coalesced.

The Prayer Ceremony

The same evening that the Society's student volunteers prepared to go "alley strolling" to deliver provisions to the poor, another group readied themselves for the prayer ceremony in honor of the young man killed by his wife. Sharmin and his wife, Zahra, joined us as we climbed back into Jabbari's car to go to the home of Mrs. Shirazi, the mother of the deceased and mother-in-law to the perpetrator, Sahar Mohabadi. Sharmin's aim was to pray for Shirazi's forbearance, as well as for the soul of her son. To do that, Sharmin and Zahra explained, "We use our own [Iranian] cultural rituals. For pious families, we draw from religious rituals, like the prayer ceremony." Upon arrival, we got out of the car and walked the rest of the way to the concrete wall interrupted by an iron-gated entrance. Just in front, a solitary eucalyptus tree swayed, lightly secreting its crisp mentholated aroma into the dry night air.

One of the volunteers rang the bell. The gate jutted open from inside, having been pulled open by a cord that snaked down a long concrete alleyway to the main living room. We followed the cord as a path to the entry, where some thirty volunteers filed in, having left their shoes in a pile in the hall. The mother of the deceased greeted us. A petite woman in a colorful chador, she pushed a walker ahead of her. She had a soft, round face and bright green eyes. In a quiet, yielding tone, she told the group to be sure to close the door.

Upon seeing the gentle demeanor of this grandmother of three, I immediately understood why so many people had told me that she was not the kind of person who would execute. The problem did not lie with her, they said, but with her children (siblings of the deceased), two of whom objected to forbearance. The biggest obstacle, Sharmin had told me on the way over, was her youngest son, Mehdi, the last one still living at home, who was still very angry with his sister-in-law. Ostensibly, the prayer ceremony was for the mother, but the Society had come to talk to Mehdi, who had stepped out just prior to our arrival. As we sat in a circle on worn Persian carpets in the sparsely furnished room, Shirazi assured us that her son would be back soon.

Sharmin sat facing Shirazi, whose back rested against a wall. Her chador draped around her small frame as her luminous eyes took in the scene unfolding before her. Sharmin called out, "God, come forth! We have much to say!"

With each person holding a small Qur'an, a young reciter opened the meeting with a brief prayer and *salavat*. Next, a female student read aloud verses from the Maryam (Mary) chapter of the Qur'an.[55] The chapter tells Maryam's story in detail.[56] In it, the word, "God," is repeatedly referred to as "al-Rahman" (the Compassionate).[57] The symbolic meaning of the reading, from the only chapter of the Qur'an named for a woman, was not lost on those in the room.[58] Nor was it lost on anyone that the chapter told the story of the deep love and connection between a mother and her son—another mother, Maryam, who had also lost her son. The passage addressed the issue of forbearance, as well, suggesting that those who express leniency through merciful acts would be recognized and rewarded in death. The reading also evoked God as the ultimate righter of wrongs and implored believers to leave punishment to the Divine.

With the evening's tone firmly established, Sharmin began,

> Tonight, we are in the service of a dear mother in pain. She raised a son and in life all that remains for her is but a knife and his death. It is very painful. God looks at people's pain and understands how much one individual feels and how hard it is.
>
> Tonight, we are here to witness and to say that we understand your pain—a mother who lost a son, who left sooner than he was supposed to, and went to heaven.
>
> Mothering for this son isn't over. She is still mothering and loving this son. A mother does what is best for her son. We come here; we want what's best for this mother. What's the best that this mother can achieve? A mother is an exemplar of God. With mothers come life. Mothers give birth.

Sharmin turned his head to look at the wall behind him, where a large framed photograph of the deceased hung.

> I see this son, who comes to life from God, through the mother. A mother is like God. Noble, Merciful, Loving. [She] wants the best for her child, like God. A mother is the outward sign of God. A child's death is the ultimate hardship, and there is no limit to the pain.
>
> She wants to go through with the punishment, and it is her right. Because of the loss that she feels, this punishment is the right of the mother. CERTAINLY! How can someone who isn't a mother say to her, "Forgo punishment!" A mother who sends her son as a groom and then retrieves him in a shroud. She is broken-hearted. What can possibly compensate for this? NOTHING! Her sweetheart is lost. This heartbreak is so bitter, so painful. A mother wants only what is best for her child.
>
> Come see which of us lives. Is it known? No! Death awaits all of us. Fate exists. We cannot escape it. God has fixed it, and no one can change it, not

even the Archangel Gabriel. After death, we will come alive again on the Day of Judgment. We all die. Lucky are those who have the love of a mother. How lucky the child is who has a mother to cry for him.

As Mrs. Shirazi watched bemusedly, Sharmin paused and asked, "What age was your son when he passed away?"

"Twenty-nine.

Sharmin continued,

So many mothers cried for children martyred in the war. How sad are those who have no mother to cry for them. Tonight, beside the tears of the mother, we pray for her son, Gholam Reza. Death to this heartache! May God grant us peace.

Now this mother has the greatest difficulty. We don't claim to understand why it is the fate of this mother to have this loss of a son. Ask Fatemeh Zahra why must we lose? Because it's been decided that you must assume that station.[59] With all the respect and love we have for this mother [Fatemeh Zahra] during the month of Ramadan, I have something to share with this mother [Shirazi].

It's the mother's right to punish her daughter-in-law—the wrongdoer who committed this injury [and who] deserves the same. I don't know the daughter-in-law, nor this mother's son. And I won't know them. On the Day of Judgment, she [the daughter-in-law] will pay for what she has done. Tonight, I have a request. With all my might, I say to this mother—Summon the slogans of paradise! The biggest act she can now do for her son is to forgive.

People mix punishment and forgiveness. Forgiveness bestows blessing and light upon the forgiver. Forgiveness is not for the daughter-in-law, but the forgiver. God will mete out a tough punishment, you can be sure. *Qisas* is blood for blood. A daughter for a son. It is one way, but forgiveness will give us a better world.

This is what a mother can do. And it turns her into a mother of a martyr and a son who is a martyr because she is on par with God, merciful, noble, and, with it, all the blessings will come. *Qisas* is your right, but forgiveness will bring you more.

Sharmin reached into his pocket and pulled out his phone. He said, "I can call now. I can get an offering," referring to an amount of compensation the family would be willing to give to the victim's family in exchange for their forbearance. Shirazi stared at him, expressionless. He continued,

These two routes exist for us. With all my being, I give this right to the mother. We will help you with that, too, but that will not become heaven for your son. This *shirzan* [lioness] has lost one life along the way, now this *shirzan* will save a life and we will fill this house with red roses. Good fortune comes to the mother who forgives, and difficulty remains for the forgiven who remains always a debtor.

Leaning towards Mrs. Shirazi, Sharmin stretched his body flat across the floor, took her bare feet into both of his hands, and kissed them. Still prostrate, he called out,

"For Gholam Reza, forgive! For these students here, forgive! Like God, forgive! Entrust her to God! The gift from God is higher!"

Mrs. Shirazi responded, "I can't. I can't satisfy my heart."

"For your son, your heart is broken."

"I worked so hard. I raised these children with such difficulty, it was such a struggle."

"What will satisfy your heart?"

"*Dar* [the noose]." Sharmin waited a moment before speaking. "Then, for me, for us, for these children here today, wait, not for one-hundred years, but, perhaps, fifty."

"Ok. I'll wait, but forgiveness won't satisfy my heart. I told the head of the Implementations Unit, 'Even if you were to execute me; I wouldn't care. I can't forgive.' My children say, 'What does your heart say?' I'll do it myself. I'll push the button."

"Carrying out the sentence will that satisfy your heart?"

"Yes—only this. Nothing else. If I go to hell or heaven, only God knows."

"*Qisas* is a right. But forgiveness is a right, as well."

"If I were going to be satisfied, during these seven years . . . I have no feet, no eyes, see what misfortune has befallen me, from your daughter," she quotes herself speaking to her daughter-in-law's father. Then back to Sharmin, "He [Sahar's father] says he's responsible. Everyone said they should have gotten divorced." Now, speaking to an imaginary Sahar, "Why did you do it? You could have gotten divorced."

"I just want peace and tranquility for you," Sharmin interjected.

"Everyone has abandoned me but Mehdi."

"Carrying out the sentence won't bring you peace. What if your son [the deceased] comes to you in your sleep?"

"He won't. He hasn't."

"Don't be hasty, maybe . . ."

"They said no executions are carried out during Ramadan, but after, I entrust her to God. I have no grudge. She said she did it intentionally. She planned it, to have him come to the park and then stab him."

Zahra Rahimi, Sharmin's wife, interjected. She told Shirazi about a case in which the family of victim did not forgive. "The mother could not escape her misery. After the violence she committed," she said, "the mother has gone mad."

Shirazi responded, "With *qisas*, I wouldn't feel pain, even in my fingernail." Then, she chided the perpetrator's family, "In four years, one time, they took me to their house." She continued her reproach, "My husband was deaf, dumb, and blind. [Before dying], he said, 'You know best. Just pull the thing [lever]. Don't look. You can close your eyes.'"

"What a joke! He told you that?" Sharmin exclaimed. "It's a person we're talking about, not a sheep!"

"Mehdi said, 'I'm nothing. You are the principal [one to decide],'" she said, emphasizing what everyone knew to be untrue.

Mehdi had returned and was standing outside the room, listening, but he refused to enter despite Sharmin's appeals that he join them. Sharmin spoke loud enough for Mehdi to hear, "God tests us all. This issue is for all of us. When accidents happen, God is testing us."

Then Mehdi entered and shouted, "My brother! This was intentional murder!"

"Yes, I know, but wait! Open your heart to peace. May God's favor be upon you." Sharmin instructed the student volunteers, "Recite a *Fatiheh* for the lost one." Then he turned to Shirazi, "Whatever your decision, may God be with you."

After the ceremony, we filed out, a bit beleaguered. I got into Jabbari's car and, along with Sharmin and Zahra, we headed directly to the perpetrator's (Sahar's) parents' home, a few blocks away. In the car, Jabbari insisted, "These are not killers. I've spoken with her. She won't do it. It's her sons; they want money."

Sharmin added, "It's a show. The mother doesn't care."

I was taken aback. It seemed to me that she did care. She was clear that she wanted *qisas*. Over time, however, I came to realize the purpose of this exercise—the audience of so many permitted the victims to expend their anger, to execrate, accuse, chastise, and blame. I noted that the serious efforts Sharmin had made to bring Mehdi into the room were precisely because he was the angriest and more staunchly against forbearance than his mother. The "show" was not, as I had at first thought, for Shirazi, but rather for Mehdi. His mother was protecting Mehdi and, in a sense, taking his anger as hers thus forming a shield between the social workers and him.

Moments later, we arrived. Despite the late hour, we found Sahar's parents outside, awaiting news. Speaking to them under a street lamp, Sharmin gave specific instructions, "Sahar's mother must go. Shirazi complained that you haven't gone to see her. You must go every day."

Sahar's parents protested, citing specific times they had paid respects to their daughter's former in-laws. They repeated that they didn't want to upset the family with their presence, a reference to the delicate balance between assuaging the victim's family, while taking care not to antagonize them. As we saw earlier, social workers marked the moment when the victim's family asks to see the perpetrator's family as a turning point to be seized upon.

Finally, Mrs. Rahimi made the strategic call, "We can't know that the victim's family will be unhappy. Right now, she is full [bursting with emotion]. She needs you to go to her." And, she added, "Sahar should call. She must call."

Then, a bit less obliquely, Sharmin laid out the strategy, "You need to cry, beg for forgiveness, fall at her feet and cry. Someone told her: 'Your anger will be relieved with her execution.' And she believes it!"

Conclusion

I began this chapter with an emphasis on female forgiveness workers. While I have shown the involvement of women in positions to forgive and in forgiveness work, the cases here also demonstrate how women find themselves in positions to ask for forgiveness. The complexities of the law, tied to deeply-rooted patriarchal social arrangements and structures, frequently place women in a position to respond to gender-based violence with violence. Many of the cases I have described emerged from broader social ills including poverty, domestic violence, and early marriage. Laws sedimented from patriarchal social structures, such as the difficulties with obtaining a divorce (which have their own social consequences) as well as seemingly neutral provisions, such as the extremely high burden of proving self-defense, albeit revised in the new laws, make women in many situations feel powerless and with no recourse other than to fight violence with violence.

The way the procedural laws operate, with the preference for quieting sexual violence in the courts and the necessary defensive anticipation of having to ask the victim's family for forgiveness, prevent women from telling their stories and having confidence that, once they do, they will win. Instead, women often conceal their abuse in order to preserve the possibility of forgiveness later. This was a lesson some people drew from Reyhaneh's case. As we saw in Sahar's case, the quietest approach did not appear to be working. Her lawyers would decide on a different strategy (Chapter 8).

The experiences with these subtle and often elusive particularities have led forgiveness workers to cultivate expertise through a repertoire of strategies and actions that are tailored to a case, in all of its affective registers. These practices work on the activists themselves as they engage in ethical self-fashioning, an aspirational molding of their adjacent selves. Over years of following many such activists, I saw them move to entirely opposing the death penalty for everyone, though their initial positions were more qualified.

By developing these diverse practices, social workers came to see themselves as singularly trained to engage in the specialized work of seeking forgiveness from victims' families. In one case, I followed, during a very tense period of negotiations between a defense lawyer and a victim's family, a social worker called me and asked that I convey a message to the defense lawyer. She complained that the lawyer had sent boxes of fruit to the victim's family. They took it to be a callous offering, a bribe of sorts, and were insulted. They refused the goods and left them on their front stoop to rot. "Tell him that if he doesn't stop this crap, he's going to get that boy killed. What does he know about getting the victims' families to forgive! He should leave that to those of us with expertise. He's a lawyer! He goes to court. Do I go to court?" She also brilliantly highlighted the different kinds of advocacy that are at play in the pre-verdict period—defensive and rights-based, and those in the post-sentencing period—appeals to humanity and charity, as forgiveness is. As I indicated, these appeals may sometimes work at cross-purposes, for one emphasizes the social context, mitigating circumstances, and defendant's rights, while the other affirms the victim's rights, as a consequence of suffering a loss, and requires pleas to charity.

One strategy that many social activists shared was to partake in a broader social project of changing the culture of how individuals viewed the rights of the victim's family. Besides seeing retribution as a right, activists emphasized that forbearance, too, was a right, and peace the higher religious value. Social activists engage in this wider societal cultural-building through the vehicles of art and aesthetics, as I will explore in the next chapter.

7

The Art of Forgiveness

Ethics and aesthetics are one.

LUDWIG WITTGENSTEIN,
TRACTATUS LOGICO-PHILOSOPHICUS (1916)

AT NINE A.M. sharp we met at the bus station just south of the city center. Several social workers had invited me to join them on a trip to Siah Kal, a town in the northwestern province of Gilan.[1] They hoped to speak with the members of a family who had lost their son, Suleiman, when he was stabbed to death in a street fight about six years earlier. The family had to decide whether to pursue retributive sanctioning of Hamid Ahmadi, the young man who had been convicted of killing Suleiman, or forgo it. So far, the social workers told me, the family had expressed their wish for retributive sentencing to be carried out, but the social workers were hoping to convince them otherwise. They thought they had a chance because they believed that the key decision-maker in the family, the mother, was open to talking about forbearance.

As with so many of the cases that the social workers pursued, this one involved an assailant who was under the age of eighteen when he committed the homicide; Hamid had been sixteen at the time. The social workers were also persuaded that enough factual ambiguities existed that made the case a sympathetic one. The parties had gotten into a fight, but other young men were involved, thus putting into question the issues of who delivered the deadly blow to the victim and whether homicide was the true intent.

The judicial system seemed equally at odds over the facts. In August of 2009, the criminal court found Hamid guilty but, soon after, Iran's Supreme Court overturned the sentence citing uncertainties in the testimony of key witnesses and sent the case back for re-trial. In the first trial, Hamid had confessed, but on appeal, he retracted his confession, arguing that it was coerced. In the retrial, Hamid was again found guilty and, in 2010, his sentence was upheld on appeal.

There was some urgency to the matter, too. Prison officials had informed Hamid's family that they would have to make a decision on his case soon. It was the month of Ramadan (July 2014) and Iranian authorities do not typically carry out executions during the holy month. Instead, those so inclined, such as the social workers and Hamid's family, intensify their efforts to achieve reconciliation. In the weeks to come, his family feared, Hamid's execution could be carried out. In addition to reviewing the case, the social workers had spoken by telephone both to Hamid's sister and the victim's mother. The social workers determined that they could make a positive intervention and decided to go.

The social workers were not working alone, however. They were joining a passionate group of thespians who were going to perform a play about capital punishment. The actors, along with the play's co-writer and director, Amin Miri, had chartered a bus to take them the 341 km (212 mi) to Siah Kal. They were going to perform in the theater of the town's cultural center, run by the Ministry of Culture and Islamic Guidance.[2]

After I caught up with my friends, they introduced me to a dozen or so performers who greeted me warmly. As we boarded the bus and arranged our luggage, several young women asked me what I was hoping to achieve. I described my project by explaining my interest in how Iran's criminal justice system integrated victims' families in sanctioning. I outlined how my work had evolved beyond purely legalistic spaces, such as the courts, into the semi-autonomous social fields in which groups like theirs operated and attempted to reach reconciliation. A woman from the troupe nodded her head in agreement and said, "That's right, we're working in a field that is devoid of law."

I also noted that in the years since I had begun studying these unregulated spaces of forgiveness work, art and aesthetics had emerged as crucial sites through which interested groups attempted to bring about reconciliation between parties and a remission of the death sentence. I told them that I was traveling with them to learn what art achieves in the context of forgiveness. How do art and aesthetics affect the people involved? Although I meant this as a bit of professorial rhetoric, a young man with a pensive gaze quickly added the phrase that I had come to hear often in my research—"We work to bring about a feeling of forgiveness in society."

Taking the cue from my interlocutors, in this chapter, I explore how the actors seek to instill a feeling of forgiveness through the dramatic arts. In order to do so, I explore the forgiveness work of artists, particularly in modern theater and poetry, which partly fills-in and shapes the unregulated spaces of forgiveness work. I consider how art and aesthetics cultivate a feeling of forgiveness, both in the families that hold the key to an offender's life and in the communities whose residents may help to produce new social conditions that render retaliation unacceptable, and even dishonorable.

I track the performance of a theatrical production in part to show the extensive efforts involved in creating such an experience. By exploring this production and the local tragedy that motivated the artists to stage it, I also investigate the complex array of meanings and the effects that forgiveness work has on the different parties involved. Appeals to empathy are not by themselves action and do not always lead to such (Bornstein 2012:145). What I offer here, instead, is a reflection on actors' attempts at cultivating a broad cultural shift, to which I earlier referred as a wave of forgiveness. Thus, I consider what compels individuals to act precisely because we know that appeals to empathy do not always result in action.

Playing for Forgiveness

The play performed in Siah Kal, *The Blue Feeling of Death*, depicts the lives of some of the adolescents housed in Tehran's Juvenile Correction and Rehabilitation Center (JCRC), where offenders convicted of murder reside until they reach their eighteenth birthday. The play was directed by Amin Miri, who is also an actor. Miri spent time volunteering at the JCRC, getting to know the youth, and collecting their stories. Together with another well-known playwright, Sajjad Afsharian, Miri then wrote the play documenting the lives of the offenders and their families. In the winter of 2013, Miri assembled a cast that included several notable actors and directed the play, which premiered in Tehran that June to rave reviews. The play was a sort of collaborative work as the actors played real life characters that they, too, had come to know during visits to the JCRC. Some even wrote and performed their lines based on the conversations they had had with the youth at the JCRC. Initially, Miri staged the play in order to raise funds for the JCRC, but its success led the actors to the loftier goals of using it to actually obtain the forbearance of a victim's family.[3]

By the summer of 2014, the play had been performed over seventy times, primarily in Tehran, but also in several provincial towns where the troupe had traveled long distances. It was no longer in full production mode nor were its performances aimed solely at raising money. In fact, the troupe had come together for this trip for the first time in over six months. I wondered why the troupe was traveling to yet another town to perform, when many of its actors and actresses had other on-going stage commitments. Once on the bus, I asked about their activities and what they hoped their performance could accomplish. Miri, the director, a tall lanky man in his forties, responded, "We try to inspire forgiveness and mercy in the hearts of the people. We want the play to produce a feeling of forgiveness throughout society," and in particular, in Siah Kal. There it was again—the *feeling* of forgiveness. In Siah Kal, a small town of about 15,000, residents did not possess the anonymity that those in sprawling urban cities did. Many of the inhabitants knew each other or one another's families and for those who did not know each other, the degrees of separation were far fewer than in the city. The people of this town could influence one another and their actions, good or bad, could reverberate throughout the town, affecting local perceptions of their family's reputation or honor. This was just what the director was hoping to do. Through coordinating with residents and local government officials, Miri, the director, aimed to capitalize on community relations in order to influence the people of Siah Kal to accept forbearance through staging his theatrical production.

Indeed, the performance had been carefully orchestrated by the offender's sister, Somayeh. She was her brother's most vocal advocate and had worked tirelessly over the years trying to persuade the victim's family to forgo retribution. She had heard about the play a year earlier and obtained a video of it. After watching it, she felt a performance in her village could leave an impression on the people, including perhaps, the family of her brother's victim. "I had a feeling it could be influential," she told me. She had contacted Miri and, with the local Minister of Culture and Islamic Guidance, Mr. Hosseini, Somayeh organized a performance in her hometown, where her brother had been imprisoned for the previous six years, awaiting a decision by the victim's family. It was also no accident that the performance would take place during the month of Ramadan, when, in addition to fasting, Muslims focus on contemplative worship, intensify attitudes of mercy, and carry out acts of forgiveness.

Miri agreed to stage the performance, while Somayeh engaged the help of others. Notably, she connected with Mr. Abdulazadeh, a wealthy village elder, who donated a house and food for the actors during the three-day trip. All involved were hoping to inspire feelings that would lead to forgiveness. Spreading knowledge about Hamid's situation, they thought, could also contribute to the broader aim of transforming retaliatory sentencing into a socially disreputable act and moving, perhaps, from an individual feeling of forgiveness to a culture of forgiveness.

Aesthetics and Emotion

The actors, director, and other interested parties were engaging in what they referred to as *farhang-sazi* (culture-building). Through their art, they work to instill forgiveness more deeply throughout society by appealing to emotion. Phrases like "feeling of forgiveness" and "appeals to emotion" came up often in my conversations with actors, social workers, and others who were working to persuade victims' families. They used "whatever rituals or means possible," one social worker had explained, with the aim of producing this emotional inspiration on the part of the already aggrieved victim's family. It goes without saying that this was no easy feat; nor was the appeal to emotion a one-way street. The possibility of backlash in the form of a change of heart, from forbearance to retribution, was present right up until each member of the victim's family had signed and notarized a statement agreeing to forgo retaliatory sentencing and then submitted it to the court.

Forgiveness workers capitalize on the connection between emotion and art. Of course, this is a relationship that has not gone unnoticed by scholars. Nussbaum argues that storytelling and literary imagining can, through the summoning of emotions, be useful in rational argument and social justice (1995). Using literary works to discuss compassion and mercy allows others to imagine what is involved in the situation of someone different from oneself (1995:xiv). Novels, to cite one example, convey certain understandings about "discretion and mercy in criminal sanctioning," which can lead adversaries to see one another as human beings (1995:xv). Using art, Nussbaum argued, can offer "a humanistic and multivalued conception of public rationality," forcing audiences to move beyond their individual perspective in considering crime and punishment as well as in considering how others grapple with disadvantage (Ibid.).

Storytelling is important precisely because the literary imagination allows individuals to visualize in specific ways how distant others struggle through hardship. Artistic expression, particularly novels, cultivate the literary imagination, which in turn creates the conditions for greater societal empathy. My interlocutors echoed this understanding. Through a contemporary medium that he and other artists refer to as *te'atr-e mostanad* (documentary theater), Miri sought to employ the more metaphorical nature of storytelling.[4] He felt that individuals burdened by trauma could be prompted to see, feel, and think empathically when other kinds of direct interaction could be experienced as confrontation and fail.

Nussbaum's work on the relationship between art and emotion helped me make sense of what inspired Miri and others to involve themselves in this project of culture-building. It was as much for themselves as for the offender, his/ her family, and that of the victim's, that Miri and his troupe wanted to partake in this work of engaging the public about the execution of adolescents and to take an ethical stance on it, to the extent that the broader social codes and laws in Iran permitted. In doing the cultural work of empathetic imagining, the artists were nurturing an imagining of a different social order, one in which individuals who had committed offenses as adolescents were not executed or, perhaps, where no one was.

Social novels of early-twentieth-century Iran carry an effect similar to that which Nussbaum describes. These novels, part of the emerging literary print culture of the time, were often written by journalists and government employees, some with religious training (Gahan 2017). Social novels told stories of human suffering in an emerging public sphere. The authors drew on the twin aims of inspiring social reform while conjuring compassionate understanding as they related stories of social suffering, often of stigmatized women of low social class, such as prostitutes. The authors also helped generate an intimate public that invoked the shared sensibilities of their community (Berlant 1997). These works also added an element of personal growth and development in which Iranians engaged not only in *khod-sazi* (self-fashioning), but also in the building up of their culture, *farhang-sazi*. As artists, Miri and the actors used their skills to engage society and to develop the thinking of its members by appealing to their moral sensibilities. The medium of theater possesses the added power of immediacy; one of the essential characteristics of live performance is that it brings spectators together in unmediated and instant engagement with the action on stage, leading to a sense of urgency, elation, or resolve.

Indeed, storytelling is an important medium of Iranian cultural production. The *naqqali*, a form of dramatic storytelling in which a narrator communicates with an audience, is one of the oldest forms of performance and dates back to the seventh century CE. In addition, while Iran's long history of performing arts is notably evidenced by *ta'ziyeh*, religious epic dramas or passion plays (Chelkowski 1979; Fischer 1980), contemporary theater is a more recent artistic venture whose history scholars trace only as far back as the early twentieth century, with distinctive creative periods in the 1950s, 60s, 70s, the early post-revolutionary period, and today.[5]

The performing arts possess historical significance as sites for didactic messaging. This newer iteration, modern theater, resonates with the older forms of performing arts and, through the loose connection with its form, theatrical production is also capable of conveying a moral lesson, albeit with modern humanistic sensibilities of empathy. With this in mind, the director and actors aimed their efforts and performance at getting the people in the town, and possibly members of the victim's family, to consider the situation that Hamid was in and to attempt to compress the social and cultural distance between themselves and him, the distant other. The actors playing characters very different from themselves essentially unified this stark otherness through their embodied portrayals.

Embodied Portraits: Golboo/Maedeh

On the bus, I sat in the front row. Thus, once we navigated out of the sprawling capital, I could view the cascading pines that lined the undulating route up to Siah Kal. I also got to talk to others who came to the front to smoke, sip tea, and chat with the driver. After some time, the bus went quiet as the actors napped, surely catching up on lost sleep given our early morning departure. I moved a few rows back to sit next to one of the actresses, Golboo, who was not asleep, but reading a novel. Invitingly, she moved her bag from the seat next to her and tucked her book into it. She removed her stylish glasses, their thick black rectangular frames giving her an intellectual mien. A broad toothy smile filled her face as she introduced herself as a writer and poet who had previously collaborated with Miri.

When not acting, Golboo submitted commissioned pieces to e-zines, journals, and publishing houses. She had published several volumes of poetry and supported herself through her artistic pursuits. Her parents were intellectuals as well, she added. Her mother read literature in several languages. Her father was more traditional, but both encouraged her creativity. They were good models for her. She still lived at home, but independently from her parents. She came and went as she pleased. Golboo turned down a scholarship to study engineering, and instead majored in journalism and cinema. Her decision worried her parents at first. After witnessing her success, however, they became very supportive and proud of her. Although in her late twenties, she felt no pressure to marry. Remaining single allowed her to travel to Europe, where she spent several months every year.

Golboo's life was a study in contrasts with the young woman whom she portrayed in the play. Golboo interpreted the role of Maedeh, a young woman whom she got to know through numerous visits to the JCRC. Maedeh was from Langerud, a village outside of Qom, about an hour south of the capital. She was married by the time she was eleven and moved to Tehran at thirteen. At fifteen, Maedeh killed her husband. He was five years older than she and was a drug addict. Maedeh told Golboo that he slept all day and then, on most nights, he went out to score drugs. Maedeh worked to support herself. Soon her husband began to take her meager earnings for his shady pursuits. To expend her resentment, Maedeh flirted with other men. This made her husband angry and started many arguments. After numerous fights where Maedeh had endured beatings, she finally resolved to kill her husband. She did so by giving him aluminum phosphide pills. In the play, Golboo portrayed Maedeh as the sweet and cooperative inmate she had become, who got along well with other prisoners and the staff. Golboo's lines were written from actual conversations she had had with Maedeh. In her depiction, Golboo sought to highlight child marriage, poverty, lack of education, domestic violence, and other social ills that had landed Maedeh in the JCRC.

As the bus rolled north, Golboo reflected on how the justice system operates and commented on the legal and moral obligation that state officials hold to pursue reconciliation. "Some judges are good. Some, many, actually, work very hard to get the victim's family to forgo retribution. The aim of all this [retributive sanctioning], after all, is to reduce crime. Some judges understand this and know that *qisas* does not achieve that."

In Maedeh's case, Golboo noted, the victim's family are her in-laws—the deceased's two brothers and their mother. "One brother is a police officer and says 'no, do not *qisas*.' But the mother and the other brother want *qisas*. The judge says 'no,' too. So, we just wait. It's important not to be showy or to make too much noise and upset the family."

Golboo observed that the current project—Miri's play—was important because it illustrated the relationship between an individual's social status and identity. "The play shows how social status produces individuals like Maedeh." Golboo continued, "Maedeh and other women in our society are under constant scrutiny because women must embody innocence, chastity, and impeccability. When they defy these roles, they can get into trouble. Now, Maedeh needs to show herself in this way in hopes of being granted forgiveness."

Golboo's remarks underscore an important linking of forgiveness and forbearance in the Iranian context. Scholars are quick to separate these concepts, and a third related notion, that of mercy (Ferguson 2012; Griswold 2007; Murphy and Hampton 1988). Indeed, many scholars hold that forgiveness is a private act that does not involve the judicial system, while forbearance (as the forgoing of a right), and mercy (as the lessening of a deserved punishment) are legal and, thus, public (Ferguson 2012:41; Murphy and Hampton 1988:167). As I have discussed earlier, the concepts are also quite distinct in the Iranian context. However, given that in Iran the right of forbearance belongs to individuals rather than the state, the relationship between forgiveness and forbearance is much closer than in western legal contexts. As a result, many conversations about forgoing this legal right also include the willingness of the victim's family to forgive. In addition, in such discussions, the notion of mercy—a lessening or a "gentleness going beyond due proportion" with regard to deserved punishment—looms large, as it is the broader logic upon which the Islamic criminal laws are said to be devised (Nussbaum 1993:97).[6]

For many Iranians, those who are in need of mercy must appear worthy of it. Mercy often requires a merciful subject. This is what Golboo was referring to when she referenced that Maedeh must now show herself in a different manner, and her portrayal of Maedeh is decidedly scripted in this compassionate light.

In western legal contexts, mercy raises a disturbing issue when the state, by virtue of its sovereign power, pardons individuals, particularly for committing private harms, such as murder.[7] In such cases, the state is not the immediate victim, and thus not the appropriate or sole authority to excuse an injury. In the Iranian context, the state delegates the right of forbearance—the right to extend mercy—to victims, or at least their families. For some family members, the decision to be merciful creates a dilemma in that they see it as forgoing a right that belongs to the deceased.[8] As we have seen, family members often only feel they can forgo retribution when they sense that the deceased has somehow communicated to them their approval or assent. This dilemma also contributes to the conflation between forgiving and forbearing for victims. For, in order to forgo a right, we find that victims' families often need to arrive at a place where they can also forgive a perpetrator. In order to achieve this initial step of forgiveness, the victim needs to see the perpetrator as an empathetic figure. This is also true of the social workers and other actors when deciding whether to support a case. Thus, creating the conditions for empathy, like those invoked by the literary imagination and generated by various forms of art, becomes a powerful tool in bringing about forbearance and forgiveness.

Settling in: *Siah Kal*

When we arrived, night had fallen and concealed the craggy mountains just outside the town. The bus dropped us off on the main street. We walked through a wide, winding alleyway that took us to the small two-bedroom house that Somayeh had secured. For the duration of the trip, she and her family would see to everyone's needs.

As we entered the dwelling, we were greeted by Abdulazadeh, the town elder who had offered the house. His aquamarine eyes lit up the night sky seemingly leading the way through a high brick wall that enclosed a generous courtyard. The women put their bags in one room and the men in another. Neatly folded bedding sets lined the walls of each room. There was to be co-operative living for the next few days. We changed into comfortable clothes, a bit distraught that our travels north did not yield cooler air, a quality this part of the country is known for and instead breathed in heavy, humid summer air.

Dressed as people would at any summer yard party—in shorts, t-shirts, and breezy summer dresses—women and men spread out in the walled courtyard. It was time to eat; the call for prayer had sounded hours earlier. We had paid little attention to the day's fast, since it was not obligatory for travelers, although some had continued to fast, even through the dusty rest stop where others feasted on kabobs. A young man started the coals on a portable barbeque as more food and drinks arrived.

As artists, the actors seemed to maintain a more relaxed attitude with respect to the cultural norms, and the people around them seemed to afford them greater social latitude. The actors' casual talk of performances and plays was mixed with the sober purpose for which they had traveled. Did we think the play could actually affect the hurt and pain this family had experienced after the death of their son? Could it be that they would attend the play and then announce their forgiveness? I asked one of the actresses, Farzaneh, who said that this was what they were hoping for. She added that it had happened before, when they staged the play in Sistan and Baluchestan, a province in southeastern Iran. "The victim's family forgave the very night of the performance," she said with a big smile. So, it was worth a try. Another actor took as a good sign that the town's representative from the local office of the Ministry of Culture and Islamic Guidance fully supported their efforts, and even offered the use of their theater for the performance.

From the humid courtyard, I moved inside the air-conditioned house. I exchanged words with other actors, now resting comfortably on the yellow chairs and blue couches set up in the living room. I introduced myself to a petite young actress, Maryam, with glowing olive skin and dark wavy hair that fell down her back. Referring to a murder case she had been asked to support, Maryam spoke with disdain of a man "who killed two people, got off [received forbearance] and lived comfortably afterwards, and then he killed his wife!" She stated unequivocally that she would never try to persuade the family of his victims to forgo their right of retribution.

Surprised by her condemnation of the system, considering she was evidently participating in it in order to secure one family's forgiveness, I interjected, "Are you against this system or is it that you think the man in that situation should not have been granted forgiveness?"

"Well, I don't believe there shouldn't be a death penalty," she stated, hesitantly employing a double-negative. "There are these types of people who will kill again. I heard about a case in Turkey where a husband killed his wife. He got twenty-five years, but after serving half, he was out! That's wrong."

Hearing our conversation, another actress, a generation older, approached, "So many men kill their wives. Grandfathers kill grandsons . . . and they are let off too easily." The woman continued, "But the underlying, real reason [for such murders] is us. It comes from us. It is dialectical; it is a boomerang. It is the system of family, education, morality, and culture; it comes from us. We learned this from the poem, *Roozi Oghabi* [The Eagle's Pride; *lit*. One Day an Eagle], that we all had to memorize in high school." The older actress recited the first few lines, then repeated the expression, *az maast ke bar maast* (from us that is to us).[9]

Maryam, the younger actress, nodded her head in agreement and said, "I'm not saying I don't believe that some people should be forgiven, but I do think that some people cannot live in society. In any case, our play gives the audience something to think about. They can see the situation of these youth and have more context about their lives and how they got to the point of killing someone." Here Maryam expressed a concern for those who killed out of extreme disadvantage, like Maedeh, but also distinguished between such cases and others that she felt were not deserving of relief.

The older actress agreed. "It's true. Some people commit such terrible crimes and will continue if freed. We cannot forgive them. In order to be able to save some, we need to acknowledge that forgiveness is not something that should be available to everyone." The actresses' views resonate with scholarly insights that forgiveness is something that is exceptional and should be difficult to obtain (Derrida 2001a).

Both of the actresses' views on the death penalty differed, however, with those of my social worker friends. Fereshteh, a petite woman in her mid-fifties, had just freshened-up and joined us. She combed her fingers through her short, light brown hair as she spoke, "I've always been against the death penalty." Describing her work, she said, "At first we worked to end the death penalty for children, but we had a lot of problems with that. We were investigated, asked all kinds of questions, 'Why do you do this? Who sent you?' Then, when we had these problems, we turned our attention to reconciliation."

Fereshteh cut a laidback figure, dressed as she was, in loose linen trousers and a white t-shirt. She explained that now she worked exclusively on forbearance and reconciliation. "The work is hard, but also very rewarding. I can't tell you the feeling I get when we are able to obtain the family's consent to forgo *qisas*."

Fereshteh recognized the personal investment that her advocacy required. On the one hand, her role was one of witnessing; on the other, it was committed, requiring her to put her feelings in with those of the parties whose emotions rise and fall with every step along the process. By doing so, she created common cause between herself and the parties, and became a support to families on either side. When I asked what she hoped to achieve with her advocacy, Fereshteh emphasized the rewards of her work.

> We do this for the sake of humanity. It's wonderful when someone forgives. It doesn't matter if there are one, two, three, or four cases. We also do it for culture-building so that forgiveness falls into place in our society. I have always been against [the] death penalty, but most people are not. For collecting money for *diya*, people are almost always willing to come forward, more so when the funds are to help prisoners' families [in cases of] forgery or robbery, and such, but not as much for murder.

As with other social workers, Fereshteh's remarks highlighted broader aims than just advocacy in one select case. Whether this particular family agreed to forgo their right of retaliation, she was working towards a broader cultural shift and saw her advocacy, and that of Miri and the actors, as part of that larger aim of *farhang-sazi*.

Fereshteh continued, "In the context of forgiveness, *qisas* creates a situation where the social worker as well as the defendant and their family members have to be very careful about what we say about the victim because this could lead the victim's family to refuse to forgive." In the absence of government experts or regulators, Fereshteh's work filled a void in which she became the figure of the professional. In the absence of a professionalized class of experts, social workers, many of whom happen to be women, step into these roles and adopt this labor as their professional work.

Around midnight, the cooks began serving dinner. We piled in around the long rectangular table and dug in to the kabobs wrapped in warmed flatbread, roasted tomatoes, tangy sumac, yogurt-cucumber dip, salad, and long-grain rice. As we finished, we took our plates to the kitchen where Somayeh, her daughter, and her mother washed, dried, and put away the dishes before returning to their nearby home.

With stomachs full and an overwhelming day ahead, the actors, one by one, unfolded the bedding sets and laid them out along the floor in no particular order. Finally, although a few insomniacs sat outside and talked, most of the troupe said goodnight. It was three a.m.

Rehearsal

At first light, actors began to shift and turn; it was not quite eight o'clock. Soon the sunlight shone so brightly that the draped windows strained to keep the large room from announcing the day. There was much to do this morning— the rehearsal and the theater to prepare. Miri wanted to put the new actors on the stage right away. The rest of the troupe stayed back to do a run-through before going to the theater for the dress rehearsal after lunch.

Somayeh and her family arrived with breakfast. They tip-toed nimbly through the labyrinth of mattresses, sheets, pillows, and blankets towards the kitchen. They carried bags filled with bread, butter, eggs, and jam and set to work preparing breakfast. The actors, laughing and joking, put away the bed sets. Slowly pajamas morphed into t-shirts, shorts, and dresses. Groups mingled around the large table, now dotted with hot cardamom-scented tea, flatbread doused in butter and jam, and bits of deep-dish omelet.

The troupe leader called the group together and asked them to break into scenes and practice their parts. In one corner an actor portrayed an adolescent about to be executed; in the hall near the front door, two others played a scene between a sister and the perpetrator, a man who had killed her brother; and, in the dining room, a group rehearsed the conversation between a man who sought forgiveness on behalf of his brother and the family of his brother's victim. After some time, the troupe came together for a formal run-through.

They pushed the furniture along the wall, assembled in the living area, and began.

The first scene opened with a dystopian air of commotion and chaotic movement produced by all of the actors shuffling back and forth across the simulated stage. The commotion suggested the angst, distress, disquiet, and foreboding associated with the uncertainties wrought by the death sentence. Abruptly, the commotion stopped as all fell to the ground and moved off-stage. A sole actress, the petite Maryam, remained—tiny and alone. Her high-pitched voice solemnly pleaded to the air above for her brother's life.

In a different scene, an actor painted the disturbing story of Mohammad Salar, a boy who had killed another boy in a fight. The audience learned that Salar loved soccer; Cristiano Ronaldo was his idol. The scene began with a soccer game. Then the action came to a sudden halt. The actor approached center stage and recited his soliloquy. "At eighteen, he goes to the prison [thus leaving the juvenile center]. According to the Persian solar [*shamsi*] calendar, he was only fourteen years and eight months old [when he committed the crime], but, according to the Muslim lunar [*ghamari*] calendar, he was fifteen-years and eight days old. Those eight days made the difference between him getting the death penalty and not." Mohammad Salar's punishment was execution, by just eight days. "If only he had been born eight days later," the actor lamented. "Even the prosecutors messed up. First, they told him he was too young to be executed. One of the investigators told him, 'This is the luckiest day of your life. Nothing will happen to you.' He went back to his office, then came out a few minutes later. 'Oh, I made a mistake. I was looking at the *shamsi* calendar. In criminal law, we go by the *ghamari*. Your punishment is death.'"[10]

As the rehearsal moved swiftly forward, the vignettes brought to life the particular time-space disorder that sets in just after a death sentence is handed down and the pleading for life begins.

Meanwhile, the family of the perpetrator, on whose behalf the troupe was putting on the play, quietly went about preparing lunch. I was seated along a wall just to the front and left of the imaginary stage. The scenes went off with ample energy and intense emotion. An actress came to the front left-side of the room, only inches from me. She played the role of a mother whose son was condemned to death. Her only possibility of saving him was to obtain forbearance from the victim's family. I studied her focus and marveled at her poise. She sat on the floor, her knees folded beneath her and stared out, seemingly facing another mother. She pleaded, begged, and cried, "I am a mother just like you." The room was silent. From my perspective, I could see the back of the room, in the kitchen, where the real mother of the condemned stood, leaning on the counter, watching the scene. At that moment, as she watched the actress plead, she turned, put both hands to her face and silently cried. While the rehearsal was moving for us all, for this mother in the very situation, it was just too much. She turned her back and went about busying herself with lunch and tea, and tears.

After the run-through, the actors broke for the midday meal before heading to the theater. It was past noon; the sun was high in the sky and outside it was warm and humid. As we ate, I sat next to Sima, a student from Tehran who had accompanied her actor friends to the performance.

"I have a lot of sympathy for the youth who are in this position," she told me. "I think this play is very effective. Of course, these are very small steps that we can take and hopefully it will lead to bigger steps, like the forgiveness of the victim's family, and then more forgiveness in society as a whole."

Her words echoed what Fereshteh, the social worker, had said the night before about changing social perceptions on execution and the death penalty. Sima broke down those efforts into small steps and even saw meaning in what the actors were doing, regardless of whether in this particular case they were able to secure forgiveness. The dramatic portrayals of the difficulties, even injustices, that the young offenders endured, she noted, could have both an educational and emotional effect on society, regardless of whether everyone actually saw the play. The play resonated on many social registers, words and feelings precipitated from it and traveled through discourse, both verbal and emotional. "There are numerous ways in which the feeling of forgiveness can move through a society and settle in," another actor, Sussan, suggested. "This is our contribution as artists."

Samira, the real Samira

After lunch, a group of us sat and spoke with Samira. She was not an actress. Rather, she was one of the characters portrayed in the play. Samira had been released from prison just two weeks earlier. Like many young people who had experienced too much while too young, Samira exuded a resigned maturity well beyond her twenty-three years. She spoke solemnly, "Politics operates according to condemnation or prohibition, and not on the basis of forgiveness, nor that of well-being."

The older actress, who had portrayed a mother, turned to the young woman. "Samira, would you mind speaking about your case? Tell us, if you don't mind, what happened?" Samira, a thin figure with tan skin and auburn hair, turned her dark piercing eyes to us. Though she was about the same age as most of the actors, she had lived a very different life from the middle-class kids she had joined on this trip. Clearly, she had been asked to tell this story before and, despite our voyeuristic intrusion, she agreed. As she spoke, she motioned with long thin fingers that punctuated her words. Her voice was gentle yet commanding. Her sentences were dramatically inflected. Only her slight lisp gave away the younger, perhaps more innocent tone of the child who had gotten mixed up in her own father's murder.

"I was fifteen and my sister was twelve. My mother hated him. My father was an addict, who constantly hit, insulted, and humiliated her. My mother felt that he would kill her one day."

"Did you ever love your father?" Asked the older actress.

"I loved him at first. But he showed us a lot of anger and the little things added up. These were the neuroses of childhood."

"Did you have a good relationship with your mother?"

"I did when I was younger. She told me things that maybe you shouldn't tell a child. But she was very young, herself, and we didn't have a big age difference. I became like a friend whom she would confide in when her husband treated her poorly. She decided that she had to do something as he would not let us leave. Then one day, she waited until he was asleep, then she choked him with her shawl. She came to me and told me to pull one end, but I said 'no, I won't do it.' My sister wasn't in the room. But when the police came to get her, she told them that we had helped. She thought it would prevent them from giving her the death penalty, since we were under eighteen. It would at least buy her some time and maybe, after a while—my grandmother and [paternal] uncles and aunt [the victim's family]—would forgive us all. My sister and I were sent to the JCRC and my mother to prison. We stayed there. My sister is still there. When I turned eighteen, I was transferred to prison. It was very bad. I thought the JCRC was terrible, but at least there, they had classes for us and we learned some skills."

"That's where you learned *monabat kari* [art of wood carving]?" Since Samira was a character in the play, some of the actresses (who portrayed her) had come to know about the details of her life in the detention center.

"Yes. My sister is still there because she wants to support my mother. She thinks she's helping to save her, but I couldn't lie anymore. Besides, it's not going to save her; it's just going to get my sister killed too."

Samira was ultimately freed when she admitted that she had not participated in the killing and gave a thorough accounting of what had happened to the authorities. Her younger sister, however, remained in prison, but could also leave if she admitted that she did not participate in the murder. The older actress then asked Samira what she had been doing since she was freed.

"I was just released two weeks ago. I have a room that my social worker helped me find. I am looking for a job." As she spoke, Samira gestured to the dining table where her social worker, a young man who had accompanied her on this trip, was seated.

The actress then delicately proposed, "I don't know if this would interest you, but you know my two daughters, she motioned to them. "Sometimes, due to rehearsals, I can't be home right when they return from school and my husband travels so much. Would you be interested? I mean, it would be a place for you to stay, too, if you like."

"I don't know," Samira politely, but resolutely, replied. "I was just released and now I have a place which is my own. I don't know if I could live with anyone right now. I just need to find a job and go to school."

"I understand. Well, just think about it."

Samira's experience highlights not only the grave situation under-age youth sentenced to death face, but also the social context of the injustices they endure. *The Blue Feeling of Death* fits in with a broader movement of activist art that circulates in multiple media to depict social injustice through the experiences of a vulnerable population—the youth. Such art, like the play, walks a fine line between political activism and humanitarian work. The play's focus on the children's vulnerability, innocence, and, in many cases, lack of appropriate familial resources, draws empathetic awareness and action in support of the youth and yet carefully avoids open critique of the laws or the government. As in Mohammad Salar's case, the play's dialogue points out the capricious result of the two-calendar system but does so without recrimination. Instead, the focus is on the individuals in the stories, their particular situations. Through such a telling, however, a subtle critique of the enormous power laid at the feet of individuals, specifically the victim's family, also emerges.

The troupe began planning their departure to the theater for dress rehearsal. They busied themselves ironing costumes and calling cabs. The social workers were going to go speak with the victim's family. "They are supposed to come, but Somayeh is worried," Mahboubeh told me. "They won't answer her calls or texts." The social workers were planning to go talk to the family anyway. They would use the invitation to the play as an excuse to go to them. Since the victim's family still had not responded to Somayeh, we began worrying about their attendance and a current of anxiety swept over the troupe. "What if the victim's family doesn't even come? This is for them."

Somayeh, a sister's story

Somayeh, fair-skinned with freckles, quieted her visible anxiety by talking. Though aggrieved and sad for her brother's situation, she was polite, warm, and often smiling when she interacted with us. A local girl, Somayeh had moved to Karaj, a suburb of Tehran, soon after she had married, some seventeen years earlier. Bright floral headscarves complemented her wavy red hair, visible just around the edges. She had been clearing the table when our eyes met. I went over to help, and Somayeh slid her ever-present phone to the side. I took a seat across the table from her and asked how she was doing.

"Well, when I spoke with them about the play, the mother, Mrs. Bandari, told me they would come. I think they will. I don't know, though." She smiled, glanced at her phone and back at me.

"How long have you been working on getting the family to forgive?" I inquired.

"It's been six years now. Two years ago, I saw the family for the first time. I went to their house. I called first; they said to come. I went and rang the bell. I waited behind the door for ten minutes before they let me in. A woman opened the gate to a small courtyard. She led me up the stairs leading to the front door. I followed her down the hall, past three rooms, and into the living space. I was going to wait to talk to the mother, then she [the woman who had answered the gate] sat down, and I understood it was the mother. I didn't know her. I only knew her son, who was there as well. He said, 'You wanted to talk, so talk.' The mother showed me a photo of a young man. It was framed. She said to me, 'your brother is the reason he is no longer living. My son was so good, so kind.'"

Somayeh continued, "I said to her, 'I can't say I know what you are going through, but I hope you will consider my brother . . . Would you? He's really a good brother . . . he always looked after me when we were kids.'"

Then Somayeh turned to me and said, "I've had these dreams about him. In one he is executed, hanged, and he sees his own tombstone. In another, he and Suleiman [the person killed] buy bus tickets to go to Karbala [in Iraq]. I told Mrs. Bandari my dream and she said that she had had the same dream." Somayeh took this as a sign that Mrs. Bandari was sensitive and reflective but, more importantly, open to dialogue.

Somayeh continued, "A few weeks ago, Hamid [her brother, the perpetrator] called me. He was feeling very bad. I went to see him that day, at ten at night. When I saw Mrs. Bandari, she asked me, 'You went to see your brother, even at that time?' I said, 'Yes.' She was surprised and told me that I was very dedicated. After our first meeting, she said to me, 'You have a daughter? You are a mother too? Bring your daughter,' and I did. I said to her, 'My brother's life is in your hands.'"

The sense of injustice against Hamid became more manifest as we learned further details of his case. Somayeh told us about another adolescent, Mohammad, who was present during the fight and later contracted a fatal illness unrelated to the incident: "On his deathbed, Mohammad told his mother that it wasn't Hamid; it was him. He told her to go and say that he did it, but she didn't. She [Mohammad's mother] wouldn't because maybe the mother would have to pay *diya*. She is a single mother and doesn't have money. She said, 'No, my son has been exonerated. I won't say he's a murderer.'"

The Victim's Family

Victims' families are often concerned with the prejudices of the many interlocutors who enter their lives. The families may feel insulted, manipulated, betrayed, and hurt when they perceive advocates to be on the side of the perpetrator—or simply against the death penalty. As the Iranian system sets up retribution as a private right and the victim's family as its sole proprietor, some families perceive a blanket prohibition on the death penalty as effectively disenfranchising them of a right that is theirs exclusively.

Thus, social activists, like the actors and social workers in this chapter, must negotiate their perceived lack of impartiality with regard for the sensitive position of the families they seek to influence. Often the first question activists have to answer before a conversation can even begin is, "Who sent you?" They must be careful that the emotions evoked and cultivated by their work do not serve the opposite ends and lead to retribution. In several notably disappointing cases, after having initially agreed to forgo retribution, families changed their minds for this very reason. The social workers I spoke with, however, saw such actions on the part of the victim's family as extracting revenge rather than exacting in-kind punishment or seeing justice carried out on behalf of their loved one.

Yet another obstacle to the activists' work was that, in cases that rise to levels of national or international notoriety as Hamid's case had, victims' families complained about the attention and sympathy that social actors and often the media expended on the perpetrator who had killed their loved one. The families felt that the media portrayed them as the wrongdoers, when in fact they were the ones wronged. If not checked, the growing resentment by members of the victim's family over efforts of outside groups to convince them of forbearance could actually trigger an insistence of carrying out retaliatory sentencing—not in spite of, but because of those pressures. Thus, approaching victims' families is always a sensitive matter.

Such was the concern in the present case. The social workers knew that a family could become more intent on seeking retribution after seeing the heightened attention paid to their son's perpetrator. At present, the Bandari family had already complained of Somayeh's too frequent phone calls. They said she was doing too much. The social workers I was with were careful to avoid any suggestion that Somayeh had sent them. Even if they did speak with her and coordinate their efforts, the social workers insisted that their intentions were separate from hers.

Indeed, the razor's edge of appealing to emotions was a path that the social workers walked in each of the cases they encountered as they made their emotional appeals to forgiveness. In spite of the inadequacies, and even hazards of appealing to emotion, such emotions, if properly delineated, could afford "a powerful, if partial, vision of social justice and provide powerful motives for just conduct" (Nussbaum 1995:xvi). The social workers were all too conscious of the delicate terrain upon which they tread. They were not only aware of this challenge, but valiantly met it head-on.

The troupe headed for the theater and we, along with a retired teacher, Mrs. Najafi, headed to the home of the victim's family. Mrs. Najafi, who was the former teacher of the father and uncles of the deceased, had arrived at three o'clock in the afternoon. She had driven her tiny hatchback straight from Tehran. Mrs. Najafi knowingly whipped through the alleyways of the town in which she was born and had lived for over half a century. As we approached, she gently guided her car over loose gravel and potholes and sidled up to a house enclosed by a brick wall with metal gated doors. She spoke rapidly in a regional accent, "The last time we met with them, they said, if we forgive, what would the neighbors say? . . . 'Oh, they washed their son's blood with money.'"

As we parked and descended from the small hatchback, we saw the doors enclosing the property open and several members of the family emerged. They were the daughter, Leila (sister of the deceased) and her husband. Mahboubeh, who had spoken with Mrs. Bandari (the deceased's mother) by telephone several days earlier, spoke first. Mahboubeh smiled as she shoved her foot inside the door and said, "We are here to speak with you about the play. We are not asking you to make any decision now. We just want you to come and watch it. These young people came all the way from Tehran just for this performance and . . ." Her words trailed off and Leila, who was trying to look stern, cracked a smile.

"I know you," Mahboubeh said, "I know you are too gentle and kind. Please let us in. We just want to talk." At that moment, Leila's husband, who was also standing at the gate intervened, "Please, no. We just want to be left alone. We are not inclined to forgive. We have to go, please. Please go."

"But I just want to say hello to Mrs. Bandari." Mahboubeh pushed open the door and we all proceeded into the yard. The small house, set back twenty yards from the entrance, sat four feet high on a bare concrete foundation. We stood in front of the house when a young man, clad in faded jeans and a black shirt appeared. He was Mrs. Bandari's son. Angrily, he shouted, "We don't want to forgive. We want *qisas*. My mother will not speak to you." Mahboubeh again intervened. "Hello, young man. Please, don't be so angry. It will make you sick. I just wanted to see your mother and say hello. Is she there . . . Mrs. Bandari? Hello?" Then, Mrs. Bandari walked out. She was dressed to leave. "Hello," she said in a somber voice. "I can't talk to you. We have to go. We are leaving right now."

Mahboubeh made her best attempt to speak quickly and effectively. The other women, too, chimed in. "Think of your [deceased] father," Mrs. Najafi, the school teacher said. Mahboubeh reminded them that violence would not calm the pain in their hearts; it would only add pain in another mother's heart. Mahboubeh added in her own experiences with letting go and encouraged them to do the same. The son continued to tell us to leave and came down the stairs of the house towards the gate. The son-in-law, seeing that we were not moving, corralled his wife and mother-in-law towards their car parked outside the gate. We followed, still pleading. "Just come see the play. The kids worked so hard on it." They filed into the car, rolled up the windows, and drove away.

Afterwards, the women reflected; each had the same opinion. "They are open to forgiveness." Fereshteh then said, "It's the mother's choice, but the son-in-law would not let her speak to us." Mahboubeh added, "He's not even a deciding member of the family," noting that he was not an immediate family member possessing the right of retribution. "Mrs. Bandari is really very sweet; she would not do this. She just doesn't dare speak in front of the others. When I spoke with her alone, she was more amenable."

As we spoke, we walked through the neighborhood ringing doorbells and knocking on doors to invite townspeople, especially the neighbors of the family, to the play. Few were home or responded, but several opened their doors or stuck their heads out from air-conditioned interiors to assure us they would go. "This is good," said Fereshteh. "Even if the family does not come, it's important that their neighbors see it." My sense was that this would contribute to the broader cultural work that my interlocutors had mentioned earlier, but Fereshteh was simultaneously referring to something more immediate— Mrs. Najafi's earlier comment about the neighbors. Mrs. Bandari was concerned that, if she forgave, then she would have to answer to her neighbors. In pressing these particular doorbells, the social workers were aiming to change the views of the neighbors, for their opinion weighed against the mother's likelihood of forbearance.

When deciding *qisas*, the victim's family suffers incredible pressures to forgo retribution. The pressures are evident in the stories I have conveyed thus far, but far from being an act of generosity, as forbearance seems to be in the eyes of many urban elite Iranians, small-town families must contend with a different kind of attitude and backlash from neighbors and friends—the fear of losing their honor and falling into disrepute.

The family's concern with a backlash from forbearance connects the cultural work that the artists were doing in the village. The artists' task was to engage an empathetic humanism to override a culture of pride and retribution.

As Fariborz, an actor, conveyed to me, "City dwellers are very different from the rural [residents]." Even though two-thirds of Iranians resides in urban areas and people throughout the country are connected by wireless communications, satellite, and social media, Fariborz emphasized the existence of a deep fissure between the rural and urban dwellers, possibly because of such technological changes over the past twenty years. He noted, moreover, that people in small rural villages assert "tradition" as a justification for continuing some practices as the basis for holding on to their identities and values. "There is something that remains. In fact, it must remain. As our society modernizes, some people want to cling to particular values that, for them, are important indicators that they are distinct from the people in Tehran, whose values they often do not abide. We try to quell the need, if not desire, for retribution because of the socially significant loss of honor."

The Plot

Once at the theater, we met with the local head of the Ministry of Culture and Islamic Guidance, Mr. Hosseini, and a county representative, Mr. Alinejad. Somayeh had first met with Hosseini, who watched a video of the play and was moved to help. Everyone had agreed that there would not be much publicity because they did not want to cause suffering to the victim's family or antagonize them in any way. Moreover, they did not want to raise the suspicion that they were working on behalf of the offender.

During the meeting, Miri and the social workers were discussing the fact that the victim's family had not accepted their invitation to attend. They were attempting one last maneuver to get them to the theater.

> HOSSEINI: We have no right to pressure the family. We are working from a foundation of art. The stories [in the play] are mostly from the perspective of the slain?
> MIRI: No, actually they are from the perspective of the offender.
> HOSSEINI: But we are not trying to force anyone.
> ALINEJAD: No one has that right.
> HOSSEINI: We are learning how to educate our children.
> MAHBOUBEH: We really wanted the family to come.
> MIRI: This play has been performed over seventy times.
> ALINEJAD: We are not talking to them about their issues. We do not want them to think, "why is everyone trying so hard to support the murderer?"
> HOSSEINI: We are not supporting the murderer, just supporting forgiveness. They can come and sit in the balcony. They do not have to see anyone or be seen and can leave quietly.

One member of the victim's family, the [paternal] uncle of the deceased, was at the meeting. As an elder, he was an important family member and was believed to have a lot of influence. "He is with us. He wants to the family to forgive." Mahboubeh said. "He wants to know how he can help convince the others."

"Call Reza," Mahboubeh suggested. Reza, another brother of the deceased, vehemently opposed forbearance. The uncle dialed and said, "I've spoken with Reza. He's very upset, but I think he will come around." Reza did not answer. The uncle lamented, "I worked hard for this, for years. Leila [his niece and sister of the deceased] did not talk to me for two years." He dialed her number. As he waited for her to pick-up, he explained that his sister-in-law, the mother of the deceased, was in great pain. "She wants to know what will calm the pain in her heart." In the end, Leila did not answer her phone either. The victim's family did not come. The pain was palpable, but the show went on.

The Performance

A run-through and dress rehearsal prepared the actors. The stage was set. The audience poured in. The hall was almost full. The only representative of the victim's family was the uncle. The house lights dimmed. The stage was black. Miri came out first and introduced the play with a prayer for the soul of the deceased. Next Hosseini appeared behind a podium at stage left. Tall and thin, dressed in a gray suit and white dress shirt, he welcomed the audience of about eighty. He officially opened the evening with the recital of a poem, *Gonjeeshk-ha* (*The Sparrows*) by a contemporary poet, Davoud Nemati:[11]

> In the hazy story of killing leopards
> All of the guns are polluted
> The sparrows did not die of natural causes
> Bloody are the sleeves of the bullets
> History is a combination of black, blue, and red blisters
> Produced from seventy colors
> We must forbear from this bitter story
> Even the sea forbears the blood of whales
> The balance of scales is not exact
> Let's bring our faith to the happy see-saw.[12]

Two elements of poetic performance are significant in this context. Because poetry is recited, the social context in which it is read is important for understanding its meaning and the purpose for which that poem was selected. Just as meaningful is the style of oration, which contributes an affective quality to the performance and indeed sets the tone for its reception, both as an expression of individual sadness but also an evocation of empathy.[13]

Similarly, with the rich visual imagery that the verses conjure, many meanings can be attributed to a poem. In the context of the play and the purpose for which it was performed, each image in the poem takes on a specific meaning. Leopards signify courage and strength, while sparrows are symbols of beauty and innocence. The death of neither leopards nor sparrows is natural; their loss, like the children depicted in the play, is unnatural, unclean, and unjust. But history is not fair; the balance of justice is not exact. By the end, however, the poem appeals to "happy" see-sawing. Where there exists forbearance, the poem suggests, it can overcome the imbalance and inexactitude of justice and allow for equilibrium and equanimity.

Persian poetic traditions, moreover, create affect through the art of recitation. Indeed, poetry does not contribute to culture-building simply by the utterance of words that conjure images. Rather, the lyricism in the poetic language serves to cultivate feelings of empathetic humanism.[14] Here I am suggesting that eloquence is a bridge between lyrical poetry and empathetic imagining that emotionally moves audiences. Persian poetry recital possesses its own affected tenor and intentionally summons emotions.[15] Dabashi notes the significance of Persian poetry's melodiousness in particular (2012:211).[16] The lyricism in the language of recited poetry confers calm and tranquility upon listeners. The serenity then permits feelings of love for humanity to emerge and, through them, forbearance and forgiveness may flow.[17]

Hosseini ended his speech with a *salavat*, again on behalf of the deceased, and added, "I wish Suleiman's family would see the play. This performance does not seek to take the right of the victim's family away from them. *Qisas* is a right; forgiveness is a grace." Speaking of the perpetrator, Hosseini said, "He was only sixteen when he committed this crime," and thus linked the play with Hamid's situation. Hosseini added, "Love consists of good works. It is Zeinab, the name of one of the Prophet's daughters, and the name of Suleiman's mother is Zeinab."[18] In the absence of the victim's mother, Hosseini here appeared to be addressing all mothers, compelling them to act.

As he prepared to leave the stage, Hosseini introduced, Mrs. Najafi, the teacher. Standing behind the podium, she told the audience that society could help young people in difficult situations. She pleaded with the crowd, "Please help prevent revenge acts from taking place. Prevent violence. This is a chance to do so in Siah Kal. Both the perpetrator and the victim are from here. We can try to bring the families together. We are working to change the system through education and awareness." She stepped down; the house lights went out.

The actors came on stage. In short vignettes over the next hour and a half, they portrayed young people who had killed. Each story proceeded through a web of conflict and pain; children's lives and often livelihoods were depicted—playing soccer, selling wares, working at home. Grieving relatives

FIGURE 6. Image from a scene of the performance, *The Blue Feeling of Death*, in Siah Kal, Gilan, July 2015. Author's photo.

were portrayed—a mother, a brother, a sister. And the juveniles themselves were represented—crying, cajoling, asking for forgiveness. Some actors portraying youth dressed in vibrant costumes, reflecting carefree adolescence, the attire contrasting sharply with the somber tones of the set or characters depicting mourning family members. Each story highlighted a case on death row. As each story revealed itself, the youth offender climbed on a stool and stood blindfolded. Hanging nooses dangled stools in mid-air.

Ultimately, the play came to its closing scene with two actors seated on the floor next to each other, portraying the same person—Samira. The first started with a soliloquy of what she did and did not do. She did not help her mother kill her father, as her mother claimed. She did not help strangle him by grabbing one end of the shawl. The first actor ended her speech and then the spotlight moved to the second Samira. She began, "I am Samira, the real Samira. The very same Samira who, for the charge of murdering her father, spent six years in prison from the age of fifteen to two weeks ago." She continued with the words that she had written herself just the day before.

> You say murderer, but you don't know. When you experience the pain of Tuesdays, when you don't know whose turn it will be at night and which of the people around you will not see the sun rise tomorrow.[19] Who can feel the pain of that night, when they take one of your cellmates to solitary? In those moments when all the people she knew and didn't know would pray for her and from the bottom of their hearts weep and beg God for one more week of life for her. You call me a murderer, but you don't know. When I see that same murderer in her white *chador*, before her prayer rug, begging God, then I don't see a criminal. In front of your eyes, in that moment, you see a human whose place can be exchanged with any other person in the world. A human, like all others, for whom death is just one moment, but for her in every moment of life, she dies a thousand times. And each time the taste of death is more painful than the time before . . .

Those lines from the real Samira closed the play. Her words, offered in tandem with the actress portraying her, brought the performance to its ultimate finale, blurring the performative aspect of the play and disrupting the suspension of disbelief that any artistic rendering requires. As she described her misery and suffering, from fear of being called away to execution to lamenting the fate of a cellmate, Samira's soliloquy provided a story of suffering in line with what Joseph Slaughter has characterized as a "metonymical claim of belonging to a common community" (2009:105). Samira's words were intended to move the audience, not by some mere empathetic imagining, but rather physically, through her presence, showing that she belongs to their world too. Her monologue was a moving "testimonial of suffering" in which Samira appeals for membership to "the universal class of humanity from which [her] suffering has effectively excluded" her (Ibid.).

The lights dimmed, then the theater went black. A resounding applause brought the actors back to the stage. They took their bows amidst a palpably emotional finish. Audience members were visibly moved, and tears flowed generously. Little by little, the crowd poured outside the theater and gathered in the cool night air. They spoke intently about Hamid's case. "Death would only bring more *gham* [sorrow]." "There is *lezat* [joy] that comes with forgiveness." Many asked what they could do to help. Someone offered to speak with the victim's family. The uncle, the only family member in attendance, responded, "Let me work on them and get back to you. I have to involve other family members." With these reactions, I saw how the culture-building that my interlocutors spoke of was intended to work on the whole community, not just the victim's family. The aim of the cultural work was twofold: to shift people's perceptions about the case at hand and to raise awareness and discussion about the death penalty, especially for youth under eighteen. As I noted earlier, this work is both subtle and courageous, given the state's sensitivities to overt activism against the death penalty.

Later that night, we were back at the house. There was a sense of quiet achievement from the performance, but the atmosphere exuded an air of duty and detail. The actors arranged their affairs and checked their phones. At nearly ten, Hamid's mother entered. She was uncharacteristically animated, and a lightness betrayed her otherwise burdened disposition. She approached us and said that she had received a call from a member of the victim's family. The sister of their son-in-law had called. She had had a dream. In that dream, Hamid was standing with a rope around his neck. Suleiman (the deceased) told her to forgive Hamid. She then removed the rope and freed him. The son-in-law's sister called the family matriarch, Mrs. Bandari, and conveyed the dream and its message; she said that they must forgive Hamid. She then called Hamid's mother and said, "Look, we feel that we will forgive. In our hearts, there is forgiveness." But she also repeated the family's wish that Somayeh refrain from intervening. "Tell no one to come. We have the feeling of forgiveness; we have opened our hearts to it, but give us some time." I ask if the son-in-law's sister had influence. Somayeh replied that the family held traditional values and that family members and village leaders could be influential; the answer was yes. On the heels of this news, plans were being made: the son-in-law's sister would speak to the mother. The uncle would meet with the family. Mr. Abdulazadeh also planned to speak with them.

Mahboubeh began preparing a celebratory *ash* (soup). She said, "I could tell from her face, Mrs. Bandari can't do this [*qisas*]. She doesn't have the heart for it."

The Final Act

The troupe, the social workers, and even I, left the next morning with a sense of achievement, even elation. Hamid's mother had offered a joyful postscript to the evening's performance. Despite the family's absence from the theater that night, this would be a success story, like other performances these players had staged. The issue of retributive killing had been presented in this small village, and with it introduced a discussion about deeply-held values related to avenging the death of a loved one.

Still, I agree with scholars who contend that even this work of producing emotion may not move people to action. From this event, however, I consider the work that it does achieve, the idea of the culture-building; it seeks to make the death penalty a dishonorable act, while reminding us, through our intimate social networks, that forgiveness is a virtuous one. Creative imagining or storytelling allows for a refinement of emotion. It permits *catharsis* or purification (of the senses) of pity and fear and helps bring about healing and relief (Heath 1996:xxxix). Catharsis "does not eliminate emotion, rather it washes away emotional excess," leaving "a more balanced state" (1996: xl). The evening's performance helped to do just that.

In her study of the advent of human rights, historian Lynn Hunt suggests that empathy for distant others is a modern sensibility that emerges in tandem with the rise of the novel in eighteenth century Europe (2007). Hunt argues that the epistolary novel permits a "learning of empathy" because there is no singular authorial point of view, but rather several, through the characters' letter-writing. This lack of authorship made possible a heightened identification with the characters, whose socio-economic position and gender are often different from those of the readers. Hunt finds that the epistolary novel produced psychological resonance in readers because its form allows access to characters' interior worlds (2007:43). Hunt distinguishes the epistolary novel from other literary forms, including theater. I suggest that the documentary form of theater, prevalent in Iran today and characterized by *The Blue Feeling of Death*, with its storytelling narratives, confessional style, and multiple points of view, contains precisely the epistolary qualities that Hunt claims permit audience members to react to the characters, albeit real personas, in similar ways.

Conclusion

I was eager and at the same time anxious to call Somayeh to learn of the denouement of the story. However, it was not the family's forgiveness that came. Instead it was a ruling by Iran's highest court. New criminal codes in effect since 2013 permit offenders between the ages of fifteen and eighteen charged with crimes of intentional murder, assault, and (others) to submit evidence demonstrating a lack of mental state or capacity. On January 21, 2015, the court determined that this law would apply retroactively. This would be a new chance for Hamid and other under-age youth to contest their convictions and hence sentences of *qisas*. Hamid's lawyer filed evidence to this effect. The requisite judicial review then proceeded. Then, on May 15, 2015, Amnesty International issued a press release warning of the possibility of imminent execution for Hamid Ahmadi, despite his case being under review.[20] From Seattle, I sent frantic inquiries to learn about Hamid's situation to Somayeh, Miri, and my social worker friends. Each conveyed the urgency of the situation and their concern for the case.

Mahboubeh had just returned from her third trip to Siah Kal since the previous summer. She had just finished a meeting with the victim's mother,

Mrs. Bandari, when I called her on May 23, 2015. She said that Mrs. Bandari had not yet decided to forgo retribution, but, "in all my years, I have not met someone as gentle and kind as Mrs. Bandari who went through with this." She added, "I cannot say with certainty what she will do, but I would be very surprised if Mrs. Bandari went through with it." Mrs. Bandari, it seemed, had still not been able to reconcile the idea of releasing Hamid from punishment, his seven years in prison notwithstanding. In her case, Mrs. Bandari felt that it would be wrong of her to forgo punishment on behalf of her son. Mrs. Bandari was still concerned that her community in Siah Kal would look askance at a mother who did not seek to avenge her son's murder. Further, her sense of detachment from the social customs of the urban social workers highlighted vast social differences in perceptions of dealing with issues of harm and compensation. While Mrs. Bandari saw Mahboubeh as an urbanite, free of the social constraints found in small towns, Mahboubeh had tried to assure her that the neighbors would be happy, even congratulate her. She would be celebrated for her compassion and generosity, as had other mothers who forwent retributive sanctioning.[21]

Mahboubeh's efforts to get Mrs. Bandari to forgo retribution notwithstanding, I also learned that Somayeh had retained a new lawyer for her brother. This lawyer had filed the petition to have Hamid's case retried under the new law. On May 30, 2015, Mahboubeh sent me an elated message conveying a new development in Hamid's case:

Hamid's sentence had been halted by the judiciary. The criminal court in Gilan would review the case in accordance with the new law. Hamid would be allowed to submit evidence of his emotional maturity, ultimately an attempt to raise doubt as to whether a sixteen-year-old Hamid had possessed the requisite intent to kill. Hamid's lawyer wrote, "Hamid is one step farther from death and one step closer to getting on with his life."

Somayeh confirmed that the case was set to be retried. Even if the hearing did not go well, Somayeh felt that it would lead to more negotiations with the victim's family. She surmised that Mrs. Bandari would rather make a deal where she would receive *diya*, than have the courts throw it out, which would leave her with nothing. While the appeal was pending, Somayeh boosted her efforts at attaining the family's forbearance. She appealed to the resources of Mr. Saheb, "the man of forgiveness" (from Chapter 6). He flew to Siah Kal in February 2017, just as Hamid's last appeal was rejected. The family decided, finally, to forgo retribution. Hamid's life was spared. Somayeh was left to raise the hefty *diya* they demanded, which required her, once again, to appeal for help to Miri, Abdulazadeh, and others for donations.

In the case at hand, as in many, it is impossible to measure the extent to which the culture-building, or what I have referred to in this chapter as the art of forgiveness, factors into both positive and negative outcomes of these cases. As this case shows, such efforts may not move the immediate audience to which they are directed—the victim's family—to action. Instead, the advocacy of so many parties, especially the performers, directed the attention of the authorities and the residents of Siah Kal to the injustices of this case, and others like it.

Even local government officials in Gilan became involved in the case and made house calls to the victim's family. Ultimately, this case demonstrates that art performs cultural work which aims to provoke empathetic imaginings that could lead to forgiveness, but may not have direct causal impact on the victims' families. Rather, artists direct their endeavors to cultivate broad cultural shifts that engage this semi-autonomous social field, devoid of law, and attempt both to shift the grounds of acceptability and to create new conditions of possibility for a humanity that engages art, poetry, and theater to stimulate the feelings of forgiveness.

8

Cause Lawyers

ADVOCATING MERCY'S LAW

LAWYERS WHO take up *qisas* cases are at the vanguard of both rights-based advocacy and forgiveness work on behalf of their clients. As a result, they simultaneously push the limits of the law and forge effective campaigns for forgiveness, sometimes at great personal risk. On the front lines, lawyers are sometimes lauded for saving a life, but, other times, they are blamed for ineffective counsel and, at times, even castigated as brazen cons seeking celebrity and international renown at the expense of their clients' suffering. Most striking, however, the lawyers' work in intentional homicide cases is characterized by the sometimes-contradictory approach that advocacy around forbearance entails. If advocacy, by its very nature, is zealous, forthright, and adversarial, forgiveness work is conciliatory, diffident, and collaborative.

Lawyers walk a fine line on several fronts. First, they must tread lightly in mounting the defense of a perpetrator before an aggrieved family whose right of retribution is like a shield drawn up to attack, and to whose forbearance the lawyer may later need to appeal. In mounting a defense, many lawyers with whom I spoke conveyed the concern of not raising the ire of the victim's family. Thus, in the adversarial setting of the Iranian courts, strategies for defending clients are limited. In addition to concerns about victims' families, lawyers also had to be mindful of legal strategies that would give the impression of challenging the judicial system's foundational principles. As we saw earlier, during my interview with Judge Aziz-Mohammadi, he asserted that he did not believe in *qisas*—an incredible claim coming from the man celebrated for having issued the most criminal sentences in all of Iran. At that utterance, immediately, another judge stepped in to clarify that the claim was the judge's personal feeling, which did not signify his disavowal of the system. But lawyers who do not possess the same degree of political capital as judges can more readily fall afoul of government. This is especially so during the sometimes public and international campaigns on behalf of their clients. The points above are not intended to suggest any bright lines, either about the limits of advocacy or government censure. Instead, both are fluid and shift with changing social, political, and economic climates. Since working on these chapters, I have seen defense lawyers go to prison and come out, only to be returned again. Others have left the country. Those who continue to practice do so under severe constraints.

Still, the new legal provisions give lawyers greater access to clients and their files. They also ensure increased protections for defendants and open a range of strategic possibilities for lawyers in the defense of their clients. It bears repeating, however, that the definition of intent in intentional murders remains very broad, and lawyers often have very little leverage with clients, many of which they are called to defend well after the perpetrator has been arrested, interrogated, and has delivered a confession. This is the case even in light of laws allowing the accused a right to an attorney at the time of arrest.[1]

In this chapter, I consider the work of several lawyers on some widely publicized and other less well-known cases, including the cases of Sina Paymard, Behnoud Shojaee, Sahar Mohabadi, and Reyhaneh Jabbari. I examine the legal advocacy of the lawyers and compare them with other activist approaches. As I explore the lawyers' strategies and why they undertook such work, which often comes at great personal risk, I situate the practices of the lawyers I came to know during my fieldwork in the literature on cause lawyering (Menkel-Meadow 1998; Sarat and Scheingold 1998).[2] In some cases, lawyers quietly work behind the scenes and are committed to paving the legal trajectory both for their clients' sakes and for the sake of developing Iran's criminal legal system. Those lawyers see themselves engaged in human rights work. In other cases, lawyers seemingly embody the 'zealous advocate' posture and push for attention on the world stage in order to appeal to the court of world opinion on their clients' behalves. In light of the legal barriers their clients face in such cases, lawyers appeal to humanitarian discourses and sensibilities to save their clients from certain death. Accordingly, this chapter engages with the politics of anti-death penalty activism as well.

Cause Lawyers

In the fall of 2014, Nasrin Sotoudeh stood in front of the Iranian Bar Association's office in Tehran every weekday morning to protest her ban on practicing law.[3] She wore her signature white headscarf and held up signs that read, "Right to Work" and "Right of Dissenters." She was often joined by colleagues, supporters, and other social activists. The year prior, in 2013, Sotoudeh had emerged from almost three years in prison for having engaged in advocacy work that Iran's judiciary, who tried her in the state's revolutionary court, found to have amounted to *moharebeh* (waging war against God and state), endangering the security of the state, and spreading propaganda against the state.[4] Her sentence was six years in prison, of which she served about half, and a three-year ban on practicing law. Her advocacy ultimately led to a lifting on the ban, and she continued her work in important ways. On June 13, 2018, authorities again arrested Sotoudeh. They deemed her defense of the "Girls of Revolution Street," the young women who publicly removed their headscarves and were arrested, as having violated Iran's public security and anti-corruption laws.[5] Through her role in defending highly sensitive cases and, at times, high profile defendants—including activists, journalists, and dissidents charged with political crimes—Sotoudeh has made a name for herself, within Iran and beyond, as one of the country's foremost defenders of human rights.

Since I began my work as a legal anthropologist in Iran over twenty years ago, I have encountered numerous dedicated, motivated, and savvy lawyers. Many have earned international human rights awards, including the Nobel Peace Prize won by Shirin Ebadi in 2003. But in the years since Ebadi's award, some Iranian government institutions have come to view such work as political activism that challenges the state's very legitimacy, thus rendering human rights advocacy increasingly risky. Such advocacy—so named—has engendered many challenges for social and legal activists (Osanloo 2013). While activists take on numerous causes and approach them in a myriad of ways, many avoid human rights language though others persist in naming their causes outright as human rights work.

I seek to understand what makes an Iranian cause lawyer, like Sotoudeh, undertake the defense of her clients, especially in light of the risk and suffering lawyers in such positions often endure. I examine how some of Iran's cause lawyers operate, what strategies they employ, and to what ends. In order to better understand the work of legal advocacy on behalf of Iran's death row inmates, I draw from the scholarship on cause lawyering (Sarat and Scheingold 1998).[6] Most of that work emphasizes advocacy, challenges, and the politics of cause lawyers in North America.[7] This scholarship helps in better understanding the pressures that Iran's legal advocates face when they, too, advocate for a cause. Cause lawyering has been defined as "lawyering for the good" and using law to promote social change (Menkel-Meadow 1998), but it is also noted for its lack of specific conceptual framework. Cause lawyers are "individuals who self-consciously commit themselves and their skills to a political cause, and for whom lawyering is not value-neutral" (Statz 2018:6). Cause lawyers share with their clients a responsibility for the moral ends that they are promoting. In so doing, Sarat and Scheingold argue, cause lawyers "reconnect law and morality" (1998:3). With this attribute of cause lawyering, we can see the distinct risks and challenges that Iranian cause lawyers face.

When cause lawyers challenge the laws, particularly if they present alternative interpretations of Islamic principles, they can be seen as questioning the state's authority. Thus, cause lawyers risk recrimination and often prosecution, as in the case of many in Iran today, including Sotoudeh. Because the state is not monolithic, lawyers' petitions may be received as legitimate in one venue (the criminal court), but then the lawyers may be harassed, threatened, or even arrested and charged in another (the revolutionary court). In such cases, cause lawyering can, and often does, amount to charges of acting against the state, as has occurred in several cases involving anti-death penalty activism.[8]

Although it is difficult to paint Iran's cause lawyers with a broad stroke, many described their work to me as compelling state authorities to follow Iran's own laws. Many also advocate legal reform, seek to draw attention to human rights, women's rights, and children's rights, and support for specific issues, such as addressing violence against women and children and halting the death penalty. Cause lawyers work in multiple sites—in the courts as well as in the domestic public sphere—through newspaper interviews and editorials, television appearances, public lectures, and even sometimes in university classrooms. Iranian cause lawyering also reaches international venues through satellite television, social media, and NGOs that work with exiled lawyers possessing knowledge of the system. For many in the last group, the issue of being co-opted by regime change politics is a constant tension.

As we saw in the previous chapter, many of Iran's anti-death penalty activists, including but not exclusively lawyers, work most overtly on anti-death penalty cases that involve individuals who are juvenile offenders. This is because Iran is a signatory to the CRC and, through its international obligations under that treaty, it is required—and has agreed—to adhere to certain international standards pertaining to the treatment of all children, including those accused of crimes. Accordingly, many of the cases of forbearance for which I found the strongest activism were those that fell into this category. Many activists, including lawyers with whom I spoke, saw this as an entry point for a public discussion on the broader issue of ending the death penalty, a kind of activism which was too risky to broach independently.

As such, one way in which I see the work of cause lawyers differing from that of other social activists is in the formers' approach to the law. These lawyers, zealous advocates, to take a term from American legal practice, engage with the law and the legal system in ways that are both respectful of it and, at the same time, attempt to stretch it, construe it, and give it shape, meaning, and effect. They are participating in rule-making in the ways that are expected of zealous advocates the world over. This aspect of their advocacy seemed quite natural given my own experiences practicing law in the U.S., but it also surprised me. Each time lawyers took one of these cases, often pro-bono, they would be putting themselves at tremendous risk. Even so, when they spoke to me about their work, they were careful yet, at the same time, matter of fact about the work; it simply had to be done and there was no regret or hesitation about it.

Part of the reason for this attitude among Iranian cause lawyers, I think, goes back to the unregulated nature of the social field in which forgiveness work takes place. The lawyers had no specific guidelines to bring about forbearance in order to save the lives of their clients. But, in order to act ethically and to do their utmost to defend their clients, they were often required to bring international attention to their cases. In turn, however, it was this very international attention that got these advocates into trouble with their own government. In what follows, I pay close attention to the legal practices that the lawyers pursue, as well as the extra-legal advocacy they engage in, particularly in the contexts of bargaining for their clients' lives in spaces devoid of regulation. Such advocacy makes use of law in unique ways.

Sotoudeh: the unquiet counselor

I encountered many of the lawyers I write about in this chapter through social and legal advocacy networks I became acquainted with in the course of my research for both the current project and a previous one (2009). I met Sotoudeh in November 2007 through a contact from another researcher. I was interested in learning about her defense of Sina Paymard, a young man on death row. Sotoudeh's zealous and innovative advocacy of Sina and others had gained her high praise throughout the world, and included several human rights awards. I had read about the case in the international press and was intrigued by her legal strategy, a highly outspoken one.

Sotoudeh agreed to meet and invited me to her home in central Tehran. When I arrived, she, a petite woman then in her early forties, greeted me in her well-appointed apartment. The apartment, though small, had an open kitchen, dining and living rooms, and offered a spacious, airy ambience. During our meeting, telephone calls often interrupted our dialogue. Those days, Sotoudeh was working from home, having months earlier given birth to her second child.

Sotoudeh graduated from the top university in the country. An avowed human rights lawyer, she was adamantly against the death penalty. She was the first person to tell me that, as things currently stood in Iran, advocacy purely for the abolition of the death penalty was impossible, so anti-death penalty advocates took different tacks to pursue their work. She, too, referred to the culture-building that had to happen in order to change the law. First, she suggested, people's beliefs and values had to change.

I turned to the subject of my visit: Sotoudeh's advocacy on behalf of Sina Paymard, the youth whose life she had been successful in saving. In 2005, Sina Paymard was sentenced to *qisas* for killing a man. A year earlier, when he was just sixteen, Sina had met the man, a young drug dealer, at a park in Tehran. He had intended to purchase hashish. The two had a dispute over the transaction and Sina stabbed him, later claiming he was under the influence of drugs at the time. Upon review, Iran's highest court had upheld his sentence.

In September 2006, after his last appeal had been exhausted, prison officials took the now eighteen-year-old Sina to the gallows, where he was to be executed. As the law requires the victim's family to be present for the execution, in Sina's case it was the victim's four brothers who were in attendance. During our visit, Sotoudeh confirmed what others had told me in this well-known case—the deceased had been long cut off from his family. The parents of the deceased had delegated all authority on the matter of their son's death to their four other sons, the eldest of whom had not seen his brother, the victim, in some fifteen years. Many social workers and lawyers I spoke with about this case saw this as an injustice. The parents gave their power of attorney to their sons for whom the death of their brother had become a windfall—a means for them to accept *diya*.

It is here that Sina Paymard's story shares a plot line with that of the social worker, Mahboubeh, who had also exercised forbearance in the murder of her brother, Behrouz. As a final wish, Sina had asked to play his *ney* and, with his elegiac performance of Rumi's opening lament about the pain of separation, he was able to delay his execution. The victim's family decided that they would consider payment in exchange for his life and forgo retribution. Judicial officials postponed the sentence for two months to allow the prisoner and his supporters, including his lawyer Sotoudeh, to negotiate the compensation.

As she continued to pursue various avenues to spare Sina, the postponement of execution allowed Sotoudeh to pursue a new legal angle as well. It was around this time that the issue of mental age for adolescent offenders was being debated in Iran's judiciary. The question of mental capacity was an important potential defense for underage offenders because it determined the legal age of competent decision-making and, therefore, intent. Accordingly, the question of adolescent mental capacity was particularly important in Sina's case. In November of 2006, even as she negotiated with the victim's family and attempted to raise compensation funds, Sotoudeh submitted evidence that her client had a disability. He was suffering from bipolar disorder and had been treated for it several years earlier. Sotoudeh argued that the court improperly failed to consider Sina's illness as a mitigating factor, which undermined the requisite intent needed for the sentence. Additionally, Sotoudeh took to the airwaves. She went on the Iranian-language Voice of America (VOA), the much-viewed satellite station beamed into Iranian households from the U.S., to plead her case before the court of public opinion.[9] She also spread word of Sina's imminent execution through local newspapers and the internet. Amnesty International, among other international human rights organizations, picked up Sina's story, which contained several emotionally appealing angles: his age, mental disability, and the dramatic last wish of playing his *ney*.

In January 2007, Sina was granted a stay of execution while the parties continued their negotiation. The victim's family had set the amount of *diya* at $90,000. Through domestic and international appeals as well as their own meager resources, including selling their home, Sina's family was able to raise only $70,000. In April 2007, when they presented the funds, the deceased's family said they wanted more. They raised their demand to $160,000, meaning Sina and his family needed to come up with another $90,000.

On July 17th, Sina sent word to Sotoudeh that he was to be sent to the gallows again. This time, Sotoudeh obtained only a ten-day reprieve. As Sotoudeh recounted these frustrating months, she noted that the bulk of the remainder of the $160,000 *diya* had been sent to her by a wealthy Iranian who had learned of Sina's plight from the press. According to her, he immediately wired her the funds.[10] But the victim's family again refused to accept payment, saying they wanted still more. Apparently, judicial officials refused to engage the additional demands of the victim's family, meaning they had to accept the $160,000 *diya* or follow through with retribution. Finally, on July 25, Sotoudeh reported that the victim's family had accepted the *diya*, and Sina was reprieved. He was released from prison on December 24, 2007.[11]

Sotoudeh's multiple-front strategy seemed to have paid off, despite her lack of guidance in pursuing forbearance. Her international advocacy possessed a strategic angle and influenced many others to follow suit. I now turn to another advocate, Mohammad Mostafaei, who went even further with his own weblog.

Mohammad Mostafaei: "lawyer of many teenagers on death row"

The first time I met Mohammad Mostafaei was in his office in central Tehran in 2008. The prosecutor I had met when I attended a hearing in Tehran's Criminal Court knew Mostafaei from law school. Both had graduated a dozen or so years earlier at the top of their class. Now they were friends outside of court, and often adversaries inside.

When we arrived, Mostafaei, himself, sitting behind the secretary's desk, buzzed us in. He greeted his old friend with warmth and then led us into his private office. The large office, with bookcases containing legal treatises, a large conference table, and a desk and chairs, exuded warmth and confidence, like Mostafaei, himself. By this point, Mostafaei, only in his early thirties, was a well-known lawyer and highly regarded for his efforts, almost exclusively, in defending under-age youth from execution. By the time I met him, he was traveling all over the country for this work. In his office, the various phones—on his desk and in his pocket—rang incessantly. One call caught my attention. The plaintiff, that is, the victim's family, was on the line. Upon Mostafaei's personal appeals to them, they were willing to forgo retributive sanctioning, but they demanded compensation from the offender. The amount they asked for, over $50,000, was well beyond the means of the offender's family, he told the person on the line. But Mostafaei agreed to convey the message and see what he could do.

Mostafaei's defense work was effective. He reported "around a fifty percent success rate" in saving his clients from the gallows but added that "forgiveness is a twisted affair." He explained that the victim's family is given the right to retribution, but they are grieving and in terrible pain. "It's the worst time to be tasked with such a decision." State officials also sometimes act in contravention of the laws. To highlight the procedural injustices, Mostafaei told me how he had recently returned from Shiraz, where his under-age client had been executed while Mostafaei was on a plane en route to see him. He was not given prior notice of the planned execution and, in violation of the law, had not been in attendance.

Mostafaei's defense of his clients went well beyond legal defense work and bargaining for forbearance. A sensitive and articulate man, Mostafaei was also an eloquent writer who had established a blog detailing his cases. This online advocacy had made Mostafaei a household name. He had taken quite aggressively to the blogosphere, laying out the cases he was defending, the conditions that many of his clients grew up in, the serious breaches of justice they faced in the legal process, and the near-extortion level sums they needed to raise, in essence, to buy back their lives. His eponymous blog carried the subtitle *Defense of the Defenseless* and quickly became an almost daily report on the precarious legal situations of his clients in Iran.

The blog also contained an educational component through which he carefully outlined legal issues that made readers, both domestic and international, aware of how these cases violate Iran's own commitments under international law, especially the Convention on the Rights of the Child (CRC). As a practitioner, Mostafaei drew attention to how the laws operate and the problems with them. This was helpful to international advocates who were unfamiliar with Iran's legal procedures. Mostafaei's ability to reach wide audiences and communicate details of the laws and specific cases through his blog ultimately drew the attention of government censors, who closed it down several times. Each time he created a new site and continued to document both his cases and his own travails. In July of 2009 Mostafaei was arrested for conspiring against the government and detained for seven days.

Undeterred, Mostafaei continued to take on the most difficult and often high-profile cases, his presence sometimes the reason a case became high-profile. Among such cases, Mostafaei was one of the lawyers for Behnoud Shojaee, an under-age offender. On his blog, Mostafaei had detailed the painful final hours of Behnoud's life on October 11, 2009:

I was waiting for time to pass, so I could go to the Evin Prison. Around 2:30 [*sic*] we went to Evin Prison. About 200 social rights activists and some mothers whose children had been killed were also present. We were waiting for the parents of the victim to come. After one hour, we saw the mother and father of Ehsan [the victim] and his sister and brother. Everyone went towards them to try to convince them to drop their complaint. The atmosphere was very dense. The door of the prison opened. The parents of the victim [*sic*] and I entered.

We waited for a while in the waiting room. We thought that after the parents of the victim dropped the case, Behnoud wouldn't be executed. After a while [*sic*] we could hear the prayers of the activists from outside the prison. After a few minutes we entered another salon. Behnoud was there, along with a few of the prison guards. When the parents of the victim entered the room, Behnoud kneeled in front of them and begged them to not execute him. The head of the convictions prepared the conviction papers. A few of the prison guards, Mr. Oliyayee, and I went towards the parents of the victim and begged them to not go through with the execution. The mother of the victim said: "I cannot think right now. I have to put the rope around his neck." After a few minutes we heard the Call for Prayer. Behnoud went to another room to say his last prayers. He went to ask God for forgiveness. After the prayer we all went to the grounds of the prison. My whole body was shaking and I didn't know what would become of this motherless boy. When Behnoud kneeled in front of the parents of the victim, he told the mother: "I don't have a mother, please, you act as a mother and tell them not to execute me." We all went to another room. In that room there was a metal stool, and a blue plastic hanging rope was suspended above it. The parents of the victim entered that room, and then they brought Behnoud to this horrible room as well. The room [was] where they did all the executions. I had never heard of specific individual executions in Evin prison, and I thought it strange that only Behnoud was being executed that night.

Maybe this was his unfortunate fate that took him to the skies all alone. The people who were there again asked the parents to forgive, and stop the execution. The mother said you have to put the rope around his neck. He went up on the stool and they put the rope around his neck. After only a few seconds the mother and father of the victim ran towards the stool and pulled it away. I could not tolerate to watch. Right when they pulled away the stool everything became dark. Behnoud had gone to the beyond.

Today, Behnoud is not among his friends in prison anymore. They feel his absence. I did everything I could, but it was not effective. I still believe that he did not deserve to die. He shouldn't have been executed. But he was executed.

Executed.[12]

Behnoud's case was a tragic portrait of how the unregulated nature of the system can lead to confusion and dismay. The case launched conversations among activists about the nature of weblog advocacy and its potential to harm rather than help. The victim's mother had originally agreed to forgo retributive punishment but, upon learning of the international efforts to save Behnoud, she became annoyed. She told social workers that it was as if he, Behnoud, were the victim and not her son.

Mostafaei's experience with the families of victims, specifically the negotiations in Behnoud's case, ultimately led him to take a lead in fund-raising for under-age defendants. On his blog, he appealed to readers to contribute to a fund he had created for paying the increasingly exorbitant sums that victims' families demanded in exchange for their forbearance. In his post on October 21, ten days after Behnoud's death, Mostafaei explained his actions in the case:

> I never thought Behnoud Shojaee would be executed, considering that in the presence of a number of popular activist artists, the family of his victim agreed to forgive him. Even in a confidential meeting, they said they would settle for "*Diya.*" Since Behnoud's family is not financially well-off, the artists opened an account to raise money to help with the payment. After opening the account, a public announcement was made in the print media that mentioned Behnoud's name. The family became upset at this and retracted their initial consent [to forgo retribution].
>
> Currently, several clients of mine who were under 18 when they committed their crime are awaiting execution. There is an urgent need to collect [*diya*] for them so that we can get the money to the victim's family for consent or forgiveness. Because the matter is extremely sensitive, I cannot release the names of my clients, but once blood money is collected and a family's consent is obtained, they will be released.

Mostafaei then announced to his readers that he had opened a bank account to receive deposits to raise funds for youth, adding that, by raising $200,000, he could save the lives of three or four teenagers.

In order to obtain consent from a victim's family, there is a need for money to be paid to the family at the time of their forgiveness. I was forced to open an account that would help save lives of offenders who were minors at the time of their crime. I say I was "forced," because I just could not find any other organization or group that I could trust with this matter.[13]

Mostafaei gave his audience information on how to make deposits into the fund and stated that he would publish the amounts collected and payments made to victims' families on his blog at the end of each month. He signed off as "lawyer of many teenagers on death row."

Despite the challenges surrounding this work, Mostafaei had many successes, which he shared with his readers on his blog. When I met him again in the summer of 2010, he similarly had many successes to report, "almost fifty," he told me.

Along with international attention, Mostafei's indefatigable advocacy brought him under the state's surveillance system. The opening of a bank account to collect funds had brought his advocacy further within the realm of suspicion. "We don't know where the funds are going," one state official said to me. Like Sotoudeh, Mostafaei's actions and advocacy give shape to the semi-autonomous social field of forgiveness work that I have been describing in these chapters. The unregulated nature of this space, devoid of law, as my interlocutors have told me, allowed for ingenuity, as in Mostafaei's case. From his blog to his fundraising, this was legal advocacy at its most resourceful and imaginative. He was also motivated, he told me, by his complete abhorrence of the death penalty and his adherence to international human rights laws, including and especially the CRC.

In the summer of 2010, Mostafaei was steeped in the defense of Sakineh Mohammadi-Ashtianti, a forty-three-year-old mother of two charged with the crime of adultery and as an accessory to the murder of her husband. Mostafaei had engaged the world stage to denounce her imminent execution, which was to be accomplished by stoning. His actions unleashed a torrent of protest.[14] Mostafaei's advocacy ultimately stopped the execution, but also became his undoing.[15] On July 26, 2010, just days after an interview he gave to the Spanish newspaper *El Pais* about Ashtiani's case, he was summoned to court. He never appeared. Instead, embroiled in his own persecution, Mostafaei fled to Norway.

Still, his advocacy did not end there. Mostafaei became an even more vocal anti-death penalty activist through a range of publications and public appearances. He also broadened his advocacy to issues of violence against women, freedom of religious belief, freedom of expression, and others. Through his NGO, *Universal Tolerance Organization*, Mostafaei continues to advance cause lawyering tactics on the international front. Not only did he make Iranian legal practice scrutable to the outside world, but he also made human rights laws legible to advocates in Iran.

Mostafaei's demonstration of a commitment to human rights and cause lawyering led him to speak out against the system, especially about its irregular procedures and officials who did not follow Iran's own laws. His work led more people to become aware of Iran's laws and to speak out against them. His strategies, which saved lives, also moved debates about Iran's criminal justice system into the domestic and international public arena. While it is impossible to measure, Mostafaei's tactics were likely influential in helping to reshape the laws regarding juvenile punishments.

Targeting a Cause: Reyhaneh revisited

Mohammad Mostafaei was the original trial attorney hired by Reyhaneh Jabbari's family to defend her against the charge of murder. Reyhaneh's case engendered legal debates as well as legal analyses that led to important public debates about the death penalty. Reyhaneh was executed on October 25, 2014.

Reyhaneh Jabbari's case became a cause-célèbre by mid-2014 when domestic and international campaigns to spare her life went viral on social media. By then Reyhaneh had already spent eight years in prison awaiting execution. During that time, the story around the death of a former Ministry of Intelligence employee allegedly at the hands of Reyhaneh circulated throughout much of Iran, the diasporic community, and human rights and women's rights outlets throughout the world. Respected Iranian actors, filmmakers, athletes, and human rights activists pleaded her case, not only to Iranian government officials and the world stage of public opinion, but also through direct appeals to the victim's family, which included the deceased's wife and four children, as well as his mother.

Many versions of the incident that led to the death of the forty-six-year-old physician, Morteza Sarbandi, circulated in the media.[16] Among the most active advocates for Reyhaneh was Mohammad Mostafaei, Reyhaneh's first lawyer, who, from exile in Norway, mounted a vociferous campaign, detailing the problematic legal issues of the case.

In 2007, Reyhaneh, then a nineteen-year-old aspiring decorator, had entered a unit in an apartment building with Sarbandi. Reyhaneh stated that she met the doctor at a coffee shop where she had been on the phone discussing interior design work. When he overheard her conversation, he approached and asked her about an office he sought to redecorate. They exchanged numbers and agreed to go to the space to see what could be done. Sarbandi picked her up at an agreed-upon location. Reyhaneh stated that a third person was in the car, a man named Sheikhi. They stopped at a pharmacy where the doctor stepped out to make a purchase while the two passengers remained in the car. Sarbandi returned with a paper bag and then drove to the destination, an apartment building. Sarbandi and Reyhaneh went up to the fifth floor. When he opened the door, Reyhaneh was shocked at the state of the place. It was in terrible shape—not at all an office in need of interior decorating. Reyhaneh and Sarbandi were in the main room, which contained an open kitchen. On the counter was the paper bag Sarbandi had brought from the pharmacy; it later turned out to contain condoms and a liquid sedative.

Reyhaneh said that Sarbandi then locked the front door from inside. He asked her to remove her headscarf; she declined. He advanced towards her and grabbed her waist. She cried out and pushed him away. He was not moved by her distress. He turned to remove his clothing down to his undergarments. She reached into her purse, where she had a knife that she carried for protection. As he again approached her, she pushed him, he turned, and she stabbed Sarbandi on his back-left side. He fell.

Reyhaneh claimed that she had injured him, but that he was alive when she fled. As she did, Sheikhi entered. Reyhaneh was relieved, believing he would seek medical assistance for Sarbandi. She waited in a nearby street until she saw an ambulance appear. It was only then that she went home. It was not until police showed up at her house at 2:00 a.m., that she realized what had happened. Sarbandi was dead, having bled to death from a punctured lung. Reyhaneh was mystified because she had seen Sheikhi enter and assumed he would help Sarbandi.

The police did not investigate many of the details that Reyhaneh gave, including the presence of the third party, whom they never located, much to the dismay of her various lawyers. Police investigators and the state's prosecutor also drew from the presence of the knife that Reyhaneh had planned the murder. Based on these elements, they charged her with intentional murder.

During her trial, the chief judge, Tardast, asserted that Reyhaneh had admitted to killing Sarbandi during her interrogation. Reyhaneh later claimed that her confession was coerced. The judges did not believe her assertions—neither that she was defending herself from sexual assault nor that she gave her confession under duress. They rejected her defense, found her guilty of Sarbandi's murder, and sentenced her to *qisas*. Her life was in the hands of the family whose patriarch she claimed had tried to assault her.

From the very start, Reyhaneh's lawyer, Mohammad Mostafaei, raised the issue of attempted rape and claimed that his client had acted in self-defense. This claim, according to Iran's criminal laws, would discharge the *qisas* punishment—if the judges believed it. From the moment Mostafaei made the claim of self-defense for his client, the story became one of Reyhaneh Jabbari's

version against that of the prosecutor and the Sarbandi family. Issues of credibility are tightly woven into questions of character, social reputation, and
moral rectitude, not just of the defendant and victim, but of their families.
These issues possess complex social dimensions, and the public campaigns
pursued by Reyhaneh's various cause lawyers and supporters subtly touched
on them with the intent to shape her public profile as a victim. This included
a series of letters Reyhaneh wrote, detailing her version of the story, including
her treatment at the hands of interrogators.

The additional element of forbearance in this case reveals the difficult arrangement of the dual defense, so to speak. Reyhaneh's case highlights one of
the main complications that exists when the suspect must defend herself
against the state's prosecution and, at the same time, plead her case for mercy
to the victim's family. The self-defense claim rested on the facts that Reyhaneh
presented, that she was the victim of an intended rape. This made her victim
a perpetrator, a would-be rapist. The victim's family was unwilling to forgo
retribution in the case where the perpetrator had accused their father of being
a rapist. It was unacceptable to them; the issue of the family's reputation was
crucial to the decision.

During a reconciliation meeting between the families, one of several organized by the state in March of 2014, the deceased's daughter, who happened to
be the same age as Reyhaneh, shouted that she would never see her father
again and that Reyhaneh's family should face the same fate. In that same meeting, Jalal Sarbandi, the victim's eldest son repeated his statement that the family
just wanted to know the truth.[17] They were willing to forgive the sentence, he
said, if only Reyhaneh revealed for whom she was working, insinuating that
their father's death was part of a broader, perhaps political, plot. On numerous
occasions, Reyhaneh and her family responded to me personally and to their
lawyers, advocates, and on social media that there was no other truth.

I queried several interlocutors about this defense posture. What if Reyhaneh simply dropped the self-defense argument and asked for forbearance?
"No, that won't work," her lawyer by then, Mohammad Ali Jedari Foroughi, told
me. If she drops the self-defense, there will be no mitigating factors, neither for
the family to consider, nor for the public campaigns. In a sense, it seemed, she
would be what the victim's family was claiming—someone with poor character
and an intent to kill—and there would be no forbearance. Foroughi saw the
family's plea to Reyhaneh of "just tell us what happened," as a ploy to get Reyhaneh to admit to something that she did not do and then be met with the
punishment of death, when the expectation would be forbearance.

As we have seen, defendants seeking mercy must present themselves as
worthy of this lessening of punishment. The problem was that the dual strategies upon which the campaigns to save Reyhaneh hinged were at cross

purposes. The self-defense approach was based on the pursuit of a legal strategy in which Reyhaneh was the victim of an aggressor. This approach—a legal
campaign—was directed at the state, especially at judicial officials. The second
strategy was legal only in the sense that it was directed towards the right of
forbearance that the victim's family possessed. This tack, in fact, was entirely
founded on equity—that she was a human—and required the victim's family
to see Reyhaneh in a merciful light. For the Sarbandi family, this was impossible when the person imploring the family for a lessening of a sanction also
accused the head of that family of a heinous crime.

Some activists I spoke with did, indeed, merge the two strategic assertions,
stating that Reyhaneh deserved mercy because she was a victim of an intended
rape; it was precisely her strong moral character that led her to defend herself.
The problem with this reasoning, however, is that it misrecognizes the giver
of mercy as the state when it is not. However, after the Supreme Court upheld
the ruling of guilt, the only recourse Reyhaneh had was to appeal to the victim's family for mercy.

The campaigns sometimes derailed into personal infighting between the
various advocates. In one surprising exchange that took place in the spring of
2014, the primary trial judge in Reyhaneh's case wrote a response to the claims
made by her first lawyer, Mostafaei. Judge Tardast wrote that all legal avenues
had been carefully considered, appeals exhausted, and legal procedures adhered to.[18] Mostafaei responded with a carefully crafted letter addressing Judge
Tardast's claims one by one.[19] Mostafaei's advocacy went beyond articles ana-
lyzing the case and television interviews. His NGO produced an animated video
about Reyhaneh's case to provide a clear and simple account of the murder
based on her assertions of self-defense. Clearly aware of the campaign to save
Reyhaneh, the Iranian government's television station, *Seema*, came up with
their own version, also animated, detailing what they claimed was Reyhaneh's
intentional killing of Sarbandi. If the government's aim was not to defend the
victim's family, it was aiming to defend its judicial process.[20]

Many with whom I spoke, both intimates of the case and those who were
distant spectators, went so far as to say that forbearance was never an option,
not only because of the victim's family, they suggested, but also because the
state would never allow the death of a former intelligence official to go unpun-
ished. "It would simply set an unacceptable precedent," said one interlocutor.
The assertion that the state would never allow Reyhaneh to escape death, however, begs the question of why judiciary officials would permit, and sometimes
facilitate, almost a decade of advocacy on her behalf. If forbearance was never
in the offing, then why did the state permit it to get to such public heights?

Just days after Reyhaneh's execution, the Secretary General of Iran's High
Council for Human Rights, Mohammad Javad Larijani, was in Geneva for

Iran's Universal Periodic Review (UPR) before the United Nations Human Rights Council (HRC). In his response to the UPR, on October 31, 2014, Larijani addressed Reyhaneh's case specifically. He asserted that the legal process was detailed and carried out with diligence, "All the judges that sat on her case in the past seven years have ruled that she has committed premeditated murder and her claims of self-defense were not convincing[21] . . . Reyhaneh Jabbari had numerous judges, numerous lawyers. The lawyers defended her. [The] court came back with an indictment that it was first-degree murder with intention, with capital punishment."[22] Larijani went on to say that he had personally asked the victim's family to forgo retribution. He then criticized western human rights groups over Reyhaneh's death, maintaining that they interfered with the government's efforts at reconciliation. "Unfortunately, we were not able [to bring about forbearance], perhaps one reason for that was the huge propaganda that was created against this case."[23] After characterizing the killing as an affair between a mistress and her lover gone awry, Larijani told the (HRC), "We were not successful to solicit [sic] forgiveness from the hearts of victims . . . We are very sorry that two nationals lost lives, but capital punishment or 'qisas' is a unique particularity of our system."[24]

Larijani defended the Iranian process as born out of different values, "The idea that only good things [exist] in western community—the 'West and the rest'—this is a very destructive idea of human rights." He went as far as suggesting that western states study Iran's legal system. He further stated that "due process and the independence of Iran's judiciary was [sic] enshrined in [Iran's] constitution and laws" and added that "judicial and prison staff were being trained in human rights." By asserting that Reyhaneh had "several defense lawyers" and highlighting the process of judicial review, Larijani conveyed the justness of Iran's legal process through western tropes of justice. His words highlighted the tensions that reference to human rights language creates in Iran's criminal justice system.

The lawyers who worked on her case, however, claimed that the problem was precisely with Iran's legal process. Mohammad Mostafaei's public (and post-exile) defense of Reyhaneh included detailed legal analyses where he took apart the state's factual assertions. In response to Larijani's claims, Mostafaei told reporters that basic legal principles were ignored and that the prosecution gave undue consideration to the victim, a former member of the intelligence service. Mostafaei said, "I was Reyhaneh Jabbari's lawyer. Mr. Larijani's statement is completely false. It is not true that she had a fair trial. Because the deceased in this case belonged to the intelligence services, the court treated the case differently, and gave undue weight to the prosecution. Key evidence in the case, and basic legal principles, were ignored."[25] A lawyer who worked on Reyhaneh's case after Mostafaei, Shadi Sadr, who herself later fled Iran, also took issue with the legal process. Contending that the judiciary had made up its mind to execute Reyhaneh from the start, Sadr stated that the first judge in the case "told all of us, the lawyers, Reyhaneh, and her family that 'I will give you the death sentence; don't waste my time because she is guilty and has to be executed.'"[26]

In the summer of 2014, I approached Reyhaneh's then-lawyer, Foroughi, an experienced business lawyer, who took on criminal defense and workers' rights cases pro bono. A calm and reserved man, Foroughi had over forty years of legal experience. He had also worked as a journalist and once ran a monthly periodical. His politics had landed him in prison on several occasions. Each time he served his term and came out more intent on representing, as he put it, "those who have no representation." I first encountered his representation of Reyhaneh in a facebook post published in the spring of 2014, during one of the many times of heightened fear that Reyhaneh's execution was close. The post, entitled "Reyhaneh's lawyer says execution not imminent," said it all. In it, Foroughi stated that legal angles and avenues towards reconciliation were still being pursued.

I contacted Foroughi, stating my interest in his advocacy on behalf of Reyhaneh, emphasizing his pursuit of the non-legal angle—forbearance by the victim's family. I first met him early in the summer of 2014 at his law office in central Tehran, where he held meetings with other lawyers to strategize about this and other cases. Foroughi maintained a steady presence on social media, where he gave updates on his clients. He kept a professional bearing and presented only the facts, delivered sensitively and prudently. He aimed to turn attention towards the legal issues, without unduly politicizing cases or insulting the opposing parties. In Reyhaneh's case, given the facts and that he had been retained in 2014 as her fourth attorney, this was nearly impossible.

In our first meeting, I encountered a man of medium build, in jeans, dress shirt, and a tie. The tie was the giveaway for his political commitments. Foroughi, who had completely shaved his head, explained that it (the bald crown) was an act of solidarity with Sattar Beheshti, the thirty-five-year-old blogger who was killed while in police custody on November 3, 2012.[27] Foroughi was not financially dependent on human rights cases and was not an activist in the same way as some of the human rights lawyers I had encountered. I wondered what motivated him to take these cases. "For only one reason," he said. "No one else will touch them. I am the lawyer where no lawyers will go." There was also a theme in his many Facebook posts—"for the sake of humanity."

One day, sitting in his office, Foroughi talked about the need to help bring a level of humanity to our perception of the people whom we often do not encounter in our everyday worlds. He believed that we, in the comforts of our western (me) or socially elite (him) surroundings, were not free of responsibility to help others—"because none of us is innocent," he told me. He expressed a conviction that I had seen with other human rights lawyers in Iran: "We want the law to be applied correctly so that people's rights are not crushed." He wanted to follow the law and see laws develop appropriately to meet the needs of justice. He believed that part of his work was to help to pave legal avenues towards justice.

With regard to Reyhaneh, Foroughi explained, "We want to clear the record; we don't need their *lotf* [grace]," he said, referring to the victim's family. "We need to find a way to save her, yes, but she acted in self-defense. It is also important to note that the wound was not the cause of Sarbandi's death." He had officially bled to death. "There is just no motivation for her to have deliberately killed him." He went on to explain Reyhaneh's situation in mythical terms, "This is the story of Icarus. You get too close, you burn. Are you familiar with the story of Icarus?" Before I could answer, however, he explained to me the story of Icarus, the son of Daedalus, who had received a pair of wings made of feathers and wax from his master craftsman father in order to seek freedom. The pair intended to use the wings to fly out of their imprisonment in Crete. Icarus, however, did not heed his father's warnings and flew too close to the sun, causing the feathers on the wings to burn and the wax to melt. Icarus plunged into the sea and died.

The moral of the mythological story is to warn against hubris. By now, it was no secret that some saw Reyhaneh as a prideful, smart, strong young woman who had sought freedom, from her family and the moral codes of the society whose rules of social order and, in this case, perhaps even hierarchy, she flouted. While Foroughi did not stress the aspect of hubris in the case, it was clear that the sun in this story was the government and Reyhaneh risked being burned by playing too close to it.

Emphasizing his fealty to law as the proper avenue of justice, Foroughi made a passing jibe at some of the social activists working on Reyhaneh's behalf and other cases. He said, "We [lawyers] are not actors; we have to defend our clients by using the law." His interest in pursuing legal channels had its own ends. He sought to advance the rule of law, constructing it to respond to the demands of justice, particularly in the difficult death penalty cases he took on. In this sense, the law was not only serving Reyhaneh, but Reyhaneh was, in some small way, also serving the law. It was at this juncture that some of the activists' efforts to secure forbearance through any means necessary conflicted with the lawyers' efforts to mete out justice through law. Lawyers did not take cases such as these lightly. "When a file like this is in your hands, it means the person's life is in your hands."

An important consequence for legal representatives in Iran's victim-centered approach to criminal sanctioning is that lawyers do not always have full control of the strategies used to free their clients. While cause lawyers may take up the cases with every expectation of zealously pursuing all avenues, they do not control the non-legal avenues, which could have important consequences for the legal ones. It goes without saying that these non-legal strategies could very seriously affect the legal ones, and vice-versa. Thus, legal strategies must be devised very carefully, and in cases where forbearance is a significant possibility, lawyers need to balance and deliberate on exactly how these strategies affect one another, especially to what extent a legal strategy might antagonize the victim's family.

In Reyhaneh's case, during the summer of 2014, the lawyers were attempting to re-open the case based on the failure of the judges to attend to certain details of the case, including the whereabouts of the presumed third party, Sheikhi. Reconciliation efforts were also on-going. Additionally, during the March (of 2014) reconciliation meeting, one of Sarbandi's sons stated that the family did not believe that Reyhaneh killed their father; they "just wanted to know the truth." Based on this assertion, Reyhaneh's parents had written queries to the most eminent *Shi'i* jurists, those who can issue a *fatwa* (legal opinion), *marja'-e taqlid* (source of emulation) or grand ayatollahs and posed the question: If the victim's family states that they do not believe someone killed their kin, can the punishment of *qisas* stand? The parents received two responses from grand ayatollahs who indicated that, in such a case, not only would *qisas* not be the appropriate punishment, but that should the family carry out *qisas*, then they would be guilty of murder and their punishment would be *qisas*.[28] Given these activities, no one I spoke with that summer could have envisioned that Reyhaneh would be executed only three months later.

In the context of balancing legal strategy with public campaigns for forgiveness, Foroughi brought up another case, that of Sahar Mohabadi Monfared, yet another young woman on death row. Sahar, who was twenty-seven in 2014, had spent the last six years in prison for having killed her husband, Gholam Reza Shirazi.[29] Reyhaneh had befriended Sahar in prison, and eventually referred her to Foroughi in the spring of 2014. Sahar was attractive, as pictures of her circulating on social media, indicated. To the extent that the pictures of Reyhaneh appeared to emphasize her youth, piety, and chastity, those of Sahar conveyed her beauty, slightness of physique, and even a quiet stoicism.

Sahar and her husband, both from Varamin, a poor suburb of Tehran, had had a difficult marriage from the start. Their families were humble and lived simply. The marriage was arranged, her parents contended, but Sahar characterized it as forced. It soon became evident to all that the couple did not agree on much. She found her husband to be lazy and he failed to provide. She had to work at a grocery store to make ends meet. Their economic situation grew

FIGURE 7. Image of Sahar Mohabadi associated with social media campaigns to prevent her execution. Used with permission.

worse after her husband was injured in a motorcycle accident soon after their marriage and had his left leg amputated below the knee. After some seven years of marriage, Sahar and her husband had agreed to divorce and had even worked out the terms to a mutual divorce. While awaiting their court date, the couple lived apart, Sahar having gone just a few blocks away to her parent's home. The couple planned to meet in a park so that Sahar could obtain her identity papers from her soon-to-be ex-husband. For reasons that were unclear, the couple got into an argument that became physical, and ended with Sahar drawing a knife from beneath her overcoat and stabbing her husband, who died shortly thereafter.

When Foroughi asked about the knife, Sahar told him that she always had a knife with her because she lived with someone dangerous, referring to her husband. She said that during the dispute, she pulled out the knife after he hit her, but just before he could grab his own knife. This set of events, as Foroughi thought, established the basis for a self-defense claim that Sahar's previous lawyer had not pursued. In a meeting that summer in his office with several young lawyers, Foroughi decided that there could be two legal avenues to pursue. First, they could move to reopen the case based on a self-defense claim that her previous lawyers never put forth.

A second tack they came up with was for Sahar to make a demand for her *mahrieh* (bride price).[30] Sahar, despite having killed her husband, still had a valid claim for her *mahrieh*. The strategy was that Sahar would make a demand for her *mahrieh*, which would have to be paid by the victim's family. Given their financial state, Sahar's lawyers opined, this might bring the family to the bargaining table. Sahar could forgo the *mahrieh* in exchange for her life. A young lawyer at the meeting brought up the sensitive politics around the strategy, "But if we think that there is a chance the family is already amenable to forbearance, and we demand her *mahrieh*, this might anger them and push them towards retribution." But Foroughi, who had employed this strategy before, said, "Look, this family is destitute. Their father is dead. The mother is very sick." He added, "They badly need the money. It would help that woman [referring to the mother of the victim, Mrs. Shirazi]."

While Foroughi was content to advocate for his clients' attaining the forbearance of the victim's family, he was mistrustful of the motives of many individuals who got involved in the cases. He looked with suspicion at the negotiations between them and victims' families. He did not trust the arbitrary features of forbearance, which were animated by its unregulated nature, the promises that social workers or others made on behalf of desperate and imprisoned defendants, and the increasingly exorbitant monies that were paid out by families of perpetrators. Foroughi much preferred to work through legal channels. He also desired to strengthen and reform the existing laws. Where laws did not exist, were untested, or vague, he sought to generate or clarify them. He also believed it was wrong to put such power in the hands of victims' families who were not only aggrieved, emotional, and prone to revenge, but he also found many, by virtue of their anguish, susceptible to manipulation by hangers-on who wanted notoriety or possibly even financial dividends. "People in this state are vulnerable," he said.

Indeed, I had seen the mother of the deceased, Mrs. Shirazi, whose home I had visited with the social workers from Imam 'Ali's Popular Students Relief Society. At the time, she walked with the help of crutches. In the weeks to come, she (too) would have a leg amputated below the knee, due to an infection caused by diabetes. The day that we had approached her, she seemed intent on seeing her son's killer, her daughter-in-law Sahar, executed. But it had not always been that way.

Early in his tenure on the case, Foroughi had achieved what he believed was a settlement between the mother of the deceased and Sahar's family. A sum had been agreed upon and the parties went to the notary, intending to have an authentic statement of the accord drawn up and signed. Once there, one of the mother's six children, her eldest daughter, telephoned and pleaded with her not to sign. The woman then grew hesitant and changed her mind, much to the distress of Sahar, her family, and Foroughi.

Sahar's father was in attendance at all the strategic meetings. He was, by all accounts, a simple man, with a thick Azeri accent, which revealed both his ethnicity and class position. He was a sheepherder by trade. By his account, he had sold most of his herd for costs related to Sahar's case, but he said he would do anything and raise whatever money that the victim's family required. In an echo of what the social workers had told Sahar's parents on the curb the night we left Mrs. Shirazi's house, Foroughi told the father that he must speak with the family. "They want to see that you care, that you, too, are remorseful."

"I have!" Sahar's father insisted. "I have gone to talk with her [the victim's mother]. She listened to me. It's not her; it's the children. They will not let her forgive Sahar."

This was the contention expressed by many whom I had interviewed in this case. Of the six children, brothers and sisters of the deceased, there were three who dismissed the idea of forbearance completely. Some believed it was because they were greedy and holding out for more compensation; others suggested that they would eventually come around, but wanted Sahar to suffer. Some, however, were loath to predict a happy ending for Sahar. "This mother has revenge in her heart," one social worker told me. Yet others I spoke with believed that the mother, who had the most to gain (financially) from forgoing retributive sanctioning, was unduly influenced by her children, and some even went so far as to say that she feared them. While negotiations continued with different visitors, social workers, and lawyers coming and going, in the months that followed, the victim's mother still held out for Sahar to be executed.

In December 2014, the lawyers, feeling that they were getting nowhere on direct negotiations with the victim's family, decided to make a formal demand for Sahar's *mahrieh*. The demand would serve as a bargaining tactic and hopefully give the family pause to consider negotiating. Sahar's *mahrieh*, one of the lawyers told me, "as a sum, was quite insignificant, especially when considered against what the family stood to receive were they to accept forbearance. It was, however, a significant sum for an impoverished family to come up with." So maybe, the lawyers thought, it would be enough to bring the family back to the bargaining table.

Over another ten months of negotiations with the victim's family and the involvement of numerous social workers, one matter was held in common: They would not take the case public any longer. They did not want the case to go the way that Reyhaneh's had, the lawyers told me. Meetings were held in secret. Trusted family members spoke with the victim's family. The victim's family finally agreed to forgo retribution. This was conditioned not only upon the payment of *diya*, but also the perpetrator's family leaving the neighborhood, which they also did, only for a time. Finally, in the fall of 2015, Sahar was released.

Conclusion

In this chapter, I have highlighted the ways in which cause lawyers maneuver within domestic laws to bargain for their clients' lives. Through their public profiles and their moral commitments, lawyers not only partake, but also pave the unregulated field of forgiveness work, resulting in finding innovative strategies to save their clients from execution. While such strategies place lawyers at the vanguard of forgiveness work, their commitment to the rule of law nonetheless places their advocacy in sharp contrast with that supported by the state. As a result, this chapter also notes the tensions between lawyers and the state. Unlike other activists, lawyers challenge the substantive laws and the legal procedures, even while they do everything in their power to spare a client from death. Lawyers' advocacy, moreover, highlights how politicized human rights work is, especially when it takes the form of anti-death penalty activism rather than appeals to mercy.

Lawyers' actions are not in vain. They serve as important experts on and witnesses to Iran's laws and legal procedures. Their advocacy, both in courts and in the broader planes of activism, both domestic and international, has led to important debates within Iran and, crucially, changes to the criminal codes even as the government also comes to terms with the unregulated and open nature of the space for forgiveness work.

Even as they insisted on the fairness of Reyhaneh's case, the legislature was embroiled in discussions about changing the law; lawyers and activists lobbied for revisions as well. Many of my interlocutors were of the opinion that the difficulty of proving the self-defense claim in Reyhaneh's case was important in changing this law. Her case, along with many others, some which I have discussed in this work, also brought to light the problems of gender-based violence, long before the #MeToo movement went viral.

When Mercy Seasons Justice

And earthly power doth then show likest God's
When Mercy seasons justice

WILLIAM SHAKESPEARE,

THE MERCHANT OF VENICE, ACT 4 SCENE 1

THROUGH ETHNOGRAPHIC portraits I have explored the deeply interpretive, intersubjective, and blended scriptural, legal, mystical, and cultural foundations animating forbearance practices in Iranian criminal sanctioning. I have aimed to show that the system, while undoubtedly based on Qur'anic verses, *ahadith*, and stories about Imam 'Ali, nonetheless, takes shape through and alongside other cultural histories, patterns, practices, and politics; the system reveals a complexity that is neither fixed nor finished. Thus, without saying as much, this book has been a story about a movement, slow-moving and itinerant, perhaps, but a movement just the same. This movement's quality, tone, and affect were reiterated for me during a meeting I attended in late-August 2018.

In a rustic cottage outside of Tehran, some fifty activists gathered to pay tribute to an imprisoned human rights lawyer who was out on furlough. The gathering was convivial, disorganized, and completely apolitical. Those present joked, connected with old friends and new, and someone jumped in the pool fully-clothed to find a set of keys.

While waiting for the catered kabobs to arrive, some of the more high-profile speakers were asked to say a few words. A woman recently released from serving ten years in prison spoke about her delight at being freed and seeing old friends again. As a member of the Bahai' faith, she said, all they wanted was equality with others. She added, "We are Iranian. This is our home. We love Iran." Another ex-prisoner, a social justice activist, spoke with great admiration for his courageous lawyer, Nasrin Sotoudeh, who had recently been arrested. Those present gave a round of applause in her honor and eternal hope for her freedom as well as that of other human rights defenders. The warmth and charitableness of these speakers struck me. Again and again they emphasized their non-political aims, their love for their country, and their desire for social justice.

It was finally time for the guest of honor to say a few words. He rose to a round of applause. He gave a faint smile in appreciation and began, "Greetings to all. I am so pleased to see you and delighted that you have come out. You have been a great support to my family and me during this time." "My friends," he continued,

> I have something I want to say, something about our situation. Here, now, is a time of change. Big changes are afoot. I want to ask something of you all here today. Do not have hatred in your hearts, not for this government, not for your fellow citizens who work in the government. Even in prison, I know, I see. I talk to the guards. Eighty percent of them are with us. They believe in our cause, in social justice. Don't spread antagonisms. Instead, be forgiving and compassionate with people. Don't show enmity for people. They are human beings who, just because they need to put some food on the table, have taken jobs that we have the luxury of being able to avoid. Try and work through compassion, love, and mercy. And together we will bring change. Perhaps not as fast as some would like, not a revolution, but incre-mentally, through reason, law, and justice. Thank you.

His speech drew a standing ovation. The spirit of the crowd was over-whelmingly charged. Lawyers and activists exchanged cards, discussed doc-trines, and shared news of cases. In a few days, certain others would be taken into custody; the man on furlough would return to prison. But the domestic struggle for justice would continue at the level of legal activism, social advo-cacy, and beyond.

The activist's words, beyond the optimistic aspirations of a human rights lawyer, underscored what has become a central tension in understanding Is-lamic justice through mercy that this book has highlighted. Indeed, mercy, as I have intimated throughout, is a fraught concept. It is only by employing it that mercy begins to take shape. Only by a study of the context through which such actions occur can we define mercy. As we have seen, however, mercy is its own *other* side of the coin. By this I mean that mercy means a lessening of deserved punishment (leniency) and, at the same time, mercy's very presence suggests injustice lies everywhere. That is, where there is mercy, there is injus-tice. Mercy can play a crucial role in bringing about justice. The insistence on mercy, even if it is a power from above, can offer a crucial corrective to injustice.

In some ways, this feature of the legal system explains the involvement of government agents in forgiveness work and suggests the basis for the state's differential treatment of anti-death penalty or human right activists versus forgiveness workers. For the latter work alongside the state, or at least do not openly challenge the laws, which are deemed to be based on *shari'a*. For this reason, forgiveness work can be both particular—on a case by case basis—and general—against the death penalty. This distinction may also shed light on why, in such cases, the state prosecutes anti-death penalty activists, who, as a result of such advocacy, are imprisoned, forced into exile, or banned from activities. However, in the context of forbearance, government officials work alongside social workers who do not flout the laws or the principles upon which they are said to be based, and instead advocate for individual forgiveness, as both the law and sacred texts permit and, indeed, encourage.

Local practices hold strategic importance in a context of a governmental backlash against mobilisation around human rights claims and anti-death penalty activism. They permit social workers to speak about the death penalty from a different vantage point, detached from its problematic political implications. References to local practices of conflict resolution may signal more pragmatic approaches to addressing an issue of human suffering. At the same time, such references draw attention to indigenous belief systems, which similarly call upon social actors to relieve social suffering and to prevent further harm to vulnerable populations. The right of retribution makes possible the forgiveness work itself, which attends to the human condition through an emphasis on mercy, grace, and forgiveness, while actively discouraging and suppressing the discourse of human rights and accountability. Given the state's stark reactions to the two approaches, a deeper consideration of their differences and efficacy is warranted.

The social activists with whom I worked looked to cultivate an ethics of care that elevates the social standing and prestige of the victim's family and which also accentuates its power over (the life of) the perpetrator. At the same time, these ethics of care avoid discussions of human rights or the rights of the defendant. Indeed, in the international case with which I opened this book, when the father of the victim publicly announced his forbearance just moments before the would-be execution of his son's killer, Iran's Islamic Human Rights Commission (IHRC) issued a press release announcing its support for the father's decision, lauding it as "a humanitarian measure" that demonstrated a "commitment to the sublime teachings of Islam." Rather than couching this act of forbearance in terms of rights or social standing, the ethics of care promulgated by the government functioned to legitimate the state's interests in promoting humanitarianism in a decidedly Muslim form.

Earlier, I explored the meaning of this act of mercy as a relationship be-tween sovereign power, human rights, and humanitarianism, the last, defined by the IHRC through the Muslim mandate of mercy (Osanloo 2006). Un-doubtedly, the underlying philosophies of the two approaches to the human condition—human rights and humanitarianism—are distinct, perhaps even contrasting. Human rights are understood to precede the state and are pre-mised on the idea that individuals, simply by virtue of being human, possess certain rights that are fundamental to their very humanity and that must be accorded some measure of protection. In the Westphalian world system, human rights compel states to act (or desist from acting) out of a commitment to recognize the dignity of humans and to permit them to attain or maintain those rights considered fundamental to what it means to be human. The latter, humanitarianism, while also premised on the dignity common to all humans, appeals to the state's discretionary powers to act in bringing relief to situations where rights and laws do not otherwise compel it to do so. In other words, it is the opposite side of the human rights coin.

With human rights, groups or individuals file complaints against the state, demanding that it either act to protect an individual or groups, or to desist in a practice that violates their basic human rights. The crucial component in demanding rights is the premise that human beings are equal and that the state must protect its citizens (and possibly others) solely on the basis of that fun-damental equality. Human rights are claims to state protection and are often long-term, on-going struggles for justice. On the other end of the justice spec-trum, humanitarian concerns draw from an essential concern with the human condition and, while the claimants often appeal to states, they are just that, pleas that the state act out of benevolence. Indeed, individuals or groups ask-ing for such humanitarian support do not rely solely on states; they also look to other individuals and appeal to their moral outlook on the world.

There is also a temporal quality to these different philosophies. Humani-tarianism, with its roots in the laws of war, has as its goal stemming the im-mediate suffering of individuals, often far-away and different from the donors. There are elements of disconnect, distance, and a charitable quality of giving when thinking about and helping the plight of humanitarian subjects. The aid is also one-off and temporary, often considered relief in the aftermath of an event, a political conflict or climate disaster, to relieve suffering during an emergency. In contrast, human rights are enduring struggles, often organized movements that include legal recognition, and which require the state to act.

In the nation-state system, however, where only states can acknowledge the humanity of individuals by extending rights to them, the distance between human rights and humanitarianism diminishes. Both, it thus appears, depend on a discretionary grant by the sovereign power. That is, if the state does not recognize the humanity of certain individuals, and, therefore, does not act according to its obligations under human rights theories, norms, or laws, there is little consequence for that state. As such, where no entity exists to compel or sanction states to abide by human rights, sovereign power proves to be one of the most lethal and omnipotent forces of our historical moment. In a world system where the nation-state is the supreme institution, calls to convince states to intervene (or desist) in the service of humanity are akin to appeals to humanitarianism or mercy. Thus, increasingly, human rights situations are repurposed into the coaxing language of humanitarianism, such as calls for aid and relief, as opposed to the taunting and mandating language of rights-based claims—of duty and obligations states owe individuals, even those who are not citizens, residents, or even in their territories, such as refugees. In the absence of any other entity to recognize individuals' rights in such a system, human rights, too, take on the form of a grant from a nation-state.

Much of the scholarly discussion on humanitarian care traces the ethics of that care to the European enlightenment, often connected to the emergence of new moral principles associated with compassion and concern for the suffering of distant others (Boltanski 1999; Fassin 2012; Hunt 2007). However, in the present context, it is not altogether off-topic to consider the relationship between the discourse of humanitarian care and human rights. Indeed, some scholars have considered the Islamic principle in relation to an ethics or an ethos of care (Benthall 2010, 2012; Benthall and Bellion-Jourdan 2009; Khan 2012; Singer 2008). Such studies have emphasized charity and aid in relation to the context of suffering and emergencies and have based their proposition of an Islamic humanitarianism almost entirely on *zakat* (almsgiving, *lit.* that which purifies), one of the five pillars of the faith.[1]

While the philosophy of care in Muslim-majority societies may have distinct, albeit overlapping, genealogies with those arising out of the European enlightenment, ethico-religious concerns for the suffering of others go well beyond charity and, in fact, I would argue, are foundational to Islam. Charity is just one manifestation within Islam of the broader calls for ethical relationships with others and attention to relieving their suffering. To codify Islamic humanitarianism solely within the obligation of almsgiving overly institutionalizes abstract arrangements within Islam's broader ethical repertoire. Using *zakat* as the sole optic to address humanitarianism is reductionist, at best, particularly if we consider the multiple dimensions of ethical concepts grounded in the scriptural texts.

As I have noted, the Qur'an articulates a set of moral principles to guide relationships between members of the community. This set of rules underlies much of the system of social ethics that drives the discourse of *ensaniat* (humanity) among the Iranian social workers whom I knew. This ethics of care, I suggest, is foundational to the philosophy of humanitarian care among the social workers and jurists in Iran. My interlocutors' interpretations of the foundational moral principles in Islam are also premised on the tensions instigated by Enlightenment-based humanitarian reason (Fassin 2012). Humanitarian care derives from compassion for other humans and is based on the belief in a fundamental equality between humans. Thus, although the politics of compassion are based on solidarity among equal individuals, our moral sentiments express care towards the less fortunate, and are therefore premised on a politics of inequality (3). This contradiction is sociological, founded on unequal social and political relations, and delivers humanitarianism its gift-like quality and, for that reason, requires examination and critique. It is this contradiction, based in social and political inequality, with which the human rights activists in Iran are engaging and which underlies their critique of the state and the death penalty. The power of gifting life, thus, becomes the condition through which the state empowers victims of violence. In this regard, some state officials and others supportive of this victims' rights-oriented system of criminal justice see it as a recognition of human equality, empowering victims to exact an equal measure of injury. Accordingly, social workers' appeals to humanitarian care and moral principles are founded on local, social, religious, and other traditions, and thus avoid critiquing the state's human rights practices. Instead, in their appeals, social workers turn towards the very individuals the law empowers to forgo the retribution and, consequently serve to legitimate, rather than challenge, the state's laws.

In the end, it is a sort of human translation of the divine; mercy is the genesis of the divine, but it is also a site of pure human translation of the divine— "when mercy seasons justice." The power to pardon interiorized in humankind, in human power, in royal power as human power, is what Portia calls divine—"it will be God-like." This "like," this analogy or resemblance, supports what Derrida calls "a logic or analogic of *theological-political translation*," in other words, the translation of the *theological into political* (2001b:197 emphasis in original).

Iran's criminal justice system allows a privileging of victims' rights over those of the state, even if the state's delegation of the right of life and death both legitimizes the system and makes the plaintiff complicit in that system. It is, above all, a victim-centered system. The exercise of mercy also approximates a conversion in the Iranian system through the act that hails or underwrites the theological dimensions of political sovereignty. But the act of forbearance creates an effect that is different, I think, from carrying out an execution.

As Derrida said, forgiveness rises above justice or law; it rises above what in justice is only law to invoke prayer (188). For Derrida, the essence of forgiveness is prayer—that of the person who requests it and that of the person who grants it; thus, between prayer and forgiveness, there exists an essential affinity. Kenneth Cragg, a scholar of Islam and an Anglican Bishop, makes a similar point—"To seek God is by the same token to seek forgiveness" (1973:111). And seeking forgiveness means "turning the human condition, collective and personal, through self-accusation towards mercy, liberty and peace" (Ibid.).

The political prisoner, whose speech I referenced at the beginning of this epilogue, illustrated this essential turn towards mercy, even towards his jailors. With a spirit of compassion, he encouraged his fellow activists to seek that essential affinity towards others, not instead of justice, but as its complement. In this way, the prisoner sought to compel what Cragg saw as the essence of a sprit of seeking forgiveness—"a constant alertness" (127).

NOTES

Introduction

1. The young man was seventeen-years-old at the time. The killing, additionally, resulted from a brawl involving a group of men. Critics argued that the element of intent was absent.

2. *Amnesty International Global Report 2016,* Amnesty International estimates that Iran carried out 567 executions in 2016. This represents a significant reduction from the previous year's number of 977 (4). As the report indicates, a majority of the executions were for drug-related convictions (32). Amnesty's report for 2017 indicates that, after the passage of legislation amending the death penalty for drug-related offenses, executions for such offenses decreased from sixty percent to forty percent of total executions (9) and the country saw an overall eleven percent reduction in executions as compared with the previous year (6). *Amnesty International Global Report 2017.* In 2018, Amnesty recorded a fifty percent drop in the country's executions, attributing it to the new law on drug-related crimes (8). *Amnesty International Global Report 2018.*

3. I distinguish retribution from revenge, as my interlocutors have indicated they do. As many have noted, including the Roman Stoic philosopher Lucius Seneca (4 BCE—65 CE), revenge is the excess of violence, while retribution is *lex talionis*—in-kind punishment (2010). Others, however, following Nietzsche (1967), have noted the violence inherent in retribution and equate it with a revenge instinct. See, Butler (2014) and Derrida (2014).

4. This productive effect of law can also be understood as "jurisgenerative," referring to the law's capacity to create a normative universe of meaning that can often escape the "provenance of formal lawmaking" to expand the meaning and reach of law itself (Benhabib 2011; Cover 1983).

5. Black-Michaud used the term "cohesive force" to describe retribution (or the blood feud) as a social force that leads to greater social cohesion within and among tribal groups. He examined the blood feud, defining it as "exact retaliation in kind" (1975:1), as both a relationship and a social system, which shapes honor within groups.

6. Over the years, this turn of phrase—the "feeling of forgiveness"—has achieved an idiomatic quality, and is frequently referenced in newspapers and television programs, as well as by my interlocutors. For instance, in the weekly journal, *Events and Surprises,* one article focused on this expression in describing a family that forgave their son's killer. In the article, entitled "The Feeling of Forgiveness: Joy," the parents explain, "Since we forgave the murder of our son, these days, all the members of our family feel a greater sense of peace. This feeling is so sweet that we are ready to endeavor and take the lead in achieving forbearance, so that other people who are in the same situation as us can savor the flavor of forgiveness" (2013:22).

7. On the seventh day after a person's death, family members commemorate the deceased in different ways, including opening their doors to visitors paying respects, offering special meals, visiting the gravesite, and making offerings of food to the needy. These rituals are performed in the memory of the deceased to exalt his/her standing before God.

8. Giorgio Agamben (2000) describes form-of-life as a life that cannot be separated from its political, social, economic, and ethical surroundings and cannot, thus, be reduced to a physical form or bare essence. Nor is a form-of-life guided only by written law; it includes rules and habits (2013). Geertz employs "form of life" to place the juridical field within larger frames of signification, observing that the cultural contextualization of legal issues is crucial to understanding their deeper meaning (1983:180–1).

9. This dialectic is indicative of a debtor-creditor relationship that such events produce, as well. Debt is incurred by the offending party upon committing the offense, the victim's family is the creditor, who calls upon the offender to pay, either with his/her life or monetary compensation. See, Derrida 2014. In Iran there are specific ritualized practices that animate this dialectic. See, Assadi 1982; Beeman 1988; Behzadi 1994.

10. The term affect, as I employ it, represents a realm of expression well beyond mere emotions. Affect is characterized by pre-linguistic registers of experience, which include the interiorized cognitive or spiritual fields that precede intersubjective relationships.

11. The *bassij* are state-protected paramilitary enforcers of the morality laws.

12. This program aired on September 13, 2013.

13. See, for example, Ameri 2014. The author adds, "the precedence of good deeds has always been emphasized (in religion)."

14. This narrative aims to invert an opposing one advanced by proponents of retribution—that it is punishment which strengthens social bonds, through the collective outrage that comes in the wake of a crime and the need to see "justice" served (Durkheim 1984). Durkheim's "*conscience collective*" in French consists of a double-entendre that entails both psychic emotion and collective conscience.

15. Bateson et al. emphasized *javanmardi* as crucial to understanding the *safa-yi batin* (inner purity), the trait they believed to be central to Iranians' image of a positive personality. The reason for this, they suggested, is because *javanmardi* exemplifies the main virtues of inner purity: heroism and spirituality (1977:262–263).

16. The title refers to one of the figurative terms for Ramadan, suggestive of one's rededication to Islam through heightened attention to worship, charity, and reflection.

17. Wrestling is Iran's national sport.

18. In Qur'an, Chapter 19 (*Maryam* [Mary]), the word for God most commonly employed is *al-Rahman* (the Compassionate). Nearly one-third of the instances in which this name is used appear here (Nasr, Dagli, and Dakake et al. 2015:764).

19. This trope is hardly unique to Iran or to women in the Middle East. Rebecca Solnit (2017) highlighted the findings of a 2000 UCLA study that challenged the perception that the human response to danger and anxiety is "fight or flight." The original study was conducted with male rats and men. In a later study with women, scientists found that the reaction is more "tend and befriend" (2017:18). Tending refers to nurturing activities designed to protect and relieve distress. Befriending consists of creating social connections to aid in the process of ensuring safety and security. Solnit observes that "much of this is done through speech, through telling of one's

plight, through being heard, through hearing compassion and understanding in the response of the people you tend to, whom you befriend" (19). Women, she says, do this more routinely than men.

20. Interviewed by *The Guardian*, the father of the deceased said that his wife had had a dream in which her other deceased son told her that they "were in a good place and for her not to retaliate . . . This calmed my wife and allowed her to think about it more" (Ibid.).

21. "Moj-e Bakhsheshha" 2014. The article attributes the spread of forbearance to several cities and attributes it to the good will that emerged after cases highlighted by the domestic press.

22. Ghaneirad 2014. The political capital to which he was referring was the election of the moderate cleric, Hassan Rouhani, in 2013, whose campaign promises referenced hope for the future.

23. Gorji 2014. These articles represent a tiny sampling of the numerous essays, opinion pieces, and investigative reporting on forbearance in the domestic press.

24. Mozzafari 2014. The author, a judicial assistant to the Minister of Justice, noted that social activists had opened spaces in the media, especially domestic, that could greatly impact victims' families. He noted, however, that it was a double-edged sword and singled out the international media for failing to understand how the Iranian system works or the pressures on victims' families. He stated that they were unlikely to forgo retribution when foreign media got involved.

25. Derrida (2001a) argued that true forgiveness cannot exist for it requires forgiving the unforgivable—a divine quality; this is one of life's aporias.

26. Notably, apology was not required in South Africa's Truth and Reconciliation Commission (Tutu 2000).

27. Seneca, for instance, defines forgiveness as "remission of deserved punishment" (2010:175).

28. Nigel Biggar, an Anglican priest and scholar, divides forgiveness into two types— forgiveness-as-compassion and forgiveness-as-absolution. The former rests on the victim's ability to see the humanity of the perpetrator and requires empathy, while the latter rests on the perpetrator's show of remorse (2008).

29. Derrida changes the French word that François-Victor Hugo (son of the famous novelist) used in the original translation of the passage from Portia's soliloquy in *The Merchant of Venice*, which begins, "When mercy seasons justice." Hugo had used the term *tempere* or to temper for "seasons." Derrida changed it to *relever* or to lift up. This term, Derrida suggests, more accurately describes what it means when mercy seasons justice and, in turn, better captures the quality of mercy (2001b:194).

30. Fischer (1990) traces the multivalent sources of law and their effects in the immediate aftermath of the Iranian revolution and the formation of the Islamic Republic.

31. Compare with the spectrum of accountability that Minow (1998) lays out from vengeance to forgiveness, which includes trials, truth commissions, reparations, and commemorations.

32. An extended textual analysis of the relationship between Islamic scriptures and mercy is beyond the scope of this work. A study of such sources would necessarily focus on the corpus of work by Ibn 'Arabi, who has given the subject thorough study in the Islamic intellectual tradition. My goal here is simply to demonstrate the relationship between the scriptural sources that

underscore retribution and compel forbearance and Iran's penal code. This section emphasizes the common tropes, themes, and sources that I encountered during my fieldwork.

33. Statistical Centre of Iran 2016. See also, Algar 2006.

34. Scholars have compared the *Fatiheh* to the "Lord's Prayer" in Matthew 6:9–13. Both invoke praise of God and acknowledge ways of virtue and common understanding.

35. The *Sura al-Fatiheh* is the subject of numerous scholarly studies. My Iranian interlocutors often cite the work of seventheenth-century CE philosopher, Mulla Sadra, whose study of the *Fatiheh* arguably highlights the centrality of mercy to Islamic daily practice. For a penetrating analysis of Sadra's reflections on mercy, see, Rustom 2012.

36. Al-Tabari's is one of the most authoritative commentaries on the Qur'an.

37. Shah-Kazemi observes that the Qur'an must be taken as a "totality, and the balance between 'the promise' and the 'threat,' between hope and fear, between gentleness and rigor, is continually maintained throughout the text." (2007:24).

38. *Ahadith* (pl.) or *hadith* (s.) are reports of the sayings, practices, and omissions of the Prophet Mohammad.

39. Shah-Kazemi notes that the core values of Islam must be taken together (2006:3). The reading of individual verses outside of the broader aims obscures their meanings. This suggests a particular methodological approach to the study and understanding of the sacred texts— historically, linguistically, and beyond.

40. On the significance of 'Ali as a righteous political and spiritual figure, see Flaskerud 2010.

41. The pairing of human transgression with God's divine forgiveness is a strong theme throughout the Qur'an (Siddiqui 2012:125).

42. See also Fischer's discussion of 'Ali in the Karbala paradigm (1980).

43. Lewisohn finds that *Sufis* are generally not *Shi'i* except in Persia (now Iran) until after the rise of the *Mujtahid*s in the Safavid era in the late-sixteenth century CE.

44. In previous years, the majority of executions resulted from drug-related offenses, which Amnesty International determined as consisting of a total of fifty-eight percent in 2016 (*Amnesty International Global Report 2016*), see note 2. Iran's deputy judicial minister, Mohammad Javad Larijani, stated in March 2014 (in advance of Iran's Universal Periodic Review review before the United Nations' Human Rights Council) that some eighty percent of Iran's executions were for drug-related crimes. "Larijani: Omidvaram" 2014. See also, "Iran Says Nearly All Executions Drug-Related" 2014. A law passed in 2017 eases the death penalty for drug-related convictions. "Iran Eases Death Penalty Laws" 2017.

45. Iran Human Rights, *Annual Report 2015*; Iran Human Rights, *Annual Report 2016*.

46. I use the figures from the Annual Reports of the Iran Human Rights organization, noting, as they do, that these numbers are only estimates. See note 45.

47. Michael M.J. Fischer has referred to "anthropology in the meantime," as an experimental method that engages ethnography through a pragmatic, patient perspective without attempting to fill in all the gaps, but rather taking the time to figure out how people intersect and interact; it is "mapping, tracking, or inquiry into cascades, changes, and implications" (2018:2–4).

48. Khosravi (2017) eloquently reflects on the fine line that anthropologists working in Iran must walk.

Chapter 1

1. The public offense for which the defendant would be sanctioned was not murder, but rather *ekhlal dar nazm-e ummumi* (disruption of public order).

2. The first codified laws emerged well before the constitutional period, during the Qajar Dynasty, with Count's Law (*Qanun-e Kunt*) of the 1860s. Kondo (2017) suggests that the Qajar Shah transferred the administration of justice from the royal court to the state during the judiciary reforms of the latter half of the nineteenth century. These reforms included criminal cases administered by the newly-created police force, which consulted *'ulama* in *hudud* or *shari'a*-related cases.

3. Some felt that the *shari'a*, itself, offered a form of codification. Enayat (2013) shows that the statesmen were rather more concerned with buttressing state power and undercutting the legal authority of the *'ulama* than with conformity to religious principles. For a broad study of *shari'a* as codification, see Fadel 1996.

4. In 1914, Mossadeq expanded the argument for a modern penal code in his widely-read pamphlet on capitulations in which he reasoned that the only way Iran could rid itself of separate consular courts was with a modern penal code. Such a code, Mossadeq noted, would reinforce the bases of Iranian laws, including Islam (Enayat 2013:116).

5. Despite popular support suggested by a referendum, the bitter disputes that took place during the drafting of the constitution revealed vast differences in how leaders understood the new system of government.

6. Iran's post-revolutionary constitution established the Council of Guardians, a body of six Islamic jurists and six legal practitioners who determine whether legislative acts conform to *shari'a*.

7. To some, the centralizing and codifying of principles, which are meant to be interpreted according to time and place, contradicted the spirit of *Shi'i* jurisprudence. Such principles require believers to find a source of moral guidance within their own communities, that is, a *marja'-e taqlid* (source of emulation)—a qualified jurist from whom individuals seek answers to questions.

8. Art. 167 requires judges' rulings to be based on Islamic sources. Where the codified laws are insufficiently responsive to the full breadth of the *shari'a*, judges must attempt to do so. Art. 167 has opened up a can of worms for its ambiguity with regard to the laws, which are ostensibly already based on the *shari'a*. Thus, legislators and jurists continue to debate interpretations and applications of certain laws well after codification.

9. The post-revolutionary government also established a Revolutionary Court to prosecute individuals charged with violating the aims of the revolution, deemed as acting against the Islamic Republic. Such crimes are tantamount to treason and include a range of offenses, such as terrorism, inciting violence, blasphemy, insulting the leader of the Islamic Republic, and smuggling.

10. Iran's *Law of Islamic Punishment* defines nine crimes in this category: *zina*, intercourse between unmarried individuals, including intercourse by force, *zina be-onf* (rape), and incest; *qazf*, false accusation of *zina*; lesbianism, sodomy, or pedophilia; procurement; insulting the Prophet or His family, which includes the charge of blasphemy; use of intoxicants; robbery; *moharebeh* (waging war against the God); and *mofsed fel-arz* (rebellion and corruption on

earth). The latter two are used for opponents of the state, although the judiciary recently defined the category of "political crimes" which appears as a separate (and sometimes lesser) offense under the criminal code's discretionary provisions (ta'zirat).

11. As with western criminal laws, a finding of intent requires both *actus reus* and *mens rea*, that is, the commission of the physical act and the state of mind to commit it. Over time, jurisdictions broadened the meaning of intent from the notion of "malice aforethought," or premeditation, to the more liberally-defined awareness or practical knowledge that the act would lead to death. Likewise, Iran's penal code defines intent in the broader manner to include the circumstances around the killing. However, unlike Iran, other jurisdictions further divide intentional murder into sub-categories of degree from greatest culpability (first-degree murder) to lesser ones (second-degree) that consider the attendant circumstances.

12. The codes and pamphlets that reference intentional murder use the legal idiom *ghatl-e amdy* (intentional murder). Many scholars have emphasized the significance of the term *niyyat* (intent) in Islamic law (Messick 2001; Moumtaz 2018; Powers 2006). The legal codes, manuals, and scholarly texts I consulted throughout my research use the terms *amd* (intent) and, to a lesser extent, *qasd* (aim) to define the legal parameters of intentional murder in Iran's criminal code. Although my interlocutors did employ *niyyat*, they did so rather sparingly, mostly in conversations exploring the foundational ethics surrounding the formulation of an intention, especially in performing a ritual act. My experience coincides with the discussion by Powers (2006) who notes that, among Islamic jurists, *amd* possesses a negative connotation, while *niyyat* contains a positive one. In addition, *amd* appears to be a "technical term for specific types of homicidal intentions" (2006:189), while *niyyat* refers to general, but more positive, intentions.

13. *Ahadith* determine the rate of *diya* as 100 camels, 200 cows, or 1,000 sheep. At the start of every calendar year, Iran's Judiciary announces the annual rate of compensation for a death. For 2018[1397], the rate was 2,310,000,000 Iranian rials, about US $55,000 at the time. This rate increases by one-third during the Muslim holy months.

14. They do not tack to the judiciary's annually-determined rate of *diya*.

15. While *ta'zir* punishments can be quite harsh, and include capital punishment, the fact that they are punishments not specified in the sacred texts produces some uneven results, particularly in cases that have both *ta'zir* and *qisas* sanctions. This is especially clear in determining criminal responsibility for juveniles. For instance, in the context of criminal responsibility, for punishments that are specified in the sacred texts, the age of maturity (at which responsibility can arise) is referenced in the sacred texts (and interpreted as eight years and nine months for females and fourteen years and seven months for males). The age for legal responsibility in *ta'zir*, however, is determined by the civil code—eighteen for both females and males. This legal distinction creates the odd disposition that a girl as young as eight-and-a-half may be a plaintiff and exercise a private right of retribution for the murder of her kin, but she may not exercise any decision with regard to financial matters, such as inheritance or, should she forgo retribution, with regard to *diya*. In such matters, the court considers her age of responsibility to be eighteen and appoints a trustee or legal guardian to make financial decisions on her behalf. The younger age of responsibility applies only in contexts in which the law is interpreted through the sacred principles—*hudud*, *qisas*, and *diyat*. The discrepancies in age of responsibility appear not only in the divisions between civil and *ta'zir* laws versus scripture-based laws, but also, as noted previously, within

the sacred laws. The age of responsibility is also gendered. For laws that are devised from sacred principles, females arrive at legal responsibility as early as nine years old and males at fourteen. The age for criminal responsibility for youth under eighteen was the subject of important revisions in the penal code, which I discuss in Chapter 4.

16. Between 1981 and 1991, the judiciary had abolished the Office of the Public Prosecutor.

17. Forbearance in a *diya* crime would reduce or erase the monetary compensation. While *hudud* technically has no forbearance, the considerations of proof aim to restrict the implementation of the sanction, as does the plaintiff's retraction of the complaint or the plaintiff's forbearance.

18. *Zina* is broadly defined as unlawful sexual intercourse, often described as including adultery and fornication, although the penalties for each differ greatly. *Zina* becomes a *hudud* crime when the issue of consent emerges or when the parties are married to other individuals and are, thus, committing adultery. (Still, consent is the core issue because a married person cannot legally consent to intercourse with another person). The rub comes with the availability of temporary and polygamous marriages to men, which are not available to women. Technically, then, a married or unmarried man could escape punishment for *zina* by claiming a temporary marriage (i.e. consent)—as long as he is with an unmarried, non-virgin woman. By contrast, a married woman or a virgin cannot contract a temporary marriage—as she has no consent to give. The virgin girl's consent belongs to her male guardian, usually her father, and a married woman has already contracted her fidelity to her husband. So, in such a circumstance, the male—married or single—could avoid punishment altogether, while the woman could only if she were divorced or widowed. However, *zina* as fornication, that is, between consenting but unlawful partners (i.e. not married to each other and single) falls under the *ta'zir* category of punishment. The penalty for the former category (*hudud*) is death, while the penalty for the latter (*ta'zir*) is flogging. Although there have been some high-profile cases of the state prosecuting *zina*, few such penalties are carried out.

19. See Bassiouni (2014:136) for examples in different jurisdictions.

20. The Principle of Doubt is a key tenet in judicial reasoning and is based in *shari'a* (Rabb 2015). This principle finds that when doubt or uncertainty about the occurrence of a crime or the necessary elements thereof are present, then the commission of the crime has not been established. Another provision that applies to doubt is *lows* (contamination), which raises the issue of doubt where the evidence is found to be tainted (*Law of Islamic Punishment*, Art. 314).

21. According to Izutsu, "The social life of the individual is ruled and regulated by a certain set of moral principles with all their derivatives. These regulations constitute what we may call the system of social ethics soon to be developed in the post-Qur'anic period into the grand scale system of Islamic jurisprudence" (2002[1959]:18).

22. Izutsu conducts a semantic analysis to identify the Qur'an's key ethico-religious principles. One of those he finds is the term *birr* (piety or righteousness) defined by a sincerity in the belief of God's oneness expressed as social righteousness, which he opposes to a rule-based religious formalism.

23. According to Hallaq, "[t]he traditional Muslim society was as much engaged in the *shar'i* system of legal values as the court was embedded in the moral universe of society" (2009:171).

24. Indeed, Muslim courts consist of "a specific and a specialized social unit that has been carved out of society at large" (Hallaq 2009:166).

25. Feminist scholars such as Fatima Mernissi (1991) have brought to our attention the stories behind what constitutes women's modest comportment, such as veiling and gender segregation. The gendered nature of the emphasis on modest comportment and its reliance on women's dress and behavior were features of patriarchal life before Islam (Ahmed 1992). Even though these practices preceded the time of the Prophet, they were likely adapted to animate the moral dimensions of the revelations.

26. Iran's penal code requires the oral testimony of four male eyewitnesses (or three male and two female or two male and four female).

27. Here I diverge slightly from Hallaq who states that the Muslim court permits the disputants to "air their views in full and without constraint" (2009:166). I agree, however, with the broader spirit of the claim, which finds that the court serves as a site where parties may expend their anger and move towards resolving the dispute.

28. This is not to say the evidence would not be presented. The judges were often aware of cases' details, based on the filings. Additionally, in many cases, the trial was held in two phases, a public hearing, then a closed one, in which the sensitive evidence would be presented.

29. Agrama explores this idea as *satr Allah* (concealment of God), which compels investigation when evil is manifest and, conversely, prohibits it when evil is not manifest (2012:62).

30. See Lucas (2011) for analysis of the various versions of this story and their consequences.

31. Iranian legal scholars, whether lay attorneys or jurists trained in Islamic seminaries, referred to these adapted provisions as *emza'ee*, referring to their quality of being confirmed or verified by the scripture. The term, *emza'ee* suggests that the revelation "signed-off" on existing practice. Scholars with whom I spoke referred to provisions that were believed not to have been derived from custom, but were revelatory innovations, as *ta'sisi*, or established by scripture. This distinction is important in the debate in determining what elements of the religious-ethical system (or laws) humans may revise, with the latter (revelation) being inviolable and the former (custom) being adaptable. See also, Mir-Hosseini (1999:265).

32. Tellenbach notes that rape is the "most important situation from which a blood feud may arise" (2006:639).

33. In his study of feuding in tribal societies, Black-Michaud argues that, while men have honor, women "have 'shame' or sexual modesty, the female counterpart of and complement to honor, which both they and their menfolk must do their utmost to defend" (1975:218). Honor affords power, leadership, and prestige in these societies (Baroja 1966; Barth 1959; Pitt-Rivers 1966).

34. From its Arabic roots, the term *awliya-ye dam* literally means the "custodians of the blood." Neither a husband nor a wife who has lost a spouse falls within the legal category of *awliya-ye dam*. Thus, a spouse never possesses the right of retribution. As we will see, however, a spouse may be a plaintiff in an unlawful death suit that seeks damages other than *qisas*. Such damages would be classified under the *ta'zir* provisions where other charges against the defendant may be filed, such as damage to property.

35. Interestingly, the word for womb, *rahem*, and the word for mercy, *rahm*, share the same Arabic root, *r-h-m*.

36. It does not make things easier that one of the affirmative defenses to intentional murder is the defense of honor. Such situations require defendants to make impossible calculations about the human psyche. By making such a claim, the defendant tries to avoid the verdict of

intentional murder, but should he/she fail, then the claim of self-defense on account of the deceased's immoral acts or behavior may have permanently poisoned the well of goodwill and thus removed the chance to receive the forbearance of the victim's family. On the other hand, should the defendant hold back his/her account of the incident, that would suppress a justifiable motive and present too simple a case of intentional murder for which the victim's family would be unwilling to forgive. I examine such scenarios in the chapters that follow.

37. Iranian laws do punish debtors with imprisonment, including offenders with *diya* debts. Various non-governmental and governmental organizations, including the semi-official organization *Diya* Headquarters (*Setad-e Diya*), provide funds to families that cannot afford to pay such debts. Families must petition for such awards and, among other things, demonstrate financial need. Most such organizations specify that their funds only support debts that arise from unintentional injuries, in other words, from *diya* crimes. The state also has a Bodily Injury Indemnity Fund for paying out insurance claims.

38. *Law of Islamic Punishment*, Art. 550. This provision specifies that "the *diya* for murder of a woman is half that of a man."

39. Quoted in Elliot 2004.

40. Individuals I spoke with were initially skeptical about the government's ability to implement equal compensation because the cost of doubling insurance pay-outs for claims associated with women's injuries or deaths would be significant. When I interviewed Dr. Rahimi-Esfahani, then head of the Insurance Ministry's Bodily Injury Indemnity Fund in July 2010, he stated that, even so, the rule was in the process of being implemented due to widespread public support and advocacy for the proposition.

41. The state closed the religious disparity in *diya* in 2002, eliminating the disparate (and lower) rate of *diya* for injuries to non-Muslims.

42. See, for example, "Barabaree-e Diya" 2016.

43. The note states that, in order to obtain the support of the national treasury, the victim's family must demonstrate financial need. Interestingly, the note that suggests this solution comes from a provision (Art. 551) that defines the rule for determining the compensation for transgender victims. The provision states that the rate of *diya* for transgender individuals is calculated based on the victim's own understanding of his/her gender.

44. Since at least as early as the 1950s, anthropologists have attempted to understand the complex and often sophisticated modes of social organization among so-called "primitive" peoples. The evolutionary language of the times notwithstanding, anthropological inquiries sought to examine the norms and rules of societies through "inductive examination" and "without any preconceived idea," writing against the evolutionary logic of the times, including that such peoples operated through instinct, were bound by custom rather than law, and lacked complex thought processes (Malinowski 1959:15).

45. For example, the "ruling motive" of Albanian blood feuds was "pride" (Hasluck 1967:390). Regardless of the family's religion, failure to exact retribution would render the family "disgraced," "low class," and "bad" (Ibid.). Distinctly, the rape of a virgin girl marked "the most important situation from which a blood feud may arise" (Tellenbach 2006:639).

46. For instance, in Khouzestan province of southwestern Iran, conflicting tribes often settled an intertribal death or other conflict by offering in marriage a young woman from the tribe of the perpetrator to someone in the family or community of the victim (Gholami 2006:461).

Likewise, the Lor people, from the Bakhtiari region of Iran, followed a tradition referred to as *khoon-bas* (blood-stop) akin to a "truce" whereby the perpetrator's family would place a rope around the perpetrator's neck, take him to the victim's family, and allow the victim's family to choose retaliation or an offer of goods (2006:461–462). The Baluch tribe had a tradition called *patar* (asylum) in which the victim's family could similarly choose to grant forgiveness or to retaliate. According to Gholami, in the above traditions, retaliation was rarely chosen and settlement by acceptance of monetary compensation was common practice.

47. For an overview of *diya*, see Ismail 2012.

48. As we saw, jurists and scholars have identified a number of other Qur'anic verses that counsel and praise forgiveness. At least one *hadith* reports that whenever a case of *qisas* was brought before the Prophet Mohammad, he counseled forgiveness (Baderin 2003:73).

49. For instance, Schacht (1964).

50. See Ben Hounet (2012) for how states with large tribal groups integrate *diya* differently.

51. For Bohannan, law is based on a "double institutionalization" (1965), first a recognition of social customs and second their codification. Using this logic, Islamic laws are based on a triple institutionalization—from custom to scriptural injunction to codified law. The delivery of codified *diya* in Iran's penal code is a case in point, which emerged earlier from custom, then Islamic principle, and then law.

52. See also Foucault (1996), who argues along similar lines—that the introduction of the public prosecutor and rules of evidence were crucial for the formation of the development and privileging of the criminal code over that of private harms or torts.

53. Braithwaite notes that, when the formation of a strong central state or a monarch shifted the focus away from harm done to an individual (tort) to harm done to the monarch, this also marked a shift away from restorative justice (2002:5).

54. Compare with Bassiouni who says that the "Islamic criminal justice system somewhat superimposed itself on indigenous systems, but regional differences were significant" (2014:121).

55. *Law of Islamic Punishment*, Art. 420 and 421.

56. Some scholarship that explores honor crimes argues that what is often termed domestic violence or violence against women in western societies is referred to as honor crimes in non-western contexts (Abu-Lughod 2011; Volpp 2000, 2011). For my part, I suggest that the violence in western societies which we name "violence against women" is a consequence of the secularizing and individuating effect of law and legal institutions. This individuating effect shifts the focus of that which we call "honor crimes" in other societies from the family to the individual, thus arriving at "violence against women." I suggest that this is because legal institutions define such violence as against the individual instead of the family. By unpacking the institutional framework of Iran's legal system, we can see the relationship between gender, honor, and tort law more clearly and better understand how, in Iran, the focus is on *both* the family and the individual, making the remedy both about honor and the individual's right to retribution. At the same time, in western contexts, as in the U.S., honor and shame are very much alive in public discourse, even if the legal codes have supplanted the language and eliminated it.

57. For example, one of Harvey Weinstein's accuser's, Louise Godbold, noted that shame was a factor that prevented her from coming forward earlier and asks, "Why do women carry the shame of their perpetrators?" Louise Godbold, "My Encounter with Harvey Weinstein and

What It Tells Us About Trauma," *ACEs Connection*, October 9, 2017, https://www
.acesconnection.com/blog/my-encounter-with-harvey-weinstein-and-what-it-tells-us-about
-trauma. With perpetrators like Matt Lauer, shame emerged as the central element of his public
apology, "I feel ashamed." See, Disis 2017.

Chapter 2

1. *Laws of Criminal Procedure*, Art. 296.

2. I define restorative justice as a feature of a criminal justice system that emphasizes reconciliation between the offender and aggrieved parties and usually includes the payment of a reparation, monetary or other, to the victims or their surviving family members, and which results
in the forbearance of their right of retribution and/or in their forgiveness of the offender.

3. This is not to say that such attempts do not exist or that there is no debate over the principles deemed to be inviolable. One reason that the penal codes took so long to finalize was
because of such debates.

4. My citational practice here and throughout this work does not distinguish between *Shi'i*
and *Sunni* cosmologies. In terms of their moral frameworks each *mazhab* (school of thought)
of Islamic jurisprudence (possibly excepting Wahabism and Salafism) stresses the considerations with tempering *hudud* and *qisas*. For a useful discussion on the distinctions between *Shi'i*
and *Sunni* legal theory, see Enayat (2013:27).

5. Mahmoudi examines bills that preceded codification and argues that they paved the way
for a criminal justice policy that dispenses restorative justice in the new code (2006b:455).
Hallaq notes that the restorative aspects of the law involve reinstating the parties to their social
status prior to the incident in the pursuit of re-establishing social order and harmony (2009:166).

6. Besides the city of Tehran, the province of Tehran includes the cities of Behan, Damavand,
Karaj, Rey, Shemiran, and Varamin and holds a population of twelve million, about eighteen
percent of the country's total population.

7. An Iranian human rights organization based in Norway confirms this finding. See, "The
Punishment of Flogging for *Hadd* Violations May Be Revised" 2016.

8. Communitarian sanctions emphasize the relationship between the perpetrator and the
community. Sanctions are intended not only to rehabilitate the perpetrator, but also to restore
and strengthen the bond between the offender and his/her community (Duff 2001).

9. For instance, in July 2018, a widely circulated image of a young man being flogged for the
offense of drinking alcohol some ten years earlier in Razavi-Khorasan province suggested that
the availability of alternative sanctions does not prevent the use of flogging. See, "Iran: Young
man flogged" 2018.

10. The alternative sanctions do not replace the *hudud, qisas, diyat,* or *ta'zir* punishments,
which are defined as "foundational" (*Law of Islamic Punishment*, Art. 14).

11. See also Bassiouni, noting that early Islamic criminal justice systems were "judge-driven"
(2014:145).

12. That is, "if sentiments, emotions, or feelings refer to subjective experience (or senses that
can be put into discourse)," then affect "refers to a sensation that may move through the subject
but is not known to it, (i.e. it is unmediated by the cognitive, or the thinking and knowing, and
talking subject)" (Navaro-Yashin 2012:168).

13. For instance, in her ethnography on Italian family firms, Sylvia Yanagisako employs senti-ment as a mechanism to "bridge the dichotomy between thought and emotion" (2002:10). Lila Abu-Lughod has suggested that sentiments "symbolize values" and that individuals' expressions of sentiment "contributes [*sic*] to representations of the self, representations that are tied to morality, which in turn is ultimately tied to politics in its broadest sense" (1986:34).

14. Hampton (1992b:14) notes that, for retributive violence to serve its purpose, it should not degrade the perpetrator, only deny him/her the position of superiority claimed by the vio-lence inflicted.

15. Some analyses contend that judges have wide discretion in adjudicating *qisas*. Bassiouni, however, notes that this discretion is constrained by broad values of fairness in Islam (2014:142). See also, Rosen (2018).

16. Additionally, the code designates a special press court and a court for juvenile offenders. In the latter case, where the alleged crime consists of the most serious (noted in Art. 302), Criminal Court I constitutes a Special Juvenile Criminal Court (*Law of Criminal Procedure*, Art. 315).

17. *Law of Criminal Procedure*, Art. 302. Within Criminal Court I, the branches are further specialized. Inside Tehran's Provincial Criminal Court I, for instance, of the ten branches, only three handled the most severe crimes, such as murder or rape.

18. *Law of Criminal Procedure*, Art. 382.

19. *Law of Criminal Procedure*, Art. 302.

20. *Law of Criminal Procedure*, Art. 296.

21. Although rare, one judge may technically perform both roles; that is, one may serve as head of his own branch and, at the same time, circulate in another branch as an associate judge. Additionally, if the chief judge is unavailable, three associate judges may preside, with the most senior judge serving temporarily in the place of the chief judge.

22. *Law of Criminal Procedure*, Art. 374 and 378. That is, assuming he is part of the majority opinion. If he is not, then the more senior of the two associate judges will sign the opinion (*Law of Criminal Procedure*, Art. 404). If the opinion is not unanimous, then the judgment should contain the majority opinion as well as the minority opinion, inserted in a reasonable manner (*Law of Criminal Procedure*, Art. 395).

23. *Law of Criminal Procedure*, Art. 380, note 1.

24. *Law of Criminal Procedure*, Art. 431.

25. *Law of Criminal Procedure*, Art. 433.

26. *Law of Criminal Procedure*, Art. 434.

27. *Law of Criminal Procedure*, Art. 427.

28. *Law of Criminal Procedure*, Art. 426. Each province has its own Court of Review.

29. *Law of Criminal Procedure*, Art. 428.

30. *Law of Criminal Procedure*, Art. 417. The regularization of the *estizan* has a history of its own. It slowly became part of the legal process, starting in the early 1990s when the Judiciary Head, Ayatollah Mohammad Yazdi, issued a circular that was to be followed by all jurisdictions. As jurisdictions throughout the country were slow to implement the policy, a number of such circulars had to be issued over the years, including by the next Judiciary Head, Ayatollah Shah-roudi. The *'ulama* found a jurisprudential basis for it in the *ahadith* as well as in the Qur'an, verse 2:178.

31. *Law of Criminal Procedure*, Art. 5 and 347.

32. *Law of Criminal Procedure*, Art. 190.

33. *Law of Criminal Procedure*, Art. 193–195.

34. *Law of Criminal Procedure*, Art. 48. In cases that violate national security, however, the law provides a one-week delay in accessing files.

35. *Law of Criminal Procedure*, Art. 272.

36. In Iran, judges are public servants. They pass an exam to enter the judiciary. Graduates from either track, with a bachelor's in law from a university or a degree from an Islamic seminary, may sit for the judge's exam. As public servants, judges have access to public pensions, but do not earn as much as lawyers in private practice. Some judges lamented to me that the status of the work was not in line with the pay. Women are (still) unable to serve as judges in many contexts, including criminal law. There are, however, women in the magisterial level, that is, in the prosecutor's office, and are referred to as *qazi* (judge).

37. However, should the two associate judges hold the majority opinion, then one of them would sign it.

38. To gain entry to the bar, law graduates must, after completing an exam and undergoing a security clearance with the Interior Ministry, complete an eighteen-month apprenticeship, consisting of courtroom observation, internship at an attorney's office, and workshops at the lawyer's bar. At the end of the apprenticeship, the legal apprentice must pass a second exam before being admitted to the bar.

39. *Law of Islamic Punishment*, Art. 428.

40. In the summer of 2016, the judiciary in the Tehran branch of the Criminal Court began installing recording devices and cameras in the courtrooms. Hand-written stenography was coming to a close. The purpose of recordings was for judges to review proceedings during deliberation or for courts or review.

41. *Law of Criminal Procedure*, Art. 396.

42. *Law of Criminal Procedure*, Art. 48, 348, and 384.

43. *Law of Islamic Punishment*, Art. 211 and 212.

44. *Law of Islamic Punishment*, Art. 160. Art. 164–173 define and elaborate confession, Art. 174–200 deal with testimony, and Art. 201–210 construe oaths. The penal code makes a distinction between two kinds of oaths, *qasaameh* and *sogand*. While both mean 'sworn oath,' the former is verbally sworn by fifty individuals and can only be employed in cases of *qisas* and *diya*. The latter refers to an individual sworn oath.

45. *Law of Islamic Punishment*, Art. 211.

46. *Law of Islamic Punishment*, Art. 212.

47. *Law of Islamic Punishment*, Art. 213.

48. This concern is also addressed procedurally with a three-judge panel in the most serious crimes.

49. *Usul-e fiqh* is the critical apparatus of interpretation over which a jurist must have mastery in order to derive rules (Fischer 1980:66).

50. Anver Emon argues for a middle ground in which codification may procedurally serve the broader aims of a robust *shari'a* (2016).

51. The victim's sense of self-respect also influences her decision to retaliate (Murphy 2003).

Chapter 3

1. The legal physician is an administrative category of medical doctor, who works in the Commission of Legal Physicians within the Judiciary and certifies parties' various medical conditions in legal matters.

2. See for instance, Ghamkhavar 2012.

3. After retiring from the bench, Aziz-Mohammadi became a criminal defense lawyer, wrote an eight-hundred-page memoir, and was the subject of a 2018 documentary, *Death and the Judge*.

4. Although we do not often think of Iran's system of jurisprudence as possessing *stare decisis*, written decisions are collected, published, and circulated, with judges citing one another's reasoning. Collections are sold in book stores and studied in legal training.

5. Ho (2006) describes this schizophrenic quality of the modern state as an effect of the bureaucratic layering of multiple methods of rule and egalitarian imperatives of social leveling combined with inegalitarian instruments of administrative authority.

6. As we will see in Chapter 4, others, like Aziz-Mohammdi, also used their positions to propose reconciliation.

7. The provision shifts the burden of proof in certain cases of self-defense as well, making the claim easier for the defendant to prove than it was previously. Under the previous version, the defendant needed to prove that the deceased had an intent to kill and that the defendant's response was narrow and proportionate. In the previous version, the defendant needed to prove the deceased's state of mind, which is very difficult. In the new version, the defendant needs to show that he/she acted out of necessity (and not that the deceased intended to kill him/her). This is an important change in the law.

8. *Law of Islamic Punishment*, Art. 429.

9. One person's share is determined by taking the number of individuals who are the victim's next-of-kin and dividing by the amount of full *diya*.

10. *Law of Islamic Punishment*, Art. 423.

11. The way age of majority works in these cases is complicated. Because *qisas* is from the *shari'a*, the age of majority is said to be based on scriptural sources, which make the age for females eight years and nine months and for males fourteen years and seven months. But, for *ta'zir* offenses, the age of majority is based on the civil laws which set the age at eighteen for both girls and boys. To complicate things further, the reason for the eight years and nine months and fourteen years and seven months, instead of nine years and fourteen years respectively is because, again, based on the idea that these ages are based on the sacred sources, the state uses the shorter Muslim lunar calendar to calculate age instead of the longer Persian solar calendar— but *only* for those crimes that are derived from Muslim sources. This creates the situation where a boy at fourteen and a girl as young as eight can not only be held criminally responsible but can also make determinations about *qisas*. For instance, this was the case in a *qisas* case in which an eleven-year-old girl decided to have the man who blinded her when she was four-years-old also blinded. According to the head of Implementations, this was only the second time such a sentence was carried out in Iran's largest province, Tehran. "Iran: Responsibility" 2016.

12. Such comments allow for an interesting reading of Hay's classic work on private property and the rise of criminal law in eighteenth century England (1975).

13. This interview took place on September 17, 2016. Bayat-Zanjani emphasized that the Qur'an gives no authority to kill. Accordingly, the only times when killing may be legitimate are in battle or self-defense.

14. Gluckman notes that the "flexible 'uncertainty' of legal concepts" allows judges to cope with social change. Gluckman sees the judicial process as "the attempt to specify legal concepts with ethical implications according to the structure of society, in application to the great variety of circumstances of life itself" (1955:24).

15. To understand discretion, Gluckman turns to ethics and notes, "reconciliation" and "the 'moulding' of peace [are] two very flexible concepts which allow judges to draw from a wide range of sources to arrive at justice" (1955:298).

16. What appeared to be happening was a legal strategy on the part of the judges. They did not want to hold an in-camera hearing on the issue of sexual violation as a possible affirmative defense because the women had no corroborating evidence. The judges, having indicated that they had read the file, were likely gesturing towards their sympathetic view of the women's plight. Given the broad definition of intentional murder and the incontrovertible evidence of their actions, the judges were bound to rule the killing intentional. Given this finding, they would have had no discretion in sentencing the women to qisas. As a result, the judges appeared to steer the testimony, through their interrogations, towards preserving the women's post-sentencing pleas for forbearance. In the post-verdict context, the judges had more of a free hand, indeed a newly-codified duty to seek reconciliation. Their efforts in the reconciliation meeting, by virtue of its extra-judicial nature, allowed for mediation.

17. The new provisions allow the court to enforce certain conditions that the parties agree upon. The court may also validate the right to qisas if a specified condition is not met. Such a condition could include failure to pay the full amount of the agreed-upon compensation, which some interlocutors had told me was a problem. *Law of Islamic Punishment*, Art. 101, 102, and 103.

18. Iran's pious Muslims recite the *salavat* frequently, in prayer but also in everyday contexts—to thank God, to wish for success, to ask for blessings. The prayer consists of repeating the phrase, *Allah umma salli 'ala Muhammad wa al-i Muhammad* (Oh God, bless Mohammad and Mohammad's family).

19. *Law of Islamic Punishment*, Art. 38(a).

20. This hearing took place in 2013, before the judiciary implemented the procedural change from a five-judge panel to a three-judge panel for such offenses.

21. "Thy Lord hath decreed that ye worship none but Him, and that ye be kind to parents. Whether one or both of them attain old age in thy life, say not to them a word of contempt, nor repel them, but address them in terms of honour And, out of kindness, Lower to them the wing Of humility, and say: 'My Lord! bestow on them Thy Mercy even as they Cherished me in childhood.'" Chapter 17 (*Isra* [The Night Journey]:23–24).

22. They were the grandchildren of the deceased. Although not next-of-kin, their mother was the victim's daughter (and the aunt of the perpetrator) and possessed the right of retribution. However, she died after the homicide. The right of retribution, like any property right, was inherited by her children (*Law of Islamic Punishment*, Art. 419). Had the aunt pre-deceased the victim (her mother), there would be no right of retribution to pass on and the cousins would not have been involved.

23. Each member of the victim's immediate next-of-kin possesses a discrete right of retribution (*Law of Islamic Punishment*, Art. 422) and must separately petition as plaintiffs against the accused. The law permits plaintiffs who want *qisas* to pay compensation to those who want forbearance—and thus (such plaintiffs can) demand the sentence be carried out (Art. 423). They are effectively purchasing the other plaintiffs' rights of retribution from them. However, if the plaintiffs who want forbearance do not seek compensation, then the payment will be made to the defendant (whose own kin will inherit it upon execution). If the next-of-kin are minors who cannot exercise the right of retribution, then the compensatory payment would be deposited into a fund until the youth reach majority. In such cases, the implementation of the sentence is suspended until the youth reach the age of majority.

24. Mitigating factors include: private plaintiff's forbearance; effective cooperation of the accused in identifying accessories, evidence, or objects used in the commission of the offense; statement of the accused prior to prosecution, or his/her effective confession during investigation and prosecution; regret; specific condition of the accused such as his/her age or illness (*Law of Islamic Punishment*, Art. 38).

25. Notwithstanding the penal code's primary emphasis on the victim's satisfaction, this trend towards alternative criminal sanctioning opens the door to restorative justice remedies (Mahmoudi 2006b:455).

26. See Giridharadas (2014) and Grosmaire (2016) for U.S. accounts of personal forgiveness with little legal impact.

Chapter 4

1. I explore Jabbari's case in Chapters 6 and 8.

2. The two phrases are distinct. Death row phenomenon refers to the harmful effects of death row conditions, while death row syndrome is the resulting manifestation of psychological illness that can occur as a result of death row phenomenon (Harrison and Tamony 2010). The first term formed the basis of the argument in *Soering v. United Kingdom* (1989) before the European Court of Human Rights. Through its ruling against extradition to the U.S., the Court recognized for the first time that the period an offender waits for execution, itself, constitutes "cruel and unusual punishment." In light of this holding, the Court ruled that European Union countries could not extradite individuals to countries where they would face such conditions. One manifestation of death row syndrome is the apparent "volunteering" for execution by inmates (Smith 2008:238).

3. In a system which grants victims' families the right to exercise or forgo retribution, those families, too, find themselves mired in a temporal agony, that of decision-making, which I examine in Chapter 5.

4. In his exploration of hope and waiting, Khosravi found that Iranian youth commonly employ the term to signify utter purposelessness and boredom (2017:82).

5. Given the possibility of forbearance, the waiting activities of death-row inmates in Iran can be distinguished from those of U.S. inmates, who are not just "doing time" but "doing death watch" (Kohn 2009:224). Kohn notes that death-row inmates have agency and then examines their forms of self-making in prison. Inmates leave vast records of their strivings to become better people, even in the face of execution. Iran's death-row inmates have an even greater

motivation to use time actively—to show evidence of rehabilitation and remorse in hopes of obtaining forbearance.

6. This coincides with the change in administration as well. Hassan Rouhani was elected president in August 2013.

7. Gilsenan also notes, "The open-ended time span gives the situation flexibility from the revengers' point of view and allows for the maintenance of self without compromise. But it generates its own uncertainties" (2016[1976]:509).

8. Das (2006) draws from Wittgenstein to engage "form-of-life" as a term to understand how human beings live in language; that is, how language serves as the matrix through which communities arrive at mutual understanding. Drawing from the two concepts of life and form, Das adds the idea of "naturalness" that acts and expressions take. Thus, understanding the expression "form-of-life" requires recognizing that form and life "are nestled in each other: sociocultural differences, or the form that human existence takes, as well as the way in which the social and the natural mutually absorb each other." Form-of-life, thus, rests on agreements by people living together in community. Such agreements are not settled; they are constantly secured through everyday practices (Han and Das 2016:3).

9. For Agamben, potentiality, in part, refers to the 'can'—to have the faculty, the ability, or, in this context, the 'right' to act or to do something and also not to do so. I use potentiality here to recognize the victim's family who *can* but does not necessarily exercise forbearance.

10. See Introduction.

11. Othman (2007) has studied this scriptural maxim, "Amicable Settlement is Best."

12. Kant outlines these views in *The Metaphysics of Morals*, originally published in 1797. Kant is in part responding to the Italian jurist, Cesare Beccaria (1764), who opposed capital punishment on the theory that it required the prior consent of individuals in a society to carry it out and people cannot consent to giving up their own lives.

13. The phrase has also been attributed to Imam 'Ali by the thirteenth-century scholar, Ibn Abi'l Hadid in his important commentary on 'Ali's *Nahj al-Balaghah*.

14. Urbanormativity is defined as "the assumption that the conditions of urbanism found in metropolitan areas are the normative" (Thomas et al. 2010:152).

15. *Arba'een*, which literally means fortieth, is the last day of a forty-day *Shi'i* ceremony commemorating the 680 CE battle of Karbala, in which Hossein, Prophet Mohammad's grandson and the third *Shi'i* Imam, along with his companions, was martyred. Pilgrims often observe the event by walking, sometimes barefoot, from the city of Najaf to Karbala, a distance of some 82 km/51 mi, taking up to six days.

16. This was a 3–2 decision (obviously issued before the laws were revised to have a three-judge panel decide such cases). "Khanevadeh 'Amr be Ma'ruf' az Qisas Gozasht Kardan" 2015.

17. Allameh Tabataba'i was a highly regarded scholar. His *Tafsir al-Mizan* is a twenty-seven-volume work of Qur'anic exegesis. In his commentary, Tabataba'i examined Qur'anic verse 2:228 and noted, "The *ma'ruf* is that which people know by insight earned by experience in social life as they live it . . . The word refers to the gifts of the intellect as well as to the assessment of the *shar'*, the generous admirable character, and the norms of good conduct . . . what people know to do intuitively" (cited in Reinhart 2017:63).

18. Nishaburi was a Persian astronomer, mathematician, exegete, jurist, and poet, known as much for his commentary on the Qur'an as for his explorations in astronomy (Morrison 2007).

19. Around this time, a bill employing this principle was winding its way through Iran's parliament on its way to becoming law, with much heated dissent among critics who highlighted its potential misuse by vigilantes against civilians. The outpouring of dissent reached a lurid pinnacle when, in October of 2014, in Esfahan, bandits riding motorcycles threw acid on eight women. Critics believed that the culprits tried to justify their vigilantism with reference to the second clause of the principle of "commanding right, forbidding wrong" because the young women were in "bad hejab." State actors I spoke with vociferously denied that actions of the vigilantes could be justified through this (or any) principle.

20. See also Deeb (2006) and Mahmood (2005) for explorations on gender, piety, and embodiment.

21. Laidlaw takes issue with ethnographic portrayals of Islamic piety as "'unthinking' habit", which depict ethics as the cultivation of a coherent disposition (2014:168). He suggests that, even if the project of living an ethical life is a consistent and intelligible one, the endeavor to live an ethical life, itself, is a lived pursuit complete with doubts, tensions, failings, and inconsistencies.

22. The CRC prohibits the death penalty for individuals under the age of eighteen. In seeking a balance between its reading of the *shari'a* and its obligations under international law, Iran waits until such offenders have reached eighteen years of age before implementing the death penalty, a practice for which it has come under heavy criticism. See *Amnesty International "Iran 2018"* (2018).

23. *Law of Criminal Procedure*, Art. 410.

24. *Law of Criminal Procedure*, Art. 286, refers to character files for youth offenders; Art. 203 refers to the same for adults.

25. For explorations of time in the furtherance of humanization and healing, see Gobodo-Madikizela (2003). We might also consider the attempt to humanize the perpetrator in comparison with victim's justice in western legal systems. There, while the legal process is quite lengthy, the focus is not on victim's justice, but rather on the state's prosecution of the public harm (for murder). In accordance with that stance, the perpetrator is rarely humanized, despite the passage of time, and the potentiality of time is not utilized to compel forgiveness.

26. *Law of Criminal Procedure*, Art. 527. Art. 90 allows a one-time reduction to the sentence based on the Center Director's report. The article allows either a reduction to the sentence or release to parental custody, provided the offender has served at least one-fifth of the sentence.

27. *Law of Criminal Procedure*, Section 10 (Art. 88- 91).

28. Children in the concrete operational stage are typically ages seven to eleven. Their thinking is more organized and rational. They can solve problems in a logical fashion but are typically not able to think abstractly or hypothetically.

29. Adolescents do not necessarily move automatically to the next cognitive stage with biological maturation. Only about 30–35 percent of high-school seniors attain the formal operational stage of cognitive development (Kuhn, Langer, Kohlberg, and Haan 1977; Eylon and Lynn, 1988).

Chapter 5

1. For Derrida (2001a), pure forgiveness is impossible; all earthly forgiveness is in some way mediated or conditioned and, therefore, impure. This view of forgiveness as aporia leaves no room for unconditional human forgiveness. Pure forgiveness, it seems, is divine. There

are, however, numerous other possibilities, all involving exchange, usually between the parties. While this may fall short of pure forgiveness, Derrida acknowledges the value in such exchanges insofar as they forge conciliation and provide other relief, such as resolution to conflict

2. Although injured parties are required to file a complaint, there is no statute of limitations on *qisas*. Upon a *qisas* verdict, plaintiffs must petition for its implementation. During the time period between the verdict of *qisas* and the petitioning for implementation, the offender is in prison. Although state officials attempt to bring cases to a resolution, the time their efforts take varies. Prior to the new criminal code, there was no limit on how long such a period could last. The new criminal code places a ten-year limit on the detention by allowing offenders to petition for release by posting a security after ten years (*Law of Islamic Punishment*, Art. 429). The practical effect of this provision may be that the state pressures the victim's family to make a decision. Otherwise, it appears, an offender could post a bond, be released, and then, at some future point, if the victim's family desires, be executed.

3. This is the reverse of the legal maxim, the exception swallows the rule. The comparable Qur'anic verse and legal maxim derives from 5:45 "retribution is your right, but forbearance is better." The cultural shift afoot in this semi-autonomous social field seeks to recast forbearance as a right, not as an exception and not exceptional. Instead of repeating that forbearance is 'better,' and characterizing it as a relinquishing of a right, the agents of this rebranding of forbearance confirm that retribution is a right, but they affirm that forbearance, too, is a right. In this formulation, forbearance carries the same weight as retribution.

4. Reports of forbearance occurring just seconds before—or after—the sentence were not uncommon. Victims' families either changed their minds in those last moments or had no intention of carrying out the sentence and had just wanted to frighten the perpetrator.

5. Gobodo-Madikizela defines empathic repair as a shared emotional state between victims and perpetrators that emerges "as a result of a pivotal turn to perspective taking and gaining an integrated view of the other" (2008:343).

6. Sogand's prison term was commuted to time served.

7. Sina played a tune written for the opening poem of Rumi's *Masnavi, Beshno az Ney* (*Lament of the Reed Flute*), which has deep emotional significance for Iranians as a song of sorrow, desolation, and pain over separation. The poem opens with the lines, "Listen to the cry of the reed flute, Listen to its song of separation," and tells the story of the reed being cut from its source, then burned, dried, hollowed, and bored with holes in order to be capable of making beautiful music. Allegorically, the message the poem conveys to humans is that they, too, are in an unnatural state of separation—from the Divine—and must go through the trials of life and learn to be that empty before they can turn suffering into joy—and into music. The pain of separation will eventually bring them back to the Divine.

8. The term is complex and has no exact equivalence in English. *Aberu* is composed of the words *ab* (water) and *ru* (face). Zaborowska (2014) explores the etymology of *aberu* and offers a socio-linguistic genealogy of its meaning in both pre-Islamic Persian and the *Shi'i* contexts. According to her, *aberu* is a shelter that provides protection for the most valuable essence of a human being—his/her dignity and character (2014:121).

9. The idea of an anonymous social force also evokes the Muslim *umma* (community of Muslims) (Ahmadi and Ahmadi 1998:213).

Chapter 6

1. This is not to say that the state does not have any mechanisms in place for arbitration or resolution of other types of conflicts. Indeed, for monetary conflicts involving small sums, the state runs *Khaneh-ye Hal-e Ekhtelaf* (Houses of Dispute Resolution) at the city and district level. Although not part of their official mandate, these dispute resolution centers also engage in forgiveness work, especially in the provinces. In addition, a semi-independent NGO, the *Setad-e Diya* (Compensation Headquarters) operates at the behest of the state to formally help families who need to raise *diya*, but its efforts are exclusively directed towards involuntary offenses.

2. For Das, ethics grow from the forms of life that people inhabit (2012:136). They rest in "the small disciplines that ordinary people perform in their everyday life to hold life as the natural expression of ethics" (2012:139). Stewart, also, has explored how the "ordinary," which she refers to as a "shifting assemblage of practices and practical knowledge," shapes subjects' "capacities to affect and be affected" (2007:1–2). Focusing on "(non)movements," in the Middle East, Bayat (2010a) has argued that ordinary people forge a ground up approach to change, not through the mobilization of social and political movements, but rather through dissipated and uncoordinated acts that amount to "passive networks" and "undeliberate linkages" (2010b:40).

3. Lambek observes that ethics is "not a matter of smoothly following the rules but of the exhilaration of self-transcendence, as well as the struggle with ambivalence and conflict" (2010:12). The social workers' self-cultivation is not unlike the embodied and affective virtuous dispositions that Mahmood (2005) and Hirschkind (2006) have written about. In this work, it is inflected through performative actions and intersubjective speech acts (Lambek 2010).

4. Peletz (2016) examines how Islamic law in Malaysia is subject to processes of bureaucratization, rationalization, and corporatization.

5. Drawing from Nietzsche's *On the Genealogy of Morals* (1967[1879]), Derrida noted that the premise of equivalence upon which the justification for retribution relied, was faulty: "whence comes this bizarre, bizarre idea, this ancient, archaic idea, this so very deeply rooted, perhaps indestructible idea, of a possible equivalence between injury and pain?" (2014:151).

6. Boyer observes embodied behavior as attuned to individuals' distinct environments "articulated through a versatile gestural grammar of reflexes and attitudes," which he refers to as "corporeal expertise" (2005:259). As I have suggested, forgiveness workers draw from prescripted socio-cultural practices to display embodied corporeal expertise as scriptural authority, caring witness, and impartial, reasoned empath.

7. For Boltanski (2012), disputes are often regulated by recourse to "a regime of justice," somewhat implicit in everyday social interaction. Such regimes are not the only avenues for resolving conflict, however. Some interventions involve selfless and gratuitous actions. As such, they operate through what he refers to as "a regime of peace" or "love." In the course of their everyday lives, Boltanski argues, people shift between the regimes of justice and love, depending on the issue.

8. Das (2010) draws from Stanley Cavell's work on the everyday quality of moral striving, suggesting that individuals' responses to how others see them and how they allow themselves to be seen shapes their moral personhood. Thus, moral striving is characterized not by the givenness of ideals of virtue nor abstract notions of the common good, but through quotidian experiences. Das notes that individuals do not imagine their moral lives through abstract

systems of value or higher ideals. Instead, their moral striving takes place through the complex range of forces and intimate aspirations they encounter in everyday situations. Das communicates the constitutive quality of moral striving through the idea of the "adjacent self."

9. Prior to this work, Mahboubeh contributed to household finances by offering private tutoring. When calls for forgiveness work started coming regularly, she had to stop tutoring, even though she had amassed a following and a tidy salary to help support her family. As a social worker, she engages in emotional affective labor (Hardt 1999).

10. Das (2010) draws from the work of philosopher, Leo Bersani (2008) to argue that love provides us with the opportunity to realize our adjacent selves.

11. It may as well be the case that some would be repelled by re-living such experiences.

12. *'Ashura*, commemorating the death of *Shi'i* Imam Hossein, falls on the tenth day of the month of *Moharram*. The entire month of Ramadan is important for contemplative worship and mercy, but the final ten odd days of the month or *Laylat al-Qadr* (the Night of the Divine) are extremely important. For *Shi'i* Muslims, the nineteenth and twenty-first of Ramadan have heightened importance because they believe their first Imam, 'Ali (the fourth Caliph for Sunnis), was wounded and died two days later. Muslims also hold the twenty-third as especially sacred because it marks the day when the first verses of the Qur'an are said to have been revealed.

13. There is likely a legal strategy for the sister's retraction. One possibility is that the sister was attempting to absolve herself of a charge of being an accessory to the crime. In addition, her brother's claim that she asked him to come over could have been a strategy on his part to tie her to the incident, both placing deliberation into question and possibly attempting to save his life by tying his deeds to that of his sister's. The suggestion was that, since she had a good relationship with her in-laws, they would be less likely to blame her for the incident, and thus, by association, less likely to have him executed.

14. As noted, forbearance requires unanimity among the next-of-kin. Otherwise, the members of the immediate family who want retribution must pay the *diya* to those who do not want retribution. If the family members do not want compensation, the *diya* would go to the perpetrator.

15. Qur'an, Chapter 2 (*Baqarah* [The Cow]):281: "And fear a Day when you will be returned to God. Then every soul will be compensated for what it earned, and they will not be treated unjustly."

16. See Ayoub 1978; Momen 1985; Shah-Kazemi 2007.

17. This idea is reminiscent of Seneca's "inclination towards leniency in punishment" (2010). Nussbaum also notes the affinity between the ability to judge the situation and the inclination towards leniency, or equity and mercy (1993:3–4).

18. In this saying there is a double-entendre; the term conveys both, "I moved on" and "I waived my claim." The term *gozasht* can also refer to time in a number of ways—to the noun form "the past" and the verb form of "passed."

19. Samira Esmeir (2012) notes the newness of the term in secular, post-colonial contexts.

20. Leila, a social worker who worked with the NGO, first introduced me to the lifeworld of forgiveness activism in 2007. She subsequently introduced me to other activists, including Mahboubeh.

21. Upon ratification on July 13, 1994, Iran took a general reservation and "reserved the right not to apply any provisions or articles of the Convention that are incompatible with Islamic

laws and the international legislation in effect." *Status of Ratification Interactive Dashboard,* http://indicators.ohchr.org/.

22. SPRC brochure, 2008. Translated by the author. http://www.irsprc.org/.

23. In these three contexts, the SPRC advocates for new laws and the reform of existing ones where Iran is not in conformity the CRC. It works to enforce existing laws to protect children, and trains and educates families, organisations, and individuals on child protection. The SPRC also engages in activities referenced by the CRC, including educational training, health care, and assistance for children injured as a result of natural disasters and living under difficult conditions, such as poverty.

24. In 2007, one of the SPRC's most important efforts (and later achievements) was advocating for revising the law for the punishment of youth convicted of intentional murder.

25. Beeman describes *kutah amadan* as a linguistic mechanism that serves "as a corrective device for interactions that somehow get out of hand" (1986:199). In an interaction that reaches a potentially explosive point, one person may stop short or acquiesce by responding with less (rather than equal or more) emotion, thus diffusing the volatility of the exchange. Individuals employ *kutah amadan* in direct repartee, but they also use it as a mechanism to draw down prolonged disputes, particularly when the ethics of status relationships among socially dissimilar groups are involved (1986:200). For instance, a mother might intervene to resolve a dispute between her husband and son, admonishing her son to stop short, out of respect for his father.

26. Mr. Saheb's work is well-known amongst people in the lifeworld of forgiveness work. Many profiles of his efforts circulate, but do not appear to have the effect of suggesting that he represents the side of the perpetrator. See, Afaf 2015.

27. Rosaldo explains that the rage is a cathartic response to loss and leads to the violence of headhunting; it is part of a grieving process. In his study of Ilongot headhunting, Rosaldo moves away from naming such ritual practices as "timeless and self-contained" processes, and exhorts social scientists, instead, to explore the cultural forces underlying such emotions, "with a view to delineating the passions that animate certain forms of human conduct" (1989:19).

28. Of course, state officials saw the preservation of the right of retribution as a measure to cordon off and staunch the excess of violence, which they believed would break out if citizens felt the state was unable to mediate disputes.

29. The Society's website boasts of some 12,000 volunteers who work throughout the country; many are university students from the eminent Sharif University (www.sosapoverty.org).

30. In a notable reversal of gender norms, volunteers referred to Sharmin by first name and his spouse by her last name.

31. The Society's activities, well-known in Iran, have also been the subject of interest in the western press. For example, Erdbrink 2014.

32. Reyhaneh Jabbari was executed on October 25, 2014, just days shy of her twenty-sixth birthday. In her defense, Reyhaneh had claimed that she did not kill Sarbandi intentionally, but stabbed him to prevent sexual assault. The case, which I explore in Chapter 8, possessed many complexities and uncertainties.

33. Messick has also referenced the unique recitational quality of the Qur'an; this "recitational logocentrism" imbues the reciter with authority (1993:25).

34. Qur'an Chapter 5 (*Maedeh* [The Table Spread]):27–32.

35. For a discussion on the differences between human rights and humanitarianism, see Wilson and Brown (2009).

36. Wilson and Brown note, "for humanitarian suffering to be elicited, it seems imperative that the narrative of suffering strongly testify to the innocence of the sufferer" (2009:23). In these cases, those suffering would be all the parties involved, including the deceased, but the victim's family, who are the creditors, are the ones who must be swayed by the notion of suffering.

37. In a reconciliation meeting in the spring of 2014, which three of my interlocutors attended, the victim's family expressed incredulity of Reyhaneh's claim of self-defense by evoking her height.

38. In the earlier case, we saw a similar situation in which the daughters of the slain man had claimed a self-defense of sorts, but, once the verdict was issued and they were in need of mercy, one of the judges intervened and evoked a middle ground in which the defendants agreed to have "made a mistake." Although the nature of that error had been left obscure, it was enough, at that emotional moment, to convince the victim's family to forgo retribution. Another important issue was the publication of the revelations. In that case, the judges worked hard to keep the testimony about sexual violence sealed, thus keeping the family's reputational concerns outside of the broader public space. In Reyhaneh's case, the sexual violence claims traveled through social media.

39. Reyhaneh Jabbari had five lawyers over the years.

40. *Kuchegardan-e Asheq* is specific to Imam 'Ali and *Eid-e Ghadir*, the *Shi'i* celebration of the Prophet Mohammad's designation of 'Ali as his successor. Among the ritual practices of this celebration is the distribution of food to those in need, much like neighborhood relief workers or good samaritans. On its website explaining *Kuchegardan-e Asheq*, the Society quotes a passage from Imam 'Ali's last will and testament to his sons, Imams Hassan and Hossein, addressing the deprivations of poverty, especially on orphans: "O God! O God! Concerning the orphans, lest they be sometimes full and sometimes hungry and deprived of their rights." https://sosapoverty.org/kuchegardan/. Author's translation.

41. The students had been distributing food throughout the month of Ramadan. That particular day was July 24, 2014, the twenty-sixth of Ramadan. At midnight, when the students would distribute food, it would be the twenty-seventh, *Laylat al-Qadr* (the Night of Power), when Muslims believe the first verses of the Qur'an were revealed to the Prophet Mohammad. Muslims believe that *Laylat al-Qadr* is found in the last ten odd nights of Ramadan. *Shi'i* Muslims regard the nineteenth, twenty-first, and twenty-third of that month as the most significant, with the twenty-third being the most important night. *Shi'i*, who consider 'Ali as the Prophet Mohammad's rightful successor, believe 'Ali died on the twenty-first, having succumbed to injuries sustained two days earlier from a fatal blow to the head during morning prayers in Kufa. For the *Shi'i* those three days—the nineteenth, twentieth, and twenty-first of Ramadan—are the most intense, and reflection, contemplation, and good deeds are paramount expressions of faith.

42. This story appears in a narrative compilation of accounts of 'Ali's example, extracted by the author from numerous sources and recounted in simple language to reach a broad audience. In the collection's foreword, the author states his intention as contributing to readers' "moral education." He notes that "ethics is a fundamental field" of Islam to which he contributes by "transmitting authentic accounts" (Mutahhari n.d.:10).

43. Qur'an, Chapter 112 (*Tawhid* [Unity]; another name for this chapter is (*Ikhlas* [Sincerity]). Nasr et al. 2015. Among 'Ali's greatest contributions was his discovery of the *tawhid*, the unity and oneness of God (Nasr 2006). See also, Nasr, Nasr, and Dabashi 1988:114 and Lakhani 2006:15.

44. The term "sustenance" is engaged through the second verse of Chapter 112. The word translated here as "eternal" is *samad* and connotes sustenance or nourishment. Bowen's interlocutors similarly referred to the power that this verse invests in those who recite it (1993).

45. Scheiwiller (2013) explores the relationship between the iterative conditions of performativity and the post-revolutionary Iranian state in different historical periods and sociocultural dimensions.

46. Sadr examines Nasir al-Din Tusi's *The Nasirean Ethics* (633/1235) in which loving kindness is described as "the principle that connects societies" (2016: 438). Tusi's work is "the best known ethical compendium composed in medieval Persia, if not in the entire medieval period of Islam" (Sadr 2016:436). According to Sadr, *The Nasirean Ethics* "is a work of practical philosophy, or ethics (*akhlāq*), and as such is highly influenced by the works of Greek philosophers such as Plato and Aristotle" (2016:437).

47. Harris (2017) describes the importance of Iran's dual welfare system, in which the post-revolutionary government maintains a state-wide system of entitlements, while the religious foundations (*bonyads*) that emerged after the revolution provide charitable relief to the needy.

48. At the time, this would have been between around $9.00 to about $9,000.00.

49. The play was written and produced by a well-known female creative artist, Sanaz Bayan. Bahareh Rahnama, a renowned actress and humanitarian, played one of the lead roles to captivated audiences.

50. A 2006 documentary about Jahed's story, *Red Card*, was banned in Iran. The third story featured a woman who had fought off a sexual predator by stabbing him with a knife. She survived by obtaining the forbearance of the victim's family.

51. De Vries and Schott emphasize the culturally-specific modalities of love (and forgiveness), but find a common thread of alertness and a cultivation of "attunement to others" (2015:2). Similarly, Jean-Luc Marion suggests that love is not a passion, but a matter of "knowledge" and a "point of view" and should not be reduced simply to the erotic. Marion stresses love's capacity to appreciate and absorb new information in different ways (2015:28).

52. The idea of self-building is not new to the post-revolutionary generation. Khomeini's speeches over the years of his leadership, especially those directed to women, included many references to this idea as he exhorted women to strive to rebuild their identities by emulating Fatemeh Zahra, the Prophet Mohammad's daughter and Imam 'Ali's wife, who, for the government, has been idealized as the "perfect" female and model for Iranian women—a justice-seeker, nurturer, and pious Muslim. See Moallem 2005 and Osanloo 2014.

53. For a discussion of Article 91, see Chapter 4. See also, Osanloo 2016.

54. Publicizing cases through virtual media sometimes produces an effect on victims' families that is the opposite of what was intended. Far from appeasing them, it shames them and can distance them from forgiveness.

55. Qur'an, Chapter 19 (*Maryam*):86–96.

56. The Qur'anic story of Maryam tracks closely to the Gospel of Luke in the New Testament. The chapter played an important role in the early history of the Muslim community. Various *ahadith* recount the travails of early Muslim refugees who fled Mecca after the Battle of

Badr (624 CE/2 AH), in which prominent Meccans were killed. Meccan leaders sent a delegation to the Abyssinian king, a Christian, demanding that he give up the refugees so that they could face justice for deaths that occurred during the battle. The king summoned the refugees, asked them to explain the teachings of their faith, and to recite from the revelations. One man, the Prophet's cousin, Jafar, also 'Ali's older brother, recited the opening verses of this chapter that narrate the birth of Jesus. When the king and his court heard the words about Mary and Jesus, they wept and refused to return the refugees, while noting the kinship between Christian and Muslims faiths (Nasr et al. 2015:764).

57. Nearly one-third of the references to God as "the Compassionate" occur in this one chapter (outside of the opening chapter, the *Fatiheh*) (Nasr et al. 2015:764).

58. Muslims consider Maryam, the mother of Jesus, to be an exceptionally pious figure. She is one of only four women considered to be spiritually perfect and she plays a significant role in defining Islamic piety (Nasr et al. 2015:763). Maryam is the only female in the Qur'an who is referred to by name. Moreover, in a text that otherwise names descendants through the male line (agnatic kinship), the Qur'an refers to Jesus as the "son of Mary," thus emphasizing the importance of motherhood.

59. The martyrdom of Fatemeh Zahra's husband, 'Ali, and sons, Hassan and Hossein, along with her own death, made her the *Shi'i* symbol of female grief, as well as piety, courage, and spirituality.

Chapter 7

1. Siah Kal is known as the site of an important uprising against the monarchy in 1971, which, for some historians, marks the start of Iran's guerrilla movement to oust the Shah (Abrahamian 1982; Mottahedeh 1985).

2. The Ministry of Culture and Islamic Guidance is a government institution that came into being after the revolution. In 1979, the post-revolutionary transitional government brought the former Ministry of Culture and Art together with that of Tourism and Information. The Ministry's responsibilities include maintaining the values of the revolution through media, such as books, artistic expression, film, news, and cultural exchange. The Ministry promotes research through grants and provides licenses for cultural and artistic production.

3. Karimi 2013. The word blue in the title of the play possesses a different symbolic meaning than it does in English. For Iranians, the blue feeling of death references a calm that accompanies resignation before dying.

4. Snyder-Young (2013) refers to a similar genre of "applied theatre" as a tactic for making social change, while recognizing the limits of the medium to lead to social change.

5. Artists introduced modern theater through translations of European plays at the end of the nineteenth century. Modern Iranian theater developed in earnest in the early 1950s, and productions were couched largely in ideological pursuits. By the 1960 and 70s, theater was marked less by ideology and more by theme. After the revolution, the theater arts entered a period marked by revolutionary theater. Each decade that followed evinced a new era of theatrical exploration (Floor 2005; Ghaderi Sohi and Ghorbaninejad 2012; Lazgee 1994).

6. Nussbaum argues that mercy is neither opposed to justice nor a relinquishing of it. Rather, she argues, mercy can allow justice because it requires attention to the particulars, mitigating circumstances, the life of the defendant, and the context in which the crime occurred. She states,

"A merciful judge need not neglect issues of deterrence, but she is above all committed to an empathetic scrutiny of the 'insides' of the individual life" (1993:115).

7. Pardon is different from mercy. While a merciful act is a lessening of deserved punishment, pardon absolves the need for punishment; it is independent of desert (Ferguson 2013:41).

8. Susan Williams clarifies this: a person who forgives has to feel she has been wronged, but mercy requires no such logic. In addition, the person forgiving may do so for no reason, while mercy must have reasons because, Williams states, "it points to a particular stance for judgment, in which the judge makes an effort to sympathetically understand the situation of the wrong-doer" (2012:277–8). In the Iranian case, then, it is the victim's family that is called upon to do both and these sometimes-contradictory feelings emerge from the enormous responsibility both of having to stand in judgment and to forgive a wrong, even if they are not the ones wronged.

9. This is a proverb, but it comes from the poem, *Roozi Oghabi* (Eagle's Pride), by Naser Khosrow Qubadiani (1004–1088 CE), the Persian poet, philosopher, Isma'ili scholar, and traveler. In the poem, an eagle is hunted by an arrow made out of eagle's feathers and states, "what came from me, returned to me."

10. Because Iranian criminal laws are codified from *shari'a*, the age of defendants is also calculated according to the Muslim calendar. This is not the same for non-*shari'a*-based *ta'zir* or civil law, in which case the Persian calendar is employed. This is why it is not entirely unreasonable that an official would make an error calculating the defendant's age.

11. Nemati is a well-known modern Iranian poet. Many in the audience were familiar with his poetry.

12. I thank Maryam Badiee for translating this excerpt of the poem.

13. Abu-Lughod likewise describes a reconciliation ceremony during which poetry is recited as an evocation of empathy (1986:25).

14. Dabashi highlights the works of three enduring Persian poets—Hafez, Sa'di, and Rumi. Together they comprise the "triumvirate" of Persian literary humanism. With them, "love has replaced fear as the modus operandi of humanity." According to Dabashi, the signature achievement of lyrical poetry is that "it is no longer the settled fragility of the doubtful human that narrates the world but the trusting confidence of the loving person that wholeheartedly embraces it and makes it trustworthy" (2012:155).

15. I am conscious of the fact that, by transcribing the words of the poem, in translation at that, I cannot convey the poem's affect adequately. I can only describe it and the significance of the recitation style.

16. Referring to an enduring aspect in the poetry of the Mughal period (1526–1857), Dabashi states, "The key to this period is the factor of musicality [. . .] We may suggest that Persian literary humanism finally found its *melos* in the Mughal Empire" (2012:211). *Melos* is a word of Greek origin that refers to the succession of musical tones that constitute a melody.

17. Similarly, in *The Unnecessary Woman*, Rabih Alameddine compares poetry, especially the rhythms of the Qur'an, with the sensuousness of love (2013:9).

18. Zeinab, a popular name in Muslim contexts, means timorous or expressing timidity, especially before God.

19. Executions are typically carried out before dawn on Wednesday mornings.

20. "Iran: Juvenile Offender" 2015.

21. Mahboubeh gave the examples of Mrs. Javanmardi (Chapter 5) and Mrs. Alinejad, of nearby Mazandaran, whose last-minute forbearance made news around the world (Introduction).

Chapter 8

1. *Law of Criminal Procedure*, Art. 5 and 48.

2. Cause lawyers believe their professional obligations entail employing their legal skills to further a moral or political commitment (Austin and Sarat 1998).

3. Esfandiari 2015.

4. The revolutionary court is a specific tribunal of the judiciary that tries suspects charged with violations deemed to threaten the security of the state and the values of the revolution.

5. As of this writing (2019), Sotoudeh is in prison and has been sentenced to a total of thirty-eight years in prison. She refused to appeal her case in protest of the charges against her. "Human rights lawyer" 2019.

6. This area of research has been conceived and developed by Austin Sarat and Stuart Schein-gold who have elaborated on it through numerous edited volumes (1998, 2001, 2004, 2005, 2008).

7. One notable exception to the North American focus of this scholarship is Sarat and Schein-gold's edited volume on how cause lawyering manifests throughout the world in the wake of globalization and the state transformations that result from that globalization (2001).

8. At times, state officials have construed challenges to the laws as challenges to the sacred foundations of those laws. In a state which has claimed a monopoly, not only on legitimate violence, but on legitimate exegesis, actions which challenge such interpretations are tanta-mount to treason, as "waging war against God," for which heavy sanctions exist. For instance, Narges Mohammadi, who worked at the *Defenders of Human Rights*, an organization founded by Nobel Peace Prize recipient, Shirin Ebadi, which state forces shut down in 2005, is serving a sixteen-year prison sentence. Atena Daemi, an anti-death penalty activist focusing on juvenile executions, is serving a ten-year sentence. Mohammad Mostafaei was a criminal defense at-torney known for defending youth subject to capital punishment, and who sought asylum in Norway in 2010. Emadeddin Baghi, a legal scholar, activist, and author, argues that the *shari'a* does not mandate a death penalty (2012). He spent five years in prison and was banned from journalistic activities for a time. Despite these restrictions, he has continued to write against the death penalty. In 2019, he published his first work of fiction on the topic, *Jan* (*Life*), which takes a more humanistic approach to anti-death penalty advocacy, appealing to a public readership rather than to scholars, who are the primary readers of his other works.

9. Although widely watched throughout Iran, Iranian officials view VOA as a U.S. govern-ment operation dedicated to regime change. This makes appearances on VOA risky for Iranian-based lawyers.

10. The funds were donated by Dr. Rassoul Ganji, a businessman and university professor. According to Sotoudeh, "It is not the first time he has paid to save someone from execution." "Iranian Teen" 2007.

11. In a strange twist of fate, Sina passed away from unknown causes just two years later (as did Ali, the perpetrator whom Mahboubeh forgave).

12. The English language entries are original translations that appeared on the now-defunct blog. The only changes I have made here are slight spelling corrections and regularization of proper nouns. This entry can be found here: https://web.archive.org/web/20141016072019 /http://mohegh.blogfa.com/8807.aspx.

13. Ibid.

14. The French press publicized a web campaign to save Ashtiani spearheaded by activist Bernard Henri-Levy. Entitled, *For Sakineh*, the site released appeals by a number of well-known French politicians, actors, and activists. Appeals called for halting the sentence in consideration of Persian culture, love, and human dignity.

15. Ashtiani was not executed. Ultimately, she was released from prison in 2014, after serving eight years on the charge of complicity in murder. I have written about this case in greater detail (Osanloo 2016). Iran's laws on stoning for adultery have changed somewhat. The punishment has been officially removed from the new penal code but remains possible by virtue of a provision that allows the imposition of Islamic punishments.

16. I draw from Reyhaneh's own letters, *delnevesheteh-ha* (heart-renderings) describing in detail what happened, (https://partov.wordpress.com/2014/05/03/vasiyatnameh-va-delneveshteh _reyhaneh_jabbari/). I also draw from the writings of her first lawyer, Mohammad Mostafaei, interviews with her parents, and another of her lawyers, Mohammad Foroughi. For Mostafaei's clarifications on the case, see, "Complete Information and Full Responses to Ambiguities of the Case of Reyhaneh Jabbari," May 5, 2014, https://www.tribunezamaneh.com/archives/47702. See also, "An Analysis of the Case of Reyhaneh Jabbari," November 29, 2009, https://web .archive.org/web/20141031173134/http://mohegh.blogfa.com/post-260.aspx.

17. He repeated this claim to the press. See, "Pesar-e Sarbandi" 2014.

18. Tardast added a two-page addendum to his decision in Reyhaneh's case, accusing the lawyer of making the case a political affair instead of defending his client. In the last part of the letter, Tardast, the judge, complains that the lawyer is defending Reyhaneh in the name of rights, when he should be doing otherwise. This is presumably a reference to the fact that her case had already been heard and upheld by the courts. The judge was implicitly suggesting that the lawyers, instead of making this an international case, which would politicize it, should be appealing to the victim's family for forgiveness. Tardast would later be transferred out of the criminal court.

19. "Response and Reflections on Interview of Hossein Tardast, Judge in Reyhaneh Jabbari's Case," April 23, 2014, https://www.tribunezamaneh.com/archives/47676.

20. One judicial official told me that these efforts were also intended to curtail the anger and pain that activists, through social media, had provoked in the victim's family, thus pushing them away from sparing Reyhaneh, "She didn't deserve it [retribution]," the official said. On October 25, 2014, the day Reyhaneh was executed, the judiciary posted a six-point defense of its process on its website. This page has been taken down, but can be found at: https://web.archive .org/web/20141025144633/http://www.dadsara.ir/Default.aspx?tabid=4058&articleType =ArticleView&articleId=89970.

21. Larijani reiterated his statements in an interview on CNN, October 31, 2014, http:// transcripts.cnn.com/TRANSCRIPTS/1410/29/ampr.01.html. See also, "Iranian official blames Western media" 2014.

22. Ibid.

23. Cited in Nebehay 2014.

24. Ibid.

25. UN Watch Briefing 2014.

26. Cited in Nebehay 2014.

27. Beheshti maintained a blog entitled *My Life for Iran* in which he criticized the Iranian government. After posting a series of such commentaries, Iran's cyber security forces (FATA) arrested Beheshti on October 30, 2012. He was charged with illegal actions against national security on social networks and Facebook. He died in prison three days later. Forty-one inmates from his ward released a letter claiming that "signs of torture were visible on the blogger's body." The death reportedly resulted from internal bleeding and a brain hemorrhage caused by beatings Beheshti sustained at the hands of his interrogator, Akbar Taghizadeh. Prior to his death, Beheshti submitted an official complaint against his interrogators. He wrote, "I, Sattar Beheshti, was arrested by FATA and beaten and tortured with multiple blows to my head and body . . . I want to write that if anything happens to me, the police are responsible." Beheshti's death triggered outrage and condemnation of Iran's harsh treatment of prisoners. Iran's parliament and the judiciary launched investigations. The judiciary tried the interrogator, found him guilty of unintentional murder, and sentenced him to three years in prison, two years in exile, and seventy-four lashes. It should not go without saying that Taghizadeh asked for the Beheshti family's forgiveness. Since he was not charged with murder, the plea for forgiveness was perhaps an act of remorse which the judiciary could take into account, rather than a plea for mercy by the victim's family. Regardless, the Beheshti family found the sentence to be profoundly lacking and did not forgive him. Iran's national police chief also dismissed the head of the cyber police unit. See, Esfandiari 2012; "Sattar Beheshti Murderer" 2014.

28. Reported by Sholeh Pakravan, Reyhaneh's mother, interviewed on Manoto television on January 11, 2014. These legal opinions, which were also reported in the Iranian press, further emphasize movement from *shari'a* as principles open to interpretation and discretion through jurisprudential analysis versus state law.

29. We encountered the mother of the victim, Mrs. Shirazi, in Chapter 6.

30. In Iran, the *mahrieh* (bride price) is the sum of money promised to the bride upon marriage. The parties determine the amount and include it in their marriage contract. Although the *mahrieh* is rarely paid during marriage, in cases of divorce, women petition for it. They use their *mahrieh* as a bargaining tool to gain a divorce by agreeing to forgo it (Osanloo 2009).

Epilogue

1. The insistence on basing Islamic humanitarianism solely on *zakat*, one of the obligatory moral imperatives of the faith, has compelled some scholars to question whether Islam can be understood as possessing a notion of humanitarianism. The suggestion is that, since *zakat* is obligatory, Muslims are charitable out of a sense of duty rather than generosity (Calhoun 2010:35).

REFERENCES

Abou El Fadl, Khaled. 2004. *Islam and the Challenge of Democracy*. Edited by J. Cohen and D. Chasman. Princeton, NJ: Princeton University Press.

Abrahamian, Ervand. 1982. *Iran Between Two Revolutions*. Princeton, NJ: Princeton University Press.

Abu-Lughod, Lila. 1986. *Veiled Sentiments: Honor and Poetry in Bedouin Society*. Berkeley, CA: University of California Press.

———. 2011. "Seductions of the 'Honor Crime.'" *differences: A Journal of Feminist Cultural Studies*, 22(1):17–63.

Afaf, Amir. 2015. "Nagoftehha-ye Mardi Ke Karesh Reziat Gereftan Ast" (The Unspoken Words of the Man Whose Work Consists of Obtaining Forbearance). *Iranian Students' News Agency*, October 18 (Mehr 26, 1394). https://www.isna.ir/news/94072616552/.

Agamben, Giorgio. 1999. *Potentialities: Collected Essays in Philosophy*. Stanford, CA: Stanford University Press.

———. 2000. *Means Without End: Notes on Politics*. Minneapolis, MN: University of Minnesota Press.

———. 2013. *The Highest Poverty: Monastic Rules and Form-of-Life*. Stanford, CA: Stanford University Press.

Agrama, Hussein. 2012. *Questioning Secularism: Islam, Sovereignty, and the Rule of Law in Modern Egypt*. Chicago: University of Chicago Press.

Ahmadi, Nader and Fereshteh Ahmadi. 1998. *Iranian Islam: The Concept of the Individual*. New York: St. Martin's Press.

Ahmed, Leila. 1992. *Women and Gender in Islam: Roots of a Modern Debate*. New Haven, CT: Yale University Press.

Alameddine, Rabih. 2011. *The Unnecessary Woman*. New York: Grove Press.

Algar, Hamid. 2006. "Shi'ism in Iran Since the Safavids." *Encyclopædia Iranica*, Online edition. http://www.iranicaonline.org/articles/iran-ix23-shiism-in-iran-since-the-safavids.

Ameri, Maryam. 2014. "Qisas Haq Ast va Zendegy Neez" (*Qisas* Is a Right, and Life Is, Too). *Ebtekar News*, April 17 (Farvardin 28, 1393).

Amnesty International. 2016. *Iran: The Last Executioner of Children*. London: Amnesty International Ltd. https://www.amnestyusa.org/reports/iran-the-last-executioner-of-children/.

———. 2017 *Global Report: Death Sentences and Executions 2016*. London: Amnesty International Ltd. https://www.amnesty.org/download/Documents/ACT5057402017ENGLISH.PDF

———. 2018. *Global Report: Death Sentences and Executions 2017*. London: Amnesty International Ltd. https://www.amnesty.org/download/Documents/ACT5079552018ENGLISH.PDF.

———. 2018. "Iran 2018." London: Amnesty International Ltd. https://www.amnesty.org/en/countries/middle-east- and-north-africa/iran/report-iran/.

———. 2019. *Global Report: Death Sentences and Executions 2018*. London: Amnesty International Ltd. https://www.amnesty.org/download/Documents/ACT5098702019ENGLISH.PDF.

Asad, Talal. 1986. "The Idea of an Anthropology of Islam." Occasional Papers Series. Washington, D.C.: Center for Contemporary Arab Studies, Georgetown University.

Assadi, Reza. 1982. "Conflict and Its Management: Iranian Style." *Anthropological Linguistics*, 24(2):201–205.

Auyero, Javier. 2012. *Patients of the State: The Politics of Waiting in Argentina*. Durham, NC: Duke University Press.

Ayoub, Mohammad. 1978. *Redemptive Suffering in Islam: A Study of the Devotional Aspects of Ashura in Twelver Shi'ism*. The Hague: Mouton Publishers.

Babul, Elif. 2016. *Bureaucratic Intimacies: Translating Human Rights in Turkey*. Stanford, CA: Stanford University Press.

Baderin, Mashood A. 2003. *International Human Rights and Islamic Law*. Oxford: Oxford University Press.

Baghi, Emadeddin. 2019[1398]. *Jan [Life]*. Tehran: Saraee Publishers.

———. 2012[1391]. *Haqq-e Hayaat [Right to Life]*. Tehran: Defenders of the Right to Life.

Baker, J. H. 2002. *An Introduction to English Legal History*. Oxford: Oxford University Press.

Banani, Amin. 1961. *The Modernization of Iran from 1921–1941*. Stanford, CA: Stanford University Press.

Bandak, Andreas and Manpreet K. Janeja. 2017. "Introduction: Worth the Wait." In *Ethnographies of Waiting: Doubt, Hope and Uncertainty*. Edited by M. K. Janeja and A. Bandak, 1–39. New York: Bloomsbury Academic Press.

"Barabaree-e Diya Zan va Mard" (*Diya* Equality Between Men and Women). 2016. *Farda News*, March 15 (*Esfand* 25, 1392). https://www.fardanews.com/fa/news/502107/.

Baroja, Julio Caro. 1966. "A Historical Account of Several Conflicts." In *Honor and Shame*. Edited by J.G. Peristiany, 79–137. Chicago: University of Chicago Press.

Barth, Fredrik. 1959. *Political Leadership among the Swat Pathans*. London: London School of Economics and Political Science.

Bassiouni, Cherif. 2014. *The Shari'a and Islamic Criminal Justice in a Time of War and Peace*. Cambridge: Cambridge University Press.

Bateson, Mary C. et al. 1977. "Safa-yi Batin. A Study of the Interrelations of a Set of Iranian Ideal Character Types." In *Psychological Dimensions of Near Eastern Studies*. Edited by C. Brown and N. Itzkowitz, 257–273. Princeton, NJ: Darwin Press.

Bayat, Asef. 2010a. *Life as Politics: How Ordinary People Change the Middle East*. Stanford, CA: Stanford University Press.

———. 2010b. "Muslim Youth and the Claim of Youthfulness." In *Being Young and Muslim: New Cultural Politics in the Global South and North*. Edited by L. Herrera and A. Bayat, 27–47. Oxford: Oxford University Press.

Beeman, William O. 1986. *Language, Status, and Power in Iran*. Bloomington, IN: Indiana University Press.

———. 1988. "Affectivity in Persian Language Use." *Culture, Medicine, and Psychiatry*, 12(1):9–30.

———. 2001. "Emotion and Sincerity in Persian Discourse: Accomplishing the Representation of Inner States." *International Journal of Sociological Language*, 108:31–58.

Behrouzan, Orkideh. 2016. *Prozak Diaries: Psychiatry and Generational Memory in Iran*. Stanford, CA: Stanford University Press.

Behzadi, Kavous G. 1994. "Interpersonal Conflict and Emotions in an Iranian Cultural Practice: *Qahr* and *Ashti*." *Culture, Medicine, and Psychiatry*, 18(3):321–59.

Ben Hounet, Yazid. 2012. "Cent dromadaires et quelques arrangements: Notes sur la diya (prix du sang) et son application actuelle au Soudan et en Algérie." *Revue des Mondes Musulmans et de la Méditerranée*, 131:203–21.

Benhabib, Seyla. 2011. *Dignity in Adversity: Human Rights in Troubled Times*. Malden, MA: Polity Press.

Benthall, Jonathan. 2010. "Islamic Humanitarianism in Adversarial Context." In *Forces of Compassion: Humanitarianism Between Ethics and Politics*. Edited by E. Bornstein and P. Redfield, 99–122. Santa Fe, NM: School for Advanced Research Press.

———. 2012. "'Cultural Proximity' and the Conjuncture of Islam with Modern Humanitarianism." In *Sacred Aid: Faith and Humanitarianism*. Edited by M. Barnett and J. Gross Stein, 65–89. Oxford: Oxford University Press.

Benthall, Jonathan and Jerome Bellion-Jourdan. 2009. *The Charitable Crescent: Politics of Aid in the Muslim World*. London: I.B. Tauris.

Berlant, Lauren G. 1997. *The Queen of America Goes to Washington City: Essays on Sex and Citizenship*. Durham, NC: Duke University Press.

Bersani, Leo. 2008. "The Power of Evil and the Power of Love." In *Intimacies*. Edited by L. Bersani and Adam Philips, 57–89. Chicago: University of Chicago Press.

Biggar, Nigel. 2008. "Forgiving Enemies in Ireland." *Journal of Religious Ethics*, 36(4):559–79.

Black-Michaud, Jacob. 1975. *Cohesive Force: Feud in the Mediterranean and the Middle East*. Bristol: Basil Blackwell Publishers.

Bohannan, Paul. 1965. "The Differing Realms of the Law." *American Anthropologist*, 67(6):33–42.

Boltanski, Luc. 1999 [1993]. *Distant Suffering: Morality, Media and Politics*. Translated by G. Burchell. Cambridge: Cambridge University Press.

———. 2012 [1990]. *Love and Justice as Competences: Three Essays on the Sociology of Action*. Translated by C. Porter. Cambridge: Polity Press.

Borneman, John. 1997. *Settling Accounts: Violence, Justice, and Accountability in Post-Socialist Europe*. Princeton, NJ: Princeton University Press.

———. 2011. *Political Crime and the Memory of Loss*. Bloomington, IN: Indiana University Press.

Bornstein, Erica. 2012. *Disquieting Gifts: Humanitarianism in New Delhi*. Stanford, CA: Stanford University Press.

Bowen, John. 1993. *Muslims through Discourse: Ritual and Religion in Gayo Society*. Princeton, NJ: Princeton University Press.

_____. 2003. *Islam, Law, and Equality in Indonesia: An Anthropology of Public Reasoning*. Cambridge: Cambridge University Press.

Boyer, Dominic. 2005. "The Corporeality of Expertise." *Ethnos*, 70(2):243–66.

Braithwaite, John. 2002. *Restorative Justice & Responsive Regulation*. Oxford: Oxford University Press.

Brennan, Teresa. 2004. *The Transmission of Affect*. Ithaca, NY: Cornell University Press.

Bromberger, Christian. 2009. "Usual Topics: Taboo Themes and New Objects in Iranian Anthropology." In *Conceptualizing Iranian Anthropology: Past and Present Perspectives*. Edited by S. Nadjmabadi, 195–206. New York: Berghahn Books.

Butler, Judith. 1993. *Bodies that Matter: On the Discursive Limits of "Sex."* New York: Routledge.

———. 2014. "On Cruelty." Review of *The Death Penalty: Vol. I* by J. Derrida. Translated by P. Kamuf. *London Review of Books,* 36(14):31–33.

Calhoun, Craig. 2010. "The Idea of Emergency: Humanitarian Action and Global (Dis)Order." In *Contemporary States of Emergency: The Politics of Military and Humanitarian Intervention.* Edited by D. Fassin and M. Pandolfi, 29–58. New York: Zone Books.

Chelkowski, Peter J. 1979. *Ta'ziyeh: Ritual and Drama in Iran.* New York: New York University Press.

Chittick, William. 1989. *The Sufi Path of Knowledge.* New York: State University of New York Press.

———. 2000. *Sufism: A Short Introduction.* Oxford: Oneworld.

———. 2013. *Divine Love: Islamic Literature and the Path to God.* New Haven, CT: Yale University Press.

Comaroff, Jean and John Comaroff. 2006. "Law and Order in the Postcolony: An Introduction." In *Law and Disorder in the Postcolony.* Edited by J. Comaroff and J. Comaroff, 1–56. Chicago: University of Chicago Press.

Cook, Michael. 2006 [2000]. *Commanding Right and Forbidding Wrong in Islamic Thought.* Cambridge: Cambridge University Press.

Corbin, Henri. 1969. *Creative Imagination in the Sufism of Ibn Arabi.* Translated by R. Mannheim. Princeton, NJ: Princeton University Press.

———. 1973. *Traites Des Compagnons—Chevaliers: Recueil de sept 'Fotowwat-Nameh.'* Téhéran: Institut Français de Recherche en Iran.

Cover, Robert. 1983. "The Supreme Court 1982 Term—Foreword: Nomos and Narrative." *Harvard Law Review,* 97:4–68.

Cragg, Kenneth. 1973. *The Mind of the Qur'an: Chapters in Reflection.* London: Allen and Unwin.

Dabashi, Hamid. 2012. *The World of Persian Literary Humanism.* Cambridge, MA: Harvard University Press.

Dahlén, Ashk. 2003. *Islamic Law, Epistemology and Modernity: Legal Philosophy in Contemporary Iran.* New York: Routledge.

Das, Veena. 2006. *Life and Words: Violence and the Descent into the Ordinary.* Berkeley, CA: University of California Press.

———. 2010. "Engaging the Life of the Other: Love and Everyday Life." In *Ordinary Ethics: Anthropology, Language and Action.* Edited by M. Lambek, 376–99. New York: Fordham University Press.

———. 2012. "Ordinary Ethics." In *A Companion to Moral Anthropology.* Edited by D. Fassin, 133–49. Boston: Wiley-Blackwell.

De Vries, Hent, and Niles F. Schott. "Human Alert: Concepts and Practices of Love and Forgiveness." In *Love and Forgiveness for a More Just World.* Edited by Hent De Vries and Niles F. Schott, 1–23. New York: Columbia University Press.

Deeb, Lara. 2006. *An Enchanted Modern: Gender and Public Piety in Shi'i Lebanon.* Princeton, NJ: Princeton University Press.

Dehghan, Saeed Kamali. 2014. "Iranian killer's execution halted at last minute by victim's parents." *The Guardian,* April 16. https://www.theguardian.com/world/2014/apr/16/iran-parents-halt-killer-execution.

Derrida, Jacques. 1988. *Limited, Inc.* Evanston, IL: Northwestern University Press.

———. 2001a. "On Forgiveness." In *On Cosmopolitanism and Forgiveness.* Translated by M. Dooley and M. Hughes, 27–60. London: Routledge.

———. 2001b. "What is a 'Relevant' Translation?" Translated by L. Venuti. *Critical Inquiry,* 27:174–200.

———. 2014. *The Death Penalty, Vol. I.* Translated by P. Kamuf. Chicago: University of Chicago Press.

Disis, Jill. 2017. "Read Matt Lauer's full apology." *CNN Business,* November 30. https://money.cnn.com/2017/11/30/media/matt-lauer-full-statement/index.html.

Duff, R. 2001. *Punishment, Communication, and Community.* Oxford: Oxford University Press.

Dupret, Baudouin. 2011. *Adjudication in Action: An Ethnomethodology of Law, Morality and Justice.* Oxford: Ashgate Publishers.

Durkheim, Emile. 1984[1933]. *The Division of Labor.* Translated by W.D. Halls. New York: Free Press.

"Ehsaas-e Bakhshesh: Lezat" (The Feeling of Forgiveness: Joy). 2013. *Haft-e Nameh-ye Havades va Shegoftiha (Weekly Newsletter of Events and Surprises),* March 2 (*Esfand* 12, 1391).

Elliot, Tim. 2004. "Blood Money: Women take on hard-line Islam in a campaign for equal rights." *New Internationalist.* https://newint.org/columns/currents/2004/02/01/blood-money/.

Emon, Anver. 2016. "Codification of Islamic Law: The Ideology Behind a Tragic Narrative." *Middle East Law and Governance,* 8:277–309.

Enayat, Hadi. 2013. *Law, State, and Society in Modern Iran: Constitutionalism, Autocracy, and Legal Reform, 1906–1941.* New York: Palgrave MacMillan.

Erdbrink, Thomas. 2014. "Mercy and Social Media Slow the Noose in Iran." *New York Times,* March 8. https://nyti.ms/1dCzjsZ.

Esfandiari, Golnaz. 2012. "'Murder': Some Accountability in Iranian Blogger Sattar Beheshti's Death." *The Atlantic,* November 14. http://www.theatlantic.com/international/archive/2012/11/murder-some-accountability-in-iranian-blogger-sattar-beheshtis-death/265203/.

———. 2015. "One Woman Stands Against the Iranian Government." *Foreign Policy Magazine,* June 16. http://foreignpolicy.com/2015/06/16/one-womans-stand-against-the-state-in-tehran-iran-nasrin-sotoudeh/.

Esmeir, Samira. 2012. *Juridical Humanity: A Colonial History.* Stanford, CA: Stanford University Press.

Eylon, B. and M. Linn. 1988. "Learning and Instruction: An Examination of Four Research Perspectives in Science Education." *Review of Educational Research,* 58(3):251–301.

Fadel, Mohammad. 1996. "The Social Logic of *Taqlid* and the Rise of the *Mukhatasar.*" *Islamic Law and Society,* 3(2):193–233.

Fassin, Didier. 2012. *Humanitarian Reason: A Moral History of the Present.* Berkeley, CA: University of California Press.

Feener, Michael. 2014. *Sharia and Social Engineering: The Implementation of Islamic Law in Contemporary Aceh, Indonesia.* Oxford: Oxford University Press.

Ferguson, Robert A. 2012. "The Place of Mercy in Legal Discourse." In *Merciful Judgments and Contemporary Society: Legal Problems, Legal Possibilities.* Edited by A. Sarat, 19–82. Cambridge: Cambridge University Press.

Fischer, Michael. M.J. 1980. *Iran: From Religious Dispute to Revolution.* Madison, WI: University of Wisconsin Press.

————. 1990. "Legal Postulates in Flux: Justice, Wit, and Hierarchy in Iran." In *Law and Islam in the Middle East*. Edited by D. Dwyer, 115–142. New York: Bergin & Garvey Publishers.

————. 2003. *Emergent Forms of Life and the Anthropological Voice*. Durham, NC: Duke University Press.

————. 2018. *Anthropology in the Meantime: Experimental Ethnography, Theory, and Method for the Twenty-First Century*. Durham, NC: Duke University Press.

Flaskerud, Ingvild. 2010. *Visualizing Belief and Piety in Iranian Shi'ism*. London: Continuum.

Floor, Willem. 2005. *The History of Theater in Iran*. Los Angeles: Mage Publishers.

Foucault, Michel. 1977. *Discipline and Punish: The Birth of the Prison*. New York: Vintage Books.

————. 1996. "Truth and Juridical Forms." Translated by L. Williams with C. Merlen. *Social Identities*, 2(3):327–41.

Gahan, Jairan. 2017. *Red-Light District: Prostitution, Intimately Public Islam, and the Rule of the Sovereign, 1910–1980*. Doctoral Dissertation, University of Toronto.

Geertz, Clifford. 1983. *Local Knowledge: Further Essays in Interpretive Anthropology*. New York: Basic Books.

Ghaderi Sohi, Behzad and Masoud Ghorbaninejad. 2012. "Ali Nassirian and a 'Modern' Iranian National Theater." *Asian Theatre Journal*, 29(2):495–527.

Ghamkhavar, Mohammad. 2012. "Nagoftehha-ye Jenaeetarin Qazi Iran" (The Unspoken Words of the Most Experienced Criminal Judge of Iran). *Mehr News*, October 21 (*Mehr* 30, 1391). http://mehrnews.com/news/1702067.

Ghaneirad, Mohammad Amin. 2014. "Gostaresh 'Bakhshesh' Nashi Az Afzayesh-e 'Sarmayeh Siasi' Ast" (The Spread of 'Forgiveness' Arises from Increased 'Political Capital'). *Shargh*, May 8 (*Ordibehesht* 18, 1393). http://www.sharghdaily.ir/?News_Id=33816.

Gholami, Hussein. 1998–1999. "The Islamitisation of Criminal Justice and its Developments in Iran." *Tilburg Foreign Law Review*, 7:213–20.

————. 2006. "Restorative Traditions in Violent Conflicts in Iran." In *Conflicts and Conflict Resolution in Middle Eastern Societies—Between Tradition and Modernity*. Edited by H. Albrecht, J. Simon, et al., 457–70. Berlin: Duncker & Humblot.

Gilsenan, Michael. 2016 [1976]. "Lying, Honour, and Contradiction." In *Transaction and Meaning: Directions in the Anthropology of Exchange and Symbolic Behavior*. Edited by B. Kapferer, 191–219. Philadelphia: Institute for the Study of Human Issues. Reprinted in *Hau: Journal of Ethnographic Theory*, 6(2):497–525.

Giridharadas, Anand. 2014. *True American: Murder and Mercy in Texas*. New York: W.W. Norton & Company.

Gluckman, Max. 1955. *The Judicial Process among the Barotse of Northern Rhodesia*. Manchester: Manchester University Press.

Gobodo-Madikizela, Pumla. 2003. *A Human Being Died That Night: A South African Woman Faces the Legacy of Apartheid*. New York: Houghton Mifflin Harcourt Publishers.

————. 2008. "Empathetic Repair after Mass Trauma: When Vengeance is Arrested." *European Journal of Social Theory*, 11:331–50.

Gorji, Ali. 2014. "Tejarat-e Hayaat Ba Arzeshtar Az Tejarat-e Marg Ast" (The Business of Life is More Valuable than the Business of Death." *Fararu*, June 1 (*Khordad* 11, 1393). http://fararu.com/fa/news/192541/.

Griswold, Charles. 2007. *Forgiveness: A Philosophical Exploration.* Cambridge: Cambridge University Press.

Grosmaire, Kathleen A. 2016. *Forgiving My Daughter's Killer.* Nashville, TN: Nelson Books.

Hage, Ghassan. 2009. "Introduction." In *Waiting.* Edited by G. Hage, 1–12. Victoria: Melbourne University Press.

Hallaq, Wael B. 2009. *Sharī'a: Theory, Practice, Transformations.* Cambridge: Cambridge University Press.

Hampton, Jean. 1992a. "Correcting Harms versus Righting Wrongs: The Goal of Retribution." *UCLA Law Review,* 39(6):1659–1702.

———. 1992b. "An Expressive Theory of Retribution." In *Retributivism and its Critics.* Edited by Wesley Cragg, 1–25. Stuttgart: F. Steiner, Verlag.

Han, Clara and Veena Das. 2016. "Introduction: A Concept Note." In *Living and Dying in a Contemporary World: A Compendium.* Edited by V. Das and C. Han, 1–29. Berkeley, CA: University of California Press.

Hardt, Michael. 1999. "Affective Labor." *Boundary,* 2(26):89–100.

Harris, Kevan. 2017. *A Social Revolution Politics and the Welfare State in Iran.* Berkeley, CA: University of California Press.

Harrison, Karen and A. Tamony. 2010. "Death Row Phenomenon, Death Row Syndrome and their Effect on Capital Cases in the US." *Internet Journal of Criminology,* 1–16.

Hascall, Susan. 2011. "Restorative Justice in Islam: Should *Qisas* Be Considered a Form of Restorative Justice?" *Berkeley Journal of Middle Eastern & Islamic Law,* 4(2):35–78.

Hasluck, Margaret. 1967. "The Albanian Blood Feud." In *Law and Warfare: Studies in the Anthropology of Conflict.* Edited by P. Bohannan, 381–408. Garden City: Natural History Press.

Hay, Douglas. 1975. "Property, Authority, and Criminal Law." In *Albion's Fatal Tree: Crime and Society in Eighteenth-Century England.* Edited by D. Hay, et al., 17–63. New York: Pantheon Books.

Heath, Malcolm. 1996. "Introduction." In *Poetics* by Aristotle. Translated by M. Heath, vii–lxxi. London: Penguin Books.

Hegland, Mary. 2004. "Zip in and Zip out Fieldwork." *Iranian Studies,* 37(4):575–83.

Hirsch, Susan. 1998. *Pronouncing and Persevering: Gender and the Discourses of Disputing in an African Islamic Court.* Chicago: University of Chicago Press.

Hirschkind, Charles. 2006. *The Ethical Soundscape: Cassette Sermons and Islamic Counterpublics.* New York: Columbia University Press.

Ho, Enseng. 2006. *The Graves of Tarim: Genealogy and Mobility Across the Indian Ocean.* Berkeley, CA: University of California Press.

Holy Qur'an. Translated by Yusuf Ali. 2002. Beltsville, MD: Amana Publications.

"Human rights lawyer Nasrin Sotoudeh jailed 'for 38 years' in Iran." 2019. *The Guardian,* March 11. https://www.theguardian.com/world/2019/mar/11/human-rights-lawyer-nasrin-sotoudeh-jailed-for-38-years-in-iran.

Hunt, Lynn. 2007. *Inventing Human Rights: A History.* New York: W.W. Norton & Company.

Ibn Abi Talib, 'Ali. 2005. *Nahjol-Balagha (Peak of Eloquence).* Translated by Sayyed Ali Reza. Qum: Ansariyan Publications.

"Iran Eases Death Penalty Laws for Drug Traffickers." 2017. *Deutsche Welle,* August 14. https://p.dw.com/p/2i9zA.

Iran Human Rights. 2016. *Annual Report 2015*. https://www.iranhr.net/en/reports/16/.
_____. 2017. *Annual Report 2016*. https://www.iranhr.net/en/reports/18/.
_____. 2018. *Annual Report 2017*. https://www.iranhr.net/en/reports/19/.
_____. 2019. *Annual Report 2018*. https://www.iranhr.net/en/reports/21/.

"Iran: Juvenile Offender Faces Imminent Execution Despite Ongoing Review of Case." 2015. *Amnesty International*, May 15. http://www.amnesty.ca/news/news releases/iran-juvenile-offender-faces-imminent-execution-despite ongoing-review-of-case.

"Iran: Responsibility of Implementing Blinding Punishment Placed on 11-Year-Old Girl." 2016. *Iran Human Rights*, November 14. https://iranhr.net/en/articles/2708/.

"Iran Says Nearly All Executions Drug-Related." 2014. *Radio Free Europe*, November 2. http://www.rferl.org/content/iran-says-executions-drug-smugglers/26670157.html.

"Iran: Young man flogged 80 times for drinking alcohol as a child." 2018. *Amnesty International*, July 11. https://www.amnesty.org/en/latest/news/2018/07/iran-young-man-flogged-80-times-for-drinking-alcohol-as-a-child/.

"Iranian Official Blames Western Media for Woman's Execution." 2014. *Radiozamaneh*, October 31. https://en.radiozamaneh.com/10382/.

"Iranian Teen Set to Escape Execution." 2007. *Daily Times*, July 26. http://archives.dailytimes.com.pk/foreign/26-Jul-2007/iranian-teen-set-to-escape-execution.

"Iranian Victims React to UN Review of Tehran's Human Rights Record." 2014. *UN Watch Briefing*, October 31. https://unwatch.org/issue-512-iranian-victims-react-uns-review-tehrans-human-rights-record/.

Ismail, Siti Z. 2012. "The Modern Interpretation of the *Diyat* Formula for the Quantum of Damages: The Case of Homicide and Personal Injuries." *Arab Law Quarterly*, 26(3):361–379.

Izutsu, Toshihiko. 2002[1959]. *Ethico-Religious Concepts in the Qur'an*. Quebec: McGill University Press.

Jackson, Michael. 2013. *Lifeworlds: Essays in Existential Anthropology*. Chicago: University of Chicago Press.

Jalali-Karveh, Mahmoud. 2006. "Theory and Practice of Arbitration as a Peaceful Means of Dispute Settlement in the Iranian Legal System." In *Conflicts and Conflict Resolution in Middle Eastern Societies—Between Tradition and Modernity*. Edited by H. Albrecht, J. Simon et al., 429–46. Berlin: Duncker & Humblot.

Jeffrey, Craig. 2010. *Timepass: Youth, Class, and the Politics of Waiting in India*. Stanford, CA: Stanford University Press.

Kamali, Mohammad Hashemi. 2008. *Shari'ah Law: An Introduction*. Oxford: Oneworld.

Kant, Immanuel. 2017. *The Metaphysics of Morals*. Edited by L. Denis. Translated by M. Gregor. New York: Cambridge University Press.

Karimi, Nasser. 2013. "Edgy new play spotlights death row teens in Iran." *AP News*, July 19. https://apnews.com/dadc320388b84e2291c138fe8a6d2544.

Kermode, Frank. 1967. *A Sense of an Ending: Studies in the Theory of Fiction*. New York: Oxford University Press.

Khan, Ajaz Ahmed. 2012. "Religious Obligation or Altruistic Giving? Muslims and Charitable Donations." In *Sacred Aid: Faith and Humanitarianism*. Edited by M. Barnett and J. Gross Stein, 90–114. Oxford: Oxford University Press.

"Khanevadeh 'Amr be Ma'ruf' az Qisas Gozasht Kardan" (Family 'Commanding Right' Forgoes Qisas). 2015. *Shargh*, August 25 (*Shahrivar* 5, 1394).

Khomeini. Ruhollah. 1981. *Islam and Revolution: Writings and Declarations of Imam Khomeini*. Translated by Hamid Algar. Berkeley, CA: Mizan Press.

———. 2001. *The Position of Women from the Viewpoint of Imam Khomeini*. Translated by Juliana Shaw and Behrooz Arezoo. Tehran: Institute for the Compilation and Publication of Imam Khomeini's Works.

Khosravi, Shahram. 2017. *Precarious Lives: Waiting and Hope in Iran*. Philadelphia: University of Pennsylvania Press.

Koenig, T. and M. Rustad. 1998. "'Crimtorts' as Corporate Just Deserts." *University of Michigan Journal of Law Reform*, 31:289–352.

Kohn, Tamara. 2009. "Waiting on Death Row." In *Waiting*. Edited by G. Hage, 218–24. Victoria: Melbourne University Press.

Kondo, Nobuaki. 2017. *Islamic Law and Society in Iran. A Social History of Qajar Tehran*. London: Routledge.

Kuhn, D. et al. 1977. "The Development of Formal Operations in Logical and Moral Judgment." *Genetic Psychology Monographs*, 95:97–188.

Kusha, Hamid. 2002. *The Sacred Law of Islam: A Case Study of Women's Treatment in the Islamic Republic of Iran's Criminal Justice System*. London: Ashgate Publishing.

Laidlaw, James. 2014. *The Subject of Virtue: An Anthropology of Ethics and Freedom*. Cambridge: University of Cambridge Press.

Lakhani, M. Ali. 2006. "The Metaphysics of Human Governance: Imam 'Ali, Truth, and Justice." In *The Sacred Foundations of Justice in Islam*. Edited by M. A. Lakhani, 3–58. Bloomington, IN: World Wisdom Inc.

Lambek, Michael. 2010. "Towards an Ethics of the Act." In *Ordinary Ethics: Anthropology, Language and Action*. Edited by M. Lambek, 39–63. New York: Fordham University Press.

Laqueur, Thomas W. 2009. "Mourning, Piety, and the Work of Narrative in the Making of 'Humanity.'" In *Humanitarianism and Suffering: The Mobilization of Empathy*. Edited by R. Wilson and R. Brown, 31–57. Cambridge: Cambridge University Press.

"Larijani: Omidvaram Shahed-e Raf-e Hesr-e Mousavi va Karroubi Basham" (Larijani: I Hope to Witness the End of House Arrest for Mousavi and Karroubi). 2014. *Islamic Students' News Agency*, March 16 (*Esfand* 25, 1392). http://www.isna.ir/news/92122717644.

Lazgee, Seyed Habiballah. 1994. *Post-revolutionary Iranian Theatre: Three Representative Plays in Translation with Critical Commentary*. Doctoral Dissertation. University of Leeds.

Levinas, Emmanuel. 1969. *Totality and Infinity: An Essay on Exteriority*. Translated by Alphonso Lingis. Pittsburgh, PA: Duquesne University Press.

———. 1985. *Emmanuel Levinas, Ethics and Infinity: Conversations with Philippe Nemo*. Translated by Richard A. Cohen. Pittsburgh, PA: Duquesne University Press.

Lewisohn, Leonard. 2006. "'Ali ibn Abi Talib's ethics of mercy in the mirror of the Persian Sufi tradition." In *The Sacred Foundations of Justice in Islam: The Teachings of 'Ali ibn Abi Talib*. Edited by M. Ali Lakhani, 109–45. Bloomington, IN: World Wisdom Inc.

Lucas, Scott. 2011. "'Perhaps You Only Kissed Her?' A Contrapuntal Reading of the Penalties for Illicit Sex in the Sunni Hadith Literature." *Journal of Religious Ethics*, 9(3):399–415.

Mahmood, Saba. 2005. *The Politics of Piety*. Princeton, NJ: Princeton University Press.

Mahmoudi, Firouz. 2006a. "Informal Justice System in Iranian Law." In *Conflicts and Conflict Resolution in Middle Eastern Societies—Between Tradition and Modernity*. Edited by H. Albrecht, J. Simon et al., 411–28. Berlin: Duncker & Humblot.

———. 2006b. "Alternative Sanctions in Iranian Penal Law." In *Conflicts and Conflict Resolution in Middle Eastern Societies—Between Tradition and Modernity*. Edited by H. Albrecht, J. Simon et al., 447–56. Berlin: Duncker & Humblot.

Malinowski, Bronislaw. 1959. *Crime and Custom in Savage Society*. Paterson, NJ: Littlefield, Adams & Co.

Manoukian, Setrag. 2011. *City of Knowledge in 20th Century Iran: Shiraz, History, and Poetry*. New York: Routledge.

Marion, Jean-Luc. 2015. "What Love Knows." In *Love and Forgiveness for a More Just World*. Edited by H. De Vries and N. F. Schott, 27–42. New York: Columbia University Press.

McCann, Michael. 1994. *Rights at Work: Pay Equity Reform and the Politics of Legal Mobilization*. Chicago: University of Chicago Press.

Menkel-Meadow, Carrie. 1998. "The Causes of Cause Lawyering: Toward an Understanding of the Motivation and Commitment of Social Justice Lawyers." In *Cause Lawyering: Political Commitments and Professional Responsibilities*. Edited by A. Sarat and S. Scheingold, 31–68. New York: Oxford University Press.

Merleau-Ponty, Maurice. 1968. *The Visible and the Invisible*. Translated by A. Lingis. Evanston, IL: Northwestern University Press.

Mernissi, Fatima. 1991. *Women and Islam: An Historical and Theological Enquiry*. Translated by M.J. Lakeland. Oxford: Basil Blackwell.

Merry, Sally. 1990. *Getting Justice, Getting Even: Legal Consciousness Among Working Class Americans*. Chicago: University of Chicago Press

———. 2003. "Rights Talk and the Experience of Law: Implementing Women's Human Rights to Protection from Violence." *Human Rights Quarterly*, 25(2):343–81.

Messick, Brinkley. 1993. *Calligraphic State: Textual Domination and History in a Muslim Society*. Berkeley, CA: University of California Press.

———. 2001. "Indexing the Self: Intent and Expression in Islamic Legal Acts." *Islamic Law and Society*, 8(2):151–78.

Meyer, Linda Ross. 2010. *The Justice of Mercy*. Ann Arbor, MI: University of Michigan Press.

Miller, William Ian. 2006. *Eye for An Eye*. Cambridge: Cambridge University Press.

Minow, Martha. 1998. *Between Vengeance and Forgiveness*. Boston: Beacon Press.

Mir-Hosseini, Ziba. 1999. *Islam and Gender: The Religious Debate in Contemporary Iran*. Princeton, NJ: Princeton University Press.

Mittermaier, Amira. 2011. *Dreams that Matter: Egyptian Landscapes of the Imagination*. Berkeley, CA: University of California Press.

Moallem, Minoo. 2005. *Between Warrior Brother and Veiled Sister: Islamic Fundamentalism and the Politics of Patriarchy in Iran*. Berkeley, CA: University of California Press.

Mohammadi, Majid. 2007. *Judicial Reform and Reorganization in 20th Century Iran: State Building, Modernization and Islamicization*. New York: Routledge.

"Moj-e Bakhsheshha be Kerman, Nishabur, va Azerbaijan Reseed" (Wave of Forgiveness Has Reached Kerman, Nishabur, and Azerbaijan). 2014. *Entekhab*, April 23 (*Ordibehesht* 3, 1393). https://www.entekhab.ir/fa/news/162498.

Momen, Moojan. 1985. *An Introduction to Shi'i Islam*. New Haven: Yale University Press.

Moore, Sally F. 1973. "Law and Social Change: The Semi-Autonomous Social Field as an Appropriate Subject of Study." *Law & Society Review*, 7(4):719–46.

Morrison, Robert. 2007. *Islam and Science: The Intellectual Career of Nizam al-Din al-Nisaburi*. New York: Routledge.

Mottahedeh, Roy. 1985. *The Mantle of the Prophet*. Boston: Oneworld Publications.

Moumtaz, Nada. 2018. "From Forgiveness to Foreclosure: *Waqf*, Debt, and the Remaking of the Hanafi Legal Subject in Late Ottoman Mount Lebanon." *The Muslim World*, 108(4):593- 612.

Mozzafari, Ahmad. 2014. "Lezat Nab-e Bakhshesh" (The Pure Pleasure of Forgiveness). *Shargh*, April 17 (*Farvardin* 28, 1393).

Murphy, Jeffrie. G. 1988. "Forgiveness and Resentment." In *Forgiveness and Mercy*. Edited by J.G. Murphy and J. Hampton, 14–34. Cambridge: Cambridge University Press.

———. 2003. *Getting Even: Forgiveness and its Limits*. Oxford: Oxford University Press.

Mutahhari, Murtada. n.d. *Dastan-e Rastan* (*Narration of the Veracious*). Tehran: Islamic Culture and Relations Organization.

Nasr, Seyyed Hossein. 2006. *Islamic Philosophy from its Origin to the Present: Philosophy in the Land of Prophecy*. Albany, NY: State University of New York Press.

Nasr, Seyyed Hossein, Caner K. Dagli, Maria M. Dakake et al., eds. 2015. *The Study Qur'an: A New Translation and Commentary*. New York: Harper One.

Nasr, Seyyed Hossein, Seyyed Vali Reza Nasr, and Hamid Dabashi, eds. 1988. *Shi'ism: Doctrines, Thought, and Spirituality*. Albany, NY: State University of New York Press.

Nateri, Mohammad Shams. 2006. "Formal and Informal Means of Conflict Resolution in Murder Cases in Iran." In *Conflicts and Conflict Resolution in Middle Eastern Societies—Between Tradition and Modernity*. Edited by H. Albrecht, J. Simon et al., 401–9. Berlin: Duncker & Humblot.

Navaro-Yashin, Yael. 2012. *The Make-Believe Space: Affective Geography in a Postwar Polity*. Durham, NC: Duke University Press.

Nebehay, Stephanie. 2014. "Iran hits back after West condemns its human rights record." *Reuters*, October 31. https://www.reuters.com/article/iran-un-rights/update-2-iran-hits-back-after-west-condemns-its-human-rights-record-idUSL5N0SQ2TG20141031.

Nietzsche, Friedrich. 1967[1879]. *On the Genealogy of Morals*. Translated by W. Kauffmann and R. Hollingdale. New York: Vintage Books.

Nussbaum, Martha C. 1993. "Equity and Mercy." *Philosophy & Public Affairs*, 22(2):83–125.

———. 1995. *Poetic Justice: The Literary Imagination and Public Life*. Boston: Beacon Press.

Osanloo, Arzoo. 2006. "The Measure of Mercy: Islamic Justice, Sovereign Power, and Human Rights in Iran." *Cultural Anthropology*, 21(4):570–602.

———. 2009. *The Politics of Women's Rights in Iran*. Princeton, NJ: Princeton University Press.

———.2013. "Human Rights by Any Other Name." In *Iran Confronting 21st Century Challenges: In Honour of Mohammad-Reza Djalili*. Edited by. H.E. Chehabi, F. Khosrowkhavar, and C. Therme, 79–95. Los Angeles, CA: Mazda Publishers.

———. 2014. "Khomeini's Legacy on Women's Rights and Roles in the Islamic Republic of Iran." In *A Critical Introduction to Khomeini*. Edited by A. Adib-Moghaddam, 239–55. Cambridge: Cambridge University Press.

———. 2016. "Women and Criminal Law in Post-Khomeini Iran." In *Social Change in Post-Khomeini Iran*. Edited by M. Monshipouri, 91–212. London: Hurst Publishers.

———. 2017. "Evidence, Certainty, and Doubt: Judge's Knowledge in Iranian Criminal Sanctioning." In *Truth, Intentionality and Evidence: Anthropological Approaches to Crime and Tort*. Edited by Y. Ben Hounet, B. Dupret, and D. Puccio-Den, 28–45. London: Routledge Press.

———. 2019. "Subjecting the State to Seeing: Charity, Security, and Faith in Iran's Theocratic Republic." In *Governing Gifts: Faith, Charity, and the Security State*. Edited by E. C. James, 59–77. Albuquerque, NM: University of New Mexico Press.

Othman, Aida. 2007. "'And Amicable Settlement is Best': Ṣulḥ and Dispute Resolution in Islamic Law." *Arab Law Quarterly*, 21(1):64–90.

Othman, Amira. 2018. "States of Wait: The Death Penalty in Contemporary Egypt." *Kohl: A Journal for Body and Gender Research*, 4(1):106–22.

Peletz, Michael G. 2002. *Islamic Modern: Religious Courts and Cultural Politics in Malaysia*. Princeton, NJ: Princeton University Press.

———. 2016. "Syariah, Inc.: Continuities, Transformations, and Cultural Politics in Malaysia's Islamic Judiciary." In *Shari'a Law and Modern Muslim Ethics*. Edited by R. Hefner, 229–59. Bloomington, IN: Indiana University Press.

"Pesar-e Sarbandi: Vaghaeat-e Ghatl Pedarmoon Bayad Moshakhas Shavad" (Sarbandi's Son: The Truth of Our Father's Murder Must Be Determined). 2014. *Asriran*, April 19 (*Farvardin* 30, 1394). https://www.asriran.com/fa/news/331423.

Peters, Rudolph. 2005. *Crime and Punishment in Islamic Law: Theory and Practice from the Sixteenth to the Twenty-First Century*. Cambridge: Cambridge University Press.

Petrushevsky, I. P. 1985. *Islam in Iran*. Translated by H. Evans. Albany, NY: State University of New York Press.

Pitt-Rivers, Julian. 1966. "Honour and Social Status." In *Honor and Shame*. Edited by J.G. Peristiany, 19–77. Chicago: University of Chicago Press.

Powers, Paul. 2006. *Intent in Islamic Law: Motive and Meaning in Medieval Sunni Fiqh*. Leiden: Brill.

Rabb, Intisar. 2015. *Doubt in Islamic Law: A History of Legal Maxims, Interpretation, and Islamic Criminal Law*. Cambridge: Cambridge University Press.

Redfield. Robert. 1964. "Primitive Law." *University of Cincinnati Law Review*, 33(1):1–22.

Reinhart, Kevin. 2017. "What We Know About *Ma'ruf*." *Journal of Islamic Ethics*, 1:51–82.

Rochard, Philippe. 2002. "Les identités du zurkhâne iranien." *Techniques et culture*, 39:29–57.

Rosaldo, Renato. 1989. *Culture and Truth: The Remaking of Social Analysis*. Boston: Beacon Press.

Rosen, Lawrence. 1989. *The Anthropology of Justice: Law as Culture in Islamic Society*. Cambridge: Cambridge University Press.

———. 2018. *Islam and the Rule of Justice: Image and Reality in Muslim Law and Culture*. Chicago: University of Chicago Press.

Rosenbaum, Thane. 2013. *Payback: The Case for Revenge*. Chicago: University of Chicago Press.

Rustom, Mohammed. 2012. *The Triumph of Mercy: Philosophy and Scripture in Mulla Sadra*. Albany, NY: SUNY Press.

Sachedina, Abdulaziz. 2001. *The Islamic Roots of Democratic Pluralism*. New York: Oxford University Press.

Sadeghi, H.M. 2016. *Offences Against the Person (Jarayem Allehe Ashkhaas)*. Tehran: Mizan Press.

Sadr, Amin Azad. 2016. "When the Subject is the Object: Islamic Advice Literature Modes and the Treatment of Slavery in The Qābūs Nāmih and The Nasirean Ethics." *Iranian Studies*, 49(3):435–49.

Sarat, Austin. 2005. *Mercy on Trial: What It Means to Stop an Execution*. Princeton, NJ: Princeton University Press.

Sarat, Austin and Stuart Scheingold, eds. 1998. *Cause Lawyering: Political Commitments and Professional Responsibilities*. New York: Oxford University Press.

———. 2001. *Cause Lawyering and the State in the Global Era*. New York: Oxford University Press.

———. 2005. *The Worlds Cause Lawyers Make: Structure and Agency in Legal Practice*. Stanford, CA: Stanford University Press.

———. 2008. *The Cultural Lives of Cause Lawyers*. Cambridge: Cambridge University Press.

"Sattar Beheshti Murderer Gets Three Years in Prison." 2014. *Center for Human Rights in Iran*, August 9. http://www.iranhumanrights.org/2014/08/sattar-beheshti-4/.

Schacht, Joseph. 1964. *An Introduction to Islamic Law*. Oxford: Clarendon Press.

Schapera, Isaac. 1972. "Some thoughts on the anthropological concept of 'crime': Hobhouse memorial lecture." *British Journal of Sociology*, 23(4):381–94.

Scheingold, Stuart, and Austin Sarat, eds. 2004. *Something to Believe In: Politics, Professionalism, and Cause Lawyering*. Stanford, CA: Stanford University Press.

Scheiwiller, Staci, ed. 2013. *Performing the Iranian State: Visual Culture and Representations of Iranian Identity*. New York: Anthem Press.

Scheper-Hughes, Nancy. 2001. *Saints, Scholars, and Schizophrenics: Mental Illness in Rural Ireland*. Berkeley, CA: University of California Press.

Seneca, Lucius A. 2010. *Anger, Mercy, Revenge*. Translated by R. Kast and M. Nussbaum. Chicago: University of Chicago Press.

Shah-Kazemi, Reza. 2006. "A Sacred Conception of Justice: Imam 'Ali's letter to Malik al-Ashtar." In *The Sacred Foundations of Justice in Islam: The Teachings of 'Ali ibn Abi Talib*. Edited by M. Ali Lakhani, 61–106. Bloomington: World Wisdom Inc.

———. 2007. *My Mercy Encompasses All: The Koran's Teachings on Compassion, Peace and Love*. London: Shoemaker Hoard Publishers.

Shambayati, Hooshang. 1997[1376]. *Criminal Law 1*, 3rd ed. Tehran: Veestar Publishers.

Shariati, Ali. 1981. *Fatima is Fatima*. Translated by L. Bakhtiar. Tehran: Shariati Foundation.

Siddiqui, Mona. 2012. *The Good Muslim: Reflections on Classical Islamic Law and Theology*. Cambridge: Cambridge University Press.

Singer, Amy. 2008. *Charity in Islamic Societies*. Cambridge: Cambridge University Press.

Singh, Bhrigupati. 2015. *Poverty and the Quest for Life: Spiritual and Material Striving in Rural India*. Chicago: University of Chicago Press.

———. 2016. "Hunger and Thirst: Crises at Varying Thresholds of Life." In *Living and Dying in a Contemporary World: A Compendium*. Edited by V. Das and C. Han, 576–98. Berkeley, CA: University of California Press.

Slaughter, Joseph R. 2009. "Humanitarian Reading." In *Humanitarianism and Suffering: The Mobilization of Empathy*. Edited by R. Wilson and R. Brown, 88–107. New York: Cambridge University Press.

Smith, Amy. 2008. "Not 'Waiving' But Drowning: The Anatomy of Death Row Syndrome and Volunteering for Execution." *Boston University Public International Law Journal*, 17: 237–54.

Snyder-Young, Dani. 2013. *Theatre of Good Intentions: Challenges and Hopes for Theatre and Social Change*. New York: Palgrave Macmillan.

Solnit, Rebecca. 2017. *The Mother of All Questions*. Chicago: Haymarket Books.

Statistical Centre of Iran. 2016. Selected Findings of the 2016 National *Population and Housing Census*. https://www.amar.org.ir/Portals/1/census/2016/Census_2016_Selected_Findings.pdf.

Statz, Michele. 2018. *Lawyering an Uncertain Cause: Immigration Advocacy and Chinese Youth in the U.S.* Nashville, TN: Vanderbilt University Press.

Stewart, Kathleen. 2007. *Ordinary Affects*. Durham, NC: Duke University Press.

Stiles, Erin. 2009. *An Islamic Court in Context: An Ethnographic Study of Judicial Reasoning*. New York: Palgrave Macmillan.

Stoler, Ann Laura. 2009. *Along the Archival Grain: Epistemic Anxieties and Colonial Common Sense*. Princeton, NJ: Princeton University Press.

al-Tabari, Abu Ja'far Muhammad b. Jarir. 1987. *Jami' al-bayan 'an ta'wil ay al-Qur'an (Collection of Statements on Interpretation of Verses of the Qur'an)*. Translated by J. Cooper. Edited by W.F. Madelung and A. Jones. Oxford: Oxford University Press.

Tavana, Mohammad. 2014. "Three Decades of Islamic Criminal Law Legislation in Iran: Legislative Analysis with Emphasis on the Amendments of the 2013 Islamic Penal Code." *Electronic Journal of Islamic and Middle Eastern Law*, 2:24–38.

Taylor, Charles. 2007. "Cultures of Democracy and Citizen Efficacy." *Public Culture*, 19(1):117–50.

Tellenbach, Sylvia. 2006. "Bloodfeuds and How to Bring Them to an End—Experiences in Turkey." In *Conflicts and Conflict Resolution in Middle Eastern Societies—Between Tradition and Modernity*. Edited by H. Albrecht, J. Simon, H. Rezaei et. al., 637–43. Berlin: Duncker & Humblot.

"The Punishment of Flogging for *Hadd* Violations May Be Revised as Well." 2016. *Iran Human Rights Organization*, November 2. http://iranhr.net/fa/articles/2688/.

Thomas, Alexander R. et al. 2011. *Critical Rural Theory: Structure, Space, Culture*. Lanham, MD: Lexington Books.

Tuckness, Alex and John Parrish. 2014. *The Decline of Mercy in Public Life*. Cambridge: Cambridge University Press.

Tutu, Desmond. 2000. *No Future Without Forgiveness*. New York: Doubleday.

UN Watch Briefing. 2014. "Iranian victims react to UN review of Tehran's human rights record," October 31. https://unwatch.org/issue-512-iranian-victims-react-uns-review-tehrans-human-rights-record/.

Vogel, Frank. 2000. *Islamic law and Legal System: Studies of Saudi Arabia*. Leiden: Brill.

Volpp, Leti. 2000. "Blaming Culture for Bad Behavior." *Yale Journal of Law & the Humanities*, 12(1):89–116.

———. 2011. "Framing Cultural Difference: Immigrant Women and Discourses of Tradition." *differences: A Journal of Feminist Cultural Studies*, 22(1):90–110.

Weber, Max. 1978. *Max Weber: Selections in Translation*. Edited by W. G. Runciman. Translated by E. Matthews. New York: Cambridge University Press.

Williams, Susan H. 2012. "A Feminist View of Mercy, Judgment and the 'Exception' in the Context of Transitional Justice." In *Merciful Judgments and Contemporary Society: Legal Problems, Legal Possibilities*. Edited by A. Sarat, 247–90. Cambridge: Cambridge University Press.

Wilson, Richard A. and Richard D. Brown. 2009. "Introduction." In *Humanitarianism and Suffering: The Mobilization of Empathy*. Edited by R. Wilson and R. Brown, 1–28. Cambridge: Cambridge University Press.

Yanagisako, Sylvia. 2002. *Producing Culture and Capital: Family Firms in Italy*. Princeton, NJ: Princeton University Press.

Zaborowska, Magdalena. 2014. "A Contribution to the Study of the Persian Concept of Âberu." *Hemispheres*, 29(1):113–25.

INDEX

Page numbers in *italics* refer to figures and tables.

criminal law: Article 612 and, 101, 111–12, 116;
art of forgiveness and, 219, 224, 238, 296n10;
cause lawyers and, 253, 263; codification
and, 62, 64–65, 70, 84, 85, 87, 283n36;
coloring in of, 62–68; Constitutional
Revolution and, 38; Convention on the
Rights of the Child (CRC) and, 142, 185–86,
244, 248, 251, 288n22, 292n23; Council of
Guardians and, 41, 43, 55, 62, 186, 275n6;
crimtorts and, 2–3, 16, 23, 30, 33–34;
discovery and, 48–50, 97; discretion and,
34, 41, 43, 62, 87, 104, 187, 216, 275n10;
exceptions and, 26, 98, 100, 154, 222, 289n3,
297n7; forbearance and, 142; forgivable
crimes and, 44–46; *Furman v. Georgia*
and, 122–23; healing and, 289n2; *hudud*
(crimes against God) and, 42–46, 62,
65–66, 84, 275n2, 276n15, 277n17, 277n18,
281n4, 281n10; Iranian version of, 38–41,
296n10; Islam and, 2, 41–43, 52, 65, 86, 88,
95, 97, 131, 219, 289n2; *Law of Islamic
Punishment* and, 42–43, 46, 63, 65–66,
99–100, 275n10, 277n20, 279n38, 281n10,
283n44, 285n17, 285n22, 286n23, 286n24;
mental age and, 246–47; mercy and, 62,
64–65, 70, 84–85, 87, 283n36; reconciliation and, 92, 95–96, 104, 120, 124, 284n12;
reform and, 29, 39–40, 43, 65, 104, 148,
244, 275n2, 292n23; restorative justice and,
60, 62–68, 103–4, 131, 134, 186, 280n53,
281n2, 281n5, 286n25; retribution and, 38–42,
45, 54, 57, 275n10, 276n11, 276n12, 280n52;
secularization and, 39–40, 57, 280n56;
unforgivable crimes and, 45–46, 124, 273n25;
U.S., 30; virtue of courts and, 48–50
crimtorts: accountability and, 17–20, 25, 29,
273n31; activists and, 1, 11, 17, 29–31, 34;
affective contexts and, 5–10, 29–34, 272n10;
codification and, 2, 5, 20–21, 25–26; compassion and, 2, 10–15, 19, 21–22, 25, 272n18,
272n19, 273n18; compensation and, 7–8,
18–20, 23–24; context of, 51; criminal
justice system and, 1–5, 25–33; criminal law
and, 2–3, 16, 23, 30, 33–34; death penalty

and, 4, 11, 17, 29, 31, 33–34, 271n2, 274n44;
defendants and, 13; defense lawyers and, 31,
34; ethics and, 8, 12–13, 16, 24–25, 29, 34,
272n8; execution and, 1, 15, 17, 27–31, 271n2,
274n44; exposition and, 31–34; faith and,
2, 9–10, 12, 16, 18; fathers and, 1–2, 6–7, 10,
24, 273n20; forbearance and, 1, 10–17,
25–26, 32; forgiveness work and, 3–5, 7, 9, 14,
17, 25, 29–34; gender and, 10–15, 26; honor
and, 9–10, 51–52, 271n5; Iranian Revolution
and, 2, 4, 16, 33, 273n30; Islam and, 2, 8, 11–14,
17, 20–25, 31, 33, 272n16, 273n30, 274n35,
274n39; journalists and, 27, 30; jurisprudence and, 21; justice and, 1–5, 8–9, 12–14,
17, 19–33, 272n14, 273n29; Juvenile Correction and Rehabilitation Center (JCRC)
and, 214, 218, 226; lifeworlds and, 5–10,
33–34; mercy and, 1–2, 5, 7, 12–13, 19–28,
32–34; methodological approach for, 29–34;
modes of accountability and, 17–20; moral
issues and, 3, 6–16, 19, 22, 25, 29, 31; mothers
and, 6–11, 14–16; murder and, 1–4, 14–15,
17, 23, 27–30, 33, 271n6; next-of-kin and, 17;
penal code and, 2–4, 11, 25–26, 33, 273n32;
performative exercises and, 9, 19–20;
plaintiffs and, 2; procedural law and, 27, 34;
Prophet Mohammad and, 10, 13, 21; prosecutors and, 27, 29–30; Qur'an and, 13–14,
21–26, 34, 272n18, 274n36, 274n37, 274n41;
reconciliation and, 2–4, 8–12, 16–18, 23–26;
reform and, 16, 29; rehabilitation and, 24;
remorse and, 7–9, 18; retaliation and, 2, 4,
8, 23, 28, 271n3, 273n20; retribution and, 1,
12, 25–26, 28, 34; revenge and, 13, 16–18, 26,
32; rights and, 1–5, 14, 18, 25, 27–28, 31, 34;
ritual and, 2–13, 19, 22, 24, 29, 34, 272n7,
272n9, 272n10, 272n15, 274n40; sanctions
and, 2–3, 12–15, 33, 275n1; settlement and,
3–4, 11, 26; "slap heard around the world"
and, 15–17; social workers and, 4–5, 10–11,
17, 29–31, 34; spectacle and, 1–5; substantive
law and, 2–3, 34; suffering and, 9, 12,
14–15; trends and, 27–28; use of term, 2;
women and, 14–15, 272n19

and, 88 (*see also* capital punishment);
cause lawyers and, 248, 255, 258, 262,
297n8; codification and, 62–70, 281nn8–
10, 286n25; complementary, 65, 118;
conditioning and, 98–104; crimtorts and,
2–3, 12–15, 33, 275n1; exemptions from, 65;
forbearance and, 125, 128, 134, 148; *Furman
v. Georgia* and, 122–23; grief and, 13;
healing and, 151–72; mercy and, 62–70,
187, 268, 281nn8–10, 286n25; reconciliation
and, 88, 90, 93, 98–99, 101, 103–4, 109,
111–12, 115–20, 123–24; retribution and, 39,
41, 43–45, 50–52, 56–60, 276n15, 277n17;
suspended, 65, 112, 118, 286n23
Sarat, Austin, 19, 242–43, 297n6, 297n7
Sarbandi, Jalal, 190–94, 254
Sarbandi, Morteza, 189–94, 252–55, 258–59,
292n32
*Sayyed*s (descendants of Mohammad), 10
Scheingold, Stuart, 242–43, 297n6, 297n7
Schott, Niles F., 202, 205, 294n51
secularization, 39–40, 57, 280n56
self-building, 202, 294n52
self-defense: cause lawyers and, 253–56, 258,
260–61, 263; killing in, 105, 193, 253–56,
258, 279, 284n7, 285n13; mediation and,
189, 193–94, 210; mercy and, 189, 193–94,
210; rape and, 189, 193, 210, 253–54,
293n38; reconciliation and, 105, 284n7,
285n13, 293n37; retribution and, 278n36
Seneca, Lucius, 271n3, 273n27
sentencing: Article 612 and, 101, 111–12, 116;
art of forgiveness and, 212, 215–16, 229;
codification and, 62, 65, 73, 86; crimtorts
and, 34; death row and, 126–27, 201, 235,
243, 245, 247–52, 259, 286n2, 286n5;
Furman v. Georgia and, 122–23; mediation
and, 211; mercy and, 62, 65, 73, 86, 211;
reconciliation and, 90, 96, 109, 111–12, 119,
122–24, 285n16; retribution and, 43, 46, 60
sentiment, 9, 19, 32; healing and, 158, 172;
mercy and, 66–67, 175, 181, 193, 269,
281n12, 282n13; negotiation and, 158;
reconciliation and, 88–89, 111, 113, 123

settlement: codification and, 68, 75;
crimtorts and, 3–4, 11, 26; forbearance
and, 131–34, 143; healing and, 158, 165, 168,
170; mediation and, 175, 179–80; meetings
for, 106–11, 131, 168, 179; mercy and, 68, 75,
175, 179–80, 261; reconciliation and, 91,
101, 103, 106–11; retribution and, 52–53,
279n46; Shahriyari and, 131–33
sex: abuse and, 52, 105–8, 186, 198–99, 199,
210; adultery and, 50, 251, 277n18, 298n15;
assault and, 45, 189, 193, 253, 292n32 (*see
also* rape); covering and, 50–51; drugs
and, 44, 48; incest and, 275n10; lesbianism and, 275n10; modesty and, 278n33;
pedophilia and, 275n10; predation and, 59,
294n50; procedural laws and, 210;
promiscuity and, 44, 46–47; self-defense
and, 50, 189, 193, 293n38, 294n50; sodomy
and, 275n10; as taboo subject, 48–49;
unlawful (*zina*), 45–46, 49, 275n10, 277n18
shackles, 64, 76, 110
Shah-Ghasemi, Ehsan, 137–41
Shah-Kazemi, Reza, 22, 24–25, 274n37,
274n39, 291n16
Shahnameh (Ferdowsi), 13
Shah Pahlavi, 39, 95
Shahriyari, Mohammad: books of, 130–31;
on execution, 135–36; forbearance
advocacy and, 125–40; on impartiality,
130–34; Kant and, 131–32, 287n12; morality
tales and, 130–31; reconciliation and,
133–34; settlement meetings and, 131–33
Shakespeare, William, 264
Shambayati, Hooshang, 104, 120
shame, 48, 50–51, 59, 161, 278n33, 280n56,
280n57, 294n54
shari'a (Islamic principles): art of
forgiveness and, 296n10; cause lawyers
and, 297n8, 299n28; codification and,
39, 41, 62–63, 71, 73, 85–87, 98, 275n3,
283n50, 296n10; Council of Guardians
and, 41, 43, 55, 62, 186, 275n6; forbearance and, 148, 288n22; healing and, 172;
mercy and, 62–63, 71, 73, 85–87, 266,

A NOTE ON THE TYPE

This book has been composed in Arno, an Old-style serif typeface in the classic Venetian tradition, designed by Robert Slimbach at Adobe.

GPSR Authorized Representative: Easy Access System Europe - Mustamäe tee
50, 10621 Tallinn, Estonia, gpsr.requests@easproject.com

www.ingramcontent.com/pod-product-compliance
Lightning Source LLC
Chambersburg PA
CBHW021112270326
41929CB00009B/837